The Other's War

The Other's War is an intervention into a set of contemporary moral, political and legal debates over the legitimacy of war and terrorism within the context of the so-called global war on terror. Tarik Kochi considers how, despite the variety of its approaches – just war theory, classical realist, post-Kantian, poststructuralist – contemporary ethical, political and legal philosophy still struggles to produce a convincing account of war. Focusing on the philosophical problem of the rightness of war, *The Other's War* responds to this lack. Through a discussion of a number of key Western intellectual traditions, Kochi demonstrates how often conflicting and contradictory conceptions of war's rightness have developed in modernity. He shows how a process of ordering violence around different notions of right has constantly redrawn the boundaries of what constitutes 'legitimate' violence. Such a process has consequences for anyone who claims to be fighting a 'just war'. Building upon this account and drawing upon the philosophical heritage of G.W.F. Hegel and Ernst Bloch, *The Other's War* proposes a new understanding of war, not just as a social condition characterized by violent conflict and struggles for power, but as the attempt of individuals and groups to realize their normative claims through violence. Kochi argues that both of these aspects of war are an expression of the metaphysics of human subjectivity. War begins with, and is the radical exaggeration of, a fundamental activity of human subjectivity, in which the subject constitutes its normative and material identity – realizing and positing itself through acts that involve negation and violence. By drawing consideration of the problem of war back to the level of a philosophical examination of the metaphysics of human subjectivity, *The Other's War* develops a novel theory of war that helps us to better understand the nature of contemporary conflict as a process of recognition. From this perspective, judgment, it is concluded, needs to be constantly guided by the effort to recognise the ethics of the other's war.

Tarik Kochi is a Lecturer in the School of Law, Queen's University Belfast. His research is in the areas of legal theory and political philosophy.

The Other's War

Recognition and the violence of ethics

Tarik Kochi

Birkbeck
LAW PRESS

First published 2009 by Birkbeck Law Press
2 Park Square, Milton Park, Abingdon, Oxon, OX14 4RN

Simultaneously published in the USA and Canada
by Birkbeck Law Press
270 Madison Avenue, New York, NY 10016

Birkbeck Law Press is an imprint of the Taylor & Francis Group, an informa business

Typeset in Sabon by Taylor & Francis Books
Printed and bound in Great Britain by MPG Books Ltd, Bodmin, Cornwall

British Library Cataloguing in Publication Data
A catalogue record for this book is available from the British Library

Library of Congress Cataloging in Publication Data
Kochi, Tarik.
The other's war : recognition and the violence of ethics / Tarik Kochi.
p. cm.
1. Just war doctrine. 2. War (Philosophy) 3. War–Moral and ethical aspects.
I.Title.
U22.K56 2008
172′.42–dc22
2008034975

ISBN10: 0-415-48270-4 (hbk)
ISBN10: 0-203-88220-2 (ebk)

ISBN13: 978-0-415-48270-7 (hbk)
ISBN13: 978-0-203-88220-7 (ebk)

For Angel and Jennifer Kochi

A Klee painting named 'Angelus Novus' shows an angel looking as though he is about to move away from something he is fixedly contemplating. His eyes are staring, his mouth is open, his wings are spread. This is how one pictures the angel of history. His face is turned toward the past. Where we perceive a chain of events, he sees one single catastrophe which keeps piling wreckage upon wreckage and hurls it in front of his feet. The angel would like to stay, awaken the dead, and make whole what has been smashed. But a storm is blowing from Paradise; it has got caught in his wings with such violence that the angel can no longer close them. This storm irresistibly propels him into the future to which his back is turned, while the pile of debris before him grows skyward. This storm is what we call progress.

Walter Benjamin, *Theses on the Philosophy of History*.

Contents

Acknowledgements

I owe this work to the guidance and friendship of Shaun McVeigh, Wayne Hudson and Valerie Kerruish. Thank you for your kindness, brilliance and generosity. I owe a great deal of gratitude also to Costas Douzinas for his unending support and assistance.

Thanks must be given to all of those who have contributed in differing ways to the production of this book through conversation, criticism and encouragement. Thanks to Shaunnagh Dorsett, Chris Butler, Bill MacNeil, Pam Adams, John Touchie, Roshan De Silva, Sue Wilkins, Dieter Freundlieb, Elena Schak, Josh Trevino, Eva Lunde, Noam Ordan, George Hull, Mehmet Baris Albayrak, Dalia Nassar, Stewart Motha, Uwe Petersen, Peter Fitzpatrick, Bill Bowring, John Strawson, Emilios Christodoulidis, Scott Veitch, Louis Wolcher, Bill Grantham, Tim Murphy, Sally Wheeler, Colin Harvey, George Pavlakos, Robin Hickey, David Dwan and Karen Brennan. Thanks also to Colin Perrin for his support and help in bringing this work into print. Thanks go to the School of Law and Human Rights Centre, Queen's University Belfast, and to all of my friends and colleagues at Queen's. Thanks to Holly Davis and Rhona Carroll for their editorial assistance and to the anonymous reviewers for their comments.

I could not have written this book without the generous financial support from a number of institutions. Thanks to the Socio-Legal Research Centre, School of Law, Griffith University and to Richard Johnstone. Thanks to the Deutscher Akademischer Austausch Dienst (DAAD), the Philosophisches Seminar, Universität Tübingen, and to Otfried Höffe and Manfred Frank. Thanks to the Altonaer Stiftung für philosophische Grundlagenforschung (ASFPG) Hamburg, and to Uwe Petersen and Valerie Kerruish.

Over the long period of writing and re-writing, my family have provided tireless support and light hearted criticism. Thank you to my parents and to Aliyah, Amirah, Hana and Khalid Kochi. For her light and for her help, thanks to Luz Flores Michel.

Introduction

I

Growing up in north-eastern Australia was peaceful. For the last half of the twentieth century it was free from war. In small town life the historical violence against the Aboriginal population was seldom talked about, if at all common knowledge for most. War, violence and killing were always things that seemed distant. Such distance was historical and physical. We were told that wars had occurred in the past and overseas – World War I (1914–18), World War II (1939–45), Korea (1950–53) and Vietnam (1954–75) – and we were asked to remember them, at least once or twice a year. As children we were told reflect upon the sacrifices made in war by those before us, by those who offered their lives for our nation, for our freedom.

On particular days of remembrance, school children would march together with ex-soldiers and widows in a parade through the main street of the town. There was usually some type of band, maybe bagpipes, a few speeches and a minute of silence. I remember in those moments of enforced silence feeling sad, feeling sorrow for those who died in the horrors of war. I remember feeling some form of connection to them, a thankfulness, but also an overwhelming weight that the image of their dead bodies and the public ritual of remembrance forced upon me. Forced also was both a sense of condemnation and justification of killing. These were tied together in an uncomfortable way: 'thou shalt not kill'; and the killing that 'saved' the nation. We were asked to remember the men, the soldiers who killed and were killed. In a sense, the birth, the defence and security of the nation, the state, the community, were bound to the killers and the killed. We were asked not to forget, so we said, 'lest we forget'. But what and who were we meant to remember?

The ritual of remembering was also one of forgetting, or ignoring. The public and official birth story of the colonies that became the Australian nation is that of 'discovery'. For many others, and most importantly for many Aboriginals, this discovery was an invasion – a public, official, drawn-out, violent process of taking the land from one group of peoples and giving it to another. A colonial legal order founded and built upon violence and the legal legitimization of this violence – an act of genocide. Such violence was never included within official public rituals of remembrance. Those killed were never offered a minute's silence. They were placed outside the register of public mourning and edification. Lest we forget.

Sitting behind the differing registers of the memory of violence are competing and often conflicting normative justifications of past and present violence. To remember some acts of war and killing and to forget or ignore others involves an act of *justification*. Public remembrance in a ritual, in a speech, or in a school textbook is built upon a justification, often after the event, of particular acts of violence as legitimate and the condemnation of others as illegitimate. The violence of the past is viewed and legitimated through the lens of the present, we call certain acts *right* or *wrong* even though we were never actually there. And even though we were not there, we claim to know what was right then in the same sense as we claim to know what is right now. But what do we know of the rightness of killing? What do we know about the right and wrong of war, terror, and violence? Such things are hard to know, even harder to know with any certainty.

The present is linked to the violence of the past. It is linked casually and this cannot be denied. The justification of violence in the present is linked to the justification of the violence in the past. However, this latter link, because it operates via memory, representation, argument and judgment, is more tenuous and it sits within a realm of social, political, ethical and legal contestation. Because the causal violence of history never exists on its own, but only within the register of our knowledge and the self-representation of our own deeds, the link between the violence of the present and the past is complicated by our ongoing, conflicting practices of justification and legitimation. In this case, our knowledge of the legitimacy or illegitimacy of past violence is shaped and manipulated by the concerns of the present and by the irresistible demands of the future.

The ethical demand of the future creates a picture of the past for us, a picture which stands as a firm foundation and a reassurance of the rightness of our actions in the present. Yet, an ethical demand of the future does not come from nowhere but responds to an image of the past – a period of glory, a golden age, a moment of moral purity, a tragic story, or a history of oppression, bloodshed, and genocide. What we claim as legitimate killing in the present, the just war, or the illegal act of terror, sits within our knowledge and self-representation of the past and the future. Each of these feed off and are constituted by the other. On the back of mumbled children's stories, broken images and grand, untrustworthy speeches we are driven into action and pass judgment on the rightness of killing that does violence to our fellow humans – and, lest we forget, an infinite violence against non-human animals.

On days of public remembrance childhood moments stay with us, they help us to keep track of our past selves marked against our changing responses to ourselves over time. In 1989, at around the age of 10, maybe close to 11, I was watching with my family a news programme on the Salman Rushdie blasphemy controversy. I remember hearing the religious edict given by Ayatollah Ruholla Khomeini that Rushdie should be killed and the next day at primary school, during a full school parade, I sat with a sign fixed to my back saying 'Kill Rushdie'. If my teachers were cautious, my father was angry, straightforward and unimpressed. My actions met with his sharp response – 'It is not right to kill anyone.' For Muslims too, the injunction 'thou shalt not kill' is central to ethical life.

Yes, 'thou shalt not kill', but we do and we do it all of the time. The present is marked by war, violence and killing justified by some and condemned by others. Terrorist bombings such as those in New York and Washington, DC (2001), and the invasion and continued occupation of Afghanistan (2001–) and Iraq (2003–) are fresh in our memories. Some also continue to remember the first Gulf War (1990–91) and the subsequent ten years of sanctions and bombing that involved the murder of tens of thousands of civilians, mostly children, legitimated by international law and carried out by the United Nations and Western liberal democracies. There have been other prominent wars, such as the 'humanitarian war' of NATO's bombing of Serbia-Kosovo (1999) and various other acts of war, civil war, revolution, terror and violence that we do not, or choose not to, remember. In light then of the very regular human practice of killing, perhaps the injunction 'thou shalt not kill' should be amended. Perhaps the injunction is better stated as follows: 'thou shalt not kill without good reasons, without a strong justification'; or, 'thou shalt kill only in accordance with *right*'. It is not killing as such, but the rightness and wrongness of killing that seem to be at issue.

When, then, is it right to kill, to launch into acts of war and terror? What is a 'good justification' for legitimate killing, and how do we determine the 'rightness' or 'wrongness' of war, violence and terror? How do we pass such an act of judgment and what distinguishes the good reasons given by a politician, lawyer or a philosopher from the judgment of a naive child who places a sign upon his back? Are we all still really children, or, do we have firm and fair accounts (ethical, political, legal or otherwise) that guide us through our judgments over the rightness and wrongness of acts of killing – and more specifically, that guide us through judgments over the legitimacy and illegitimacy of acts of war, violence and terror?

II

The central question is, when it is *right* to use war, violence and terror? This question can be thought of as the question of the *rightness of war*, sometimes referred to as the question of *just war*. The question should not, however, be confined merely to a consideration of inter-state war. Rather, the question of the rightness or justness of war needs to be understood in a broad sense so that the question takes into consideration a number of differing forms of public and social violence. Such a question thusly does not view the issue of the rightness of 'war' in the abstract but considers this as part of a wider framework involving the various judgments we make about the legitimacy and illegitimacy of forms of public violence. The question of the rightness of violence can be called more generally the 'problem of war'.

A number of prominent Western, twentieth-century intellectual traditions have attempted to better understand and provide answers to the problem of war. Generally these approaches have focused upon the question, how can ethical, political and legal philosophy produce good or convincing reasons that justify the act of killing and violence in some circumstances and condemn similar acts within others? Further, some approaches supplement this question by placing it within the context of an investigation of the role and operation of violence in public and social life and within a consideration of a certain 'violence' situated within historical, social and intellectual discourses. There is much to learn from twentieth-century approaches to the problem of war. However, looking over a number of approaches, it appears that contemporary ethical, political and legal philosophy still struggles to produce a convincing account of the rightness of war.

One prominent twentieth-century approach to the problem of war views the question of the rightness of war primarily as a question of politics. A broad tradition, sometimes referred to within international relations literature as 'realism', looks back to ancient Greek accounts of the *polis*, or the city-state, in which the question of ethics, right and the good are bound up with the continued existence of the political community. The question of the rightness of war, of killing and violence, is understood in terms of its relation to the 'good' of the *polis*. This includes not only the security of the city-state, but of also its collective and strategic interests and its glory. Realism takes aspects of this conception of the good of the ancient Greek city-state and transfers it to a consideration of the modern territorial nation-state. Such an approach often considers the question of the rightness of war to be a question of 'national interest' or the 'right of state'. War is not justified by universal Judaeo-Christian forms of moral reasoning or by reference to an international legal order. Rather, the rightness of war is determined by the interests of the nation-state and the pragmatic negotiation of the state's interests with its competing others. Drawing upon thinkers such as Thucydides,[1] Niccolò Machiavelli[2] and Thomas Hobbes,[3] aspects of such an approach to the problem of war can be found in the writings of thinkers such as Heinrich von Treitschke,[4] Hans Morgenthau,[5] and Carl Schmitt.[6]

The tradition of realism broadly defined presents a number of insights into the problem of war. The approach, which often takes a darker view of human social relations, pays attention to the way in which individuals conduct much of their moral life in a manner that is highly dependent upon their political community.[7] The tradition understands that social life, and the individual's freedom, are linked to the violence of the political community which has developed via a history of the acquisition of territory from other peoples.[8] The tradition also helps us to understand that the operation of war and the justifications that surround it often simply involve the assertion of one state's interest together with its similarly interested 'friends' against its 'enemies'. Further, that this dichotomy, linked to the *realpolitik* of global power relations, underlies much high-sounding moral rhetoric that attempts to justify historical violence and present and future acts of war.[9]

The tradition, however, struggles to produce a comprehensive answer to the problem of war.[10] For many, realism presents an account of the rightness of war that is disturbing and highly dangerous. By appropriating an ancient Greek idea for modern times the tradition makes a significant conceptual jump from the life of a small *polis*, to the modern territorial nation-state under the conditions of capitalism. Realism's attempt to define the 'common good' or the 'national interest' of the state is highly problematic. Such justifications too often hide the interests of capital and governing elites.

Further, reducing the question of the legitimacy of war to that of the 'right of state', opens up an aggressive power politics that refuses to be curbed by any external normative rules or demands. Such an approach to the justification of war may have had a certain degree of practical legitimacy within the practice of limited warfare between ancient Greek city-states, or within the context of pre-industrial European warfare. However, given the revolutionary developments in the practice and technology of warfare within the past hundred years via its mechanization, industrialization, atomization and computerization,[11] realism's model of the legitimate use of warfare to secure national political objectives leads towards apocalyptic, doomsday scenarios.

In response to the mass slaughter caused by the use of mechanized warfare during World War I and the use of the atomic bomb dropped by the USA on Hiroshima and Nagasaki (1945), many have turned away from the prospect of realism offering a convincing answer to the question of how war is, or should be, justified. In response to the horrors of war and the threat of nuclear apocalypse, there are good reasons to turn towards some form of cosmopolitan or universal conception of right that can be drawn upon to judge the legitimacy or illegitimacy of massive acts of public violence. The establishment of the United Nations (1945) was a historical cosmopolitan move in this direction. With this institution and the passage of history, many strong critiques of purely statist accounts of political life and the rightness of war have emerged. Such critiques draw attention to the radically changed nature of the global social order involving the increased inter-dependency of economic, juridical and cultural relations between political communities driven by trade, capital flows, cross-cultural immigration, and a global movement of information.[12] Within the context of a complicated global picture of international relations, a purely statist approach may not be fully adequate to come to terms with the modern problem of war.

In the second half of the twentieth century a growing dissatisfaction with the philosophy of utilitarianism[13] led in part to a renewed popularity of approaches to ethics and political and legal philosophy influenced by Kantian philosophy.[14]

Such approaches look towards the possibility of determining universal standards of right that may be used to guide us through the maze of social conflicts both within the state and internationally. With regard to war, such approaches attempt to discern universal, cosmopolitan principles of right and justice upon which our judgments over violence may be grounded. One example of a major figure within this tradition is John Rawls.[15]

Rawls' Kantian philosophy attempts to discern a way of thinking about justice which is universal and is not hamstrung by the differences within a political community or between political communities. Rawls' thought experiment of the 'original position' attempts to think through the question of justice from behind a 'veil of ignorance' so as to determine the universal principles of justice that might be valid for everyone and which are not merely contingent upon social status or political persuasion. Such a form of Kantianism which is historically comfortable with the emergence of international institutions such as the United Nations, attempts to morally regulate the operation of war so as to realize global peace, and in pragmatic or 'reasonably utopian' terms, global justice. The approach morally critiques the *realpolitik* of wars fought for power and national interest and attempts to solve the war problem by convincing states to become moral agents who direct their action in accordance with universal moral principles.

A Kantian tradition broadly defined offers a number of benefits to the consideration of the problem of war. In one sense it attempts to re-draw the boundaries of what we consider to be the 'political', and following this the position of ethics as related to the political. From a cosmopolitan position, the political is understood no longer simply as the sphere of the state, but that of the inter-state, the inter-connectedness of diverse political communities whose differences make up a global whole.[16] The tradition re-works the question of the 'common good' of the community as one that must account for the plurality of perspectives within a universal, cosmopolitan, global political community. In attempting to think through what this good might be, as a conception of right or justice, and in particular, as it relates to the issue of war, the tradition provides a method of attempting to discern universal principles of right (the categorical imperative; the original position – the veil of ignorance) which avoids merely re-affirming the preferences of particular cultural values or prejudices or national interests. At least, the tradition offers a method of determining what might be 'thin' universal principles of right that can guide decisions about the legitimacy and illegitimacy of war.

The approach, however, does not produce a convincing account of, or set of answers to, the problem of war. Compared to realism, the Kantian tradition, such as in the approach of Rawls, is often too abstract and is unable to conceptualize the destructive potential and violence contained within efforts to realize universal values such as peace, freedom, justice and human rights. The tradition frequently abstracts from the role of historical violence and from ongoing forms of social violence and relies too heavily upon an optimistic liberal modelling of human social relations based upon notions of autonomy, choice, rationality and freedom of action. The tradition can produce what seems to be convincing accounts of how to morally regulate war on paper or at a theoretical level. However, when put into practice, the attempt to realize universal moral principles via war can be just as destructive as a war waged purely in terms of national interest. Such a moral tradition is often caught within a paradox of advocating war as a means of realizing peace, or, of violating human rights in an effort to protect them. The tradition also has trouble with coming to terms with the manipulation of the language of universal moral values and principles by actors who use a moral rhetoric to mask and legitimize their use of violence for power and self-interest.

While the tradition puts forward a method that aims at determining 'universal' principles of right and justice, often what is offered by thinkers such as Rawls are highly particular and parochial principles embedded within the historical traditions of liberalism and capitalism. Such accounts have led many to be sceptical of the possibility of Kantian or Rawlsian methods of moral reasoning ever completely escaping from the blind spots of residual cultural, moral and political presuppositions.[17] Most significantly the liberal cosmopolitan effort to realize 'universal' principles via the use of physical force does 'violence' to other intellectual, cultural and political conceptualizations that are conceptually and practically excluded.

In this respect, Kantian moral approaches to the problem of war are often undermined by their inattention to a certain 'violence' of the *word*. Thinkers such as Rawls ignore a type of violence contained within their own moral reasoning and fail to consider its operation when making judgments about the legitimacy or illegitimacy of war. Because the tradition does not account for the operation of 'conceptual' or 'discursive' violence, it often ends up producing 'solutions' to the problem of war that compound the operation of social violence. Such inattention leads to the exacerbation of conflict rather than its resolution. While the Kantian tradition is generally well intentioned, its limitations point to the need to take into account both historical violence and the more subtle operation of discursive violence if we are to properly come to terms with the contemporary problem of war.

The latter half of the twentieth century was marked by an increasing scepticism of Enlightenment claims over human rationality, the ability of moral reasoning to make 'objective' judgments, and the idea that political and legal institutions can establish fair and just systems of social life. The Nazi genocide of countless Jews, Slavs, Poles, Sinti, Roma, the Left, Soviet soldiers and the disabled, threw caution to the notion that the ideas of the Enlightenment were bound necessarily to the notion of human progress. The mass killings, absence of democracy, cultures of surveillance and control and endless purging of elements political opposition in the Soviet Union, Communist China, East Germany, and within many other systems of state socialism globally, highlighted the dark reality of attempts to radically transform whole spheres of social, cultural and economic material life against the weight of an internal and international status quo. Such attempts also exposed the tendency of many former revolutionaries to fall into the authoritarian roles and practices of the old governing elites. In many cases the socialist project of revolution driven by the demand for justice and human dignity came unstuck. Too often it was impaled upon its reliance upon violence to sustain radical social transformation and to defend against counter-revolutionaries and attacks by capitalist states.

The massive violence that was always attached to what was described by some as 'good reasons', was not limited to fascism and communism. Western liberal democracies have also shown themselves to be profoundly violent and have spent the past hundred years carving up the world outside of Europe and North America into colonies and zones of economic control. For so-called 'good reasons', liberal democracies throughout the twentieth century have continually slaughtered indigenous peoples, stolen material and economic resources, suppressed local democracies, installed puppet governments and have controlled the capital flows and trade relations of the bulk of the earth's peoples. The USA, whose birth story was that of a liberal-bourgeois revolution in the name of 'life, liberty and the pursuit of happiness', has continually fought aggressive wars of conquest and control against its indigenous population, its neighbours and its global 'enemies'. The twentieth century and beginning of the twenty-first were and are stained in blood. All forms of political organization have been complicit in massive acts of killing and all have done so within, and by paying homage to, a heritage of the Enlightenment – all have claimed to have carried out this violence in accordance with 'reason'.

Given this historical context, it is understandable then that intellectual traditions have emerged that seek to pay attention to the violence attached to, if not contained within, Western claims to reason, rational action and moral judgment. Following in the wake of Karl Marx's analysis of the creation of inequality, poverty, alienation and commodification within capitalist economic and social relations,[18] Friedrich Nietzsche's project of unearthing the hidden resentment, shame and will to power within reason and Judaeo-Christian morality,[19] and of Sigmund Freud's identification of the repression and sublimation of sexual desire within bourgeois rationality,[20] many traditions have emerged to develop powerful tools that critique aspects of Western rationality and its claims to moral, political and juridical authority. The tradition of 'post-structuralism', or what is sometimes called 'post-modernism', is one such tradition. Its focus upon the operation of power and violence within Western rationality adds much to the consideration of the problem of war.

One major figure within a general tradition of post-structuralism is Michel Foucault.[21] Foucault's post-structuralist philosophy unearths some of the darker moments within modern conceptions of rationality and within institutional and moral behaviour. His account draws sharp attention to the operation of violence and power within modern thinking and in particular within social-historical-intellectual modes of thinking or 'discourses'. Foucault traces a modern discourse of the disciplining and control of forms of knowledge and the human body. The disciplining of knowledge emerges in the eighteenth and nineteenth centuries as forms of knowledge are forced into particular orders of 'science' which, then, through their claims to higher legitimacy, exert power over differential forms of human knowledge about the world in general. The process is not simply intellectual but exerts power as 'scientific knowledge' over the human body through its practice within institutions such as the medical clinic, asylums and prisons.

The increasing influence of disciplinary power over the construction of knowledge within the modern state leads to the increased regulation of forms of knowledge and human life more generally. The operation of what Foucault terms 'bio-power' develops as a form of violence that impacts upon all aspects of human life. Such an account helps us to understand that the exercise of power and violence is not simply a juridical function carried out by an army at war or a police force putting down a riot. Rather, the notion of bio-power identifies the operation of power and violence within all aspects of modern thinking within the social world – this includes the attempt to discern moral 'universals'.

Discursive violence and bio-power can be seen to occur in the way a normative discourse *excludes* particular modes of thinking and particular human actors in a manner that has dire consequences for those who are excluded. Through affirming what is understood as the 'same' and excluding the 'other', a discourse (whether as the discipline of natural science, clinical, institutional, or bureaucratic practice or as a normative tradition of liberalism or socialism) may carry out a violence of the word against particular actors. The violence of the word translates into physical violence, coercion and oppression when realized within the activity of public institutions and government regulation. Power and control are exercised and violence is carried out via the regulation of everyday life within the modern world through the managing of mortality and the quality of life via government agencies and by way of governmentality, that is, through the adoption of self-regulatory, self-disciplinary, habitual practices by the populace.

The expression of bio-power can also be seen in the ambiguous workings of a Western discourse of social Darwinism with its notions of 'civilization' and 'progress' attached to notions of 'racial purity'. Thinkers such as Edward Said, concentrating on the colonial and post-colonial, have highlighted how a discursive violence of exclusion has played a major role in the way liberal democracies have attempted to justify and legitimate endless colonial wars against the so-called 'unreasonable', 'unclean', 'uncivilized' non-Anglo-European 'other'.[22] Such accounts of discursive violence are not irrelevant today to the question of how Western governments portray and identify the threat of the so-called 'Islamicist terrorist' in relation to Muslim communities globally.

Post-structuralist perspectives add much to the consideration of the problem of war. The tradition helps re-frame the question of war back within the context of a wider assessment of the operation of power relations and discursive violence within human society more generally. Such accounts help us to consider the problem of war as one related to the way we reflect upon human life. By building upon such accounts we can re-position the problem of war within the framework of a broader consideration of the relation between *thinking*, *action* and *violence* located at the centre of human life and the practice of living. However, while the tradition offers a strong set of critical tools for analysing the operation of war in terms of discursive violence and bio-power, it suffers from an inability to present convincing accounts for determining how we *ought* to organize social, political and juridical affairs.

To be fair, a tradition that has developed by way of criticising the exercise of power and discursive violence within governing social and political paradigms should hardly be expected to produce a universal social and political programme. However, the tradition is haunted by its inability to put forward a convincing account of how we can or should organize our social, political, ethical and legal affairs so that we minimize the activity and consequences of violence. In a sense, the tradition is so captured by the violence of not only fascism, communism and liberalism, but also of modern human life in general, that it is unable to put forward an alternative account of how to organize human social relations. The preoccupation with power and violence hamstrings the tradition – post-structuralism demands a future world of non-violence, however, it is unable to conceive of a non-violent means of realizing or creating such a social order. This inability forces post-structuralist approaches into a corner. Against competing intellectual and institutional discourses, the tradition can only offer critique, it cannot fight back, so to speak, with a convincing alternative vision of the future and because of this, it risks increasing marginalization within a modern world whose primary political concept is still that of *action*.

At a more limited level, the tradition's scepticism of normative universals means that it is unable to put forward practical criteria for judging between legitimate and illegitimate violence. Without such criteria the tradition is open to attacks that it descends into some form of relativism. While this criticism is partly unfair, the tradition either refuses to engage with or is unable to answer the question of, when is it right to go to war? While the tradition still broadly adheres to modern normative concepts such as freedom, human dignity and justice, it struggles to produce an account that explains when violence can be used to realize these normative demands.

One brief example of post-structuralism's inability to fully come to terms with the problem of war is given in the philosophy of Jacques Derrida. Derrida, who early on identified a certain violence of the word,[23] drew upon the philosophy of Emmanuel Levinas as a means of setting out a radical, cosmopolitan ethic of openness to the other – an ethic guided by the attempt to create a non-violent relationship to the other. The approach leads Derrida to construe the notion of ethics, or justice itself, as *impossibility*. This involves the sense that the demand to do justice to the other and to all others cannot be carried out without, in some way, doing violence to some of our others.[24]

The critique is radical and worth holding onto. However, it is symptomatic of a difficulty contained within post-structuralism itself at the end of the twentieth and beginning of the twenty-first centuries. In one sense the notion invites a cautionary approach to ethical and political acts. It involves an attention to and a worrying about the violence contained implicitly within ethical and political action. On the other hand, the notion marks out a stalemate or inactivity that is representative of many post-structuralist approaches to war and violence.[25] The 'impossibility' of ethics and justice invites an impossibility of ever adequately judging between 'legitimate' and 'illegitimate' violence. Further, impossibility invites an attitude of inaction. One must constantly be concerned with the ethical demand not to do violence to the other. However, because it is impossible ever to carry out non-violent ethical activity, or a non-violent politics, then one is placed within the position of not being able to act at all. For some inheritors of this tradition, all radical ethical and political action becomes impossible.

A further sense of how post-structuralist approaches struggle with the problem of war stems from their presupposition of a particular metaphysics. Post-structuralist accounts that concentrate upon exclusion, sameness, difference, and otherness inherit and engage with a metaphysics of subjectivity and identity that has developed through numerous long traditions of Western philosophy. The analysis of the metaphysics of subjectivity reached its historical apex with a tradition that is broadly referred to as German Idealism, or German transcendental philosophy. Broadly defined, its major figures include Kant, Johann Gottlieb Fichte, Friedrich Schelling, G.W.F. Hegel, Ludwig Feuerbach, and Marx.

Post-structuralism, drawing upon the writings of Nietzsche, Edmund Husserl, Martin Heidegger, and to an extent Alexandre Kojève, critically engages with and often rejects many of the dominant claims about the metaphysics of subjectivity made by German transcendental philosophy, especially many of the claims made by Hegel. However, while the tradition attempts to set itself aside from this old tradition, its forms of thinking are still, in many significant ways, trapped within a metaphysics of subjectivity as set out by the tradition it seeks to move beyond.[26] Post-structuralism is still caught by and finds itself working though a number of key questions of the metaphysics of subjectivity as set out by German transcendental philosophy in general, and by the philosophy of Hegel in particular.

One way of understanding post-structuralism's difficulty with fully coming to terms with the war problem is by considering its problematic relationship with the philosophy of Hegel. Post-structuralism misses many of Hegel's key insights into the metaphysics of subjectivity. Significantly, it overlooks the highly original way in which Hegel grasped the operation of conceptual or discursive violence contained within the metaphysics of subjectivity, operating as *negation.* Well before Foucault and Derrida, Hegel drew attention to a central relationship between *thinking*, *action* and *violence* contained within the metaphysics of subjectivity. Further, he showed how the operation of conceptual violence extends through our ethical traditions and judgments occurring via the operation of *normative force* and *normative contradiction*. Hegel's philosophy has much to say about the status of conceptual and physical violence within the normative traditions of social-material life and within ethical and political action. Hegel's philosophy also has much to say about the violence contained within universal judgments and of the historical violence contained within the founding and continuation of political communities.

Given that the major lines of modern thought have struggled to fully come to terms with the problem of war, it might be worth taking a few steps back and re-investigating the problem through the lens of the tradition of German transcendental philosophy and, in particular, the philosophy of Hegel. Such an account may help to overcome some of the limitations of post-structuralist approaches to violence. Further, a contemporary, critical re-interpretation of Hegelian philosophy that pays attention to post-structuralist concerns may also help to produce an account that brings together the insights of realism and Kantian cosmopolitan approaches. In the face of the challenges of the present what is needed is a theoretical approach to the problem of war that holds onto the key insights given by the traditions of realism, Kantian cosmopolitanism and post-structuralism. Such an approach must also overcome the limitations and oversights of these traditions if it is to produce a convincing account of the rightness of war. In late modernity the problem of war has not yet been fully understood, let alone, answered. There remains much work to be done.

III

One aspect of the problem of war is the sense that it involves something of a 'war' at the level of ideas, at the level of thought. What we understand as war is not simply the act of physical violence but more importantly conflicts between forms of human thinking. These ideas do not emerge from a vacuum but are the product of differing social and material conditions of human life often understood and enunciated by human subjects in objectified, reified and fetish forms. Every act of war involves not only clashes between military forces, but also conflicts between human ideas – a war of thoughts against thoughts, a war fought out between differing thoughts, between differing forms of thinking, between differing conceptions of the world. Most often this war of thoughts against thoughts involves a conflict between competing normative claims over the legitimacy, justness or rightness of acts of violence. War is not so much a battle of might against might as it is a conflict of right against right. Every warring actor, together with those who look on in support and condemnation, claims to have *right* on its side. Each warring actor claims that its particular war is right, legitimate and just and each actor is comforted and pushed on by the assumed righteousness of its violence and the absence of right on the side of the enemy. The critics of war also seem to hold a monopoly upon right, each critic claims that a particular act of war is *not right*, or, that some wars are more right than others.

Holding onto the differing approaches to the problem of war helps to show more clearly the wider dimension of a war fought at the level of ideas. The conflict between differing notions of right is not merely confined to intellectual discussions but rather, this conflict plays a major role in the physical-material world. Wars are driven by thoughts of national interest, ideas of the right and good of the state which come into conflict with competing claims of other states. Further, universal, moral justifications for violence are claimed by numerous sides who go to war in the name of freedom and justice. Such universal moral claims are not monopolized by liberal democracies but are claimed also by many others, such as, for example, many radical Islamicist political actors – those whom we all too readily dismiss as 'crazy, religious terrorists'. For all sides the thinking of right is bound up with the activity of war. Right and war cannot be separated, they seem to run together with, or at least parallel to, a relationship between thinking and action

If we are to properly comprehend the problem of war, then it is not enough to describe the operation of a chaotic war of ideas by overly simplistic concepts such as the 'clash of civilizations'[27] or as a 'battle between ideologies'[28] playing out through history. Such simplifications miss the question of how a notion of right not only frames a form of action but also how such a notion tempers and propels human subjects into differing forms of violent action. Further, rational choice and game theories do not offer complete solutions here, something more complicated and blurred is at work. There are external aspects of normative human life that are so ingrained within the internal view of subjectivity that they blow apart any attempt to produce atomistic models of 'rational' human behaviour. There is something about the pressing, futural demand of a norm which seems to force the behaviour of a human subject into violent action and which also blocks, for that human subject, alternative understandings of the justification of violence carried out in the present and the past.

Something more mischievous is at work within the problem of war, a trickiness, but also a darkness, that demands further investigation. Given the scope of the issues contained within the problem of the rightness of war, we need to attempt to build a more convincing philosophy of war. Such an account would need to explain how norms are connected to and organize violent action, and of how the activity of normative thinking is related to violence within human subjectivity.

My approach attempts to develop a philosophical account of war. The method involves the re-examination of a set of modern, Western, political, ethical and legal traditions of how we think about the rightness of war. Such an approach builds upon the insights of realism, Kantianism and post-structuralism and attempts to push beyond their theoretical limitations. The re-investigation of a number of central traditions of thinking about the rightness of war is made in light of both the profound violence that has taken place throughout the twentieth century and the inability of many dominant Western traditions of philosophy to properly come to terms with this violence. My theory of war has three elements: (1) that the rightness of war is something that is *ordered*; (2) that war is an *act of positing*; and (3) that the appropriate response to war is the development of a *praxis of recognition*.

The rightness of war is something that is *ordered*. Ordering occurs as an activity within human thinking that determines and sets out the boundaries of the legitimacy of violence in response to particular circumstances. There is no such thing as an act of violence which is inherently or naturally right or wrong, legitimate or illegitimate. Rather, the rightness of war is produced by the activity of human thinking and by historical, social, intellectual and cultural traditions (or discourses) of thought. The argument is not simply that the rightness of war stems from a social or cultural context. What is more central is the manner in which the rightness, or normative value, of every act of violence is ordered, arranged or organized by particular modes of thinking in particular ways so as to achieve a consistent account of the legitimacy of violence within a particular society and territorial space at a particular point in time.

Rather than viewing particular acts of violence as inherently wrong, we need to understand how the wrongness and rightness of particular acts of violence are ordered and thus produced by human thinking. One example is the prohibition of murder. This prohibition is not in anyway inherent to reason, but instead it emerges through a process of the ordering of the relative normative value of a number of acts of violence within a historical-social sphere. The content of what lies within the boundaries of the concept of 'murder' is always something that is ordered and this content is related to the way the legitimacy of war is ordered more generally. That is, the prohibition upon murder emerges only through a process in which a society or a juridical-political community (or its elites) determines the boundaries of the legitimate and illegitimate use of violence. In many ways the prohibition upon murder comes after the justification of war.

Holding onto a notion of the ordering of war allows us to situate our own conceptions of what we think is a right or just war within a social-historical framework. In attempting to outline a number of the dominant modern traditions of the ordering of war, I show how our thoughts about contemporary wars play out many of the limitations within, and conflicts between, differing traditions of the ordering of war. Such an argument, while important, is not particularly controversial. It is only controversial for those who assume that particular acts of violence, such as acts of terrorism carried out by radical Islamicist political organizations, are inherently wrong. A clearer position is to understand that the wrongness of such acts stems from their breaching the ordered lines of the 'legitimacy' of violence within particular social and territorial spheres. These ordered frames of legitimacy are held in place by relations of power and by the social-material conditions of differing forms of human life.

In this respect the 'wrongness' of such acts emerges not only via the challenge to the organized lines of the legitimacy of violence, but more directly from the way such acts challenge the institutional power of those who claim a legal, political and moral authority *to order* the rightness of violence within the present. My argument is that before we rush to condemn or legitimate particular acts of violence we need to understand how our own concepts of the rightness of war are ordered – that is, we need to get our concepts about war and right into some form of order.

The second aspect of my theory of war involves the argument that *war is an act of positing*. War involves the effort to posit, put forward and realize a norm. This norm is contained within an ethical, legal, political, economic or religious claim situated within the historical conditions of social and material life. In one sense war as positing involves the operation of war as an *act*, as an instrument, within social and material life. Such a sense is nothing new. For Hugo Grotius, war is a dispute of rights by force.[29] For Carl von Clausewitz, war is an act of force used to compel the enemy to do one's will, and further, war is an instrument that allows the continuation of policy and politics by other means.[30] Thinkers, such as Schmitt, Kojève,[31] and Raymond Aron,[32] have all grasped this instrumental element of war and have shown how it describes political and ethical conflict within differing historical circumstances.

However, something more than an instrumental account is contained within my theory of war as an act of positing. War is not merely an instrument used by human agents, it is something more fundamental. War is a central moment in the life of a human subject as it itself is posited by the force or power of a normative, futural demand that is a dominant content of any subjectivity's social-material life. War as positing is a *creative-destructive activity* and *process* central to the operation of human subjectivity as it exists within a material life-world of thick normative content. In a sense, the term 'war' is somewhat misleading here. 'War as an act of positing' is a shorthand way of referring to a specific account of human subjectivity existing within a world of conflicting normative demands. My argument is that by understanding the operation of *positing* at the level of the metaphysics of subjectivity, we can better understand the operation of the rightness of war, violence, and terror within the wider world.

My use of the term 'positing' draws upon an interpretation or re-reading of the metaphysics of subjectivity developed in differing ways by Fichte and Hegel. Within such an account, the self or the 'I' is constituted through its relation to the 'not-I' or what is other than itself. In a general sense, the term 'positing' refers to the *activity* occurring transcendentally within thought and also within the inter-subjective context of a social-material life in which a human subject knows itself (as an identity) and acts in relation to its others.[33] Subjectivity is posited by an activity – subjectivity is the activity of the self positing itself in and through its relations to its others. In the act of positing itself as an identity, the self *excludes* something other than itself and this exclusion involves *negation.* At a purely conceptual level such negation is not yet violence. However, when occurring within social-material life, the operation of negation, bound to the activity of positing, is very often violent or has violent consequences.

Existing within inter-subjective, social-material life, the self contains a thick normative content which is not external to it but is built into its notion of self-identity by way of its historical, social, ethical, cultural and economic production or co-constitution. While the self claims a degree of autonomy, choice and decision over its normative content, it still exists in the sense of being the agent of a wider normative institutional and cultural content that exerts or posits itself through the activity of human subjectivity. Such normative content does not have a 'life' of its own but it does have an existence within social-material life and it contains a restlessness related to its unfulfilled conceptual potentialities.[34] That is, the normative content of social and material life contains a radical, futural dimension that stems from the operation of potentiality within norms – each of which demands immediate realization in the present. The radical futural demand of the normative content of social and material life exerts a force upon human subjects – 'it' posits itself through the activity of human subjects and these subjects, who self-legislate the external norm as their own, posit themselves and their normative claims against their others in the world. This activity of the subject *as positing* and *being posited* through negation constitutes the basis of a theory of war – war is the extrapolation and radical exaggeration of the act of positing.

The third aspect of my theory of war involves the argument that the appropriate response to contemporary acts of war is to develop a *praxis of recognition.* Holding onto both the historical and discursive operation of the ordering of the rightness of war, and the activity of war as positing built upon the metaphysics of subjectivity, the continued war of all against all (and of some against some) fought out at the level of ideas and through public, physical violence, may not be resolved by further acts of positing that attempt to bring the chaos of war into order. Instead of the condemnation of the other's war, what is required is the development of a stance or attitude that attempts to grasp the legitimacy of the other's violence. At a practical level, this involves the effort to *recognize the ethics of the other's war.*

Through my accounts of ordering, positing and recognition I attempt to set out a philosophical account that assists us in both better coming to terms with the modern problem of war and in responding to contemporary violent conflicts. While my approach is ambitious in that it endeavours to produce a philosophical theory of war, it does have a number of immediate limitations. One limitation arises out of the focus upon ethics, politics and the juridical. Because of this, my approach does not attempt to produce a complete and comprehensive philosophy of war, to do so, one would need to give full treatment not only to the Foucauldian question of bio-power, but also to various psychological, anthropological and feminist accounts of violence, and perhaps also to the question of 'species war' – the violence carried out by humans against non-human animals. A complete and comprehensive philosophy of war would also need to defend the particular account of the metaphysics of subjectivity presented here against American pragmatist and post-Wittgensteinian approaches within analytic philosophy and against accounts of subjectivity given by analytic approaches to the philosophy of mind more generally. An inclusion of and defence against these various traditions of thought would be asking too much for this present work. It is enough to note that there are many pressing questions relating to the problem of war which demand continued investigation.

With this said, the arguments I am presenting here are relevant and important to better understanding the problem of war within the present. If we are to come to terms with the problem of war, then we need to take seriously the links between the operation of war, the way we justify and legitimate violence, and the metaphysics of subjectivity. These are not separate questions to be pursued by different spheres of philosophical endeavour. Further, while we know that politics is violent, we need to begin to pay more attention to the violence that is produced by and contained within our own ethical demands. Comprehending the role and operation of violence within ethics and of how this relates to the activity of human subjectivity is fundamental to understanding how we make judgments about the legitimacy and illegitimacy of violent action and of how we can plan for the future in the interest of minimizing violence and harm. Any reconsideration of the future of socialism, or of a politics of radical or revolutionary social transformation, needs to come to terms with the violence of positing, a certain violence of the metaphysics of subjectivity, that is fundamentally linked to any effort to realize some form of the good.

Finally, I am presenting the case for a darker account of the metaphysics of subjectivity. A theoretical approach in this direction always runs the risk of being appropriated by a conservative or fascist politics with the interest of attempting to legitimize some horrendous violence or form of oppression. Any such appropriation of a darker metaphysics of subjectivity must be openly rejected in favour of a radical politics focused upon the realization of human emancipation, dignity and economic and social equality and happiness. Any such ideal, however, cannot be achieved on the basis of a social theory guided by a 'relationship of non-violence with the other'. As much as a radical or socialist politics might hold onto this utopian ideal as an (impossible) end, it should not let it obscure the comprehension of the darker moments of a human ontology (of positing and negation) which any politics must pay careful attention to and develop strategies for coming to terms with.

IV

With regard to the structure of the work, Chapter 1 opens with an engagement with contemporary 'just war' theory and its popular proponent, Michael Walzer. Through a discussion of classical just war doctrine as presented in the work of Francisco de Vitoria, the chapter offers a critique of just war theory and its modern re-appropriations. I argue that just war theory is an inadequate approach to the problem of war and that many just war theorists do not really take the problem of war very seriously. The following four chapters attempt to take the problem of war seriously and do so by looking at a number of ways in which the notion of the rightness of war has been ordered by differing intellectual traditions in modernity. Through these chapters I show how differing conceptions of what constitutes legitimate authority, sovereignty, morality, and the causes of conflict have led to the production of often conflicting accounts of 'legitimate violence' – the 'right' and 'wrong' of war.

In Chapter 2, I begin the modern story of the ordering of war by focusing upon the production of the notion of Westphalian, European state sovereignty, through the theories of Grotius and Hobbes. I call this tradition the *juridical ordering of war*. In Chapter 3, I discuss how aspects of this form of war's ordering are inherited and critiqued by Rousseau and Kant. Beginning with a discussion of Kant's epistemology which grounds his moral theory, I examine Kant's project of the *moral ordering of war* and show how both his approach and contemporary cosmopolitan approaches are significantly limited. I show how, at their worst, cosmopolitan moral approaches to war present a new form of secular, and sometimes fanatical, just war.

In Chapter 4, I discuss how, through the philosophy of Fichte, Hegel inherits and builds upon Kant's epistemological theory to develop a theory of intersubjective recognition. My reading of Hegel interprets his theory of recognition as an epistemic and normative theory in which the act of positing, involving both moments of affirmation and negation, sits at the foundation of mental and physical acts within human subjectivity. By showing how the theory of recognition underlies Hegel's mature political and legal philosophy, I offer an interpretation of Hegel's theory of war as explaining an ethics of exclusion that resides within the ethical life (*Sittlichkeit*) of the state. With an emphasis upon the role of recognition and misrecognition, negation and the ethics of exclusion, I argue that Hegel's theory presents an *ethical ordering of war*.

In Chapter 5, I discuss aspects of Marx's inheritance of Hegel's theory of recognition and his critique of Hegel's notion of the state. I show how Marx's analysis of economic coercion, alienation and commodification within modern capitalism, leading to his theories of social and class conflict, has been inherited by a number of thinkers who constitute a tradition of the *political ordering and disordering of war*. Through a discussion of Lenin's notions of class and imperialist war and Schmitt's examination of the twentieth-century phenomenon of 'partisan war', I outline the breakdown of classical notions of inter-state war and the emergence of non-sovereign war which prefigures and helps us to better understand the contemporary figure of the 'terrorist'.

In Chapter 6, I draw together the analysis of the different traditions of war's ordering and attempt to develop a contemporary theory of war. Drawing upon Hegel's theory of subjectivity, Marx's theory of labour and Ernst Bloch's critical utopian philosophy of the 'not yet' (*noch nicht*), I develop a theory of *war as positing* in which acts of violence constitute both the affirmation of right and negation. By viewing contemporary acts of war as moments of positing and counter-positing, driven by normative force and normative contradiction, I conclude the work by examining the possibility of there being any objective position of judgment over the rightness of war. In Chapter 7, I argue that one way of developing something of an 'objective' standpoint of judgment on the rightness of war is through the development of a praxis of recognition, that is, through recognizing the ethics of the other's war. For those in the West, this means attempting to recognize the ethics of acts of terrorism carried out by militant, Islamicist political organizations.

Notes

1 Thucydides, *The History of the Peloponnesian War*, trans. R. Warner, London: Penguin Classics, 1954.
2 N. Machiavelli, *The Prince and the Discourses*, ed. M. Lerner, trans. L. Ricci, New York: Random House, 1950.
3 T. Hobbes, *Leviathan*, ed. R. Tuck, Cambridge: Cambridge University Press, 1996.
4 H. Treitschke, *Politics*, trans. H. Kohn, New York: Harcourt, Brace and World Inc., 1963.
5 H.J. Morgenthau, *In Defence of the National Interest*, New York: Alfred A. Knopf, 1952.
6 C. Schmitt, *The Nomos of the Earth*, trans. G.L. Ulmen, New York: Telos Press, 2003.
7 Many communitarian and constructivist approaches to international relations pick up on this point, and, drawing upon Hegelian and post-Hegelian accounts of ethical life mediate such an account with modern cosmopolitan political and ethical concerns. See generally: C. Brown, *Political Restructuring in Europe: Ethical Perspectives*, London: Routledge, 1994; M. Frost, *Ethics in International Relations: A Constitutive Theory*, Cambridge: Cambridge University Press, 1996; K. Hutchings, *International Political Theory*, London: Sage, 1999; A. Linklater, *The Transformation of Political Community: Ethical Foundations of the Post-Westphalian Era*, Cambridge: Polity Press, 1998.
8 Schmitt draws attention to the notion of the 'appropriation of land' (*Landnahme*) as one of the foundational concepts of law. See C. Schmitt, *The Nomos of the Earth*, pp. 42–49.
9 See C. Schmitt, *The Concept of the Political*, trans. G. Schwab, Chicago, IL: University of Chicago Press, 1996. Consider also: G. Simpson, *Great Powers and Outlaw States*, Cambridge: Cambridge University Press, 2004.
10 In my approach to the problem of war in this work, I will not follow the standard line, as commonly presented in international relations textbooks, of dividing approaches to war in terms of 'realist' and 'normative'/'moral' approaches (with sometimes 'historical', 'constitutive' and 'post-modern' approaches thrown in for good measure). While this standard division has some merits, it has the fault of obscuring the fact that both 'realist' and 'normative' approaches within international relations draw upon particular ideas about the legitimacy of violence which are inherently *normative*. That is, even a political 'realist' who views the international sphere as a war of 'all against all', fought for reasons of state interest, and being impossible to morally regulate, still assumes particular normative notions about the legitimacy of violence held by the sovereign in relation to other domestic

and external actors. The question of how the legitimacy of violence is *ordered* is one of the questions I am following here. It is a question that is generally assumed and not asked within a great deal of international relations literature. It is a question that precedes the problem of how states should act in relation to one-another.

11 Consider P. Hirst, *War and Power in the 21st Century*, Cambridge: Polity, 2001.

12 Consider the various accounts given in J. Habermas, *The Postnational Constellation: Political Essays,* trans. M. Pensky, Cambridge: Polity Press, 2001; M. Hardt and A. Negri, *Empire*, Cambridge, MA: Harvard University Press, 2001; Z. Bauman, *Liquid Modernity*, Cambridge: Polity Press, 2000; U. Beck, *Risk Society: Towards a New Modernity*, London: Sage, 1992; A. Giddens, *Modernity and Self Identity*, Cambridge: Polity Press, 1991.

13 This is not to say that utilitarianism is irrelevant, only that dissatisfaction with a number of the answers it produces has led to a large shift within liberal moral and political philosophy towards deontological approaches. For utilitarian approaches that are still highly relevant to pressing social questions, see P. Singer, *Animal Liberation*, New York: Random House, 1975; P. Singer, *One World: Ethics and Globalization*, New Haven, CT: Yale University Press, 2002. Within legal theory, the turn towards deontological approaches occurs also due to the dissatisfaction with theories of legal positivism given by Austin and Hart. See J. Austin, *The Province of Jurisprudence Determined*, London: Weidenfeld and Nicolson, 1971; H.L.A. Hart, *The Concept of Law*, 2nd edn, Oxford: Oxford University Press, 1994.

14 For alternative Kantian-cosmopolitan approaches to the questions of war, international relations and globalization, see generally O. Höffe, *Demokratie im Zeitalter der Globalisierung*, München: Beck, 2002; T.W. Pogge, *World Poverty and Human Rights: Cosmopolitan Responsibilities and Reforms*, Cambridge: Polity, 2002; O. O'Neil, *Faces of Hunger: An Essay on Poverty, Justice and Development*, London: Allen and Unwin, 1986. For a more radical cosmopolitan approach, see D. Held, *Democracy and the Global Order: From the Modern State to Cosmopolitan Governance*, Cambridge: Polity Press, 1995.

15 J. Rawls, *A Theory of Justice*, Cambridge, MA: Belknap Press, 1971; J. Rawls, *Political Liberalism*, New York: Columbia University Press, 1993; J. Rawls, *The Law of Peoples*, Cambridge, MA: Harvard University Press, 1999.

16 See, generally, D. Archibugi and D. Held (eds) *Cosmopolitan Democracy: An Agenda for a New World Order*, Cambridge: Polity Press, 1995; P. Cheah and B. Robbins (eds) *Cosmopolitics: Thinking and Feeling Beyond the Nation*, Minneapolis, MN: University of Minnesota Press, 1998.

17 The inability to escape from, or often be aware of certain presuppositions of liberalism and capitalism which govern their mode of thinking about the world severely curtails the possibility of forms of Anglophone legal philosophy ever producing a truly universal account of right. Accounts such as that given by Rawls and Richard Dworkin suffer from an overly naïve assumption that liberal conceptions of subjectivity and rights are universal and natural. Such theorists are blocked by a refusal to thoroughly reflect upon the historical, economic and material contingency of what they claim as being 'universal' values or principles. See R. Dworkin, *Law's Empire*, Cambridge, MA: Belknap Press, 1986.

18 See, generally, K. Marx, 'On the Jewish Question', in L.H. Simon (ed.), *Karl Marx: Selected Writings*, Indianapolis, IN: Hacket Publishing, 1994; K. Marx, *Economic and Philosophic Manuscripts of 1844*, trans. M. Milligan, Amherst, MA: Prometheus Books, 1988; K. Marx, *Capital*, Vol. 1, trans. B. Fowkes, London: Penguin Classics, 1992.

19 F. Nietzsche, *The Basic Writings of Nietzsche*, ed. P. Gay, trans. W. Kaufman, New York: The Modern Library, 2000.

20 S. Freud, *The Ego and the Id*, ed. J. Strachey, New York: W.W. Norton & Co., 1962; S. Freud, *Totem and Taboo*, ed. J. Strachey, New York: W.W. Norton & Co., 1950; S. Freud, *Civilisation and its Discontents*, ed. J. Strachey, New York: W. W. Norton & Co., 1961.

21 See, generally, M. Foucault, *Madness and Civilisation: A History of Insanity in the Age of Reason*, New York: Random House, 1965; M. Foucault, *Discipline and Punish: The Birth of the Prison*, trans. A. Sheridan, New York: Vintage Books, 1977; M. Foucault, *The Order of Things: An Archaeology of the Human Sciences*, New York: Random House, 1970; M. Foucault, *Society Must Be Defended*, trans. D. Macey, London: Penguin Books, 2003.

22 E.W. Said, *Orientalism*, London: Routledge and Kegan Paul, 1978. Consider also G. Agamben, *Homo Sacer: Sovereign Power and Bare Life*, trans. D. Roazen-Heller, Stanford, CA: Stanford University Press, 1998.

23 J. Derrida, 'Violence and Metaphysics: An Essay on the Thought of Emmanuel Levinas', in *Writing and Difference*, trans. A. Bass, Chicago, IL: University of Chicago Press, 1978.

24 See J. Derrida, *The Gift of Death*, trans. D. Wills, Chicago, IL: University of Chicago Press, 1995; J. Derrida, 'The Force of Law: The Mystical Foundation of Authority', trans. M. Quaintance, in D. Cornell, M. Rosenfeld, and D.G. Carlson, *Deconstruction and the Possibility of Justice*, New York: Routledge, 1992; J. Derrida, *Specters of Marx: The State of Debt, the Work of Mourning and the New International*, trans. P. Kamuf, New York: Routledge, 1994; J. Derrida, *On Cosmopolitanism and Forgiveness*, trans. M. Dooley and M. Hughes, London: Routledge, 2001. Consider the reformulation of this approach as a post-modern ethics: D. Cornell, *The Philosophy of the Limit*, New York: Routledge, 1992; C. Douzinas, *The End of Human Rights: Critical Legal Thought at the Turn of the Century*, Oxford: Hart, 2000.

25 A similar notion is developed within Jean-Luc Nancy's account of community. See J. Nancy, *The Inoperative Community*, trans. P. Conner *et al.*, Minneapolis, MN: University of Minnesota Press, 1991.

26 See the accounts in J. Habermas, *The Philosophical Discourse of Modernity*, trans. F.G. Lawrence, Cambridge, MA: MIT Press, 1990; P. Dews, *The Logics of Disintergration: Post-Structuralist Thought and the Claims of Critical Theory*, London: Verso 1987; P. Dews, *The Limits of Disenchantment: Essays on Contemporary European Philosophy*, London: Verso, 1996; M. Frank, *What is NeoStructuralism?*, trans. R. Gray, Minneapolis, MN: University of Minnesota Press, 1989; G. Rose, *Dialectic of Nihilism: Post-Structuralism and Law*, Oxford: Basil Blackwell, 1984; G. Rose, *The Broken Middle: Out of Our Ancient Society*, Oxford: Blackwell, 1992; R. Pippin, *Modernism as a Philosophical Problem: On the Dissatisfactions of European High Culture*, Malden, MA: Blackwell Publishers, 1991; J.P. Butler, *Subjects of Desire: Hegelian Reflections in Twentieth-Century France*, New York: Columbia University Press, 1987. An account of some of the ways central questions of post-structuralist philosophy are caught within or play out the central concerns of German transcendental philosophy, and in particular the philosophy of Hegel, is given by Slavoj Žižek. While Žižek takes many of the questions of war and violence back to a metaphysics of subjectivity grounded in German transcendental philosophy his account is restricted by his Lacanian interpretation of subjectivity which too often reduces the futural demands of the normative content of social-material life to psychological concepts of 'lack' and 'the void'. See S. Žižek, *The Sublime Object of Ideology*, London: Verso, 1989; S. Žižek, *Tarrying with the Negative: Kant, Hegel and the Critique of Ideology*, Durham, NC: Duke University Press, 1993; S. Žižek, *Welcome to the Desert of the Real! Five Essays on September 11 and Related Dates*, London: Verso, 2002; S. Žižek, *Iraq: The Borrowed Kettle*, London: Verso, 2005.

27 See, for example, S.P. Huntington, *The Clash of Civilizations and the Remaking of World Order*, New York: Touchstone, 1996.
28 See, for example, F. Fukuyama, *The End of History and the Last Man*, New York: Avon Books, 1992.
29 H. Grotius, *The Rights of War and Peace*, ed. R. Tuck, Indianapolis, IN: Liberty Fund, 2005.
30 C. von Clausewitz, *On War*, ed. M. Howard and P. Paret, New York: Everyman's Library, 1993.
31 A. Kojève, *Outline of a Phenomenology of Right*, ed. B. Frost and R. Howse, Lanham, MD: Rowman and Littlefield, 2000.
32 R. Aron, *Peace and War: A Theory of International Relations*, Garden City, NY: Doubleday and Co., 1966.
33 Here the historical and discursive practice of 'ordering' is situated within the transcendental operation of positing within subjectivity. The activity of positing then is always an activity of *the self ordering itself* and its others in relation to itself.
34 My account broadly attempts to re-conceptualize Hegel's notion of *Geist* or *spirit* by drawing upon the Marxist philosophy of Ernst Bloch. See E. Bloch, *Natural Law and Human Dignity*, trans. D.J. Schmidt, Cambridge, MA: MIT Press, 1996; E. Bloch, *The Spirit of Utopia*, trans. A. Nassar, Stanford, CA: Stanford University Press, 2000; E. Bloch, *The Principle of Hope*, trans. N. Plaice and S. Plaice, Cambridge, MA: MIT Press, 1995.

Chapter 1

A critique of just war

1

Many people have an opinion on war. When it comes to justifying or condemning a particular war, many are quite ready to voice their opinion, to shout their belief out loud, to shout down others. In the context of what is commonly called the 'war on terror' our ears are pounded and battered by ever constant proclamations that this 'war' is 'just' and that it is the 'right' thing to do. More sporadically, more dispersed, but perhaps no less powerful, stands a groundswell of opinion that murmurs and mutters its discontent with such proclamations. Sometimes this muttering breaks out into public demonstration with an anger that shouts back that the war is unjust, illegal, illegitimate, or most basically, that it is not right. It is easy to say that a particular war is 'right' or that it is 'not right', however, it seems that it is more difficult to explain what is meant by this. What is the rightness of war? What place do concepts of right have in helping us judge acts of war? Are there differing concepts of right contained within our opinions on war? Taking the problem of war seriously involves asking and pursuing these types of questions.

Under the shadow of the so-called 'war on terror' this chapter offers a critique of a discourse commonly known as 'just war theory'. Just war theory dominates many contemporary debates related to war and terror. It is not merely an academic discourse, it is also widely invoked by politicians and many within the media to both justify and condemn acts of war, humanitarian intervention, and terrorism. This chapter will briefly look at a popular account of just war theory offered by Michael Walzer and point to the general inadequacy of his approach. Walzer's just war theory fails because of its uncritical reliance upon a number of assumptions about the nature of 'morality', 'justice' and 'reason'. Due to these assumptions his pronouncements about what does or does not constitute a 'just cause' resemble little more than the private and dubious opinions given by politicians and so-called media 'experts'.

The chapter probes a little deeper into some of the assumptions that are relied upon by Walzer and other just war theorists. By looking at the classical just war theory of Francisco de Vitoria, the chapter examines the way in which a well-meaning, careful, and principled approach to war via just war concepts too often ends up as an apology for, and justification of, aggressive violence and conquest. By situating Vitoria, one of the 'early fathers' of just war theory, within the colonial context, some of the inadequacies of the abstract nature of just war thinking come more readily to the surface. By holding on to this context, modern re-appropriations of just war theory are shown to be increasingly suspect and, at times, rather dangerous.

II

The bombings in New York and Washington, DC, in the USA in 2001 may be thought generally to have opened a period of conflict described as the 'war on terror'.[1] The invasions of Afghanistan in 2001 and Iraq in 2003 by the USA and its allies along with a number of terrorist bombings carried out by 'militant Islamicist political organizations'[2] in Indonesia, Spain, Saudi Arabia, Pakistan, Turkey and Great Britain are generally seen as moments within this conflict. The main sites of the 'war on terror' are the continued wars of occupation fought by the USA and its allies in Afghanistan and Iraq against Afghani and Iraqi guerrilla resistance forces and ongoing acts of terrorism carried out by militant Islamicist political organizations across the globe.

For many the 'war on terror' is a just war. The conflict is described as representing a legitimate moral struggle in the defence of freedom, human rights and the values of modern, Western liberal civilization against those (i.e. the 'terrorists') who desire to destroy this. For many, it is a war in which the Western values of freedom, human rights and democracy are pitched against the forces of evil.[3] US President George W. Bush's response to the bombings in the USA in 2001 framed the 'war on terror' within a broad moral sense of representing a just war in defence of freedom and civilization.[4] Such a justification could be seen in a number of moments within a speech given on the 20th of September, 2001. Bush stated:

> Tonight we are a country awakened to danger and called to defend freedom. Our grief has turned to anger, and anger to resolution. Whether we bring our enemies to justice, or bring justice to our enemies, justice will be done.[5]

Further, that:

> These terrorists kill not merely to end lives, but to disrupt and end a way of life. With every atrocity, they hope that America grows fearful, retreating from the world and forsaking our friends. They stand against us, because we stand in their way.[6]

Further, that:

> We are not deceived by their pretences to piety. We have seen their kind before. They are the heirs of all the murderous ideologies of the 20th century. By sacrificing human life to serve their radical visions – by abandoning every value except the will to power – they follow in the path of fascism, and Nazism, and totalitarianism. And they will follow that path all the way, to where it ends: in history's unmarked grave of discarded lies.[7]

Further, that:

> This is not, however, just America's fight. And what is at stake is not just America's freedom. This is the world's fight. This is civilization's fight. This is the fight of all who believe in progress and pluralism, tolerance and freedom.[8]

The portrayal of the 'war on terror' as a just war, a war of freedom against unfreedom, a war of civilization against barbarism, is not universally accepted. Many question the moral legitimacy of not only the wars carried out by the USA in Afghanistan and Iraq but also the legitimacy of new forms of security legislation and the US imprisonment and torture of enemy soldiers. For many, the invasion of Iraq by the USA in 2003 was in breach of international law and represented a war crime. Further, many are sceptical of the use of a moral language and the ambiguous use of terms such as 'freedom', 'human rights', 'democracy' and 'civilization' to justify particular acts of state violence when it seems that behind this powerful language often reside the workings of political, strategic and economic interests.

One means of coming to terms with the competing claims over the justness of the 'war on terror' is to turn towards an intellectual tradition known as the just war tradition. At first glance this tradition might offer some assistance in addressing the ambiguity of the moral concepts and language bound up with competing justifications and condemnations of war. In recent history one of the popularizers of just war theory is Michael Walzer.[9] Walzer argues for the contemporary importance of the notion of just war and his work has been highly influential in reviving this tradition of thought against legal positivism and 'reason of state' theories. For Walzer, just war theory involves a set of moral arguments about the moral legitimacy or illegitimacy of particular acts of war and the manner in which they are conducted. It involves moral judgment over the legitimacy of acts of war (*ius ad bellum*) and moral judgement over the conduct of participants within war (*ius in bello*).[10] It is worth here drawing attention to what Walzer describes as the sphere of 'morality' which informs a notion of just war. Walzer argues:

> I want to account for the ways in which men and women who are not lawyers but simply citizens (and sometimes soldiers) argue about war, and to expound the terms we commonly use. I am concerned precisely with the

present structure of the moral world. My starting point is the fact that we do argue, often to different purposes, to be sure, but in a mutually comprehensible fashion: else there would be no point in *arguing*. We justify our conduct; we judge the conduct of others. Though these justifications and judgments cannot be studied like the records of a criminal court, they are nevertheless a legitimate subject of study. Upon examination they reveal, I believe, a comprehensive view of war as human activity and a more or less systematic moral doctrine, which sometimes, but not always, overlaps with established legal doctrine.[11]

Further, that:

> I shall always refer to the laws of international society (as these appear in legal handbooks and military manuals) as *positive* laws. For the rest, when I talk of law, I am referring to the moral law, and to those general principles that we commonly acknowledge, even when we can't or won't live up to them.[12]

And:

> Throughout the book, I treat words like aggression, neutrality, surrender, civilian, reprisal, and so on, as if they were terms in a moral vocabulary – which they are, and always have been, though most recently their analysis and refinement have been almost entirely the work of lawyers.
>
> I want to recapture the notion of just war for moral and political theory. My own work, then, looks back to that religious tradition within which Western politics and morality were first given shape, to the books of writers like Maimonides, Aquinas, Vitoria, and Suarez – and then to the books of writers like Hugo Grotius who took over the tradition and began to work it into secular form.[13]

With regard to what Walzer precisely means by 'morality' or the 'moral law', he argues:

> There is a particular arrangement, a particular view of the world that seems to me the best one. I want to suggest that the arguments we make about war are most fully understood (though other understandings are possible) as efforts to recognize and respect the rights of individuals and associated men and women. The morality I shall expound is in its philosophical form a doctrine of human rights, though I shall say nothing here of the ideas of personality, action and intention that this doctrine probably presupposes. Considerations of utility play into the structure at many points, but they cannot account for it as a whole. Their part is a subsidiary to that of rights; it is constrained by rights. That is above all true of the

> classical forms of military maximization: the religious crusade, the proletarian revolution, the 'war to end all war'. But it is true also, as I will try to show, of the more immediate pressures of 'military necessity'. At every point, the judgments we make (the lies we tell) are best accounted for if we regard life and liberty as something like absolute values and then try to understand the moral and political processes through which these values are challenged and defended.[14]

It should be noted that Walzer positions his work as a 'practical morality'[15] and he tries to develop his moral account of war through the use of case studies and by contrasting historical examples. With this said, however, Walzer makes many very broad assumptions over what constitutes 'morality' and thus upon what should be drawn upon as a notion of right when judging the legitimacy of an act of war. Walzer assumes that there is a 'common morality' and he asserts that the content of this common morality is human rights. Judgments about the rightness or wrongness of going to war are to be based upon an assessment of how the use of violence relates to the common morality of human rights.

Generally, in relation to the *ius ad bellum*, Walzer's just war theory operates in two senses. In one sense, the theory operates negatively or critically, in that wars normally legitimated by political, economic and power interests, and even those justified by positive law or notions of utility, may be condemned as unjust because they threaten a common morality of human rights. In another sense, the theory operates positively, in that it offers a ground for legitimating war in the name of protecting and safeguarding the rights of individuals who are threatened or injured by some form of violence or coercion.

Walzer sets out a number of arguments under which the positive sense of just war is limited and restricted, and generally the notion is usually limited to instances of self-defence. However, Walzer also outlines other broader possibilities of the use of force as being *just* in the context of: a perceived immediate threat; the necessity of humanitarian intervention; and, in situations of 'extreme emergency'. Each of these notions allows exceptions from the more restrictive aspect of his theory. It is at the point of these exceptions to a restrictive just war theory and their opening onto a more proactive use of the intellectual discipline of just war theory to legitimate sometimes aggressive acts of international violence, that is of concern and which brings a popular just war theory like that of Walzer into question.

From his notion of morality *as* human rights, Walzer passes judgment on particular acts of war in history. It is questionable whether such an approach is an example of what it means to take the problem of war seriously. Is it enough for a scholar to simply assert what a 'common morality' apparently *is* and then say 'I think' that such and such an act of war is just or unjust?[16] Does this kind of approach lead thinking out of the ambiguous use of moral statements made all too often by politicians in their justification of killing, or does it lead straight back into a realm of moral ambiguity?

By simply declaring what he thinks morality *is* and then proceed to judge the justness of war from this basis, Walzer overlooks a deeper question lying at the heart of war. This question is centred around a relationship between war and right. The term 'right' here refers not to the limited sense of legal rights or human rights, but denotes a broader concept encompassing differing notions of ethics, morality, law, justice and the good.[17] In this latter sense, the term right refers to a broader sphere of thinking about the ethical or normative arrangement of human lives in the world. Thought in this sense, what is being overlooked by thinkers such as Walzer (and by politicians who speak in a similar language) is the possibility of a deeper relationship between war and right which marks, frames and even organizes our thinking about war in general. This relation has developed historically over a process of ongoing attempts of human ethical thinking to come to terms with the role and status of killing and violence in general and the act of war in particular.

Certainly Walzer argues that his concern is not with a historical question and that rather, his approach is focused upon the 'present character' of the moral world.[18] Yet, in making such a claim and attempting to name the present character of morality as human rights, Walzer confuses *one* form of right (human rights) with the *whole* of right (containing a number of different, inter-related forms). Further, he suppresses the continuing role and significance of other forms of right which are essential to his and other's judgments upon the justness of particular acts of war. By not acknowledging the role these other, often competing, forms of right play within the 'moral' judgment over war,[19] Walzer presents only a thin, surface level account of just war which does not differ substantially from much of the just war rhetoric given by state propaganda and sorry apologists.

A theory of just war that attempts to take the problem of war seriously would need to investigate what a notion of 'right' or 'justice' meant in a broader historical and philosophical sense. Such a theory could not simply assume, as Walzer does, that there is a 'common morality' and then make judgments about 'just cause' from that basis. Rather, a theory of just war would need to, at least, present a compelling account of right or justice and show how the status of violence operates within this wider moral, legal and political framework. What might be some of the forms of right that a theorist would need to consider? A non-exhaustive list might include: the question of 'legitimacy' of the state and international law; competing notions of sovereignty; moral and legal justifications of violence and coercion; differing accounts of individual and group rights; secular and religious conceptions of political community; differing forms of ethical life; and, competing notions of the 'good', 'democracy' and 'freedom' enunciated both historically and in the present.

In this sense, an approach that takes the problem of war seriously would have to move beyond the style of merely making assumptions about what aspects of these notions constitute a 'common morality' and would need to engage with the problem of war in a critical manner. That is, the question of just war would need to be considered as a proper philosophical question and not merely as an issue of applied ethics, to which the question of legitimate violence is simply tacked onto a religious or secular, liberal (or conservative) ideology. Further, the problem of just war as a philosophical question would need to consider the relationship between right and violence as a philosophical problem.

Thus, there is a deeper set of questions involving the complex relationship between war and right that lie beneath the just war language of theorists such as Walzer or politicians such as George W. Bush. While certain theoretical approaches, such as Walzer's, give the appearance of engaging with these questions, what they are really doing is suppressing them in an effort to present an account of just war that is 'useful' and digestible. There are of course other scholars within a contemporary just war discourse who approach questions of 'just cause' with a greater degree of care than that of Walzer.[20] Yet, these approaches, and the just war tradition as a whole, are still limited by particular assumptions they make about justice, legitimate authority, and moral reasoning, in relation not only to war, but in relation to violence in general. For the purpose of looking a little deeper into some of these assumptions it may be helpful to consider one of the 'early fathers' of the just war tradition, Francisco de Vitoria.

III

Vitoria is generally considered to be one of the major historical figures within the just war tradition. His writings helped to draw together the disparate Christian just war concepts put forward by Augustine of Hippo and Thomas Aquinas into a more comprehensive account of just war that also drew upon and responded to elements of humanist and republican thinking of the time. Significantly, Vitoria, a Catholic, Dominican theologian attempted to develop a theory of just war upon natural law principles in response to the Spanish conquest of America – a conquest which was an act of genocide.[21] Vitoria's natural law theory of just war was not only influential upon Spanish theologians and jurists but was also heavily influential upon early secular natural law theorists such as Hugo Grotius, a thinker who shaped many of the principles that lie at the basis of modern international law. Many contemporary just war theorists still draw a great deal from Vitoria and see in his writings an honest and genuine attempt to set out principles of just war that cautiously restrict and limit the legitimate causes of war and regulate its conduct.

Vitoria's writings on just war survive by way of copies made by his pupils of his lectures or *relectiones*, in the form of the texts, *On the American Indians* (1539) and *On the Law of War* (1539).[22] These texts are written in the colonial context of the Spanish conquest of America. They deal with problems ranging from: the question of ownership or dominion over land in America; the question of forced conversions to Catholicism; the legitimate causes of waging war against the indigenous population; and, the general treatment of the indigenous inhabitants by the Spanish. A sense of Vitoria's own complex standpoint on these issues can be gleaned from a letter written by Vitoria to a religious superior in 1534 on the subject of the conquest of Peru by Francisco Pizzaro and the plunder taken by his *peruleros* ('Peruvian adventurers'):

> But *if utterly forced* to give a categorical reply, in the end I say what I think. Some of these Peruvian adventurers, *I fear*, may be the type '*that desire to be rich* [and fall into temptation]' (1 Tim. 6:9), of whom it was said '[it is easier for a camel to go through the eye of a needle than] *for a rich man to enter the kingdom of heaven*' (Matt. 19:23–24). Here, since the property belonged to someone else, they can allege no title other than *the law of war*.
>
> *First*, I do not understand the justice of the war. I *do not dispute* the emperor's right to conquer the Indies, which *I presuppose* he may, most strictly; but as far as I understand from eyewitnesses who were personally present during the recent battle with Atahuallpa, neither he nor any of his people had ever done the slightest injury to the Christians, nor given them the least grounds to making war on them.
>
> *But*, the defenders of the *peruleros* reply that their soldiers were not obliged to examine this, but only to obey and carry out their captain's orders.
>
> *I accept this response* in the case of those who did not know that there was no other cause for this war than sheer robbery – which was all or most of them. Other more recent conquests have, I think, been even more vile. But I cannot let the matter rest at this. I grant that all the battles and conquests were good and holy, but we must still consider that this war *by the very admission* of the Peruvian conquistadors is not against strangers, but against true vassals of the emperor, as if they were natives of Seville; *and furthermore, truly ignorant of the justice of the war*, convinced that the Spaniards are tyrannical oppressors waging unjust war on them. Even if the emperor has just titles to conquer them, the Indians do not and cannot know this. *They are most certainly innocents in this war*.
>
> But even *supposing the justice in the war is all on the side of the Spaniards, hostilities may not proceed* beyond subduing them and compelling them to accept the emperor as prince *with the infliction upon them of as little damage as possible*. This does not mean robbing them and leaving them destitute *of everything regarding their temporal goods*. War, especially against one's vassals, must be undertaken and waged for the good of the vassals and not the prince, '*if there is any truth in the oracles of the seers*' (Ovid, *Metamorphoses* XV. 879) – that is, of the saints and doctors of the church. I know no justification for the robbing and plundering the unfortunate victims of defeat of all they posses and even what they do not possess.
>
> In truth, if the Indians are not men but monkeys, *they are incapable of injury*. But if they are men, and our neighbours, and *as they claim* vassals of the emperor, I cannot see how to excuse the conquistadors of utter impiety and tyranny.[23]

Vitoria's response to the questions raised by this colonial context and delivered in the form of scholastic theological inquiry set out a number of principles that today echo throughout modern international law. Vitoria denied that the Pope had any claim to dominion or ownership over America and instead he affirmed and recognized on the basis of natural law the right of the Amerindians to ownership of their lands. He denied that the Amerindians were 'natural slaves' in any Aristotelian sense and argued that they be recognized, as humans, who were to observe and be treated in accordance with the law of nations, the *ius gentium*. He argued that forced conversion to Christianity was inconsistent with Christian doctrine and hence that wars were not justified on the basis of religious conversion. Further, he argued for the limitation of the legitimate or just causes of war to self-defence and to the avenging of injury.

Given this list of arguments, what makes Vitoria such a profound figure in the history of the just war tradition, and within the history of international law, is the fact that his claims, based upon a set of natural law principles, lay out criteria that legitimate and justify the Spanish conquest of America – that is, the colonial appropriation of land and the assumption of political authority founded upon *just war*. To understand how this seemingly contradictory moment in Vitoria takes place it is necessary to briefly discuss aspects of Christian just war thinking outlined by Augustine and Aquinas which form part of the background of Vitoria's thought.

While Augustine did not develop a comprehensive theory of just war as such, his comments have been highly influential upon the tradition. In the *City of God* (426),[24] Augustine responds to the initial prohibition of killing contained within the Decalogue and the Christian Gospels and in this sense engages with an early Christian tendency towards non-violence and pacifism. Since the conversion of the Emperor Constantine to Christianity, theologians like Augustine were faced with the demand to reconcile pacifist injunctions with the pragmatic demands of a Christian city or empire previously governed by Roman law. Augustine attempted to find ways of justifying the use of violence by Christians to maintain public order or to fight wars against non-Christians. With regard to the commandment 'Thou shalt not kill', Augustine states:

> But the divine authority itself has made certain exceptions to the rule that it is not lawful to kill men. These exceptions, however, include only those whom God commands to be slain, either by a general law, or by an express command applying to a particular person at a particular time. Moreover, he who is commanded to perform this ministry does not himself slay. Rather, he is like a sword which is the instrument of its user. And so those who, by God's authority, have waged wars, or who bearing the public power in their own person, have punished the wicked with death according to His laws, that is, by His most just authority: these have in no way acted against that commandment which says, 'Thou shalt not kill'.[25]

Regarding an express command by God to kill, Augustine gives the example of Abraham who was commanded by God to kill his son.[26] With regard to those bearing public power, Augustine imputes that the role of public office (the Christian monarch), which is necessary to maintain public peace and order against crime and civil war, allows a legitimate use of violence that is exempt from the prohibition on killing.[27] For Augustine, such acts of justified killing are bound up with the 'wretchedness of man's condition'.[28] This involves the misery of living in the condition of sin and the role of the public official, guided by the law of God, who may legitimately use violence to punish those who sin. Yet, such a wretchedness of the fallen condition of man also involves the operation of error within human judgment and the possibility of public authorities sometimes torturing and killing the innocent.[29] In this respect while a war fought against a harmful or threatening enemy may be a 'just war' it is certainly not celebrated or romanticized by Augustine. He argues:

> Let everyone, therefore who reflects with pain upon such great evils, upon such horror and cruelty, acknowledge that this is misery. And if anyone either endures them or thinks of them without anguish of the soul, his condition is still more miserable: for he thinks himself happy only because he has lost all human feeling.[30]

Elements of Augustine's account were inherited and developed by Aquinas and organized around the notions of legitimate authority, just cause and intention. In the *Summa Theologiae* (1266–73),[31] Aquinas, in response to the question of whether war is always sinful, argues:

> There are three conditions for a just war. First the ruler under whom the war is to be fought must have the authority to do so. A private person does not have the right to make war since he can pursue his rights by appealing to his superior. In addition a private person does not have the right to mobilize [*convocare*] the people as must be done in war. But since the responsibility for the commonwealth has been entrusted to rulers, it is their responsibility to defend the city or kingdom or province subject to them. And just as it is legitimate for them to use the material sword to punish criminals in order to defend it against internal disturbances – as the Apostle [Paul] says in Romans 13, 'He does not bear the sword without cause, for he is a minister of God, an avenger in wrath against the evildoer' – so they also have the right to use the sword of war to defend the commonwealth against external enemies ...
>
> Secondly, a just cause is required – so that those against whom the war is waged deserve such a response because of some offence on their part. Augustine says, 'Just wars are usually defined as those that avenge injuries, when a nation or city should be punished for failing to right a wrong done by its citizens, or to return what has been taken away unjustly.'

> The third condition that is required on the part of those making the war is a right intention, to achieve some good or avoid some evil. St. Augustine says in his book, *On the Words of the Lord*, 'For the true followers of God even wars are peaceful if they are waged not out of greed or cruelty but for the sake of peace, to restrain evil doers and assist the good.' Yet it may happen that even if the war is initiated by a legitimate authority and its cause is just, it can become unjust because of evil intentions.[32]

This latter point relates to what is sometimes called the principle of double effects and the notion of proportionality. Aquinas argues:

> One act may have two effects, only one of which is intended and the other outside of our intention. Moral acts are classified on the basis of what is intended, not of what happens outside of our intention since that is incidental to it ... The action of defending oneself may produce two effects – one, saving one's life, and the other, killing the attacker. Now an action of this kind intended to save one's own life cannot be characterized as illicit since it is natural for anyone to maintain himself in existence if he can. An act that is proportionate to the end intended. This is why it is not allowed to use more force than is necessary to defend one's life. However, if moderation is used in repelling violence, this is justified self-defence, for according to the [canon] law, 'It is legitimate to meet force with force if it is an act of innocent self-defence and exercises restraint.' It is not required for salvation that a man not carry out actions of proportionate self-defence in order to avoid killing another person, for a man is more obliged to provide for his own life than that of another. However, because killing is only allowed by action of public authority for the common good, it is not lawful for someone who is acting in self-defence to intend to kill another man – except for those who in the exercise of public authority justify the act of self-defence as related to the public good. This is the case of a soldier fighting against the enemy or an officer of the law combating robbers – although these too commit a sin if they are motivated by private animosity.[33]

For both Augustine and Aquinas, the question of 'legitimate authority' was central to any notion of the just use of violence by Christians. For Augustine, part of what was at stake in the use of violence by the individual was the loss of an attitude or state of love and its replacement by the motivations of greed, lust and hatred. However, Augustine saw the possibility of public officials adopting a more detached emotional standpoint for the purpose of public duty and thus not using violence because of hatred but instead acting out of the motivations of charity and love. As F.H. Russell notes:

> Recognizing that the legitimacy of warfare had to be grounded in evangelical precepts, Augustine sought support in one of the touchstones of this thought,

> the notion of charity. Punishment of evil-doers that prevented them from doing further wrong when administered without being moved by revenge or taking pleasure in suffering was an act of love. The precept 'resist not evil' (Matt. 5:39) did not prohibit wars, for the real danger in soldiering was not military service itself but the malice that so often accompanied it, and the command to 'turn the other cheek' (Luke 6:29) referred to the inward disposition of the heart rather than the outward deed. Patience and benevolence did not always conflict with the inflicting of physical punishment, for when Moses put sinners to death he was motivated not by cruelty but by love. Hatred was to be overcome by a love of one's enemies that did not preclude a benevolent severity. By this distinction between the inward disposition of the heart and outward acts, to be accepted without serious question in the Middle Ages, Augustine claimed to reconcile war and the New Testament. Since according to the 'inwardness' of his ethics the intention rather than the hostile act was normative, any hostile act was justified provided it was motivated by charity. The spirituality of the Sermon on the Mount that had induced earlier Christians to renounce war now justified it. To treat evangelical precepts in this way was to revalue them politically such that warfare now became necessary rather than inherently sinful. Love for one's neighbour could legitimate his death, and not to resist evil became an attitude compatible with outward belligerence toward him. The new *miles Christi* now fought other men as well as sin and the devil.
>
> Augustine's intellectual revaluation denied the use of physical violence to private persons. A private Christian could not kill an attacker in self-defence, for that would entail hatred and loss of love. In such cases Augustine bore witness to the pacifist tendencies of the early Church. Only rulers and officials acting in the line of duty were able to kill without giving vent to hatred and other sinful passions. Private pacifism was thus joined to a justification of public warfare that underscored the later medieval emphasis on the legitimate authority necessary to wage wars.[34]

Such a justification that allowed monarchs and public officials to carry out violence for the purpose of love was accepted by latter just war thinkers such as Aquinas and Vitoria. It is not too difficult to see the continuation of this idea in the contemporary notions of humanitarian intervention and wars carried out in the name of humanity. These modern forms of war sit within a just war framework in that they are motivated not only by the desire to preserve peace, but also, out of love for fellow humans. Just like the earlier Christian wars of love, these modern, secular wars of good conscience are easily manipulated and used as a pretext for gaining greater wealth and power.

Sitting beneath the accounts of Augustine and Aquinas is the assumption that the political authority of Christian monarchs is derived from the authority of a Christian God over the universe. Aquinas married Christian theology with

Aristotelian philosophy. He followed Aristotle's conception of a community organized for the sake of securing the 'bare needs of life' and of developing the 'good life', that is, of a *polis* directed towards the realization of justice.[35] This for Aquinas, is to be secured by a monarch.[36]

For Aquinas, the universe is governed by God's divine providence and reason which acts as an 'eternal law'. Rational creatures such as humans who follow their natural inclinations participate in eternal reason through their knowledge/inclination of 'natural law'. Particular dispositions arrived at by humans through reason deduced from the universal precepts of natural law are called by Aquinas 'human laws'. In addition, humans have access to 'divine law' as revealed to them in religious scripture.[37] Through this hierarchy of laws which link the governance of human social life to the Christian God via natural inclination and reason, Aquinas is able to demonstrate how earthly legal and political institutions such as monarchies draw their authority from both the Aristotelian desire for the good life and justice, and, from the divine reason of a Christian God. The earthly authority of the monarch derives its authority from the word of God by way of a cosmic chain of being mediated through the differing hierarchies of law and reason. Earthly justice and divine justice are linked together through a natural order of the world ordained by God through grace and reason.

In this sense, the precept of 'legitimate authority' within the just war tradition is situated firmly within a Christian world view that sees its religious texts and subsequent doctrines as universal truth.[38] The earthly authority of the Christian monarch, and thus its right to carry out war and violence stem from both the ruler's agency per Paul, as a 'minister of God'[39] and from the cosmic chain of reason (eternal-natural-human-divine law) that legitimates earthly authority via God's *logos*. Significantly, because of the universality of natural law, such a line of argumentation opens onto the possibility of non-Christian polities being recognized as holding 'legitimate authority' to the extent that they are organized around Aristotle's concept of the good life.[40] Such an opening by way of natural law is taken up later by Vitoria and used to develop his account of the 'just' legal relations between Christians and the Amerindians via the *ius gentium*.

Vitoria inherits and to a great degree accepts such a Christian world view and Aquinas's explanation of the universe and human life ordered by way of divine reason and natural law. In presenting his account of just war within the context of the Spanish conquest of America, it is the conceptual framework of Aquinas and the theory of natural law that Vitoria turns to and further develops. In *On Civil Power* (1528), Vitoria presents a scholastic account of political authority beginning with the argument that the 'final cause' of civil power is 'natural necessity'.[41] He quotes Aristotle and argues that the political form of organization – cities or commonwealths – is not an invention of humans but, is 'a device implanted by nature' for their safety and survival.[42] Further, he argues that communities cannot exist without some form of public power or ordering force to guard public property and look after the common good.[43] In this respect, for Vitoria, the final cause or justification for secular power is natural necessity.[44] However, the 'efficient cause' of civil power is God. He argues:

> *The efficient cause of this power* can easily be deduced from the preceding argument. If, as we have shown, public power is founded upon natural law, and if natural law acknowledges God as its only author, then it is evident that public power is from God, and cannot be over-ridden by conditions imposed by men or by any positive law.[45]

From this point, Vitoria argues that the 'material cause' of civil power is the commonwealth which, as required by divine and natural law, is to govern and administer for the sake of the common good.[46] Further, the authority of the commonwealth to kill a human is derived from divine and natural law and that this authority to take a man's life is not held by a private citizen.[47] For Vitoria, the material power of the commonwealth is invested in sovereigns, the best form of which he describes as being monarchy or kingship.[48] In this respect, Vitoria justifies royal power and authority on the basis of both divine and natural law.[49]

On the back of this account of natural law Vitoria argues that non-Christian monarchs may hold legitimate authority regardless of their unbelief, unless they commit some form of injustice.[50] And further, that monarchs do not receive their temporal power from the Pope.[51] Each of these arguments plays a significant role in Vitoria's just war account set within the context of Spanish imperial conquest.

In *On the American Indians* and *On the Law of War*, Vitoria approaches a set of theological questions relating to what constitutes a 'just war'. These respond critically to various arguments peddled at the time and used to justify Spanish conquest and also relate to concerns held by some Spanish about the brutal treatment of the Amerindians. Vitoria considers the issue of whether the Amerindians lack political authority over themselves or ownership over their lands and possessions – the question of public and private dominion.[52] In this respect he considers whether the Amerindians can be considered in an Aristotelian sense as either 'true masters' or 'natural slaves'.[53] Vitoria's conclusion is that the Amerindians are true masters and cannot be disposed without just cause,[54] and that they are neither deprived of their dominion by way of being sinners nor because of unbelief.[55] Further, he argues that the Amerindians should not be deprived of dominion on the basis of arguments made at the time that they were irrational, were children or were mad. Rather, he insists that they exercise judgment in their affairs, such as through the organization of cities, laws, industry and commerce and religion; all of which indicate the exercise of reason.[56]

By establishing that the Amerindians are rational humans who are not to be considered natural slaves, Vitoria is able to extend his theory of natural law to govern the relations between Spanish and Amerindians and thus argue for a need to respect and recognize their property rights and political institutions.[57] On a similar basis, Vitoria is able to argue against any claim that the Spanish emperor is 'master of the whole world' because the dominion of other peoples is guaranteed by natural law.[58] Further, Vitoria also argues against any claim by the Pope to be the civil or temporal master of the whole world[59] and in this respect he challenges aspects of the authority of the Papal Bulls that had previously divided the 'undiscovered world' between Spain and Portugal.

For Vitoria, because the Amerindians had legitimate political authority and ownership of their lands under natural law, they could only be dispossessed by the Spanish if some 'just cause' existed. Vitoria argues, following Augustine, that a Christian may lawfully fight and wage war to avenge an injury and for the purpose of both peace and security of the commonwealth, and for the 'good of the whole world'.[60] In setting out what constitutes a just war, Vitoria denies that it is lawful to wage war because of difference of religion, for the purpose of enlarging an empire or for the personal glory of a monarch.[61] In this respect, Vitoria's notion of just cause appears very limited in that he argues that the only just cause for waging war is when a harm has been inflicted, and further that, not every injury gives sufficient grounds for waging war.[62] Thus, on the face of things, Vitoria's account of just war, when applied to the Spanish context in America, severely restricts any grounds that justify the conquest. He argues that the Amerindians, even if they reject the Christian faith, offer no just cause to the Spanish to carry out war against them if they do no wrong or do not cause injury to the Spanish.[63]

However, when Vitoria discusses the role of Spanish 'travellers' and missionaries in America he enunciates some startling arguments that point to the Spanish having a just cause to wage war. Not only this, but he sets out the possible theological justification on the basis of natural law for the 'injured' Spanish and the Spanish crown to take possession of property, enslave parts of the population and assume political authority, all on the basis of self-defence, the avenging of injury, security and the common good. What initially appears as a theory of just war aimed at limiting violence and aggression, turns quickly into a profoundly disturbing political text that justifies the Spanish conquest and does so via an honest and genuine, if fundamentally naïve, attitude of love, charity and good conscience shaped by a Christian world view. It is through such a well-intentioned apology for theft and barbarism that the worst of the just war tradition shines through and puts us on notice that we should remain wary of its reappropriation and championing in the present.

Vitoria sets out a number of 'just titles' through which the land and bodies of the Amerindians pass under the authority of the Spanish crown. He argues that on the authority of the law of nations (*ius gentium*), which is derived from natural law, the Spanish have a right to travel and dwell in America as long as they do not harm the local inhabitants.[64] Further, the Spanish have a right to lawfully trade[65] and possess forms of property that are held in common (i.e.

digging for gold on common land or in rivers).[66] He argues that if the Amerindians deny the Spanish these rights and do not listen to the reasoning and persuasion of the Spanish and instead inflict violence (even if only out of fear), then the Spanish have a just cause to go to war in self-defence to redress or avenge the injury done to them. He notes that such a war should be exercised with moderation as it is defensive.[67] However, he claims:

> [I]f all other measures to secure safety from the barbarians besides conquering their communities and subjecting them have been exhausted, the Spaniards may even take this measure. The proof is that the aim of war is peace and security, as St Augustine says in his letter to Boniface (*Ep* 189.6). Therefore, once it has become lawful for the Spaniards to take up war or even to declare it themselves for the reasons stated above, it becomes lawful for them to do everything necessary to the aim of war, namely to secure peace and safety.[68]

And, further:

> [O]nce the Spaniards have demonstrated diligently both in word and deed that for their own part they have every intention of letting the barbarians carry on in peaceful and undisturbed enjoyment of their property, if the barbarians nevertheless persist in their wickedness and strive to destroy the Spaniards, they may then treat them no longer as innocent enemies, but as treacherous foes against whom all rights of war can be exercised, including plunder, enslavement, deposition of their former masters, and the institution of new ones. All this must be done in moderation, in proportion to the actual offence.[69]

Following this, Vitoria then argues that Christians have the right to preach and announce the Gospel in America.[70] And, further:

> [I]f the barbarians, either in the person of their masters or as a multitude, obstruct the Spaniards in their free propagation of the Gospel, the Spaniards, after first reasoning with them to remove any cause of provocation, *may preach and work for the conversion of that people even against their will*, and may if necessary take up arms and declare war on them, insofar as this provides the safety and opportunity needed to preach the Gospel.[71]

Vitoria notes that the resulting war with its massacres and pillage may obstruct the process of conversion rather than encourage it, and that while the method is lawful *per se*, his fear is that some actions have gone beyond the permissible bounds of justice and religion.[72] In discussing further grounds for legitimate title, Vitoria delivers an argument reminiscent of contemporary notions of humanitarian intervention and so-called 'regime change'. Whereby, if the political leaders of the Amerindians are tyrants or carry out oppressive laws such as human sacrifice, then the Spanish have a lawful right to intervene, and if necessary, to depose their political leaders and their laws and set up new ones.[73]

Vitoria sets out another possible ground under which the Amerindians and their lands may come into the possession and the authority of the Spanish, this relates to the just cause of fighting on behalf of allies and friends. He gives the example of the alliance between the Spanish conquistador Hernán Cortés and the Tlaxcaltecs against Montezuma's Aztec confederacy in which, per Vitoria, Cortés was promised whatever his forces might win in return for his assistance.[74] Vitoria argues that confirmation of this principle is provided by the Romans who extended their empire by way of coming to the aid of their friends and allies and thus profiting by the opportunity to declare just wars and obtain new provinces by the laws of war. Vitoria notes that the Roman Empire was declared legitimate by both Augustine and Aquinas.[75]

IV

Vitoria's theory of just war, especially when read in light of his letter of 1534, appears to be written by someone who was appalled by the treatment of the Amerindians at the hands of Spanish conquistadors motivated not by a sense of love and Christian mission, but by greed, ignorance and hatred. In this sense, his theory of just war operates as an attempt by a Dominican theologian to clarify the limits by which Christians can legitimately wage war and the motivations or right intentions that should govern their actions. Indeed, he offers words of restriction to his account of just war stating that 'everything is to be done for the benefit and good of the barbarians, and not merely for the profit of the Spaniards'.[76] In this respect, Vitoria stands within a side of a just war tradition that attempts to carefully proscribe the limits of the operation of war and which argues against a 'holy war' or a Christian Crusading tradition happy to justify expansive and aggressive wars for the sake of converting and destroying infidels and capturing their territory.[77]

To this extent, Vitoria's account limits the legitimate claims of the Spanish crown's conquest of America. One might even claim that Vitoria's principles of just war could portray the Spanish conquest as illegitimate, *if* in every concrete case, it could be shown that the Amerindians did not cause injury to the 'visiting' Spanish. However, Vitoria's lectures do not do this, but the opposite, so that he justifies and legitimates the Spanish conquest on the basis of just war.

One major problem within Vitoria's theory of just war is his scholastic theological approach which relies heavily upon principles that float above, or are disconnected from, the realities of the historical and political situation of his time. His principles are too 'abstract' in the sense of not being tied to the practicalities of the colonial experience. Because of this, Vitoria's use of the concepts of 'injury', 'just cause', 'proportionate punishment' and so on offer a specific meaning for those who have a particular world view or who pick and choose their historical examples sporadically.[78]

An example is Vitoria's declared right of the Spanish to 'travel' and 'trade'. This misdescribes completely the historical situation of the Spanish in America, who since Columbus, had from the very beginning engaged in the activity of conquest, land appropriation, enslavement and religious conversion in the name of the Spanish crown and Catholicism. Any effort to describe the activities or the intentions of the Spanish in a less vindictive way is either naïve or ideologically biased. Indeed one of Vitoria's pupils, Melchor Cano, criticized this depiction of the Spanish as well-intentioned, travellers, traders and ambassadors, by asking: 'Who would have described Alexander as a traveller?'[79]

Another example is Vitoria's depiction of Cortés and his winning of just title for the Spanish through wars fought in the aid of particular Amerindian allies. The example allows Vitoria to impute a good and noble intention, that of helping friends and thus of carrying out a war motivated by love, when it is doubtful whether the conquest carried out by Cortés could have met the criteria of right intention. In this very crucial manner Vitoria's account misrepresents the Spanish as innocent 'visitors' who are forced to defend themselves against the injuries done to them by the Amerindians.

Such an abstract use of just war principles, tied to a sporadic use and somewhat biased interpretation of historical examples, allows Vitoria to outline a justification of the Spanish conquest by way of a set of theological and natural law principles which give the appearance of being 'neutral' and 'objective'. Through his account of a natural law-based theory of just war Vitoria helps to establish some of the early colonial foundations of modern international law – a set of seemingly 'objective' rules and principles which, when applied in carefully selected ways, allowed European nations to colonize the bulk of the world in accordance with the rule of law, for the purpose of the 'common good', and in good conscience.[80]

The links between Vitoria's natural law theory and account of the law of nations (*ius gentium*) and his legitimization of colonial conquest have been airbrushed away by many scholars in a similar manner to the way that Vitoria himself airbrushes the role played by the Spanish in America.[81] Yet, doing this denies the close historical links between both modern international law and the just war tradition within a history of the European colonization of the non-European world. Modern just war theories, such as that presented by Michael Walzer, which do not pay enough attention to the colonial heritage of the just war tradition and rely merely upon abstract principles, replicate the same problems and difficulties that plague Vitoria's account – they often present a 'principled' justification for neo-colonial, ideological or politically motivated violence.[82] Furthermore, it is not too difficult to discern similar rhetorical games made by politicians and international lawyers in the present who mischievously misrepresent historical events and apply the rhetorical move of innocence and good intention to depict an otherwise aggressive war as a 'just war', a 'pre-emptive strike' and a 'humanitarian intervention' against the threats made and injuries caused by a tyrant.[83]

Another problem with Vitoria's theory of just war is his assumption of particular forms of legitimate authority based upon Catholic theology and a particular Christian world view. While Vitoria recognizes the political authority of Amerindian leaders over their territory by way of his account of natural law, he also assumes the authority of a Christian God over the universe and thus, the authority of the Pope and the Spanish crown to teach the religious 'truth' to the Amerindians. Vitoria's natural law rights of individuals to travel and of Christians to preach are built upon a world view shaped around the Christian mission that render the political authority of Amerindian communities subservient to a greater 'spiritual' sovereignty of Christianity and the Pope.

For Vitoria, Amerindian political leaders do not have the authority to exclude Christian missionaries from their territory or to stop them from preaching. Further, Vitoria's right of Christians to spread the Gospel, clothed as a neutral, natural law right to visitation and free travel, is not considered at a level of genuine reciprocity. That is, it is doubtful whether Vitoria would have extended the right of non-Christians to preach their religion in Spain and following this, the possibility that non-Christians would have a just cause to go to war, conquer or enslave the Spanish peoples if Christian Spanish monarchs had caused them injury. Such a lack of reciprocity highlights again the way seemingly 'neutral' and 'objective' just war or natural law principles grant particular rights to some and not others based upon assumptions of legitimate authority sustained by a religious or ideological world view. Given that Christian Spain had been conquered by an Islamic empire 500 years earlier, the possibilities of thinking about this kind of reciprocity were not completely beyond the modes of thought that governed Vitoria's intellectual universe.

Again, Vitoria's ascribed right of Europeans to preach a Gospel of 'universal truth' to innocents, the ignorant and unbelievers finds a certain resonance in the present, albeit in a secular mode of preaching. A modern 'humanist' language of the 'universal truths' of 'freedom', 'democracy' and 'human rights' are preached as a form of Gospel by many Anglo Europeans of the North Atlantic world to their others in a manner that is reminiscent of old-fashioned Christian preaching. These claims to truth or concepts raised to a level of transcendent authority are also used to legitimate contemporary just wars as humanitarian interventions, and as holy wars or crusades waged brutally against modern 'heretics'. In Vitoria's time, the so-called 'universal truth' preached was really only *one* version or interpretation as enunciated by one Christian sect, Catholicism (albeit with degrees of internal divergence within a Catholic framework). Today, while universal concepts such as 'freedom', 'democracy' and 'human rights' are invoked by Western political leaders and their lawyers, what is being preached and often violently inflicted upon the world, is only *one* particular interpretation of these concepts – an interpretation which is fundamentally limited and shaped by a system of modern capitalism.

To this extent contemporary humanitarian just wars are often as unholy and ungodly as those waged by the Spanish conquistadors against the Amerindians, or by the earlier Christian Crusaders against the empires of Islam. Drawing the links between religious just wars of the past and modern or post-modern humanitarian just wars of the present, Costas Douzinas argues:

> Not unlike contemporary humanitarianism, just war theory was a marriage of convenience between prudence and morality consecrated by the establishment of the day. As a result of the religious-moral influence, medieval political theology became preoccupied with the justice of the cause, which was sought in the Bible and the disputations of natural law. A just war should be conducted in line with its declared aims. Little attention was paid to the means used. The divine duty to punish the infidel and evil-doer made the prosecution of some wars limitless. It justified unremitting violence of the Crusades, the genocidal attacks on the Indians and indigenous peoples of the newly discovered lands and, later, the atrocities of the religious wars, which, conducted on both sides in the name of true faith, knew no limit in their attempt to annihilate the morally degraded enemies.[84]

The problems inherent within Vitoria's approach are not merely limited to his religious just war account but rather, they point to a deeper set of difficulties contained within just war theory more generally. These difficulties limit the discourse's ability to effectively come to terms with the problem of war. One difficulty centres upon the notion of 'just cause' and the assumption by just war thinkers that their moral theory, either in a secular or religious form, can be used to determine a 'just' as opposed to an 'unjust' cause.

Most moral judgment involves some reflection upon, and the weighing up of, differing reasons and motivations for acting in one way and not in another. Just like other approaches to moral judgment, such as utilitarian, Kantian/deontological, or virtue ethics approaches, a just war approach encounters moments where it is difficult to determine what is the 'right' thing to do. This difficulty is faced by all forms of moral reason and does not, on its own, discredit just war theory. However, where just war theory comes unstuck is in its attempt to pick out one cause (i.e. an injury done or a threat perceived) from an infinite number of causes which might justify recourse to violence.

In a sense, just war theory mirrors the approach of criminal law in many domestic jurisdictions when considering legal defences to assault or murder. In both cases a set of criteria are used (i.e. self-defence, provocation by an injury, the existence of threat) to help determine when the use of violence is justified or not. However, in contrast to domestic criminal law, which more often or not, considers the acts of violence carried out by one individual against another, just war theory considers the action of communities or states involving hundreds, thousands or millions of connected individuals. Inter-communal violence, when considered historically, involves an infinite number of inter-related actions between members of communities. These actions are not simply the bare violence of a physical act, but also involve actions within the context of political, legal, cultural and economic systems which link and form the often porous boundaries between communities. The attempt to isolate one cause, or a set of causes of injury or threat, that crosses a conceptual threshold and amounts to a 'just cause' is an overwhelmingly difficult empirical exercise of data collection. Yet, most just war theorists, such as Walzer, do not present piles of historical and empirical data and instead merely point to a particular 'cause' by way of a cursory reading of contemporary events or history.

In the case of inter-communal violence, there are often simply too many historical, social and physical causal factors involved. One only needs to think about the ongoing cycle of reciprocal violence that has occurred between the populations of Israel and Palestine in the twentieth century to get a sense of the difficulties in determining a 'just cause' for the parties involved. All members of these communities have been victims of some form of violence and injury and all lay claim to some form of justification for violent action. Each party will lay claim to a historical 'first cause'. Each will invoke a set of rights, customs and laws to help them distinguish 'just causes' out of the infinite manifold of violent acts. Each will have recourse to the notions of self-defence, the avenging of injury, and action in response to perceived threat.

When we consider that perhaps all states have their origin in some form of violence, or the theft of property by one group from another, then how is the just war theorist to define the parameters that mark out which causes are considered relevant and which are not? Even if the theorist's approach is not, like Vitoria's approach, highly ahistorical and instead tries to comprehend the entirety of a historical and political situation, how is the just war theorist to adequately rank the significance of these historical causes in an 'objective' manner?

Some contemporary just war theorists acknowledge the difficulties involved in such attempts to pass judgment on history. They argue for a degree of caution to be taken when looking at the notion of just cause and endeavour to take a broader, historical view of conflict, examining the rights and interests of both parties when naming a 'just cause'. A.J. Coates argues for taking a 'bilateral' approach to the notion of just cause. He states:

> Viewed bilaterally, therefore, the question of just cause appears in a different, more muted light. The recognition of the rights and interests even of an unjust aggressor, along with the acknowledgement of one's own moral fallibility and partial responsibility for war, rule out the moral triumphalism engendered by a more unilateral moral approach, as well as the ruthless prosecution of war that is the natural outcome. This essential moral blurring of the conflict underlines the need to limit severely the action taken as well as the need to define the aims of war conservatively and the terms of peace generously and sympathetically. Understood in this

> way, the bilateral understanding of just cause appears not as a threat to just recourse but as an essential prerequisite. The position of the just belligerent is more that of an impartial judge who seeks to do justice to both sides in a dispute than that of an accuser or plaintiff.[85]

Such a response perhaps moves closer to framing just war theory within a post-Grotian conception of limited European war between states where each views the other as the just enemy, and further understands war more like a dispute resolution mechanism of last resort. The approach is cautious and is aimed at using the notion of just cause as a critical and limiting mechanism, thus attempting to narrow the legitimate causes of war while accepting the practicalities of wars being claimed as 'just' by both sides within a conflict. Such an approach can be distinguished from less careful approaches (i.e. Walzer) and from ideologically driven theories of just war, peddled, for example, by Jean Bethke Elshtain.[86] The distinction between these careful and less careful approaches within just war theory also mirrors contemporary legal approaches to humanitarian war and humanitarian intervention. Less careful approaches throw about the rhetorical language of human rights to justify all sorts of state violence and neo-colonial endeavours. More careful approaches on the other hand are aware of the limitations of the use of force for the purposes of humanitarian intervention due to the possibilities of these violent actions injuring the individuals who were meant to be saved.[87]

While some just war approaches recognize the difficulties involved in isolating a just cause and attempt to move just war theory away from the dangers of ahistoricism, they still struggle to provide a convincing solution to how we should comprehend and respond to the problem of war. Much of what creates difficulties for just war theory are the assumptions made about 'legitimate authority' and the way this blocks the tradition's ability to comprehend important aspects of violent conflict. As was shown in relation to Vitoria's theory of just war, assumptions about what constitutes a legitimate authority form part of the moral background or moral grammar that is drawn upon when judging whether a particular act constitutes a just cause. Moral determinations about just cause take place within, and are orientated by, an overarching conception of *justice* which may have both cosmic and temporal elements. For example, the concept of legitimate authority in Vitoria's scholastic account operated in a dual sense. Through a theory of natural law both Christian and non-Christian commonwealths had the authority to use violence internally for the sake of order and externally in war. Yet, Vitoria's almost 'quasi-secular' natural law theory of political authority was situated within a particular Catholic conception of universal justice which, in certain crucial respects, privileged Christian peoples and their monarchs over others. Vitoria's moral judgments about what constituted a 'just' cause were influenced by his cosmic conception of the absolute, legitimate authority of the Christianity – a 'higher' sense of right that framed all moral judgment.

Modern, secular just war approaches continue this linkage in that moral judgments about just cause are influenced by their assumptions of what constitutes an absolute, legitimate authority. For some, like Walzer, this absolute legitimate authority is made up of a conception of liberal, human rights, and at a secondary level, the sovereignty of nation-states and their historical boundaries. For others, like Elshtain, this absolute, legitimate authority is the global mission of the USA as the voice of 'freedom' within a chaotic world. The judgments of each with respect to what constitutes a 'just cause' in a particular historical case is framed, guided and shaped by their notions of legitimate authority. For Walzer and Elshtain, like the bulk of just war theorists, what constitutes 'legitimate authority' is often a matter of assumption and opinion, rather than a matter of theoretical or historical inquiry.

In contradistinction to many modern just war approaches, thinkers like Aquinas and Vitoria treated the concept of legitimate authority as a serious theoretical (and theological) question. For many modern just war theorists like Walzer and Elshtain, any similar depth of theoretical inquiry has been dispensed with. Such a dispensation allows particular actors (i.e. states) to assume something of an *a priori* sense of legitimacy and others an *a priori* sense of illegitimacy (i.e. 'terrorists') with respect to acts of violence. These lines which mark the boundaries of legitimate violence in contemporary conflict are not theoretically justified by most just war theorists but are merely assumed. If we are to seriously respond to the contemporary problem of so-called 'terrorist' violence by non-state actors, then operating by way of mere assumption is inadequate. Something more is required.

Some contemporary just war theorists lament the modern tradition's refusal to treat the concept of legitimate authority as a serious theoretical question. Coates, for example, argues: 'The criterion of legitimate authority has become the most neglected of all the criteria that have been traditionally employed in the moral assessment of war. Nowhere is this more evident than in the popular assessment of contemporary terrorism.'[88] While recognizing this difficulty, more cautious just war theorists like Coates still do not seem to probe deep enough into the question of legitimate authority. While he and others might slightly adjust traditional conceptions of sovereignty with reference to a greater historical appreciation of the role of revolutionary violence, generally they do not specifically investigate the relationship between the concept of legitimate authority and violence. In this respect both cautious and non-cautious approaches within just war theory overlook something crucial about the nature of war and violence. That is, often what is at stake within war and conflict is a contestation or struggle between parties over what form of *authority* is *legitimate* – over authority as a particular instantiation of justice. In this respect, the notion of legitimate authority is not merely one criterion which can be assumed as a given, even if slightly problematic. Rather, the question of just war is itself a question of what constitutes legitimate authority, over who has authority, over who has sovereignty, over whose conception of authority, sovereignty and justice is legitimate, universal, or the 'truth'.

A sense of this can be seen in Vitoria and in his response to the colonial context of a conflict between competing conceptions of political authority and sovereignty. His method is an attempt to develop a theoretical justification of justice and authority that allows smaller temporal claims but which effectively trumps any absolute universal claims made by the Amerindians. Vitoria's theory is an example of the intellectual production of a claim to moral and political authority, a claim to justice, used as a weapon in conflict against an other. If we are to take the problem of war seriously what is needed is an investigation into the differing ways in which a language of right and justice is produced as both a means of coming to terms with the problem of conflict and as a weapon within conflict itself.[89] While some just war theorists pay attention to this at a historical level, their analysis too often trails off and loses focus in the present.[90] What is required is a more thorough, theoretical consideration of how the concepts of moral and political authority, and right and justice, have been constructed in modernity and play out in the present through war and violence.

Following on from this, one final and major inadequacy of the just war tradition is its lack of appreciation of the critique of reason in modernity. Generally, just war theorists overlook the way moral 'reason', drawn upon to deliberate over the issues of just cause, legitimate authority and right intention, is itself a participant in struggle and conflict between parties asserting the universality and thus supremacy of a particular version of right and justice. For most just war theorists, access to, or the use of, something called 'reason' is generally assumed or invoked without question.

For example, Vitoria recognizes that princes and private subjects can be in error when making moral judgments over the justness of war. He argues that while they think that they are acting justly, their minds may be swayed or influenced by one passion or another. Hence, for Vitoria, 'Any man's opinion is not sufficient to make an action good.'[91] Rather, invoking Aristotle, he claims that determinations of just war should be based upon the judgments of a 'wise man'.[92] In contrast, Walzer does not appear to be interested in the way in which the critique of reason might be relevant to the consideration of how we think about the rightness or justness of war. It seems that his 'practical morality' has little time for such reflection. He argues:

> I did not begin by thinking about war in general, but about particular wars, above all about the American intervention in Vietnam. Nor did I begin as a philosopher, but as a political activist and a partisan. Certainly, political and moral philosophy ought to help us at those difficult times when we choose sides and make commitments. But it does so only indirectly. We are not usually philosophical in moments of crisis; most often, there is no time.[93]

Such a so-called 'practical' approach is symptomatic of a tradition which in modernity too often invokes a form of moral reasoning and fails to question what form of 'reason' is being invoked, or of how reason plays a role as a participant in conflict. Just war assumptions about the nature of human reason, either at the level of invoking the dispassionate 'wise man' or an ambiguous 'practical morality' are no longer adequate given the wealth of different approaches within modernity that have criticized and analysed the role of reason and rationality within moral judgment.

In recent history, one very popular account of the critique of reason is that developed by French post-structuralist or post-modernist thinkers such as Michel Foucault and Jacques Derrida through their re-appropriation of Friedrich Nietzsche's (and Sigmund Freud's) critique of the Western philosophical tradition's conception of rationality. Yet, the critique of Western philosophy's conception of rationality and the critique of 'common-sense' assumptions about reason are not limited to the thought of Nietzsche and his post-modern inheritors. Various lines of critique can also be found within the writings of Thomas Hobbes, Benedict de Spinoza and G.W.F. Hegel. Hobbes and Hegel, like Spinoza and Nietzsche, show an acute awareness of the way in which the operation of thinking, or reasoning, is driven by the passions or desires and that 'neutral' or 'objective' claims to reason hide particular social and cultural contents as well as drives towards empowerment and mastery. In particular, Hegel shows how violent conflict is in part a product of the desire of human rationality to posit or realize itself.[94]

Given this wealth of philosophical perspectives that contribute to the critique of reason, there is no excuse for a theorist to not consider at least some of these when thinking about moral judgments over the rightness or justness of war. Such a meta-reflection upon the role of reason within moral reasoning about war (the thinking of thinking, or the critique of concept formation) is not simply a luxury of philosophy. Rather, it is instead a practical demand of our age and will continue to be so for as long as politicians, and so-called 'wise men' and 'practical philosophers' claim to engage in some form of 'moral reasoning' when passing judgment on just and unjust wars. If just war theory cannot incorporate the critique of reason into its intellectual discourse, then we are probably better off setting the theory aside. A mode of theorizing about war which does not or cannot consider how competing concepts of justice and authority, and the desires for empowerment and realization within human rationality, *together*, underlie violence, conflict and war, is not an adequate or sufficient theoretical approach. Opposed to the inadequacy of the just war tradition, theoretical approaches that pursue these significant questions need to be developed.

Notes

1 The term 'war on terror', while ambiguous and grammatically dubious, will be used here simply because through its constant use by Western media, governments and commentators it has become a term of common parlance. The term should be

approached cautiously since it is in many respects a propaganda and rhetorical device and its continued use helps to frame conflicts in a manner that is advantageous to particular interests and disadvantageous to others.

2 The term 'militant Islamicist political organization' is used to distinguish particular groups from the majority of Islamicist political organizations around the globe which are non-violent and do not carry out acts of war or terror. Heated, rhetorical terms such as 'Islamic terrorists' and '*Jihadis*' will not be used here. For a discussion of how such organizations fit into a historical context of the twentieth-century tradition of Islamic reformism or revivalism, see I. M. Abu-Rabi, *Intellectual Origins of Islamic Resurgence in the Modern Arab World*, Albany, NY: SUNY Press, 1996; J. Esposito, *The Islamic Threat: Myth or Reality*? New York: Oxford University Press, 1999; L. Esposito (ed.) *Voices of Resurgent Islam*, New York: Oxford University Press, 1983. See, more generally, S.H. Nasr, *The Heart of Islam*, New York: HarperCollins, 2002; T. Ramadan, *Islam, the West and the Challenges of Modernity*, trans. S. Amghar, Leicester: The Islamic Foundation, 2004.

3 Consider the accounts given in M. Ignatieff, *The Lesser Evil: Political Ethics in an Age of Terror*, Edinburgh: Edinburgh University Press, 2004; J.B. Elshtain, *Just War Against Terror: The Burden of American Power in a Violent World*, New York: Basic Books, 2003.

4 G.W. Bush, 'Address to a Joint Session of Congress and the American People', 2001, http://www.whitehouse.gov/news/releases/2001/09/20010920–28.html (accessed 9 June 2008).

5 Ibid.

6 Ibid.

7 Ibid.

8 Ibid.

9 M. Walzer, *Just and Unjust Wars: A Moral Argument with Historical Illustrations*, 3rd edn, New York: Basic Books, 2000; M. Walzer, *Arguing about War*, New Haven, CT: Yale University Press, 2004.

10 While Walzer concentrates on both the *ius ad bellum* and the *ius in bello*, and shows important inter-relations between the two, I will restrict my approach to a focus upon the former.

11 M. Walzer, *Just and Unjust Wars*, p. xix.

12 Ibid., pp. xix–xx.

13 Ibid., p. xx. He goes on to argue that:

> But I have not attempted a history of just war theory, and I quote the classical texts only occasionally, for the sake of some particularly illuminating or forceful argument. I refer more often to contemporary philosophers and theologians (and soldiers and statesmen), for my main concern is not with the making of the moral world but with its present character.

14 Ibid., pp. xxi–xxii.

15 Ibid., p. xxii. With regard to his account of morality Walzer, at p. xxi, argues:

> I am not going to expound morality from the ground up. Were I to begin with the foundations, I would probably never get beyond them; in any case, I am by no means sure what the foundations are. The substructure of the ethical world is a matter of deep and apparently unending controversy. Meanwhile, however, we are living in the superstructure. The building is large, its construction is elaborate and confusing. But here I can offer some guidance: a tour of the rooms, so to speak, a discussion of architectural principles.

In *Arguing about War*, at p. x, Walzer argues:

> But *just* is a term of art here; it means justifiable, defensible and even morally necessary (given the alternatives) – and that is all that it means. All of us who argue about the rights and wrongs of war agree that justice in the strong sense, the sense that it has in domestic society and everyday life, is lost as soon as the fighting begins. War is a zone of radical coercion, in which justice is always under a cloud. Still sometimes we are right to enter the zone.

16 This is not to say that the 'I think' should be removed from the consideration of war. Indeed, the 'I think' stands at the centre of modern Western philosophy, it appears as a major question engaged with by numerous traditions. What Walzer does is remove all questions from the 'I think' and speak from a position of self-proclaimed authority over the rightness of war. It is such unquestioned claims to authority taken by contemporary philosophers and politicians with regard to war which is both inadequate and dangerous. I try to present a more careful discussion of the relation between the 'I think' and violence in Chapter 4.

17 In this sense, 'right' refers to also the ethical norms contained within both subjective morality, within customs and conventions and within positive law.

18 M. Walzer, *Just and Unjust Wars*, p. xx.

19 Walzer does engage with these questions to a degree, and in his later work, *Arguing about War*, he pays more attention to them. The problem is, however, that Walzer never examines these questions as foundational questions and does not acknowledge their place within his conception of morality and justice.

20 See, for example, J.T. Johnson, *The Just War Tradition and the Restraint of War*, Princeton, NJ: Princeton University Press, 1981; A.J. Coates, *The Ethics of War*, Manchester: Manchester University Press, 1997.

21 For an early account of Spanish brutality, see B. Las Casas, *A Short Account of the Destruction of the Indies*, trans. N. Griffin, London: Penguin, 1992. In the *Short Account* (1552), written as a petition to the King of Spain, Bartolomé De Las Casas offers a chilling account of the violence carried out by the Spanish. At p. 32 he states:

> From the very beginning, Spanish policy towards the New World has been characterized by blindness of the most pernicious kind: even while the various ordinances and decrees governing the treatment of the native peoples have continued to maintain that conversion and the saving of souls have first priority, this is belied by what has actually been happening on the ground. The gulf that yawns between theory and practice has meant that, in fact, the local people have been presented with an ultimatum: either adopt the Christian religion and swear allegiance to the Crown of Castille, or they will find themselves faced with military action in which no quarter will be given and they will be cut down or taken prisoner. It is as though the Son of God, who gave his life for every living soul, when he instructed His followers with the words: 'Go ye therefore, and teach all nations,' intended heathens, living in peace and tranquillity in their own lands, to be confronted with a demand that they convert on the spot, without their ever hearing the Word or having Christian doctrine explained to them; and that, should they show any reluctance to do so and to swear allegiance to a king they have never heard of nor clapped eyes on, and whose subjects and ambassadors prove to be cruel, pitiless and blood-thirsty tyrants, they should immediately surrender all their worldly goods and lose all rights to their land, their freedom, their womenfolk, their children and

their lives. Such a notion is as absurd as it is stupid and should be treated with the disrespect, scorn and contempt it so amply deserves.

22 F. de Vitoria, *Political Writings*, ed. A. Padgen and J. Lawrance, Cambridge: Cambridge University Press, 1991.
23 Ibid., pp. 331–3.
24 Augustine, *City of God against the Pagans*, ed. R.W. Dyson, Cambridge: Cambridge University Press, 1998.
25 Ibid., p. 33. It should be noted that these comments are made within the context of Augustine's discussion of suicide and his condemnation of suicide as murder. At this point Augustine also makes an important distinction between the killing of humans and the killing of plants and animals. For Augustine, the commandment 'thou shalt not kill' does not extent to the killing of plants and animals of which he claims that their 'life and death are subject to our needs'.
26 Ibid.
27 Ibid., pp. 944–5.
28 Ibid., p. 928.
29 Ibid., pp. 927–8.
30 Ibid., p. 929. Augustine, at p. 104, with regard to a number of wars carried out by Rome in defence of its territory, argues:

> Clearly, however, the Romans did have a just defence for undertaking and waging such great wars. They were compelled to resist the savage incursions of their enemies; and they were compelled not to do this by greed for human praise, but by the necessity of defending life and liberty.

Augustine, at p. 39, exempts soldiers from the prohibition on killing. He argues:

> But when a soldier, obedient to the power under which he has been lawfully placed, slays a man, he is not guilty of murder according to any laws of his city. On the contrary, if he does not do so, he is guilty of desertion and contempt of authority. If he had done this of his own will and authority, however, he would have fallen into the crime of shedding human blood. Thus, the deed which is punished if he does it when not commanded is the same as that for which he will be punished if he does not do it when commanded.

31 Aquinas, *St. Thomas Aquinas on Politics and Ethics*, ed. P. Sigmund, New York: Norton & Co.: 1988.
32 Ibid., pp. 64–5.
33 Ibid., pp. 70–1.
34 F.H. Russell, *The Just War in the Middle Ages*, Cambridge: Cambridge University Press, 1975, p. 17. See also the discussion in P. Ramsey, *War and the Christian Conscience: How Shall Modern War Be Conducted Justly?* Durham, NC: Duke University Press, 1961; L.J. Swift, *The Early Fathers on War and Military Service*, Wilmington, DE: Michael Glazier, 1983; S. Windas, *Christianity Versus Violence*, London: Sheed & Ward, 1964.
35 Aristotle, 'Politics', in *The Basic Works of Aristotle*, ed. R. McKeon, New York: Modern Library, 2001, p. 1129. Aristotle states:

> When several villages are united in a single complete community, large enough to be nearly of quite self-sufficing, the state comes into existence, originating in the bare needs of life, and continuing in existence for the sake of a good life.

At p. 1130:

> A social instinct is implanted in all men by nature, and yet he who first founded the state was the greatest of benefactors. For man, when perfected, is the best of animals, but, when separated from law and justice, he is the worst of all; since armed injustice is the more dangerous, and he is equipped at birth with arms, meant to be used by intelligence and virtue, which he may use for the worst ends. Wherefore, if he have not virtue, he is the most unholy and the most savage of animals, and the most full of lust and gluttony. But justice is the bond of men in states, for the administration of justice, which is the determination of what is just, is the principle of order in political society.

36 Aquinas, *St. Thomas Aquinas on Politics and Ethics*. At pp. 17–18, he argues:

> Among the bees there is one king bee, and in the whole universe one God is the Maker and Ruler of all. This is in accord with reason since every plurality derives from a unity. Therefore since art imitates nature and a work of art is better to the degree that it resembles what is in nature, it follows that it is best for a human group (*multitudo*) to be ruled by one person.

37 Ibid., p. 46.
38 Though, through Aquinas and others, this Christian worldview is re-built upon the philosophy and political theory of both Greek pagan texts and the wealth of Islamic scholarship that had, before Aquinas, reconciled 'reason' with a monotheistic (Judaeo-Christian-Islamic) religious worldview. This Islamic heritage upon which the Christian West was dependent in its emergence from its own 'dark ages' has usually been purged from Western Christian accounts of history. The present Catholic Pope, Benedict XVI has continued this historical denial and in doing so has missed a chance to comprehend the historical and intellectual links that bind together the Christian and Islamic worlds. For a somewhat clumsy account of this, see T. Kochi, 'The Pope and the Ethics of Exclusion', *Logos*, 6(3), 2007.
39 Aquinas, *St. Thomas Aquinas on Politics and Ethics*, p. 64. Note the comment by Joan D. Tooke that Aquinas's category of 'legitimate authority' overlooked the political realities of his time under feudalism and imperialism where there could be a number of kings and princes as well as an emperor all competing for the claim of holding 'legitimate authority'. See J.D. Tooke, *The Just War in Aquinas and Grotius*, London: SPCK, 1965, p. 26.
40 Such moments of cross-cultural recognition and regulated conduct between polities under the *ius gentium* are also to be found and have their sources in Roman and Islamic law. This historical background is, however, too broad to be dealt with here.
41 F. Vitoria, *Political Writings*, p. 6.
42 Ibid., p. 9.
43 Ibid.
44 Ibid., p. 10.
45 Ibid.
46 Ibid., p. 11.
47 Ibid., p. 12.
48 Ibid.
49 Ibid., p. 17. Vitoria argues:

> And therefore we must say about royal power exactly what we have asserted about the power of the commonwealth, namely that it is set up by God

> and the natural law. This agrees with Holy Scripture, and with common practice, which calls kings 'ministers of God' not 'ministers of the commonwealth'.

50 Ibid., p. 18.
51 Ibid., p. 29. For a more general discussion on the scholastic debates on political authority, see Q. Skinner, *The Foundations of Modern Political Thought*, Vol. 2, Cambridge: Cambridge University Press, 1978, pp. 135–48.
52 For a discussion of the concept of dominion and its differing treatment in scholastic and humanist debates, see R. Tuck, *Natural Rights Theories: Their Origin and Development*, Cambridge: Cambridge University Press, 1981.
53 F. Vitoria, *Political Writings*, p. 239.
54 Ibid., pp. 240, 250–1.
55 Ibid., pp. 240–6.
56 Ibid., pp. 250.
57 See the discussion in A. Padgen, *The Fall of Natural Man: The American Indian and the Origins of Comparative Ethnology*, Cambridge: Cambridge University Press, 1982. At pp. 104–5, Padgen argues:

> *De indis* effectively destroyed the credibility of the theory of natural slavery as a means to explain the deviant behaviour of the Indian. After Vitoria's analysis it was clear to all his followers that as a model, as a paradigm, it had failed dismally to satisfy the evidence it was intended to explain. Henceforth the Indian would cease to be any form of 'natural man' – however that ambiguous phase might be interpreted. He was now, whatever his shortcomings, like all other men, a being whose actions could only now be adequately explained in terms of his culture. This 'barbarian', by definition an 'outsider', had now been brought 'in'; 'in', it is true, at the lowest possible social and human levels: socially as a peasant, a brutish creature living outside the discrete web of affiliations, patterns of behaviour, modes of speech and of expression, which made up the life of the civil man; psychologically as a child, that unreflective, passion-dominated, half-reasoning being. But 'in' none the less.

For a more general account of the European construction of the non-European other in relation to America, see D.F. Silva, *Toward a Global Idea of Race*, Minneapolis, MN: Minnesota University Press, 2007; E. Dussel, *Beyond Philosophy*, ed. E. Mendieta, Lanham, MD: Rowman & Littlefield, 2003.

58 F. Vitoria, *Political Writings*, p. 256.
59 Ibid., p. 260.
60 Ibid., pp. 297–8.
61 Ibid., pp. 302–3.
62 Ibid., pp. 303–4.
63 Ibid., pp. 270–2.
64 Ibid., p. 278.
65 Ibid., p. 279.
66 Ibid., p. 280.
67 Ibid., p. 282.
68 Ibid., p. 283.
69 Ibid. Following this, Vitoria notes that as per the law of nations (*ius gentium*) 'everything captured in war belongs to the victor'.
70 Ibid., p. 284.
71 Ibid., p. 285.

72 Ibid., p. 286.
73 Ibid., p. 288.
74 Ibid., p. 289.
75 Ibid. At pp. 291–2, In his conclusion, Vitoria argues that if the Amerindians inflict no injury and therefore did not offer a just cause for war, then the Spanish might be limited to only trading with them in a manner similar to the Portuguese and occupy only vacant land. He argues further, however, that once a large number of Amerindians had converted to Christianity, it would be no longer be expedient or lawful for the Spanish crown to abandon the administration of the territories.
76 Ibid., p. 291.
77 On the distinctions between a more limited natural law theory of just war (i.e. as presented by Vitoria) and a more expansive 'holy war' tradition, see J.T. Johnston, *Ideology, Reason, and the Limitation of War: Religious and Secular Concepts 1200–1740*, Princeton, NJ: Princeton University Press, 1975. Johnston argues that a comprehensive just war doctrine emerges out of these disparate traditions only after 1500.
78 A similar critique is made by Carl Schmitt. See Carl Schmitt, *The Nomos of the Earth*, trans. G.L. Ulmen, New York: Telos Press, 2003, pp. 102–22.
79 Quoted in the 'Introduction' to F. Vitoria, *Political Writings*, p. xxvii.
80 For differing accounts of Vitoria's role in establishing the colonial foundations of international law, see C. Schmitt, *The Nomos of the Earth*; R. Tuck, *The Rights of War and Peace: Political Thought and the International Order from Grotius to Kant*, Oxford: Oxford University Press, 1999; C. Miéville, *Between Equal Rights: A Marxist Theory of International Law*, London: Pluto Press, 2006; A. Anghie, *Imperialism, Sovereignty and the Making of International Law*, Cambridge: Cambridge University Press, 2005. See also D. Kennedy, 'Primitive Legal Scholarship', *Harvard International Law Journal*, 27(1), 1986, 1–98.
81 See, for example, J.B. Scott, *The Spanish Origins of International Law: Francisco De Vitoria and His Law of Nations*, Oxford: Clarendon Press, 1934.
82 Michael Walzer's 'selective' historical treatment of Israel when discussing the notion of just cause is one such 'principled' move. Walzer's lack of appreciation of the colonial aspects of the just war tradition is curious given that, in part, his work is a response to the USA's bloody neo-colonial adventure in Vietnam.
83 The manipulating of facts and imputing of good intentions by politicians, bureaucrats, media 'experts' and international lawyers aimed at justifying the invasion and occupation of Iraq by the USA and the UK in 2003 took place in a just war rhetorical style that was not too distant from some of the arguments given by Vitoria.
84 C. Douzinas, *Human Rights and Empire: The Political Philosophy of Cosmopolitanism*, Abingdon: Routledge-Cavendish, 2007, p. 238.
85 A.J. Coates, *The Ethics of War*, p. 154.
86 J.B. Elshtain, *Just War Against Terror*. Elshtain uses just war theory as an ideological tool to attempt to legitimate the aggressive wars carried out by the USA in contemporary times.
87 For a critique of humanitarian intervention more generally, see A. Orford, *Reading Humanitarian Intervention: Human Rights and the Use of Force in International Law*, Cambridge: Cambridge University Press, 2007.
88 A.J. Coates, *The Ethics of War*, p. 124. See also J.T. Johnson, *Morality and Contemporary Warfare*, New Haven, CT: Yale University Press, 1999, pp. 102–12; O. O'Donovan, *The Just War Revisited*, Cambridge: Cambridge University Press, 2003, p. 14.
89 I develop this line of thinking in Chapters 4, 5 and 6.

90 James Turner Johnson's historical work on just war is very good in this respect. See J.T. Johnston, *Ideology, Reason, and the Limitation of War*. However, his discussion of just war in the present offers less probing insights.
91 F. Vitoria, *Political Writings*, p. 306.
92 Ibid.
93 M. Walzer, *Just and Unjust Wars*, p. xvii.
94 In Chapters 4 and 6, I draw upon these ideas within Hegel's theory of recognition to develop a modern theory of war.

Chapter 2

The juridical ordering of war

I

There have been many differing accounts of war, many different ways of thinking about war and about public and private violence more generally: in short, many different orders of war. Historically we know of some of these, most, however, have been lost to us, just as the words and deeds of our modern age will also be lost. When we think of human thoughts and actions in the context of celestial and natural histories stretching out over millennia, then much of our petty squabbling and squeaking fades away from central view. In wider terms, old questions are still relevant here: what does my justification for an act of violence mean to the stars? Such questions will not and cannot go away. However, the daily mess and busyness of life in the present do not spare too much time for broader, perhaps cosmic, modes of contemplation. Human beings kill, our social and public lives contain much violence. In determining how we are to live among ourselves and, in focussing upon the desire for a future which might be better than the present, the question of how war is ordered is a pressing one.

The previous chapter considered the limits and inadequacies of modern just war theory and did so through examining one of the historical fathers of the just war tradition, the scholastic theologian, Francisco de Vitoria. This chapter presents an approach to the problem of war which inherits the natural law theory of Vitoria, but which departs from scholastic natural law so as to develop a secular natural law of minimum content. This thin version of natural law is developed in part by Hugo Grotius and then more fundamentally by Thomas Hobbes. Hobbes's approach attempts to de-theologize and de-moralize the problem of war and can be termed the *juridical ordering of war*. This involves a re-thinking, or re-ordering of the relationship between right and violence around the juridical figure of the sovereign with an emphasis upon the concepts of peace and survival. The tradition begins to remove the language of 'justice' from of the consideration of war and instead lays the groundwork for a modern conception of the legitimacy of violence centred upon the figure of secular state sovereignty.

This chapter will present the way in which a particular historical, intellectual tradition *re-orders* the relationship between violence and legitimacy. This occurs as a response to a set of political circumstances in which the previous theological conception of Christian just war was deemed to be inadequate to resolve the problem of religious 'holy war' between Protestants and Catholics in Europe. In the context of a Western Christian worldview that had splintered into rival sects, each positing their conception of justice through violence, thinkers like Hobbes saw that a just war theory based upon a thick, theological conception of natural law and Christian justice was part of the problem and not the solution.

Hobbes's approach develops a secular account of political authority and sovereignty that underlies the modern conception of the state and international law. However, what is potentially more valuable is the way in which he depicts a relationship between violent action and moral claims of authority. Hobbes is perhaps one of the fist modern thinkers to pay attention to how the linguistic, moral and political positing of authority (or claim to authority) is in some senses linked to the *act* of violence. His appreciation of this in the context of civil war, and his response, continues to be relevant to the attempt to come to terms with the problem of war in the present.

II

Grotius and Hobbes inherited the problem of war in a time of radical religious upheaval. The historical context involved the breakdown of a singular religious-political order of the Catholic Church in the Middle Ages into multiple claims over truth and over religious and political authority through the emergence of differing Christian confessions. Ultimate claims of political and legal right had throughout the Middle Ages been grounded upon, or at least mediated through, a religious concept of the 'universal authority' of a Catholic Pope who claimed authority under God. The splitting of the Western church into competing confessions prompted a re-analysis of questions of authority, legitimacy, and power, especially in relation to the use and limits of violence within social and political life.

The political empowerment of the Protestant confessions threw a long held Christian conception of 'just war' into internal conflict and contradiction. The doctrine had well served various Christian monarchs in legitimating violence against the Islamic world during the Crusades and in justifying the colonization of America. However, when the political conflicts between the hegemonic aspirations of European monarchs and princes came to be coloured by and take on the character of wars between differing Christian confessions, the Christian doctrine of just war revealed itself as somewhat self-destructive. The high point of this chaos could be thought to involve a bloody period of intra-state civil war between Christian confessions known as the Thirty Years War (1618–48). This series of conflicts, driven in the most part by the competing claims to power by European monarchs and princes had nevertheless a strong religious character. Each, church, sovereign and army claimed to have God on their side and each claimed to be the legitimate inheritor of divine truth. In this respect, the conflict, when viewed within the wider process of the Reformation and Counter-Reformation had framed questions of legal, political and moral authority and legitimacy as questions of theology and theologically grounded natural law. In this context, such intra-state civil war and the horrors of destruction it caused in central Europe, were driven, or at least energized by competing claims over religious *truth*.[1]

The Peace of Westphalia (1648) marked something of an end to this destructive and chaotic period of intra-state civil war between the Christian confessions. For international lawyers, much has been made of the Peace of Westphalia as the beginning or moment of foundation of the modern period of international relations. On the significance of Westphalia, J.L. Brierly argues that 'The Peace of Westphalia, which brought to an end in 1648 the great Thirty Years War of religion marked the acceptance of the new political order in Europe.'[2] Arthur Nussbaum has given a somewhat more cautious account of Westphalia's significance. He argues:

> The Thirty Years War (1618–48), probably the most devastating European conflict since the barbarian invasion, constitutes the dominant event of the seventeenth century. It was at once the climax of, and practically the last of, the religious wars. The war was ended by the Peace of Westphalia after negotiations had dragged on for more than three years simultaneously at Münster and Osnabrück ... For at least a century it remained the framework of Europe's political organisation. Characteristically, a number of important publications in the history of international law have taken the Peace of Westphalia as the starting point. In fact, the Peace has sometimes been represented as the inception of the European law of nations. While this view is unwarranted, the Peace is a landmark in the development of international law.[3]

Much can be made of the importance of the Peace of Westphalia in the foundation of international law. Yet, as with all claims to 'foundations', the significance of Westphalia needs to be treated with caution, and a degree of scepticism. There is certainly value within the argument that the idea that modern international law was founded upon the treaties of Münster and Osnabrück is not much more than a 'myth'.[4] One must be careful not to overstate the importance of treaties and 'events' and thus reduce complex historical and institutional processes to a mythic symbol that might be polemically regurgitated as a claim to authority within the present.

What is of concern here is not the central importance of Peace of Westphalia itself as an event, but the intellectual and historical shift of thinking it represents in relation to war and the justification of the legitimacy of violence. In this respect, the image or symbol of Westphalia is drawn upon to help mark an important shift within the traditions of natural law developing *before* and *after* the treaties of Münster and Osnabrück. What might be described as a *heritage* of Westphalia embraces a form of thinking which moved towards the de-theologization of religious conflict and the ordering of the legitimacy of violence around a secular (in the sense that this involved an authority which was not the Church) figure of the sovereign. Elements of this heritage might be seen in the work of thinkers such as Jean Bodin, Alberico Gentilli, Hugo Grotius, John Selden, Thomas Hobbes and Samuel Pufendorf.[5] The importance of this heritage of Westphalia is expressed by Ian Hunter. He argues:

> First, at the interstate level, the Westphalian order was dedicated not to the elimination of war – which it treats as a permanent feature of interstate relations – but to its regulation. On the one hand, by tying the European states into a system of reciprocally guaranteed security, and by treating territorial states as sovereign in relation to all other temporal or spiritual powers, Westphalia was designed to banish ideological wars of annihilation from the European heartlands. The system of pacts backed by great-power guarantors was not intended to preclude territorial infringements or conflicts, but to ensure that these would take the form of contests between 'just enemies' – rather than wars of extermination against heretics – thereby avoiding the cycle of outrage and revenge that had made the religious wars so savage and so difficult to end. On the other hand, this entirely concrete re-spacialization and de-theologization of the European order was dependent on the existence of an extra-European colonial world …
>
> Second, the restriction of war to a domain of regulated conflicts between states depended on the de-sacrilization of politics inside them. Here we have observed that Westphalia marked the tentative emergence of the first forms of religious toleration that would lead to the separation of state and church. It was only when a secularized political jurisprudence permitted social peace to displace religious truth and moral right from the political arena that Catholics and Protestants could reach a compromise in the distribution of religious rights and possessions. This substitution of worldly security for theological truth, which entailed a major curtailment of the sovereign's rights in religious matters, was the first step towards the norm of the state's neutrality in religious affairs.[6]

By looking briefly at Grotius and then at the political philosophy of Hobbes it will be seen how aspects of this 'secularized' political jurisprudence help to reframe the approach to the problem of war.

III

Grotius developed a theory of just war which inherited and owed much to the natural law theory of just war presented by Vitoria. In contrast to the scholasticism of Vitoria's thought, mired within the theological worldview of Aquinas, Grotius's intellectual background was broadly humanist and he drew as much on the thought of Cicero as on Christian theology. Grotius is sometimes portrayed as a father of the modern, secular law of nations.[7] Like Vitoria, Grotius's supposed status as a 'father' of modern international law needs to be set within its colonial context. Some attention should be paid to the way in which Grotius developed arguments that lent support to Dutch colonial interests. In the colonial sphere, against non-European peoples, Grotius can be interpreted as presenting a more expansive just war theory than that of Vitoria. In *The Rights of War and Peace* (1625),[8] he argues:

> We must also know, that Kings, and those who are invested with a Power equal to that of Kings, have a Right to exact Punishments, not only for Injuries committed against themselves, or their Subjects, but likewise, for those which do not peculiarly concern them, but which are in any Persons whatsoever, grievous Violations of the Law of Nature or Nations. For the Liberty of consulting the Benefit of human Society, by Punishments, which at first, as we have said, was in every particular Person, does now, since Civil Societies, and Courts of Justice, have been instituted, reside in those who are possessed of the supreme Power, and that properly, not as they have an Authority over others, but as they are Subject to none. For, as for others, their Subjection has taken from them this Right. Nay, it is so much more honourable, to revenge other Peoples Injuries rather than their own, by as much as it is more to be feared, lest out of a Sense of their own Sufferings, they either exceed the just Measure of Punishment, or, at least, prosecute their Revenge with Malice ... For the same Reason we make no Doubt, but War may be justly undertaken against those who are inhuman to their Parents, as were the *Sogdians*, before *Alexander* persuaded them to renounce their Brutality; and against those who eat human Flesh, from which Custom *Hercules* compelled the ancient *Gauls* to desist, as *Dio dorus* relates and against those who practice Piracy.[9]

Following this:

> And so we follow the Opinion of *Innocentius*, and others, who hold that War is lawful against those who offend against Nature; which is contrary to the Opinion of *Victoria*, *Vasquez*, *Azorius*, *Molina* and others, who seem to require, towards making a War just, that he who undertakes it be injured himself, or in his State, or that he has some Jurisdiction over the Person against whom the War is made. For they assert, that the Power of Punishing is properly an Effect of Civil Jurisdiction; whereas our Opinion is, that it proceeds from the Law of Nature.[10]

Commenting on these passages, Richard Tuck argues:

> It is remarkable – and, I think, completely unrecognized by modern scholars – that Grotius specifically aligned himself with Innocent IV against Vitoria on this crucial issue. The idea that foreign rulers can punish tyrants, cannibals, pirates, those who killed settlers, and those who are inhuman to their parents neatly legitimated a great deal of European action against native peoples around the world, and was disconcertingly close to the extreme pre-Vitorian arguments used by the Spaniards in America ... The central reason why Grotius had developed his argument in this direction was, I think, that the Dutch had begun to change the character of their activity in the non-European world since his earlier works, and in particular had begun to annex territory.[11]

Grotius's expansive just war theory as a method of justifying colonial conquest in the non-European world sits in contrast to his desire for peace within Europe, for which he argues for the peaceful settlement of disputes through dialogue and arbitration. He states:

> Now War is Matter of the weightiest Importance, since it commonly brings many Calamities, even upon the Innocent, and therefore when there are Reasons on both Sides of the Question, we ought to incline to Peace.[12]

While the question of how Grotius fits within history of the just war tradition is an interesting one, it will not be pursued further here. Given the critique of just war theory that was enunciated in the previous chapter, it is of little importance to consider further the exact outlines of Grotius's theory of just war. What is of greater relevance, and is perhaps more interesting, is the issue of how Grotius re-frames the tradition of natural law and of how this begins to re-order the notion of legitimate authority in relation to the use of violence – a move that opens the way for a radicalization of the theory natural law by Hobbes and a re-conceptualization of the relation between right and violence.

One of Grotius's achievements was to de-theologize or 'secularize' natural law. Ernst Bloch argues:

> Grotius was the first to clearly separate human natural law as a creation of human reason from the theological context – the ancient relationship that united *jus naturae* and *lex divina* is broken. The law of reason, said Grotius, is valid even if – *per impossibile* – there was no God; the identification of natural law with the Decalogue, as well as with the Sermon on the Mount, is abandoned.[13]

Grotius inherits at theory of natural law like that developed by Vitoria, in which natural law sits between and is linked to God's eternal law and human law, and with divine, Biblical law connected at the side. Like Vitoria, Grotius deduces the political authority of the sovereign on the basis of natural law, or natural necessity, via the idea that humans who need to gather together in societies for their mutual advantage also need some form of power above them to oversee their actions and judge between their disputes. This law of nature, while derived from the natural condition or nature of humans flows ultimately from God.[14] For Grotius, the content of natural law belongs to humanity's desire for sociability and the principles of natural law can be identified by 'right reason'.[15] He thinks that human laws should be established, via right reason, in accordance with natural law, and thus the law of nations, which although arising out of custom and consent between states, should also by guided by the principles of natural law.[16]

Grotius's theory of natural law does, however, develop in a different direction from the scholastic theories of natural law as developed by thinkers such as Vitoria. Grotius emphasizes the centrality of a natural law based upon human nature and human reason and in this respect pushes the role of God out of the centre and to the periphery. He argues that natural law remains valid even if God did not exist.[17] In the context of rabid religious intra-state civil war being waged between Catholic and Protestant confessions, such a secularization of natural law makes a great deal of sense. It allows Grotius to assert a natural law that remains 'universal' and which can be relied upon by all conflicting parties because of its apparent neutrality on the question of whose version of God is the truth.

Grotius's argument also paves the way for the recognition of the temporal authority of Protestant sovereigns on the basis of natural law in a way which is not too dissimilar from Vitoria's recognition of the sovereignty of Amerindian monarchs. Such a theory makes available to Protestant monarchs a concept of sovereignty that precludes their reliance upon recognition by a Catholic Pope. For Grotius, temporal sovereignty can be derived via right reason from the principles of natural law, linked to God's eternal reason, but no longer mediated through the institutional framework of the Catholic Church.

Grotius's secular re-conceptualization of the basis of sovereignty also partly moves away from a thick conception of the good life as conceived by Aristotle and Aquinas. In its place, Grotius presents a thin, minimalist, natural law whose content is grounded upon the notion of peaceful sociability. The move away from a communitarian conception of natural law as the good life also involves a shift towards a more individualistic conception of natural rights over the person and property. In such a shift, what is 'right' is not so much a notion of justice mediated through and dependent upon the interpretation of cannon and scholastic law,[18] but is instead a more personalized, individualistic right directly accessible by all human individuals by their use of reason.[19] The move, which is later taken up and developed by Hobbes, involves a partial shift away from natural law and towards a more dominant notion of natural rights. Grotius states:

> There is another Signification of the Word *Right* different from this, but yet arising from it, which relates directly to the *Person*: In which Sense *Right*

> is a *moral Quality* annexed to the Person, *enabling him to have, or do, something justly* ... Civilians call a *Faculty* that Right which a Man has to his *own*; but we shall hereafter call it a *Right properly, and strictly taken.* Under which are contained, 1. A Power either over our selves, which is term'd *Liberty*; or over others, such as that of a *Father over his Children*, or a *Lord over his Slave*. 2. Property, which is either *compleat*, or *imperfect*. The last obtains in the Case of *Farms*, for Instance, or *Pledges*. 3. *The Faculty of demanding what is due*, and to this *answers the Obligation of rendering what is owing.*[20]

Grotius's re-conceptualization of the content of natural law (and the shift towards natural rights) allows him to re-think the nature of what it means, in the language of the just war tradition, to be a 'legitimate authority'. His raising of the principle of peaceful sociability to be a central tenet of natural law grounds the authority of the sovereign on a 'secular' basis and begins to re-shape the boundaries of what counts as legitimate violence. When such a theory of natural law is taken up and radically re-interpreted by Hobbes, then the question of what counts as 'legitimate violence' is moved quite far away from a language of justice and the good life and more closer to the sovereign's role in maintaining peace for the purpose of securing the natural rights to life and property of its citizens. Such a movement which secularizes and re-conceives the nature of political and legal authority has the follow-on effect of re-conceiving the meaning of a 'just' war. It is important to note that this movement takes place not merely as an intellectual exercise, but is itself a response to the violence of intra-state religious civil war.

Grotius, in attempting to find a solution to the problem of war considers the 'nature of war'. He argues:

> Being then to treat of the Right of War, we must consider what that *War* is which we are to treat of, and what the *Right* is which we search for. *Cicero* defines WAR *a Dispute by force*. But Custom has so prevailed, that not the Act of Hostility, but the State and Situation of the contending Parties, now goes by that Name; so that War is the State or Situation of those (considered in that Respect) who dispute by Force of Arms. Which general Acceptation of the Word comprehends all of the kinds of War which we shall hereafter treat, not even excluding single Combats, which being really ancienter than Publick Wars, and undoubtedly of the same Nature, may therefore well have one and the same Name.[21]

Beginning with this general approach Grotius asks whether war, defined as a form of social violence more generally, is legitimate, or is in accordance with natural law.[22] In questioning the status of war in relation to a concept of right Grotius gives central emphasis to the notion of 'preservation'. Grotius argues that 'Among the First impressions of Nature there is nothing repugnant to

War.'[23] He claims that the aim and end of war is the preservation of life and limb and the keeping or acquiring of things useful to life.[24] Further, he argues that, at times, it is necessary to achieve these ends through use of force.[25] However, what remains a fundamental question is the extent to which the use of force might come into conflict with society and the taking away of the rights and possessions of others.[26]

One way in which the right to violence comes to threaten peaceful sociability and endanger the lives and property of others occurs where there exists no *body* in the position of authority to *judge* between conflicting claims of right. When every actor presides as the judge of their own claims, then it is difficult to distinguish the legitimacy of any claim from pure self-interest. For Grotius, where there does exist the possibility of a body that can judge between conflicting claims, then, in the interest of securing peace, the grounds to determine the legitimacy of violence should be handed over to this authority. Grotius's approach to this long-running question over who or what has *the authority to judge the legitimacy of violence* is to de-legitimize private violence and vest the legitimacy of violence in the legal-political figure of the sovereign. Grotius argues:

> That some Sort of private War may be lawfully waged, as far as respects the Law of Nature, I think has been fully proved by what I have said above, where it was shewn, that it is not repugnant to the Law of Nature, for any one to repel Injuries by Force. But perhaps some will think, that it is not lawful, at least since the establishment of publick Judges, for tho' Courts of Justice are not from Nature, but human Appointment; yet, since it is much honester, and more conductive to the Peace of Mankind, that Differences should be decided by a third Person that is disinterested, than that every Man should be allowed to do himself Justice in his own Cause, wherein the Illusions of Self-Love are much to be apprehended: Equity itself, and natural Reason, advise us to submit to so laudable an Institution.[27]

The rule of right reason which holds peaceful human sociability as a central concept, demands the renunciation of the private right to violence. For Grotius, this includes giving up the private right to rebel against the sovereign. Grotius argues:

> Indeed all Men have naturally a Right to secure themselves from Injuries by Resistance, as we said before. But civil Society being instituted for the Preservation of Peace, there immediately arises a superior Right in the State over us and ours, so far as it is necessary for that End. Therefore the State has a Power to prohibit the unlimited Use of that Right towards every other Person, for maintaining publick Peace and good Order, which doubtless it does, since otherwise it cannot obtain the End proposed; for if that promiscuous Right of Resistance should be allowed there would be *no longer*

> *a State*, but a Multitude without Union, such as the *Cyclops* were, *every one gives the Law to his Wife and Children*. A Mob where *all are Speakers, and no Hearers*. Or the *Aborigines*, *Sallust* mentions as a wild and savage People, without Laws, without Government, loose and dissolute. And in another Place the *Getulians*, who had neither Customs, Laws, nor Magistrates. So we find that the Resistance in Question, is looked upon as unlawful, according to the Usage of all States. *All human Societies* (St. *Augustine* tells us) unanimously agree to obey Kings.[28]

This movement can be understood as the *juridical ordering* of the concept of war. The concept of war becomes re-defined and re-organized around the legitimating figure of the sovereign state.[29] In this movement there emerges the beginning of a *modern legal concept of war*[30] which contains a number of elements. In one sense, the legitimacy of violence is tied to particular actors, these being sovereign states. Further, war comes to be understood as 'sovereign war' and the legitimacy of violence is bound to legal-political sovereign authority. The natural law de-legitimization of the right to private violence in the name of peace creates what Max Weber later describes as the 'state's monopoly upon the legitimacy of violence'.[31] In this respect, war occurs as a form of violence waged between sovereigns,[32] who hold a particular *status*. The concept of war is developed through the identification of the rightful enemy who might only rightfully be another sovereign. By this definition violence carried out by the state against a non-sovereign group is excluded from the realm of 'war proper' as is private violence which is re-cast as crime.

Further, while thinkers like Grotius still tried to set out the conditions defining the legitimacy or illegitimacy of a particular sovereign's act of war via just war concepts, the conceptual foundations of just cause and legitimate authority had shifted significantly. The determination of the just cause of war and the determination of what acts of violence formally amounted to 'war' were no longer directly mediated through any transcendent or religious authority. While the sovereign was still partially bound to a quasi-religious natural law, the determination of whether there was a right to war in particular circumstances was understood thoroughly as the operation of a *sovereign decision*.[33]

Such a theory of natural law, that privileged the category of peaceful sociability, limited and undermined any attempt to legitimize war on the grounds of moral or divine authority. The positing of the figure of the secular sovereign as the only possible authority who could preserve social peace undercut the moral and theological authority of the Catholic Church and Protestant confessions who could not effectively perform this function. This movement of the de-sacralization of politics can also be thought of as a co-constituting relationship between the concepts of sovereignty and war. On the one hand, secular sovereignty is raised as the only solution to the problem of religious civil wars. On the other, the concept of war is re-defined as a properly sovereign function, a juridical function that no longer belongs to the Church. The development of this concept of sovereignty out of the context of civil war and the natural law de-legitimation of the right to private violence in favour of the sovereign's monopoly upon the legitimacy of violence was developed further by Hobbes.

IV

With regard to the issues of war and international law, Hobbes is quite often interpreted as presenting an account of a warlike sphere of international relations in which higher claims of justice are mere idealizations in relation to the 'real' operation of the might and right of individual states.[34] In this interpretation, Hobbes is often placed within a 'realist' or 'reason of state' account of international relations.[35] While the similarities between Hobbes's warlike 'state of nature' and the operation of inter-state relations are a significant point of interest,[36] such a focus obscures more central elements of Hobbes's political philosophy that are of greater importance to the consideration of the problem of war.

Of central importance within Hobbes, and especially in the interpretation of the *Leviathan* (1651),[37] is the manner in which Hobbes responds to the problem of *civil war* and the issue of how his account of sovereignty and the de-legitimation of private violence in favour of sovereign violence stems from this context. Hobbes's moral and political philosophy is interpreted here as a response to the problem of civil war. Hobbes can be read as responding to a context of highly charged, moral, political, religious and ideological conflicts which threw Europe into chaos and had plunged England into the violence and terror of bloody civil war and revolution.[38] Like Grotius, Hobbes's interest lay in finding a political and juridical solution to the chaos of civil war. Similarly, Hobbes's solution lay in looking towards the minimization of internal social violence and giving emphasis to the category of peace.

In *On the Citizen* (1642), Hobbes notes that part of the reason for his hurry to produce that particular work was in response to the political climate and seething questions on the right of government and obedience of citizens proceeding and leading up to the outbreak of civil war.[39] With regard to the reasons for writing *On the Citizen* Hobbes argues:

> I did not do this to win praise (though if I had done so I could use the defence that few except those who love praise do anything to deserve it), but for your sake, Readers. My hope is that when you have got to know the doctrine I present and looked well into it, you will patiently put up with some inconveniences in your private affairs (since human affairs can never be without some inconvenience) rather than disturb the state of the country. My hope is that you will measure the Justice of what you are thinking of doing by the laws of the commonwealth, not by the talk or counsel of private citizens, and no longer allow ambitious men to get power for themselves by shedding your blood. My hope is that you will

> think it better to enjoy your present state (though it may not be the best) rather than to go to war, and after you have been killed or died of old age, leave other men in other times to have a better life. As for those who refuse to be subject to the civil Magistrate and want exemption from public burdens and yet demand to be in a commonwealth and to be protected by it from violence and wrongs, I hope that you will regard them as enemies and saboteurs and not gullibly accept all that they put before you openly or secretly as the Word of God.[40]

Further, Hobbes claims his work to be: '[N]ot the words of a partisan but of one who has a passion for peace, whose justified grief at his country's present calamity reasonably merits some indulgence.'[41] Hobbes can be read as attempting to set forth a science, or account of philosophy as 'right reason'[42] which attempts to come to terms with the chaos of civil war and navigate through the various truth claims, religious and political rhetoric, and sceptical disputes over human knowledge that underlie social violence.[43] Hobbes develops an approach that has consequences for how war is thought about. Such a style of thinking focuses upon the question of: who or what has not only the authority, but also the capability, to judge the legitimacy of an act of violence? In Hobbes, the question of judgment over the legitimacy of acts of violence is framed in terms of a wider question involving the possibilities and more importantly, the limitations, of human knowledge. The issue of judgment over war is situated within a theoretical context which emphasizes the finitude, frailty, and errors of *human knowledge*.

Hobbes's approach to the problem of civil war takes seriously the challenge scepticism poses to claims of *authority* within moral and political philosophy. By focusing upon the categories of peace and self-preservation, Hobbes attempts to present an account of a basic ground of moral and political philosophy which cannot be eroded by scepticism.[44] In this respect Hobbes's response to civil war does not involve the common misconception that Hobbes based his moral and political philosophy upon an anthropology in which humans were understood as primarily selfish and self-interested.[45]

For Hobbes, social violence is not caused primarily by selfishness or greed but rather by the inability of human actors in the social world to adequately judge or measure the correctness of their claims of right or truth against their others. In this respect the central problem of war spins around the inability to resolve fundamental disputes of belief from a human epistemic standpoint. On this point, Richard Tuck argues:

> The prime source of the conflicts of the state of nature, for Hobbes, is thus epistemic in character: it is the differing judgments which people make about their own relative power, and about all other matters of importance to them. These judgments need not, strictly speaking, be driven by self-interest

> *at all*, since they may arise simply from the fact that there is no objective standard of truth.[46]

Understood in this sense, Hobbes's approach to the problem of war can be seen to bring together a general scepticism about basic forms of human knowledge and judgment, and in particular, a scepticism about moral and religious forms of speaking about the world (including the emotive power of religious, political and moral rhetoric), with an attempt to come to terms with the violence occurring during the English Civil War (1642–51). The problem of a bloody war playing out as a struggle for power between various religious and political beliefs is situated within a context of an irresolvable conflict over the validity of human *beliefs* themselves. Hobbes's approach attempts to side-step or short-circuit the ongoing conflict between moral, political and religious beliefs by moving to a juridical solution: the identification of the basic conditions of a natural law that might allow peaceful human sociability.

Hobbes's most famous section of the *Leviathan* in which he introduces the notion of a state of war ('*warre*') 'of every man, against everyman',[47] a condition of fear and the danger of violent death, where the life of man is 'solitary, poore, nasty, brutish and short',[48] is contained within the first section of the *Leviathan*, entitled 'Of Man'. This section is devoted to a theoretical account of the possibilities and limitations of human knowledge. It covers topics such as sensory input, speech, logical reasoning, the passions, rhetoric, manners and religion. When placed within this textual and theoretical context Hobbes's use of the term 'war' can be understood to occur in two connected senses. In a literal sense, 'war' involves the ongoing social violence represented by the chaos of religious and political civil war. In a more figurative sense, 'war' occurs as a war of beliefs, ideas, opinions, judgments and interpretations contained within all aspects of the human social and material world. In some interpretations of the *Leviathan* Hobbes's account of linguistic and epistemic conflict are suppressed or are treated as unrelated to Hobbes's account of the warlike state of nature.[49] Such interpretations overlook the importance of Hobbes's grounding of the causes of war in *epistemic conflict* and his efforts to deduce a solution to this problem through right reason by drawing attention to the importance of the categories of the preservation of life and peace.

In giving an example of the frailty and self-conflicting nature of human knowledge, Hobbes argues:

> For though the nature of that which we conceive, be the same; yet the diversity of our reception of it, in respect of different constitutions of the body, and prejudices of opinion, gives every thing a tincture of our different passions. And therefore in reasoning man must take heed of words; which besides the signification of what we imagine in their nature, have a signification also of the nature, disposition, and interest of the speaker; such as are the names of Vertues, and Vices; For what one man calleth

> *Wisdome*, what another calleth *feare*; and one *cruelty*, what another *justice*; one *prodigality*, what another *magnanimity*; and one *gravity*, what another *stupidity*.[50]

For Hobbes, it is not only the situation that the frailties of human knowledge and public reasoning cause conflict, but that moral and political claims are drawn into violent dispute by parties who are willing to re-interpret facts to further their own interests. Hobbes argues:

> [T]he doctrine of Right and Wrong, is perpetually disputed, both by the Pen and the Sword ... For I doubt not, but if it had been a thing contrary to any mans right of dominion, or to the interest of men that have dominion, *That the three Angles of a Triangle, should be equal to two Angles of a Square*; that doctrine should have been, if not disputed, yet by the burning of all books of Geometry, suppressed, as farre as he whom it concerned was able.[51]

In this respect the condition of 'fear' which for Hobbes occurs within the state of war can be understood as an epistemological condition. Fear occurs as an anxiety over both the unknown causes of things and an anxiety over what is to occur in the future, both in this life and after death.[52] In this wider context, Hobbes introduces the notion of 'equality' within the state of nature. Hobbes's notion can be interpreted as an equality with regard to the problems of knowledge and judgment shared between all humans as much as it refers to a basic equality in the physical vulnerability of being killed. Individuals are not only equally vulnerable to being killed, they are also equally unable to pass judgments objectively that could otherwise resolve their conflicting claims of belief.

Hobbes's expression of a lack of a 'common power which keeps men in awe' can be understood to refer not merely to political power and coercion, but equally, to the lack of any authoritative and objective standpoint of judgment that can prevent conflict over differing beliefs. As such, notions of right and justice have no place within the 'state of nature'.[53] Instead, these conceptions are the subject of dispute themselves; war occurs as the dispute and struggle over the differing conceptions of right and justice and the attempt to bring one particular conception into the condition of universal validity that governs by way of political power.[54]

Within the condition of war, where all claims and opinions are open not only to dispute, but involve self-deception and error, Hobbes attempts to set out the minimal conditions of a natural law upon which humanity might be able to come to some kind of basic agreement. With similarity to the approach of Grotius, Hobbes turns towards the development of a natural law of minimal content. Hobbes's approach follows Grotius's question of asking, what might be the basic conditions of securing peaceful human sociability? In Hobbes's account, the basic condition upon which there can be no disagreement is the centrality of the preservation of human life.[55] For Hobbes, the requirement of the preservation of human life precedes any debate over *how* such a life is to be lived. On this point, H.L.A. Hart[56] cites the importance of Hobbes who, he argues, has seen 'in the modest aim of survival the central indisputable element which gives empirical good sense to the terminology of Natural Law'.[57] Hart argues:

> We wish to know whether, among these social arrangements, there are some which may illuminatingly be ranked as natural laws discoverable by reason, and what their relation is to human law and morality. To raise this or any question concerning *how* men should live together, we must assume that their aim, generally speaking, is to live.[58]

In pointing to the notion of survival as the most basic category of natural law, Hart makes the claim that survival is a *necessary* condition for all law. The question of *how* a social life is to be organized, of how life is to be lived, presupposes the existence and continuation of life. Survival is seen as necessary to the question of law in the sense that other claims about life (about quality, preference, modes of organization) cannot be made without, and are dependent upon, survival as a basic category. Hart argues:

> Even if we think of it in this common-sense way, survival has still a special status in relation to human conduct and in our thought about it, which parallels the prominence and the necessity ascribed to it in the orthodox formulations of Natural Law. For it is not merely that an overwhelming majority of men do wish to live, even at the cost of hideous misery, but that this is reflected in whole structures of our thought and language, in terms of which we describe the world and each other. We could not subtract the general wish to live and leave intact concepts like danger and safety, harm and benefit, need and function, disease and cure; for these are ways of simultaneously describing and appraising things by reference to the contribution they make to survival which is accepted as an aim.[59]

For Hobbes, the categories of preservation of life and peaceful human sociability could be determined by 'right reason' as the basic requirement of what is necessary for a functional social life.[60] By applying a test of whether particular acts were either conducive or disruptive to peaceful social life Hobbes thought that he could undercut sceptical claims and rhetorical redescription and determine 'scientifically' virtue from vice.[61] Hobbes's approach differs from Grotius's in that Hobbes considered that what remained problematic was an individual's judgment over how their own life was to be preserved. That is, while the value of peace might be agreed upon, conflicts and disputes would still continue between individual judgments over the *means* by which life could be preserved and peace achieved. Such dispute potentially aggravated the condition of social violence. Hobbes's solution is for individuals to renounce their 'right of nature' and hand this right over to a sovereign. Hobbes argues:

> The Right of Nature, which Writers commonly call *Jus Naturale*, is the Liberty each man hath, to use his own power, as he will himselfe, for the preservation of his own Nature; that is to say, of his own Life; and consequently, of doing any thing, which is in his own Judgment, and Reason, hee shall conceive to be the aptest means thereunto.[62]

And, following this, he enunciates as a rule of right reason the pursuance of peace. Hobbes argues:

> That a man be willing, when others are so too, as farre-forth, as for Peace, and defence of himselfe he shall think it necessary, to lay down his rights to all things; and be contented with so much liberty against other men, as he would allow other men against himselfe.[63]

Hobbes agues that to 'lay down' a 'right' involves the divesting of an individual's liberty of hindering another of the benefit of the other's right to the same.[64] Contrary to authoritarian interpretations of Hobbes, Hobbes's argument does not involve the giving up of all private rights and liberties and entering into an obligation of absolute obedience to the sovereign in exchange for protection.[65] Rather, what is primarily being renounced is the 'natural right' to judgment over how an individual can best preserve its own life. Further, it is not the bare right of self-preservation that is renounced, but rather, the right to use one's own judgment about preservation which is handed over to the sovereign.[66] That is to say, what is given over to the sovereign by Hobbes is the right to pass judgment over public opinions and doctrines that might threaten domestic peace and throw the commonwealth back into the chaos of civil war.[67] In many ways the line Hobbes treads between liberalism and absolutism is defined by the threat, or the appearance of the threat, to internal peace and the sovereign's judgment to carry out what is 'necessary' to safeguard peace and avoid civil war. In the pursuit of peace much faith is placed in the sovereign's judgment and in the sovereign's decision. For many, this faith continues today.

In such a manner Hobbes attempts to come to terms with the chaotic social violence of religious and political conflict present within the conditions of civil war. The competing moral, political and religious claims over justice and the good life cannot be reconciled by the tradition of Christian just war nor by an old form of religious natural law. Rather, all that could be salvaged is a natural law of minimal content which holds onto the basic significance of the preservation of life and peace. Yet, while there might be agreement over the category of peace, the continuing dispute over how it is to be brought about pushes Hobbes towards developing a juridical solution: the renunciation of the right of private judgment to determine the means for the preservation of life and the renunciation of the right to private violence, together with the affirmation of the sovereign's right to violence and judgment over how peace is to be secured within the commonwealth.

V

Hobbes's juridical ordering of war moves towards treating social violence as a predominantly public concern that is to be dealt with by the juridical figure of the sovereign at the head of a social-contractual notion of political community. As a public juridical concern, the question of the legitimacy of violence is no longer primarily a question of morality and religion. While decisions over what acts of state violence are legitimate to preserve peace or defend the commonwealth may be influenced by moral and religious considerations, under the juridical ordering of war the act of judgment over the legitimacy of violence remains firmly a *sovereign decision*. The control over the right to violence within the commonwealth, and violence external to the commonwealth, and the right to judge when the use of violence is necessary, is vested firmly within the sovereign's authority. As with Grotius, Hobbes de-legitimizes private violence and orders the legitimacy of violence around the notion of war proper, war undertaken and decided upon by the sovereign. In *On the Citizen*, Hobbes argues:

> It is useless for men to keep peace amongst themselves, if they cannot protect themselves against outsiders; and it is impossible to defend themselves if their strength is not united. It is therefore *necessary* to the preservation of individuals that there be some *one assembly* or *one man* who has the right to arm, muster and unite, on each occasion of danger or opportunity, as many citizens as the common defence shall require, taking into account uncertainty about the number and strength of the enemy; as well as the right to make peace with the enemy when advantageous. It must therefore be recognized that the individual citizens have transferred the whole of this *Right of war and peace* to one *man* or *assembly*. And this right (which we may call the *Sword of war*) belongs to the same *man* or *assembly* as the *Sword of justice*. For the only one who can rightly compel the citizens to arms and the expenses of war is the one who has the right to punish anyone who disobeys. Both swords, therefore the *Sword of war* and the *Sword of justice* are inherent in sovereign power, essentially and from the very nature of the commonwealth.[68]

Further, that: 'All *judgment*, therefore, in a commonwealth belongs to the possessor of the swords, i.e. to the holder of sovereign power.'[69] In Hobbes, what can be seen is a form of *positing* of the scope and boundaries of legal authority, including the authority to pass judgment over the legitimacy of violence. This positing of the law takes the shape or is presented through an agreement of community or social contract.[70] The form of positing in Hobbes occurs as a movement in which humanity, based purely upon its own use of 'right reason' and through its own 'will', creates for itself a political and juridical authority that determines the scope and breadth of individual rights and obligation. Such a form of positing can be thought of as 'modern' in the sense that it begins to move away from the reliance upon religious and transcendent forms of authority (dominant in the ancient and medieval worlds) to ground the basic rules of human, social behaviour. In another sense, however, this movement might also be seen to involve the positing of a new form of non-theological divinity, the divinity of the sovereign state, which over time attempts to unseat the authority of God and claim much of this old authority for itself.

At the least, what can be seen as following on from the process of juridical ordering in Grotius and Hobbes is the re-description and ordering of territory and space around the figure of sovereignty and through inter-sovereign relations. A manner of looking at and comprehending the social world is posited by the juridical ordering of war, one in which the legitimacy of human action and violence is bound up with the question of sovereign authority. Such a conception had partially existed in differing forms before the formulations of Grotius and Hobbes. However, what is of importance is the manner in which the form of the juridical ordering of violence around the secular sovereign within the Westphalian heritage of the natural law tradition has come to regulate and re-shape the relations between right, territory and violence in a manner that continues to influence human social relations today.

One radical aspect of the juridical ordering of war involves the re-framing of human social relations as relations between sovereign bodies, between monarchies, commonwealths (and later nation-states). In some respects the inter-sovereign relation presents a chaotic and violent picture similar to that of the war of all against all within the conditions of civil war. Hobbes makes such a characterization. He argues:

> But though there had never been any time, wherein particular men were in a condition of warre one against another; yet in all times, Kings, and Persons of Soveraigne authority, because of their Independency, are in continual jelousies, and in the state and posture of Gladiators; having their weapons pointing, and their eyes fixed on one another; that is their Forts, Garrisons, and Guns, upon the Frontiers of their Kingdoms; and continuall Speyes upon their neighbours, which is a posture of War.[71]

From one perspective Hobbes might be charged with bringing a solution to one problem (i.e. civil war) but of ignoring the challenges of another (i.e. inter-sovereign war). However, a better formulation involves the suggestion that it is only through the process of juridical ordering given by thinkers such as Grotius and Hobbes that contemporary thinking draws such a sharp distinction between the problem of civil war and the problem of inter-state war: between war proper and non-sovereign violence. In other words, the suggestion is that the framing of the war problem *as a problem of inter-state war* has developed historically, in part, through the work of thinkers such as Grotius and Hobbes. In responding to one form of social violence, this Westphalian heritage of the natural law tradition has framed and produced a specific account of the problem of war and has developed a style of thinking about war, right and international relations that continues to exert influence within late modernity.

There are a number of critiques of the movements within Grotius and Hobbes which cannot be discussed in detail here but, should at least be mentioned. It should be noted that the juridical ordering of war carried out by both Grotius and Hobbes takes place within the emerging nature of bourgeois economic relations and modelling of human nature and the development of legal justifications for the European colonization of the non-European world.[72] In this respect, the process of juridical ordering and its formulation of the sovereign's monopoly over the legitimacy of violence cannot be completely abstracted from the workings of forms of political economy.[73] The de-legitimation of private violence, the opening of a sphere of peaceful sociability within the state and the justification of the state's right to war independent of theological considerations, took place within the breakdown of feudal economies and the growing mercantile interests of emerging European economies. This development was probably only made possible by the imperial conquest of the non-European world by Europeans.

Further, the juridical ordering of war developed by Grotius and Hobbes needs to be viewed in the light of late twentieth-century deconstructions of the notion of the social contract. Accounts that attempt to found a legal order upon a social contract or agreement within a community run into some difficulty as they presuppose questions of origin within the notion of community itself. Jean-Luc Nancy points to Jean-Jacques Rousseau's suggestion that the notion of community contains an *aporia*: 'the *aporia* of a community that would have to precede itself in order to constitute itself'.[74] Nancy also draws attention to the fact that any moment of 'foundation' of political community contains a hidden account of a politics of exclusivity and exclusion.[75] In one respect the accounts presented by Grotius and Hobbes can be interpreted as efforts to legitimate particular forms of sovereign authority through the *fiction* of the social contract. This fiction involves the notion that sovereign authority is legitimated by, either a practical, historical, social contract, or by the so-called 'logical' claim that all sovereign authority is grounded upon and legitimated by its maintenance of peace and security.

Among the women, children, the working poor and the internal enemies of the state who are excluded or precluded from the historical or 'logical' social contract stand also non-European peoples excluded through the category of the preservation of life. The colonial subject generally stands outside of the narrative of the Westphalian heritage of the natural law tradition. The history of the killing of non-European peoples by Europeans whose 'right' to violence was substantially orientated around the emerging figure of state sovereignty, somewhat upsets the 'neutral' category of the preservation of life.[76] Within this category lies heavy differentiation over the relative *values* of differing forms of human life. The history of European colonial conquest was built upon theories of race that justified the slaughter and not the 'preservation' of non-European human life. In this respect the category of the preservation of life cannot be too far abstracted from the historical shedding of much blood.

Further, the typical narrative of European secularization and the development of a secular natural law is also not unproblematic.[77] Any such 'secular' movement needs to be understood as having developed within the boundaries of a wider European, Christian worldview. While the process of 'secularization' managed to resolve a number of conflicts within Europe, at their borders, Europeans engaged in quite openly religious conflicts between their Christian worldview and numerous other non-Christian religious and cosmic worldviews. Considered in this respect, one should be careful not to simplistically assume that the creation of public 'secular' sphere of law or politics equates to a 'neutral' sphere or that such a sphere can simply be reapplied to contemporary conflicts between a 'secular' West and actors within the Islamic world.

Such criticisms, while important, do not derogate completely from the theoretical and historical significance of the tradition of the juridical ordering of war. Within this tradition a modern concept of war was produced through which the right to violence is held by the sovereign and is understood as partly constitutive of the definition of sovereignty. War is de-sacralized and de-moralized and the only actors who are understood to hold a legitimate right to use violence are sovereigns.

Within the territory of the sovereign state, the sovereign body holds the monopoly upon the legitimacy of violence. What might have formerly been comprehended as disputing claims of a 'just' war within the territory of the state is now de-legitimized. In the process of de-legitimization, acts of civil war, violence and terror are criminalized; they are conceptualized as crimes against the state and against the peaceful social order. One citizen's violence against its others is not understood via the legal category of war but is understood as a domestic or internal legal category of murder, or even treason. On the flip side, the state's violence against its own citizens is no longer viewed as war but, rather, as police action, as lawful coercion and as punishment. In this context what constitutes 'war' proper is bound to the status of sovereignty and sovereign decision.

For the tradition of legal positivism and its comprehension of international law, often the concept of 'war' is equated with 'state war' and all other forms of violence, including civil war, terror, revolution, and murder, are expunged from the categories and laws of war developed by international treaties and frameworks. In the sense of the grand legal positivist distinction drawn by John Austin between 'laws properly so called' and 'laws improperly so called',[78] forms of violence that are carried out by non-sovereign actors stand on the 'improper' side of juridical characterization. As such, because non-sovereign acts of violence stand outside or do not correspond to the modern legal concept of war developed by the tradition of juridical ordering, many positivist lawyers (or at least those who recognize international law today as 'law properly so called') simply cannot understand how non-sovereign violence might be described as 'war'.

In such a light, it is worth paying attention to the fact that the distinction between war proper and war improper, or non-sovereign violence, has developed within a particular historical and intellectual tradition and that the content of a modern concept of war is not set in stone. Further, the boundaries and content of this concept of war have been sustained by sovereign states and legal and political actors who continue to re-inscribe the importance of war's juridical ordering. As such, the content of such a concept has no *a priori* validity and continues to hold force only until the moment the content is changed under the pressure of differing social and material conditions.

Of continuing significance is the act and function of *ordering* occurring within the thought of both Grotius and Hobbes. Within each, the lines and boundaries of the legitimacy of human violence are demarcated and are set or moulded into an enduring juridical form. The juridical ordering of war has endured over time. The tradition has established a *form* or shape of thinking through which many humans have come to view and comprehend the relation between violence and right over centuries. Such a form has been adopted by political actors and interpretive communities and exerts the normative force of a dominant historical tradition which heavily influences the way we speak and think about the legitimacy of violence today. The tradition is not, however, the sole form of the ordering of war, it is inherited, critiqued and challenged by others.

Notes

1 Such an account is put forward by Martin Heckel. See M. Heckel, *Deutchsland im konfessionellen Zeitalter*, Göttingen: Vandenhoeck-Ruprecht, 2001, pp. 39–40.

2 J.L. Brierley, *The Law of Nations: An Introduction to the International Law of Peace*, Oxford: Clarendon Press, 1936, pp. 5–6.

3 A. Nussbaum, *A Concise History of the Law of Nations*, New York: Macmillan, 1947, p. 36. See the discussion also in K.L. Holsti, *Peace and War: Armed Conflicts and International Order, 1648–1989*, Cambridge: Cambridge University Press, 1991. At p. 38, he argues:

> The religious issue, the overriding source of increasing chaos, brutality, and intolerance throughout Europe for the proceeding century, was resolved according to the principles with which the rulers and dynasts of the day, if not the Popes, could live. No war occurring after 1648 – wars against the Ottomans excepted – derived primarily from religious issues. The Westphalia religious formula, moreover, was so successful that it served as a model for numerous other treaties, such as the Peace of Oliva (1660) ending the Swedish-Polish war.

> Westphalia, in brief, resolved an issue that had generated numerous wars in the past. Domestic intolerance continued in many countries and caused frequent diplomatic frictions, but the dynasts never again went to war against each other carrying the banners of Protestant or Catholic faiths.

4 On the argument that Westphalia represents a 'myth', see S. Beaulac, *The Power of Language in the Making of International Law*, Leiden: Martinus Nijhoff Publishers, 2004. See also: O. Elias, 'Regionalism in International Law-Making', in C. Harding, and C.L. Lim (eds) *Renegotiating Westphalia*, The Hague: Martinus Nijhoff, 1999.
5 See also the account of this movement in C. Schmitt, *The Nomos of the Earth*, trans. G.L. Ulmen, New York: Telos Press, 2003; T.J. Knutsen, *A History of International Relations Theory*, Manchester: Manchester University Press, 1992; I. Clark and I.B. Neumann (eds) *Classical Theories of International Relations*, London: Macmillan, 1996.
6 I. Hunter, 'Westphalia Calling', unpublished research paper, p. 11. On this heritage more generally as an intellectual movement, see the discussion in I. Hunter, *Rival Enlightenments: Civil and Metaphysical Philosophy in Early Modern Germany*, New York: Cambridge University Press, 2001. As this relates to contemporary critical legal scholarship, see D. Saunders, *Anti-Lawyers*, London: Routledge, 1997.
7 See H. Lauterpach, 'The Grotian Tradition in International Law', *British Yearbook of International Law*, 23, 1946, 1–53; H. Bull, *The Anarchical Society*, London: Macmillan, 1977.
8 H. Grotius, *The Rights of War and Peace*, ed. R. Tuck, Indianapolis, IN: Liberty Fund, 2005.
9 Ibid., pp. 1021–123.
10 Ibid., p. 1024. Although Grotius's comment at p. 1027 should also be noted:

> As therefore, with Respect to the Civil Laws, the Ignorance of them, or of their true Meaning excuses a Fact, so, with Respect to the Laws of Nature, it is reasonable that they should be excused, who either through Weakness of their Judgment, or their ill Education, violate those laws. For as the Ignorance of the Law, if it is invincible, entirely exculpates one, so when attended even with Negligence, it lessens the Fault. And therefore those Barbarians who offend in these Matters, by Reason of their bad Education, *Aristotle* compares to such as have their Appetites vitiated by some Distemper.

11 R. Tuck, *The Rights of War and Peace: Political Thought and the International Order from Grotius to Kant*, Oxford: Oxford University Press, 1999, p. 103.
12 H. Grotius, *The Rights of War and Peace*, p. 1120. See also the discussion in E. Keene, *Beyond the Anarchical Society: Grotius, Colonialism and Order in World Politics*, Cambridge: Cambridge University Press, 2002.
13 E. Bloch, *Natural Law and Human Dignity*, trans. D.J. Schmidt, Cambridge, MA: MIT Press, 1996, p. 50.
14 H. Grotius, *The Rights of War and Peace*, p. 91.
15 Ibid., p. 87. At p. 150, Grotius claims:

> NATURAL RIGHT *is the Rule and Dictate of Right Reason, shewing the Moral Deformity or Moral Necessity there is in any Act, according to its Suitableness or Unsuitableness to a reasonable nature,* and consequently, that such an Act is either forbid or commanded by GOD, the Author of Nature.

16 Ibid., pp. 93–5.

17 Ibid., p. 89.

18 There is also an inheritance here by Grotius of certain notions from Roman law.

19 On the Protestant influences on this shift in natural law more generally, see E. Bloch, *Natural Law and Human Dignity*; Q. Skinner, *The Foundations of Modern Political Thought*, Vol. 2, Cambridge: Cambridge University Press, 1978; R. Tuck, *Natural Rights Theories: Their Origin and Development*, Cambridge: Cambridge University Press, 1981.

20 H. Grotius, *The Rights of War and Peace*, pp. 138–9.

21 Ibid., p. 134.

22 Ibid., p. 180.

23 Ibid., pp. 182–3.

24 Ibid., p. 183.

25 Ibid.

26 Ibid., p. 184. Grotius argues:

> But Right Reason, and the Nature of Society, which is to be examined in the second and chief Place, does not prohibit all Manner of Violence, but only that which is repugnant to Society, that is, which invades another's Right: For the Design of Society is, that every one should quietly enjoy his own, with the Help, and by the United Force of the whole Community.

27 Ibid., pp. 240–1.

28 Ibid., pp. 339–40.

29 The term 'state' is used here only tentatively in the sense that the modern territorial state was only beginning to emerge at this point in time. With Hobbes, and his discussion of a commonwealth situated in England, it is perhaps easier to use the term 'state'.

30 This 'public' nature of war which distinguishes it from 'crime' is argued for also by Alberico Gentilli. In *De Jure Belli Libri Tres*, he argues:

> In fact, war is nothing if not a contest, and it is a contest of arms because to wage war in one's mind and not with arms is surely cowardice and not war ... Furthermore, the strife must be public, for war is not a broil, a fight, the hostility of individuals. And the arms of both sides should be public, for *bellum*, war, derives its name from the fact that there is a contest for victory between two equal parties and for that reason it was at first called *duellum*, a contest of two. Therefore that definition which appeared after ours, 'war is armed force against a foreign prince or people' is shown to be incorrect by the fact that it applies the term 'war' also to the violence of private individuals and brigands.

Cited in L. Kotzsch, *The Concept of War in Contemporary History and International Law*, Geneva: Librairie E. Droz, 1956, pp. 35–6.

31 M. Weber, 'Politics as a Vocation' in H.H. Gerth and C.W. Mills (eds) *From Max Weber: Essays in Sociology*, New York: Oxford University Press, 1958, p. 78.

32 H. Grotius, *The Rights of War and Peace*, at pp. 248–50:

> Publick Wars are either *Solemn, according to the Law of Nations*, or *not solemn*: What I here term *Solemn* is generally called *Lawful*, or *made in Form*, in the same Sense as a *Will* is termed *Lawful*, in Opposition to a *Codicil*; or a *Marriage Lawful*, in Opposition of the *Cohabitation of Slaves* ... Two Things then are requisite to make a War solemn by the Law of Nations. First, that it be made on both Sides, by the Authority of those that have the Sovereign

Power in the State: And then, that it be accompanied with some Formalities; of which we shall treat in its proper Place.

33 Lothar Kotzsch gives a very neat summary of this movement. L. Kotzsch, *The Concept of War in Contemporary History and International Law*, at p. 37, he argues:

> The period of transition from the medieval doctrine of just war through the formalisation of that theory until its reshaping at the hands of Grotius can be summarised under the following headings:
>
> 1 The existence of war is conditioned on an initiator having *summa potestas*.
> 2 The *iusta causa*, formerly bound up with the concept of justice conformable to Christian morality is more and more subordinate to the sole judgment of the sovereign.
> 3 The former alternative between just and unjust war is transformed into a new alternative between war and no war at all.
> 4 The competence of the Pope in having the last word for the legal qualification of armed conflicts no longer had any relevance. The question of deciding whether at a given moment war is being carried on or not is to be settled exclusively by the temporal sovereign.
> 5 The idea of the just war is formalized into that of the just enemy.

34 For such an account, see H. Bull, *The Anarchical Society*; and D. Boucher, *Political Theories of International Relations: From Thucydides to the Present*, Oxford: Oxford University Press, 1998.
35 Other 'realist' thinkers might include H. Treitschke, *Politics*, trans. H. Kohn, New York: Harcourt, Brace and World Inc., 1963; H.J. Morgenthau, *In Defense of the National Interest*, New York: Alfred A. Knopf, 1952; and K. Waltz, *Man, the State and War*, New York: Columbia University Press, 1959.
36 Chapter 3 shows how this characterization of inter-state relations is inherited by Kant and used to develop an approach to the ordering of war.
37 T. Hobbes, *Leviathan*, ed. R. Tuck, Cambridge: Cambridge University Press, 1996.
38 For an introductory account which firmly places Hobbes within the context of civil war in England and more broadly in Europe, see R. Harrison, *Hobbes, Locke and Confusion's Masterpiece*, Cambridge: Cambridge University Press, 2003, pp. 1–42.
39 T. Hobbes, *On the Citizen*, ed. R. Tuck and M. Silverthorn, Cambridge: Cambridge University Press, 1998, p. 13.
40 Ibid., pp. 13–14.
41 Ibid., p. 15.
42 Ibid., pp. 4–5. Hobbes argues:

> In treating of figures it is called *Geometry*, of motion *Physics*, of natural law, *Morals*, but it is all *Philosophy*; just as the sea is here called British, there Atlantic, elsewhere Indian, so called from its particular shores, but it is all Ocean. The Geometers have managed their province outstandingly. For whatever benefit comes to human life from observation of the stars, from mapping of lands, from reckoning of time and from long-distance navigation; whatever is beautiful in buildings, strong in defence-works and marvellous in machines, whatever in short distinguishes the modern world from the barbarity of the past, is almost wholly the gift of Geometry; for what we owe to Physics, Physics owes to Geometry. If the moral Philosophers had done their job with equal success, I do not know what greater contribution human industry could have

made to human happiness. For if the patterns of human action were known with the same certainty as the relations of magnitude in figures ambition and greed, whose power rests on the false opinions of the common people about right and wrong [*ius et iniuria*], would be disarmed, and the human race would enjoy such secure peace that (apart from conflicts over space as the population grew) it seems unlikely that it would ever have to fight again. But as things are, the war of the sword and the war of the pens is perpetual.

43 The interpretation taken here differs from the view given by Leo Strauss that Hobbes's political philosophy expresses a 'pre-scientific', 'new moral attitude' hidden by an account of psychology and a 'scientific' approach to the problems of human knowledge in general. See L. Strauss, *The Political Philosophy of Hobbes: Its Basis and its Genesis*, trans. E.M. Sinclair, Chicago, IL: University of Chicago Press, 1963. Consider also the 'anti-systematic' interpretation given by Warrender. See H. Warrender, *The Political Philosophy of Hobbes: His Theory of Obligation*, Oxford: Clarendon Press, 1957. Against these interpretations, Hobbes's account of human psychology, and elements of his materialism continue to play a role in how he conceives the fundamental basis of human conflict and his efforts to determine a solution. Consider the account of Hobbes's 'scientific approach' in J. Hampton, *Hobbes and the Social Contract Tradition*, Cambridge: Cambridge University Press, 1986. At p. 49, Hampton argues: 'It is Hobbes's deepest faith that he can show a *necessary causal connection* between at least one cooperative project (i.e. the institution of the sovereign) and peace.'
44 For Hobbes's position in relation to the challenges of scepticism, see M. Oakeshott, *Hobbes on Civil Association*, Indianapolis, IN: Liberty Fund, 1975. Consider also L. Strauss, 'On the Spirit of Hobbes's Political Philosophy', in K. Brown (ed.) *Hobbes Studies*, Oxford: Blackwell, 1965.
45 Something of this view is emphasized by Carl Schmitt, who, when speaking about, among others, Hobbes, argues: '[A]ll genuine political theories presuppose man to be evil.' See C. Schmitt, *The Concept of the Political*, trans. G. Schwab, Chicago, IL: University of Chicago Press, 1996, pp. 58–60. While such a claim that Hobbes' possessed a pessimistic human anthropology is not completely untrue, it needs to be placed within a general context of the 'dark' view of human nature contained in Calvinist theology, and such a Calvinist environment in which Hobbes was educated. Hobbes's philosophy should not be reduced to any such dark anthropology. On Hobbes's work placed in a Calvinist context, see A.P. Martinich, *The Two Gods of the Leviathan: Thomas Hobbes on Religion and Politics*, Cambridge: Cambridge University Press, 1992. For a refutation of the claim that Hobbes presents a 'psychological egoism', see B. Gert, 'Hobbes's Psychology', in T. Sorell (ed.) *The Cambridge Companion to Hobbes*, Cambridge: Cambridge University Press, 1996.
46 R. Tuck, *The Rights of War and Peace*, p. 131.
47 T. Hobbes, *Leviathan*, p. 88.
48 Ibid., p. 89.
49 For interpretations that give little attention to Hobbes's account of epistemic problems in the first portion of the *Leviathan*, see H. Warrender, *The Political Philosophy of Hobbes: His Theory of Obligation*, Oxford: Clarendon Press, 1957; F.C. Hood, *The Divine Politics of Thomas Hobbes*, Oxford: Clarendon Press, 1964.
50 T. Hobbes, *Leviathan*, p. 31.
51 Ibid., p. 74.
52 Ibid., pp. 74, 76.
53 Ibid., p. 90.

54 Richard Tuck makes a similar point See R. Tuck, 'Introduction', in T. Hobbes, *Leviathan*, pp. xxvi–xxix.
55 T. Hobbes, *Leviathan*, p. 117.
56 H.L.A. Hart, *The Concept of Law*, 2nd edn, Oxford: Oxford University Press, 1994, p. 193. Hart's adoption of a 'natural law of minimal content' is sometimes overlooked by many who consider Hart to put forward a strictly 'legal positivist' theory of law.
57 Ibid., p. 191.
58 Ibid., p. 192.
59 Ibid., p. 192
60 T. Hobbes, *Leviathan*. Described as a 'precept or, general rule of Reason', Hobbes argues at p. 92: 'That, every man, ought to endeavour Peace, as farre as he has hope of obtaining it; and when he cannot obtain it, that he may seek, and use, all helps, and advantages of Warre.'
61 Q. Skinner, *Reason and Rhetoric in the Philosophy of Thomas Hobbes*, Cambridge: Cambridge University Press, 1996, p. 341.
62 T. Hobbes, *Leviathan*, p. 91.
63 Ibid., p. 92.
64 Ibid.
65 Such an 'absolutist' interpretation is taken by Schmitt in his drawing upon a relation of 'protection and obedience' to de-legitimize a pluralistic state. See C. Schmitt, *The Concept of the Political*, pp. 52–3. For a critique of Schmitt's interpretation of Hobbes, see U. Steinvorth, 'On Carl Schmitt's Interpretation of Hobbes', in L. Foisneau, J. Merle and T. Sorell (eds) *Leviathan Between the Wars*, Frankfurt am Main: Peter Lang, 2005. Note the comment by Leo Strauss in L. Strauss, 'On the Spirit of Hobbes's Political Philosophy', in K.C. Brown (ed.) *Hobbes Studies*, Oxford: Blackwell, 1965, at p. 13:

> If we call liberalism that political doctrine which regards as the fundamental political fact the rights, as distinguished from duties, of man and which identifies the function of the state with the protection or the safeguarding of those rights, we must say that the founder of liberalism was Hobbes.

66 R. Tuck, 'Introduction', in T. Hobbes, *Leviathan*, p. xxxii. Tuck argues:

> In other words, it is the right to use one's own judgment about preservation which is in fact the right of nature, not the bare right of self-preservation. The right of nature rests on the recognition of the salience for everybody of their own survival, but like any right it is renounceable, and its renunciation is the heart of Hobbes's theory.

67 T. Hobbes, *Leviathan*, p. 125. Hobbes states:

> It belongeth therefore to him that hath Soveraign Power, to be Judge, or constitute all Judges of Opinions and Doctrines, as a thing necessary to Peace; thereby to prevent Discord and Civil Warre.

68 T. Hobbes, *On the Citizen*, pp. 78–9. See also T. Hobbes, *Leviathan*, p. 126.
69 T. Hobbes, *On the Citizen*, p. 79.
70 T. Hobbes, *Leviathan*, p. 121.
71 Ibid., p. 90.
72 Aspects of this critique will be addressed in Chapter 6. See generally the critiques in C.B. Macpherson, 'Hobbes's Bourgeois Man', in K.C. Brown, *Hobbes Studies*,

Oxford: Blackwell, 1965; R. Tuck, *The Rights of War and Peace*; E. Bloch, *Natural Law and Human Dignity*. Bloch, at p. 47, argues:

> Hobbes obviously possesses a purely bourgeois ideology and his convoluted natural law is at its service; but one must not forget that despite Salböl and Olymp, the absolutism of the seventeenth century possesses a thoroughly bourgeois function and is closely and complexly entangled in the economy of the state, that is, with the mercantile system. Absolutism, otherwise called the dictatorship of the national state, which is incarnated in it, broke the local, feudal, economic order in the interest of the grand bourgeoisie; the exercise of absolutism, as it occurs in Hobbes, does not contradict the anti-feudal tendency of classical natural law.

73 This question is taken up again in Chapter 5.

74 J. Nancy, *Being Singular Plural*, ed. R.D. Richardson, trans. A.E. O'Byrne, Stanford, CA: Stanford University Press, 2000, p. 24.

75 Ibid.

76 On the problematic notions of 'preservation of life' and 'bare life' lying at the heart of particular Western conceptions of sovereignty, see G. Agamben, *Homo Sacer: Sovereign Power and Bare Life*, trans. D. Roazen-Heller, Stanford, CA: Stanford University Press, 1998; M. Foucault, *Society Must Be Defended*, ed. D. Macey, London: Penguin Books, 2003.

77 For critiques of the notion of 'secularism', see W.E. Connolly, *Why I Am Not a Secularist*, Minneapolis, MN: University of Minnesota Press, 1999; J. Milbank, *Theology and Social Theory: Beyond Secular Reason*, Oxford: Blackwell, 1993.

78 J. Austin, *The Province of Jurisprudence Determined*, London: Weidenfeld and Nicolson, 1971, p.1.

Chapter 3

The challenge of morality

I

The previous chapter outlined the development of the initial moments of a modern concept of war. Through the natural law theories of Grotius and Hobbes the relation between the concepts of war and right were ordered around an emerging notion of secular, European sovereign authority. 'War proper' was framed as a particular form of violence between sovereigns rather than as social violence between humans in general. The juridical ordering of war helped to formalize a trend towards the de-theologization and de-moralization of war. In this process, acts of terror and civil war were de-legitimized and even criminalized through an emphasis upon the sovereign's monopoly upon the legitimacy of violence. In such a configuration the notions of peace, security and the preservation of life took centre stage.

Within the outlines of the Westphalian tradition the question of the rightness of war came to be understood as a question pertaining to the status and limits of sovereign authority. When thinking about the problem of war in contemporary times this line of inheritance remains significant. The sovereign authority of the state remains a primary organ or persona through which social-political relations and the legitimacy of acts of violence within the world are arranged and understood. Yet, today, within a global system of international law the state sovereign's right to war is limited by the notions of international peace and cosmopolitan human rights. On the back of these notions, the act of aggressive war is condemned and, to an extent, is criminalized. This chapter examines one line of inheritance of the problem of war in which these contemporary conceptions are seen to emerge theoretically: *the moral ordering of war*.

This chapter focuses upon how the approaches to the problem of war taken by Grotius and Hobbes are inherited and taken up by Immanuel Kant through his re-framing of the problem of war as a moral problem. While Kant continues to hold onto the importance of the category of peace and the notion of war proper as state war, he attempts to reorder the question of the legitimacy of state violence via the categories of freedom and moral duty. Further, Kant institutes a radical, theoretical account of human reason and moral thinking that is no longer reliant upon nature to provide a measure for judgments over war. Kant's fundamental break with the depiction of reason given by his predecessors helps to usher in a modern form of approaching war in which the activity of human thinking – and the human responsibility for its own *acts* of thinking – begin to come into prominence.

In historical terms, Kant's moral ordering of war anticipates and occurs as a forerunner to the developments of international law within the twentieth century. These developments involved attempts to legally regulate state violence, the outlawing of aggressive war and the predominant use of a moral language drawn upon to both justify and condemn acts of war. Through focusing upon Kant's approach we might better come to terms with the *Janus face* of the contemporary moral ordering of war. On the one hand, the moral ordering of war offers a powerful and radical sense of hope. It posits an idea that may be believed in by millions that war can be overcome and that the world should be re-ordered in a manner that secures not only peace, but also freedom, human dignity and cosmopolitan justice. Further, the moral ordering of war presents a strong critique of the petty justifications for war, aggression and colonialism so often peddled by lawyers, leaders and heroes. Yet, on the other hand, the moral ordering of war opens onto the possibility of its own abuse. The moral ordering of war plunges the problem of war back into the chaos of competing moral claims over the right to violence. Also, the emergence of the moral validation of war develops as a modern form of secular, 'just war'.

By way of introducing a number of concepts that are drawn upon and developed by Kant, the chapter will begin by briefly discussing aspects of the moral and political philosophy of Jean-Jacques Rousseau. Following this, the chapter will examine Kant's moral philosophy – underlaid by his epistemology – by looking at the way in which he draws upon a 'universal' moral theory to come to terms with the problem of war. While Kant's cosmopolitan approach to the problem of war has many merits, his approach suffers from a number of severe limitations stemming from the inability of his moral theory to properly account for the role of violence within moral action and the status of violence at the foundation of legal institutions. Such a limitation in Kant's theory renders problematic the many contemporary 'cosmopolitan' approaches that follow in his footsteps.

II

For the purpose of examining Kant's moral theory and his approach to the problem of war it is necessary to briefly consider a few elements of Rousseau's moral and political philosophy. One way in which Rousseau can be seen to be relevant to the Kantian tradition of the moral ordering of war is through Rousseau's abridgement and criticism of Abbé Saint Pierre's *Perpetual Peace* (1712) published in its whole after Rousseau's death as the *Project of Perpetual Peace* (1782).[1] In the text, Abbé Saint Pierre puts forward the idea of a federation of states, which could bring to an end the problem of war between European monarchs and solve conflicts in a peaceful manner. The argument, which involves setting up an inter-state parliament, prefigures both Kant's proposal of an inter-state federation and the institutionalization of such a proposal in the twentieth century through the League of Nations (1919) and the United Nations (1945).

Rousseau, while sympathetic to the project, was sceptical of the possibility of it being realized within the political conditions of his time. For Rousseau, the idea of a federation of states instituting perpetual peace was 'too good to be adopted' and 'an absurd dream'.[2] Rousseau noted that the strategy of going to war to secure their own interests was too engrained within the attitudes of princes and their advisors.[3] Further, he argued that the creation of any inter-state federation could not simply be brought about by discussion, but instead, would need to rely on force.[4] This criticism, as will be shown later, troubles both Kant's approach to the problem of war, as well as contemporary, cosmopolitan approaches. Early on, Rousseau saw part of the paradox clearly. That is, the creation and realization of a formal, legal, inter-state institution designed to achieve peace would have to rely upon violence and war to achieve its objective.

While Rousseau's critique of the notion of perpetual peace is interesting, what is more relevant to the discussion here is the way in which Rousseau develops a theory of freedom which was influential upon not only Kant's moral philosophy but also upon a modern tradition of revolutionary war. While not a revolutionary himself, there is a revolutionary sap that bleeds from Rousseau's texts. This radicalism, standing in an ambiguous relationship with the Jacobins of the French Revolution (1789), expresses a critical and forward-yearning account of natural law in which the strategy of violence is directed by the futural, and sometimes romantic, demand for freedom. Commenting upon this radical tendency, Ernst Bloch states:

> *The Social Contract* (1762) thus became the Bible of the Jacobins, or one might even say, in an anachronist image, that it became the Sermon on the Mount of a rejuvenated people. For the sake of the hymn to liberty, which here is an inalienable liberty, natural law prevails. It was a revolutionary act when Rousseau, going far beyond Grotius, completely erased the contract of domination form the social contract; there is nothing left of the original subjugation in Rousseau's social contract. The absolute *inalienability of the person* – that is the novum that Rousseau introduced into classical natural law. The problem of an ideal law was this: to find a form wherein *individual freedom* could not be abdicated ('to find a form of association that defends and protects the communal force of the person'). The solution Rousseau offers to this truly difficult problem is twofold: first, to point to the voluntariness with which the individual enters into the social contract; and second, to show the immediacy with which the individual relates to the ensemble of communality, and is therefore not alienated.[5]

Rousseau's radical moral and political theory of freedom sits within, inherits and develops aspects of broad natural law tradition contributed to, in differing ways, by Grotius, Hobbes and John Locke. With some similarity to Locke, Rousseau develops an account of natural law that is both critical and transformative and which radically challenges the authority and legitimacy of a monarch via a social contract model of popular sovereignty. Such an approach frames a notion of natural law around an idea of liberty. On some interpretations, the different natural law accounts presented by Locke and Rousseau pave the way for the potential, legitimate use of violence against the unjust incursions upon liberty (and property) by a monarch. Aspects of a potential natural law legitimation of revolutionary war can be found within particular readings of Locke's *Two Treatises of Government* (1689–90).[6] Locke argues:

> The *State of War* is a State of Enmity and Destruction; And therefore declaring by Word of Action, not a passionate and hasty, but a settled Design, upon another Mans Life, *puts him in a State of War* with him against whom has declared such an Intention, and so has exposed his Life to the others Power to be taken away by him, or any one that joyns with him in his Defence, and espouses his Quarrel: it being reasonable and just I should have a Right to destroy that which threatens me with Destruction.[7]

And, that:

> [W]henever the *Legislators endeavour to take away, and destroy the Property of the People*, or to reduce them to Slavery under Arbitrary Power, they put themselves into a state of War with the People, who are thereupon absolved from any farther Obedience, and are left to the common Refuge, which God hath provided for all Men, against Force and Violence. Whensoever therefore the *Legislative* shall transgress this fundamental Rule of Society; and either by Ambition, Fear, Folly or Corruption, *endeavour to grasp* themselves, *or put into the hands of any other an Absolute Power* over the Lives, Liberties, and Estates of the People; By this breach of Trust they *forfeit the Power*, the People had put into their hands, for quite contrary ends, and it devolves to the People, who have a Right to resume their original Liberty, and, by the Establishment of a new Legislative (such as they shall think fit) provide for their own Safety and Security, which is the end for which they are in Society.[8]

Locke, arguing against the absolutism present within the social contract theories of Grotius and Hobbes, helps to reframe the notions of legitimate authority and legitimate violence around an idea of popular sovereignty and consent.[9] In Grotius and Hobbes, the sovereign's authority and its claim upon the monopoly of the legitimacy of violence are grounded upon the sovereign's ability to secure internal peace within the state and thus safeguard the lives and property of its citizens. Locke extends this formulation in a direction that insists upon the preservation, of not just the lives, but of the liberty and property of individual citizens.[10]

In this sense, the social contract that grounds legitimate authority, is for Locke one where individual liberty and property rights sit on a par with peace and the preservation of life. In such a move, legitimate sovereign authority is split between the executive and the populace (or its representatives). Such a splitting or sharing of authority has consequences for the notion of what counts as 'legitimate violence'. The old, ambiguous natural law right of tyrannicide is given theoretical and political meat: when individual liberty and property are threatened by the monarch, the natural law contract that constituted political authority is dissolved, and so with it, the monarch's right to the monopoly upon the legitimacy of violence. Or in other words, legitimate violence is held in reserve by popular sovereignty (the constituting power) to be used when the executive-sovereign (the constituted power) acts in a way which is illegitimate. An era of eighteenth-century revolutions, North American, French and Haitian, bear witness to and enact this radical natural law re-casting of moral and political authority and with it, 'the people's' (or 'man's') right to engage in 'legitimate violence' (violent rebellion and revolutionary war) against an unjust or oppressive monarch.

While building upon Locke, Rousseau develops a notion of moral and political freedom that attempts to move beyond the limitations of Locke's liberal rights framework. Rousseau sets forth an account that further radicalizes Locke's reformulation of political authority and popular sovereignty. In the *Discourse on the Origin of Inequality* (1755),[11] Rousseau develops a social theory that attempts to explain the development of inequality, conflict and unfreedom within modern social life and does so by drawing much from and setting himself against (sometimes only rhetorically) the theories of the social presented by Grotius and Hobbes.

After describing the 'natural' state of humanity as one in which the physical drive for self-preservation is tempered by the sentiments pity, compassion and love,[12] Rousseau goes on to chart the origins of social inequality and alienation.[13] Rousseau presents an account of humans who through cleverness, cunning, reflection and 'mechanical prudence' determine novel ways of acting and behaving, alone and in community with others, in ways which help to preserve their lives and realize their desires. For Rousseau, these humans in reflecting upon their achievements, feelings of empowerment and success, began to develop a sense of individual pride.[14] The individual's *amour-propre*, or generally the feeling of pride, self-esteem and the desire to be valued highly and desired by others, is identified by Rousseau as a core reason for the development of feelings of competitiveness and the conditions of social conflict.[15] Such a desire also leads to individuals making value judgments over the worth of others and the entrenchment of judgments over differential forms of life-value within social and legal systems as inequality and unfreedom.[16] In one example of the operation of *amour-propre*, Rousseau argues:

> People grew accustomed to gather in front of their huts or around a large tree; song and dance, true children of love and leisure, became the amusement or rather the occupation of idle men and women who had flocked together. Each one began to look at the others and to want to be looked at himself, and public esteem had a value. The one who sang or danced best, the handsomest, the strongest, the most adroit or the most eloquent became the most highly regarded. And this was the first step toward inequality and, at the same time, toward vice. From these first preferences were born vanity and contempt on the one hand, and shame and envy on the other. And the fermentation caused by these new leavens eventually produced compounds fatal to happiness and innocence.
>
> As soon as men had begun mutually to value one another, and the idea of esteem was formed in their minds, each one claimed to have a right of it, and it was no longer possible for anyone to be lacking it with impunity. From this came the first duties of civility, even amongst savages; and from this every wrong became an outrage, because along with the harm that resulted from the injury, the offended party saw in it contempt for his person, which was often more insufferable than the harm itself. Hence each man punished the contempt shown him in a manner proportionate to the esteem in which he held himself; acts of revenge became terrible, and men became bloodthirsty and cruel.[17]

To a certain extent, Rousseau's account of the origins of social conflict, driven by conflicting desires, feelings of pride and jealousy, and drives towards self-empowerment, is not too distant from an account presented by Hobbes. Yet, in other crucial respects, especially in relation to the emphasis Rousseau places upon the production of social inequality, Rousseau was not convinced that a model which grounded political authority upon the idea of preservation of life, peace and security, was an adequate solution to multiple social ills. Indeed, Rousseau saw in the theories of political authority proposed by Grotius and Hobbes the entrenchment of the conditions of inequality and unfreedom through law and legal violence. Rousseau argues:

> They all ran to chain themselves, in the belief that they secured their liberty, for although they had enough sense to realize the advantages of a political establishment, they did not have enough experience to foresee its dangers. Those most capable of anticipating the abuses were precisely those who counted on profiting from them; and even the wise saw the need to be resolved to sacrifice one part of their liberty to preserve the other, just as a wounded man has his arm amputated to save the rest of his body.
>
> Such was, or should have been, the origin of society and laws, which gave new fetters to the weak and new forces to the rich, irretrievably destroyed natural liberty, established forever the law of property and of inequality, changed adroit usurpation into irrevocable right, and for the profit of a

> few ambitious men henceforth subjected the entire human race to labour, servitude and misery.[18]

Under the conditions within which the otherwise 'legitimate authority' of the state and its law operates as a form of mastery and oppression, entrenching inequality and enslavement, then for Rousseau, such a political authority cannot be viewed as holding moral or political legitimacy – any contract and its claim to establish legitimate authority and legitimate sovereign violence is *dissolved*. When the state is merely the political and legal form that affirms the empowerment of some over others through legal force, then the state can equally be disposed of by a countering, and now legitimate, violence. He argues:

> Here is the final stage of inequality, and the extreme point that closes the circle and touches the point from which we started. Here all private individuals become equals again, because they are nothing. And since subjects no longer have any law other than the master's will, nor the master any rule other than his passions, the notions of good and principles of justice vanish. Here everything is returned solely to the law of the strongest, and consequently to a new state of nature different from the one with which we began, in that the one was the state of nature in its purity, and this last one is the fruit of an excess of corruption. Moreover, there is so little difference between these two states, and the government contract is so utterly dissolved by despotism, that the despot is master only as long as he is the strongest; and as soon as he can be ousted, he has no cause to protest against violence. The uprising that ends in the strangulation or dethronement of a sultan is as lawful an act as those by which he disposed of the lives and goods of his subjects the day before. Force alone maintained him; force alone brings him down.[19]

Judgment upon the illegitimacy of a monarch or government of a state (or the state itself) who claimed to hold legitimate authority would be dependent upon certain criteria. For Rousseau, the criterion for judging political and legal authority is the concept of freedom. In *On the Social Contract* (1762), Rousseau outlines a form of moral and political organization that attempts to overcome social conditions of alienation and oppression by developing a novel theory of freedom. His efforts respond to a problem which he states as:

> Find a form of association which defends and protects with all common forces the person and the goods of each associate, and by means of which each one, while uniting with all, nevertheless obeys only himself and remains as free as before.[20]

Rousseau sets out a theory of political authority, based upon a form of social contract, in which the individual is both governor and governed. Under this conception, sovereignty is re-formulated as a mode of *self-legislation* in which individual citizens collectively constitute the sovereign body via the notion of the 'general will'.[21] Rousseau's re-conceptualization of sovereignty as popular sovereignty, and as a form of political being which is *singular-plural*,[22] is guided by his notion of moral and civil freedom.

Within his account, Rousseau contrasts 'natural liberty' to 'civil' and 'moral' 'liberty'.[23] Very generally, Rousseau considers natural liberty to be somewhat egoistic, as it involves the sense of an individual being interested in only realizing its own desires. In part, he sees the theories of Hobbes and Locke as presenting an account of natural liberty, whereby, personal and private 'natural rights' are held by individuals who want to safeguard their rights from being infringed upon by other individuals or by the state. Within this early liberal social contract tradition some of these natural liberties are handed over to the state on the condition that the state maintains an internal sphere of peace within which the remaining natural liberties of individuals may be enacted. For Rousseau, such an account represents a limited view of freedom, it reinforces a social condition of self-interest, pride, and dominance and thus inequality and unfreedom for many within the populace. In its stead Rousseau suggests a notion of freedom in which individuals gain their liberty through the constitution of a political institution as a joint, or communal, exercise. For Rousseau, the individual gains its liberty *through law* and through a change in *self-conception* which alters the individual's outlook in a positive way.

In a political and legal sense, the freedom of Rousseau's individual becomes explicitly linked to other individuals who form and constitute the sovereign body. Rights and liberties are not something fixed or taken from 'nature' but are constructed out of the social body itself and are gained rather than given up. Freedom, which lifts all citizens equally out of inequality and domination, is produced by the state and by the citizen's participation in the general will. In a moral sense, Rousseau's individual is drawn out of its narrow, egotistical interests and comes to acknowledge and affirm the interests of its fellow citizens. Each individual, understanding itself as part of the community, part of the sovereign body, becomes de-centred and 'ennobled' through the knowledge that moral freedom and conscience now occur as an exercise which considers the interests of others together with the interests of the self. Moral judgment is to be guided by the universal interest of the community of citizens who make up the sovereign body and the general will. Rousseau argues:

> This passage from the state of nature to the civil state produces quite a remarkable change in man, for it substitutes justice for instinct in his behaviour and gives his actions a moral quality they previously lacked. Only then, when the voice of duty replaces physical impulse and right replaces appetite, does man, who had hitherto taken only himself into account, find himself forced to act upon other principles and to consult his reason before listening to his inclinations. Although in this state he deprives

> himself of several of the advantages belonging to him in the state of nature, he regains such great ones. His faculties are exercised and developed, his ideas are broadened, his feelings are ennobled, his entire soul is elevated to such a height that, if the abuse of this new condition did not often lower his status to beneath the level he left, he ought constantly to bless the happy moment that pulled him away from it forever and which transformed him from a stupid, limited animal into an intelligent being and a man.
>
> Let us summarise the entire balance sheet so that the credits and debits are easily compared. What man loses through the social contract is his natural liberty and an unlimited right to everything that tempts him and that he can acquire. What he gains is civil liberty and the proprietary ownership of all he possesses ... To the proceeding acquisition could be added the acquisition in the civil state of moral liberty, which alone makes man truly the master of himself. For to be deprived of appetite alone is slavery, and obedience to the law one has prescribed for oneself is liberty.[24]

Rousseau's conception of the social contract, with its ambiguous notion of the general will opens onto the possibility of absolutist political formulations. His comment that individuals who refuse to obey the general will, will be 'forced to be free',[25] sounds somewhat ominous. Yet, his theory enunciates an idea of freedom which breaks out a natural law tradition of fixed, so-called 'natural' rights. With Rousseau, 'freedom' becomes something produced by the social body, something communal, which emerges only when the problem of political alienation is resolved. For Rousseau, the problem of freedom is a problem of self-legislation – individuals can only be understood as free when they are able to determine the content of the laws which regulate their daily activities within social and material life. Because individuals live in community, then this self-legislation, on Rousseau's account, must accommodate some form of communal self-legislation.

Rousseau's social contract occurs in this sense as an act of self-positing: the act in which individuals posit their own freedom through others, through the social body. The positing of the social order, in which Rousseau shares elements with the artificial and human self-creation of the social order given by Hobbes, is directed towards, the *self-positing of freedom*. In part, the concept of freedom moves from being some *thing*, present in nature, to more properly being a human *act*. Johann Wolfgang Goethe's claim that '*in the beginning was the deed*'[26] might be thought, partially, as a mirroring of this emerging modern conception of freedom: freedom as a human *act*, as the self's (or the community's) positing of itself, and as the act or work of the human hand, or fist (*Faust*) in this process.

If the form of the political and legal institutions which Rousseau suggests is interpreted as being insufficient for realizing freedom as communal self-legislation, that is, if aspects of his political architecture and strategy are considered inadequate, then there still remains a further kernel of merit within

Rousseau's account that can be held onto. The normative, radical utopian idea of freedom which Rousseau demands, remains valid today as an emancipatory ideal to which political institutions might strain towards and be judged by. Further, even if one were to dismiss this radical, utopian element, then at least, Rousseau identifies a fundamental *aporia* within a Western tradition of legal and political philosophy which remains unresolved. This being: the problem of freedom as self-legislation by individuals whose existence involves a necessary dependency upon others within a society or community.[27] Drawing upon and moving beyond the natural law theories of Grotius, Hobbes and Locke, Rousseau helps to draw this *aporia* to the centre of modern, legal and political philosophy.[28]

With regard to the problem of war Rousseau's account helps to re-formulate a rival notion of legitimate violence that sits within, and in contestation to, the Westphalian juridical conception. The sovereign's monopoly upon the legitimacy of violence resides not necessarily with a political institution but with the community, or party, or faction that claims the mantle of popular sovereignty and claims to act in the name of the 'general will'. Whether in power as the government of the state, or in search of political power as a rebellious or revolutionary organization, the notion of 'legitimate violence' is re-organized around a communal demand for freedom. Following on from Rousseau's account, in response to the conditions of social, political and legal oppression and alienation, the future demand of freedom is to be realized through the constitution or construction of a free community of self-legislating citizens. Under the conditions of injustice this constituting power may posit itself and its freedom through the act of revolutionary violence. If such an argument is not directly expressed by Rousseau, then it is at least one possible formulation drawn from his theory which has been inherited and further enunciated by many revolutionaries, 'freedom fighters' and 'terrorists' who throughout history have attempted to justify acts of violence in the name of freedom.

The inheritance of this line of thought and a number of differing ways in which the legitimacy of revolutionary and 'non-sovereign' violence is ordered will be taken up later.[29] For the moment, another line of inheritance of Rousseau's conception of freedom remains to be discussed. Immanuel Kant, horrified by the Terror of the French Revolution, took certain aspects of Rousseau's theory of freedom as self-legislation and left to the side other elements of political radicalism.[30] Kant drew upon Rousseau's attempt to overcome political and moral alienation and developed this in the direction of a proposed universal moral theory which was then applied to the problem of inter-state war.

IIII

Kant can be seen to inherit and develop an understanding of Rousseau's conception of freedom and locate it as the central category of his conception of law. In Kant's account of law presented in *The Metaphysics of Morals* (1797), particularly Part I, the *Metaphysical First Principles of the Doctrine of Right* (*Rechtslehre*),[31] law is conceptualized through a meditation upon the category of freedom. Kant's accounts of law and freedom need to be situated within the context of Kant's 'critical philosophy' developed in the *Critique of Pure Reason* (1781).[32] The *Critique of Pure Reason* inherits a problem similar to that faced by Hobbes where thoughts and ideas are at war with one another. Kant calls this a 'battlefield (*Kampfplatz*) of metaphysics'.[33] For Kant, a war of all against all rages through metaphysics itself. In this sphere there seems to be endless controversy, endless conflict and very little peace and stability. In the face of a war within metaphysics rises the demand for peace, the demand for some form of sovereign authority, an objective position of judgment to bring an end to the endless conflict and establish a reign of peace. Hobbes's demand for a sovereign authority to be raised to end ongoing disagreement and civil war is echoed and radicalized by Kant. For Kant, such a 'court of justice' (*Gerichtshof*)[34] must be raised within the realm of metaphysics. He argues:

> One can regard the critique of pure reason as the true court of justice for all the controversies of pure reason; for the critique is not involved in these disputes, which pertain immediately to objects [*Objekte*], but is rather set the task of determining and judging what is lawful [*die Rechtsame*] in reason in general in accordance with the principles of its primary institution.
>
> Without this, reason is as it were in the state of nature, and it cannot make its assertions and claims valid or secure them except through *war*. The critique, on the contrary, which derives all decisions from the ground-rules of its own constitution, whose authority no one can doubt, grants us the peace of a state of law [*eines gesetzlichen Zustandes*], in which we should not conduct our controversy except by *due process*. What brings the quarrel in the state of nature to an end is *victory*, of which both sides boast, although for most part there follows only an uncertain peace, arranged by an authority in the middle; but in the state of law it is the *verdict*, which, since it goes to the origin of the controversies themselves, must secure a perpetual peace. And the endless controversies of a merely dogmatic reason finally make it necessary to seek peace in some sort of critique of this reason itself, and in a legislation grounded upon it, just as Hobbes asserted, the state of nature is a state of injustice and violence, and one must necessarily leave it in order to submit himself to the lawful coercion which alone limits our freedom in such a way that it can be consistent with the freedom of everyone else and thereby with the common good.[35]

Kant's raising of a court of justice within metaphysics shares some aspects with Hobbes's positing of a regime of sovereign law. However, Kant's approach represents a radical departure not only from the philosophy of Hobbes but from that which had preceded it within the history of the philosophy of metaphysics. Kant's approach presents a wholesale change of perspective, the consequences of which rattle and continue to shake the relationship between thinking, action and violence well into the present. While the radicality of Kant's 'Copernican revolution' within metaphysics has been appreciated by a number of traditions of philosophy, the significance of his revolutionary act has perhaps, not yet, been fully comprehended by those who have turned their thinking to the problem of war.

A certain positivism of Hobbes created a firm break with an old thick, Scholastic natural law which grounded itself upon religious and transcendent realms of authority. However, Hobbes's natural law of minimum content, while elevating the position of man, still took many of its cues from nature and looked towards modelling human social relations upon a certain geometry of nature and the sense of necessity and predictability of laws that could be 'found' in nature. In this sense, for Hobbes the solution to human social violence involved the development of moral and legal philosophy as a 'science' that might discover and outline the basic, universal human natural laws in a similar manner to the way in which natural science might 'discover' the universal laws of nature.

Kant also wanted to place metaphysics (and following from it, moral philosophy) on the 'secure path of science',[36] however, he rejected any approach that attempted to 'find' or 'discover' these laws within nature. For Kant, such approaches put the cart before the horse. For Kant, what we claim as 'universal laws' are not found or discovered in nature, but are produced by the activity of human thinking and its use of concepts that puts questions to nature rather than subserviently following nature's lead. For Kant, a sense of the appreciation of this *critical standpoint* is already contained within the methods of mathematics and physics and needs to be comprehended more fully within the field of metaphysics (and following this, moral philosophy). Kant argues:

> When Galileo rolled balls of a weight chosen by himself down an inclined plane, or when Torricelli made the air bear a weight that he had previously thought to be equal to that of a known column of water, or when in a later time Stahl changed metals into calx and then changed the latter back into metal by first removing something and then putting it back again, a light dawned on all those who study nature. They comprehended that reason has insight only into what it itself produces according to its own design; that it must take the lead with principles for its judgments according to constant laws and compel nature to answer its questions, rather than letting nature guide its movements by keeping reason, as it were, in leading-strings; for otherwise accidental observations, made according to no previously designed plan, can never connect up into a necessary law, which is yet what reason seeks and requires. Reason, in order to be taught by nature must approach nature with its principles in one hand, and, in the other hand, the experiments thought out in accordance with these principles – yet in order to be instructed by nature not like a

> pupil, who has recited to him whatever the teacher wants to say, but like an appointed judge who compels witnesses to answer the questions he puts to them. Thus even physics owes the advantageous revolution in its way of thinking to the inspiration that what reason would not be able to know of itself and has to learn from nature, it has to seek in the latter (though not merely ascribe to it) in accordance with what reason itself puts into nature. This is how natural science was first brought to the secure course of a science after groping about for so many centuries.[37]

Kant's position involves a revolutionary change in comprehending how human thinking relates to the world. It places a realm of *a priori* concepts *between* reason and the world and shows how human concepts make the world appear in a certain way *for us*, a way which may be very different from how the world is *in itself*. For Kant, humans are only able to discern universal laws within nature because the operation of the concepts within our thought allows this to be so. In one dazzling moment, Kant shifts the balance of power away from nature and towards the activity of human thought in its construction of how it views the world. As if it were the price paid for this power in a bargain with the Devil, Kant cuts human knowledge off from the true nature of objects in the world – sets these objects apart from us, as the unknowable *thing in itself*.[38]

For Kant, it is not the case that we have an immediate access to objects in the world, that strike our eyes, so to speak, and from which we learn how the world is. Rather, in Kant such an over-arching passivity is done away with and in its place is positioned the *activity* of human thinking in which objects in the world are grasped only through the framing and ordering of these objects by our own *concepts*. Kant sets forth the radical argument that what we 'know' of the world, we only know, *through* our concepts.[39] For Kant, our knowledge of the world is produced through the human activity and faculty of cognizing.

If, for Kant, objective knowledge is possible (and in his view mathematics and theoretical physics show that it is), then there must be an *a priori*, universal, objective, character in this faculty and its conceptual contents operating as the ground of knowledge for all humans. Following this, in the realm of metaphysics, the search for an objective position of judgment is not directed outwards towards some 'thing' in nature, but rather, it is directed inwards towards the operation of human reason itself and to the possibility of determining an objective, *a priori* realm underlying human reason that guides and governs *our* thoughts about the world. In Kant's view, the *Critique of Pure Reason* can be called a 'court of justice' because it brings to an end a long-running battle of metaphysics by identifying and justifying (deducing) the universal, objective set of *a priori* concepts that ground our cognition and knowledge of objects of experience.[40]

Kant's account relies upon a particular 'architectonic' that forms the structure of human cognition. For Kant, we have no direct access to objects in the world but only have an *experience* (*Erfahrung*) of them made possible by a faculty of *intuition* (*Anschauung*) and its *a priori* forms, space and time. The experience of sensible and empirical objects only involves a certain *appearance* (*Erscheinung*) of these objects made possible by intuition and does not involve a grasping of the objects as they are in themselves. For Kant, the manifold of the complex and confused content of what we experience through intuition is *ordered* and rendered comprehensible by a *spontaneous* faculty of cognition called the understanding (*Verstand*).[41] The understanding has concepts (the categories), which for Kant are *a priori* and which, via a transcendental deduction, can be justified and shown to be objective. These concepts make our cognition of the objects of our experience possible. For Kant, the faculty of reason (*Vernuft*), thinks (orders) these concepts at the level of ideas. It can be called pure reason because it is separated from the objects of experience. While reason can *think* of the objects generally, it cannot *cognize* them[42] as this cognition occurs solely within the understanding in relation to objects of experience given by intuition in the forms of space and time.

Kant's assumption of such an architecture of cognition leads to a number of consequences. In one sense a certain space is opened up that explains the possibility of objective *a priori* concepts, and then synthetic judgments over these made by the faculty of pure reason. These judgments are shielded from the empirical world as they only relate to concepts, which in turn are shielded from the world itself as they only cognize the appearance of objects made possible by experience grounded in intuition. In this manner the field of pure reason is made to shrink.

For Kant, pure reason is rendered problematic when judgments do not confine themselves to a consideration of the concepts of the understanding (and their inherent principles) but instead attempt to grasp the *unconditioned*, the totality, which involves the effort of comprehending objects beyond the boundaries of experience.[43] For him, when pure reason ventures beyond experience, or attempts to grasp the absolute 'unity of reason', then it runs into irreconcilable antinomies or contradictions:[44] the '*Antinomy of Pure Reason*', which for Kant, confirms his limitation of pure theoretical reason to the realm of experience (alternatively, that cognition is only of appearances).[45]

Kant has a decision (*Entscheidung*) as regards all four antinomies: the arguments of both sides fall to the ground since they make a false assumption. That is, Kant asserts that the conflict that arises between each side of the antinomies represents an 'illusion' because each is based upon the application of an idea of absolute totality, a consideration of things in themselves, and not as merely as they are in the realm of appearance.[46] For Kant, this critical decision must be made otherwise reason is caught in a conflict with itself and cannot be that supreme authority which will terminate a war of metaphysics. For Kant, if pure reason is directed not towards grasping an absolute totality, but instead of only thinking about objects as they are in the realm of appearance, then the antinomy or contradiction goes away.

Importantly, Kant has a resolution (*Auflösung*) for the dynamical antinomies (3 and 4) but not for the mathematical antinomies (1 and 2). He argues that while all four antinomies were initially dismissed as based on false presuppositions on each side, there is a presupposition within the dynamical antinomies that might coexist with the pretensions of reason. This presupposition relates to a certain activity of human intelligence.[47] In this respect, the separation between the knowledge of objects only in their appearance and a thinkable but unknowable aspect of objects as they are in themselves, has positive, practical consequences. Kant thinks that limiting the sphere of pure reason opens a space for *pure practical reason*[48] as (pursuant to the resolution of the third antinomy) it allows causality to be comprehended in a dual sense. Kant argues:

> Now if we were to assume that the distinction between things as objects of experience and the very same things as things in themselves, which our critique has made necessary, were not made at all, then the principle of causality, and hence the mechanism of nature in determining causality, would be valid of all things in general as efficient causes. I would not be able to say of one and the same thing, e.g., the human soul, that its will is free and yet that it is simultaneously subject to natural necessity, i.e., that it is not free, without falling into obvious contradiction; because in both propositions I would have taken the soul *in just the same meaning*, namely as a thing in general (as thing in itself), and without prior critique, I could not have taken it otherwise. But if the critique has not erred in teaching that the object should be taken in *a twofold meaning*, namely as appearance or as thing in itself, if its deduction of the pure concepts of the understanding is correct, and hence the principle of causality applies only to things taken in the first sense, namely insofar as they are objects of experience, which things in the second meaning are not subject to it; then just the same will is thought of in the appearance (in visible actions) as necessarily subject to the law of nature and to this extent *not free*, while yet on the other hand it is thought of as belonging to a thing in itself as not subject to that law, and hence *free*, without any contradiction hereby occurring. Now although I cannot *cognize* my soul ... nevertheless, I can *think* freedom to myself, i.e., the representation of it at least contains no contradiction in itself, so long as our critical distinction prevails between the two ways of representing (sensible and intellectual), along with the limitation of the pure concepts of the understanding arising from it, and hence that of principles flowing from them.[49]

For him, this distinction between two ways of representing – sensible and intellectual – opens up a notion he terms 'transcendental freedom' which forms the basis of constructing an objective set of practical moral laws that are not grounded upon the dictates of nature but upon a certain form of intellectual causality occurring as a (f)act of reason. For Kant, the notion of transcendental freedom develops from an appreciation of two differing types of causality: that according to nature and that from freedom.[50] With regard to the first, Kant argues that in a world of sense experience each appearance rests upon temporal conditions, upon the preceding state, which occurs as a cause of what has subsequently (in time) arisen.[51] In terms of the causal law every appearance is conditioned, in the manner that it is reliant upon something before it, which was necessary for its emergence or appearance in the world. Distinguished from this, Kant argues for a second way of thinking about causality. He argues:

> By freedom in the cosmological sense, on the contrary, I understand the faculty of beginning a state *from itself*, the causality of which does not in turn stand under another cause determining it in time in accordance with the law of nature. Freedom in this signification is a pure transcendental idea, which, first, contains nothing borrowed from experience, and second, the object of which also cannot be given determinately in any experience, because it is a universal law – even of the possibility of all experience – that everything that happens must have a cause, and hence that the causality of the cause, as *itself having happened* or arisen, must in turn have a cause; through this law, then, the entire field of experience, however far it may reach, is transformed into the sum total of mere nature. But since in such a way no absolute totality of conditions in causal relations is forthcoming, reason creates the idea of spontaneity, which could start to act from itself, without needing to be preceded by any other cause that in turn determines it to action according to the law of causal connection.
>
> It is especially noteworthy that it is this *transcendental* idea of *freedom* on which the practical concept of freedom is grounded, and the former constitutes the real moment of the difficulties in the latter, which have long surrounded the question of its possibility. *Freedom in the practical sense* is the independence of the power of choice from *necessitation* by impulses of sensibility. For a power of choice is *sensible* insofar as it is *pathologically affected* (through moving-causes of sensibility); it is called *animal* power of choice (*arbitrium brutum*) if it can be *pathologically necessitated.* The human power of choice is indeed an *arbitrium sensitivum*, yet not *brutum* but *liberum*, because sensibility does not render its action necessary, but in the human being there is a faculty of determining oneself from oneself, independently of necessitation by sensible impulses.[52]

Kant believes that the notion of transcendental freedom allows a realm of pure practical reason in which *a priori*, universal, objective laws aimed at morally guiding human behaviour can be justified or deduced.[53] The determination of such objective *a priori* laws is to bring to an end a war of metaphysics within the moral realm and is to prove the foundational touchstone from which all human practical activity can be based, or at least, measured against. By putting forward such a theory Kant takes large steps away from Hobbes's approach to the conflict between moral and political ideas within the social realm and ushers in the possibility of a complete canonical regulation of the public, social sphere as a solution to conflict. This canonical regulation is *morality* as re-framed by Kant. In Kant's view, there need not be such widespread conflict between moral and political claims because pure practical reason sets moral philosophy upon the secure path of science to which politics should attend.

For Kant, a public morality is rendered possible because a universal law can be derived *a priori* to serve as a foundation upon which moral judgments can be made. In the *Groundwork of the Metaphysics of Morals* (1785),[54] Kant sets out what he sees as an objective, universal rule, determined by human thinking for itself, independent of sense experience. Kant calls this the 'categorical imperative': 'Act only in accordance with that maxim through which you can at the same time will that it become a universal law.'[55] This includes the variant, that: 'Act as if the maxim of your action were to become by your will a universal law of nature.'[56] To this is attached the injunction, that: 'So act that you use humanity, whether in your own person or in the person of any other, always at the same time as an end, never merely as a means.'[57] Through deducing the *a priori* laws of pure practical reason Kant thinks that moral action can be ordered universally. Kant believes we are able to judge the validity of moral acts by measuring moral content, or 'maxims', against the standard of the categorical imperative. Moral judgment is asked to test its maxims against the categorical imperative and if these maxims fall into contradiction, then they cannot be considered to be appropriate maxims for moral action. In this respect, pure practical reason operates as a negative test, it gives only negative instruction.[58] Like pure reason, pure practical reason occurs for Kant as a 'science' that can bring to an end seemingly endless dispute. However, the focus of pure practical reason is upon the practical, moral world, it is directed towards resolving moral disputes in every day life which include not only 'wars' within the realm of moral ideas but also physical wars within the political world.

Kant's approach can be thought of as fully modern in the sense that it has not only broken from the old dictates of religion and nature, but further, in that it has ushered in a novel way of comprehending the relation between human thinking and the world. Through Kant, the activity of human thinking becomes central. This activity is spontaneous and creative and constructs our view of the world in a particular way through forms of intuitions, concepts and ideas. For Kant's many inheritors, this insight is radicalized in ways that completely transform how many humans understand themselves, and their social and natural world.[59] Such an inheritance is still ongoing and its consequences are perhaps yet to be fully borne out in history. What can be grasped, however, is the immense sense of power that is placed within the hands of humans as a result of a notion such as that of 'transcendental freedom'. It tears apart an old relation to the world in which man is bound by nature and beholden to it. Instead of this bond where the human is perpetually the child or the student, the human being is jettisoned into a new modern realm of intellectual and moral self-consciousness – one in which it knows and grasps itself in relation to its moral world, and knows itself as a creative partner in its relationship with nature.

In a wider sense, Kant's development of a universal moral law and the idea of practical human freedom arising from the notion of transcendental freedom inherits and builds upon the modern idea of *positing* present within the self-creation and construction of human social orders, and the self-authorization, of these orders, given, in differing senses, by Hobbes and Rousseau. Kant's radical idea of the *spontaneity* of human thinking can be understood as a further development of this modern form of thinking in which the activity and deeds of human thinking play a foundational, creative role in the production of the social and material world and its normative standards. Developing Rousseau's idea of moral freedom as a form of self-legislation, Kant's notion of pure practical reason presents a conception of human moral thinking that thinks its own law (or posits its own law) for itself. That is, for Kant, pure practical reason creates its own set of standards by which humans ought to abide in public life and is a theory of morality in which the individual is both governor and governed. This function of thinking can be viewed as a form of ordering. It is not so much reliance upon a pre-established authority, but rather, it occurs as a critical self-ordering of human thinking by itself within the practical realm – the creative and constitutive ordering of the otherwise chaotic public, moral life.

Kant may also be thought here to be re-moralizing the public realm. Kant, following Rousseau, moves towards re-conceptualizing the European territorial state in a manner coordinated by a public notion of the good. In Kant, the good is re-framed by a proscription of universal moral rules about how individuals in public life ought to behave.[60] While, for him, the moral law of the categorical imperative underlies social life, it is also limited. In his view, the sphere of moral duty is limited by and held distinct from the realm of law.

Within the *Metaphysics of Morals*, which Kant separates into the *Rechtslehre* and the *Tugendlehre*, Kant attempts to draw a distinction between the spheres of law or legality and morality or moral duty. For him, the latter involves an internal or subjective principle of action (which may or may not adhere to the *moral law* of the categorical imperative) while the former relates to the limits of external action.[61] According to Kant, law is defined in relation to the concept of freedom. He defines the 'universal principle of right' as:

> Any action is *right* if it can coexist with everyone's freedom in accordance with a universal law, or if on its maxim the freedom of choice of each can coexist with everyone's freedom in accordance with a universal law.[62]

This definition involves a certain negative sense. For Kant, a universal law of freedom places a limit or constraint upon external action, that is, an individual must not act so as to impair the freedom of another.[63] In a sense somewhat reminiscent of Hobbes, Kant's notion of law involves the social contractual idea of limiting one's freedom in a way that might be consistent with the freedom of everyone else. This notion of limitation impacts upon Kant's account of coercion.

Kant defines a 'wrong' (*Unrecht*) as any act that hinders another's freedom, or more precisely, that which hinders everyone's freedom in accordance with a universal law.[64] Linked to this is Kant's conception of the relationship between right (the legal sense of right) and coercion.[65] Kant argues that coercion is a hindrance of that which resists freedom. For him, as coercion is opposed to wrong (coercion as the hindrance of a hindrance to freedom), it is consistent with freedom in accordance with universal laws, and as such, right.[66] He notes that connected with the notion of right, by the law of contradiction, is the authorization to coerce someone who infringes upon right.[67] In this sense, it appears that for him that the idea of coercion is not something brought after, or subsequent to, the obligation of law. Rather, the construction of the concept of legal right includes, *a priori*, the idea of coercion.[68] He argues: '[O]ne can locate the concept of right directly in the possibility of connecting universal reciprocal coercion with the freedom of everyone.'[69] While legal coercion cannot be reduced to a concept of violence, it can be assumed that violence is one element within the operation of coercion at the heart of law. In one respect, he can be thought to be instituting a shift in the justification of the sovereign's right to the monopoly over the legitimacy of violence. The violence of the law is not merely grounded upon law's role in the preservation of life and securing of social peace, but upon a higher standard, the securing of freedom. There is, however, a tension within Kant's account and one which displays the competing inheritances of Hobbes's sovereign law that secures peace, and Rousseau's positing of the social contract to construct a sphere of freedom.

In pragmatic terms, freedom in Kant's sense depends upon the presence of a law backed by sovereign power and violence. While for Kant the regulating and motivating idea of law is the idea and demand of freedom, when a tension arises between peace and freedom, Kant might be seen to favour the former over the latter. One example is Kant's approach to the act of revolution. In this example, peace and the internal security of the sovereign state are placed above freedom, even in the face of tyranny. For Kant, there is no right of rebellion against a head of state even in the case of an unbearable abuse of authority.[70] He argued that if a right of rebellion against a tyrant were made into a universal maxim then such a right would lead back into the situation where each individual acted as a sovereign judge over the state.[71] More drastically, for Kant, not only is there no right of rebellion, there is no right to inquire into the historical origin of the state. Kant argues:

> A people should not *inquire* with any practical aim in view into the origin of the supreme authority to which it is subject, that is, a subject *ought not*

> *to reason subtly* for the sake of action about the origin of this authority, as a right that can still be called into question (*ius controversum*) with regard to the obedience he owes it. For, since a people must be regarded as already united under a general legislative will in order to judge with rightful force about the supreme authority (*summum imperium*), it cannot and may not judge otherwise than as the present head of state (*summus imperans*) wills it to. – Whether a state began with an actual contract of submission (*pacta subiectionis civilis*) as a fact, or whether the power came first and law arrived only afterwards, or even whether they should have followed in this order: for the people already subject to civil law these subtle reasonings are altogether pointless and, moreover, threaten a state with danger. If a subject, having pondered over the ultimate origin of the authority now ruling, wanted to resist this authority, he would be punished, got rid of, or expelled (as an outlaw, *exlex*) in accordance with the laws of this authority, that is, with every right. – A law that is so holy (inviolable) that it is already a crime even to call it in doubt *in a practical way*, and so to suspend its effect for a moment, is thought of as if it must have arisen not from human beings but from some highest, flawless law-giver; and that is what the saying 'All authority from God' means. This saying is not an assertion about the *historical basis* of the civil constitution; it instead sets forth an idea as a practical principle of reason: the principle that the presently existing legislative authority ought to be obeyed, whatever its origin.[72]

In this regard, while Kant's account establishes morality as a sphere that might stand above positive law and critique it and while he places freedom as an *ought* to which all positive law must aspire, he gives up on the *radical* demand of freedom as expressed by Rousseau: the demand of freedom which asks individuals to wager the possibility of being free through instability and even social violence against the conditions of inequality and unfreedom maintained by sovereign law. Kant's account of freedom is not expressed as a radical demand; it does not take a certain *risk* of freedom, involving the *leap* into uncertainty that might render the possibility of freedom possible. Rather, it is a more cautious account of freedom and one which falls back onto the Westphalian ordering of violence around the sovereign in order to attempt to secure freedom on the often tenuous grounds of preserving peace and security.

Most drastically, the radicalism of Kant's critical philosophy does not extend to hard foundational questions involving the relationship between the origin of legal-political orders, moral thinking and human action. He does not seem to grasp, or does not dare to grasp, the fact that a war of ideas within a moral or legal realm (or between realms) revolves, in part, around the central question of the historical-foundational violence of sovereign states and social contracts. On this point, Kant fell back into a little bit of a 'dogmatic slumber' and because of this, his philosophy of morality and law cannot bring to an end the war of ideas. While Kant's philosophy of morality and law might try to bring an end to war, its self-induced blind spot means that it can only contribute to further wars and forms of violence in a non-objective, non-universal, partisan manner.

IV

Kant inherits the Westphalian conception of war as inter-state war. His approach affirms the modern legal concept of war developed by Grotius and Hobbes in which the institution of the European territorial state occurs as the principal legitimate actor in the sphere of violent relations. With Hobbes, in condemning the legitimacy of acts of rebellion and revolution, Kant affirms the state's monopoly upon the legitimacy of violence. However, in viewing the relations between states, Kant is strongly critical of the state's claim to an absolute right to war or rights to expansive, colonial wars justified (in the manner of Grotius) by tenuous accounts of the *ius gentium*. Following Abbé Saint Pierre, Kant condemns the state's right to war and does so in the name of 'peace'. Drawing upon the notion of practical reason, Kant attempts to re-order the problem of war. In his account, there is a degree of ambiguity over whether his approach amounts to a legal or a moral ordering of the problem of inter-state war. It is argued here that Kant's approach involves the latter: that his re-framing of the problem of war through the concepts of peace and freedom amounts to a moral ordering of the problem of war.

It is important to note that Kant's account of war includes a teleological approach in which the negativity and destructiveness of war are given a sense of historical, positive moral value. In 'The Idea of a Universal History with a Cosmopolitan Purpose' (1784),[73] Kant describes an 'unsocial sociability' which drives men towards a process of enlightenment and points towards the design of a wise creator.[74] Further, a theory of historical development guided by 'providence' is also present in Kant's essay 'Perpetual Peace: A Philosophical Sketch' (1795).[75] While this account of war in terms of providence is a relevant point within Kant's moral philosophy more generally, it needs to be put to the side and will not be considered in this discussion.[76]

Relevant to Kant's process of the moral ordering of war is an inheritance of Hobbes's conception of the state of nature. In Hobbes, it was shown how the notion of the state of nature was described as a state of war and this was used to portray both a lack of internal peace where a powerful sovereign was absent and also the chaotic and threatening relation that existed between states. Kant takes up Hobbes's conception of the relation between states as a warring condition of nature in which there exists a lack of a legal authority or higher power to judge between competing claims of right. Kant argues: 'War is only a regrettable expedient for asserting one's rights by force within a state of nature, where no court of justice is available to judge with legal authority.'[77] In this sense, Kant frames the problem of war between states in the same manner as Hobbes's account of civil war, each occur, in part, as a problem of judgment.

Violence occurs through the lack of an authority to judge between particular claims and disputes arising out of conflicts between beliefs, opinions and even claims over truth. For Hobbes, this problem was resolved internally through a natural law of minimal content which gave authority to a sovereign body of law on the basis of securing peaceful human sociability. In Hobbes, the figure of a world-sovereign is absent. Kant's account replicates the movement of Hobbes's social contract at grander level and suggests the idea of ending of war through a contract between states.[78] Kant's account can be thought as putting forward a notion of a global form of *sovereignty*, occurring not as a world state, but as a federation of nations designed to secure peace.[79]

One significant point in which Kant re-interprets Hobbes's conception of the problem of war and, more generally the problem of social violence, is Kant's attempt to relate war to the question of freedom. For Kant, the development of peace and justice *within* a particular state is dependent upon the development of peace and justice *between* states.[80] By making the problem of freedom within the state *subordinate* to the problem of war between states, Kant makes a powerful move in the thinking of legal and political philosophy. In one sense, Kant suggests an inter-dependence between the state's external and internal affairs,[81] in another, he introduces a truly *global* perspective to thinking about problems of peace, freedom and justice. Further, Kant also develops something of a juridical solution to the problem of war. The notion of a federation of states presents the possibility of an independent position or institution of judgment on inter-state disputes guided by the global sovereignty of practical reason. Yet this vision, while inheriting significant elements of the juridical ordering of war given by Hobbes, substantially breaks with the Westphalian conception of the state's inherent right to war. Such a right is morally condemned by a cosmopolitan conception of humanity.

Kant's approach to the problem of war involves an ambiguous relationship with the figure of state sovereignty. The ambiguity might be seen as an inheritance of a conception of war given by Rousseau, who argues:

> War is not therefore a relationship between one man and another, but a relationship between one state and another. In war private individuals are enemies only incidentally: not as men or even citizens, but as soldiers; not as members of the homeland but as its defenders.[82]

In this passage, Rousseau, in part, affirms the Westphalian conception of war as state war and excludes from the definition of war 'private war', duels and other forms of private combat.[83] Yet in contrast to the account given by Grotius and Hobbes, Rousseau strips away the inherent legitimacy of state war by de-idolizing the state and viewing it as a 'thing'. The state as a thing is an object, albeit a necessary social arrangement, serving as an artificial convention for the sake of freedom. In Rousseau, 'man' and humanity's freedom are placed as central categories. The social order exists only as the foundation, establishment and test of human freedom. Set against the freedom of humanity the state is a thing, an object, which should not be confused with the human freedom that it serves.[84] In this respect, Rousseau claims that, 'It is the relationship between things and not that between men that brings about war.'[85]

Further, for Rousseau, the position of the state sovereign as a legitimate authority and the sovereign's monopoly upon the legitimacy of violence is not guaranteed, especially when it represents a regime of oppression and unfreedom. Following Rousseau's account, sitting behind the state's right to war is the spectre of popular revolt or revolutionary war claiming legitimacy under the banner of human freedom. The state and its right to war are re-positioned as something secondary to the concept of human freedom. In such an account the institution of the state is placed after 'man'. Man as 'human' is given central position in the effort to determine the concept of right. While Kant does not endorse the suggestion that revolutionary war might be a form of legitimate violence, he does endorse part of Rousseau's formulation which places the state after human freedom. In developing the cosmopolitan strains of Rousseau's thought Kant attempts to re-order the traditional Westphalian rights of states in accordance with the demands of human freedom. For Kant, the rights of states need to be limited by what he sees as 'human rights', which in part, Kant describes under the notion of 'cosmopolitan right'.

In contrast to the notion of civil right (*ius civitatis*) and international right (*ius gentium*), Kant puts forward the notion of cosmopolitan right (*ius cosmopoliticum*) which refers to the notion of both individuals and states co-existing as citizens of a universal community of humanity.[86] Through this separation Kant can be seen to accept the 'form' of the modern legal concept of war as 'state war' but not its inherent scope of legitimacy. The state's right to war is limited by a higher right, cosmopolitan right. This development of a Stoic[87] and Enlightenment[88] conception occurs as an effort to re-shape and re-conceptualize the emerging global social order. On the basis of this higher and universal right of humanity,[89] Kant not only critiques the state's right to war, he also critiques a long tradition of violent colonialism carried out by European nations which, he argues, offends the universal law of cosmopolitan hospitality.

From the perspective of the right of humanity, Kant condemns both the state's act of war which leads away from the possibility of securing inter-state peace[90] and philosophers and jurists whose conceptions of international right lead away from the idea of cosmopolitan peace and, are instead, used as justifications of military aggression. For Kant, thinkers such as Grotius, Pufendorf and Vattel are nothing but 'sorry comforters' of both state aggression and the rabid, violent, process of the European colonization of the rest of the world.[91] The term, 'sorry comforters', is not out of place today. However, in the context of the moral ordering of war, the use of the term is not unproblematic.

Kant's moral ordering of war does not merely aim to limit war but condemns it. For Kant, standing above states and their warring relations is a higher moral law under which the conduct of states is to be regulated. Kant argues:

'[R]eason, as the highest legislative moral power, absolutely condemns war as a test of rights and sets up peace as an immediate duty.'[92] For Kant, while the condition of states in a state of nature might be devoid of law and legal authority, this does not mean it is devoid of morality or the moral law. Rather, for Kant, the warlike state of nature is governed by a moral ought, the imperative that peace and freedom be secured through the attempt to establish a viable form of international law. In this sense while the inter-state relation resembles a Hobbesian condition of injustice, Kant places states under a moral obligation to act in accordance with practical reason and the categorical imperative and to act so as to bring into realization a universal condition of freedom and justice. In such a form of ordering of the inter-state relation, Kant asks that the juridical persona of states adopt a distinctly moral persona – states are conceptualized and expected to act as if they are moral persons.

For Kant, the attempted solution to the problem of war is moral action. Peace might only be secured if states become moral actors and fulfil a moral obligation to erect a viable form of international law. The universal rule for state action is action in accordance with moral duty. In this respect, Kant introduces a new form of 'judgment' into the inter-state relation. Judgment is not reliant upon a higher institutional power but becomes the moral self-judgment of particular states who in accordance with practical reason are asked to judge not only their own action but the acts of their others.

His moralization of the figure of the state occurs through the mediating conscience of the politicians or statesmen who direct these respective monarchies and republics. He draws upon two contrasting figures: the 'moral politician' and the 'political moralist'.[93] He argues that the evil which stands in the way of perpetual peace results from the fact that the political moralist starts out from the position where the moral politician rightly stops, that is, the political moralist makes moral principles subordinate to political ends.[94] In contrast, the moral politician follows the formal principle: 'Act in such a way that you can wish your maxim to become a universal law (irrespective of what the end in view may be).'[95]

In contrast to the political moralist, who treats problems of political, international and cosmopolitan right as merely technical or instrumental tasks, the moral politician views these in terms of a moral task.[96] The moral politician sees that the bringing about of peace is not just desirable as a physical good, but that it is a 'state of affairs which must arise out of recognizing one's duty'.[97] Kant gives the following advice: 'Seek ye first the kingdom of pure practical reason and its *righteousness*, and your object (the blessing of perpetual peace) will be added unto you.'[98]

The separation of the international order between moral politician and political moralist combined with the figure of the unjust enemy points towards a stark moral ordering of the problem of war. Under Kant's re-conceptualization war becomes a *moral problem*. It results from the failure of states (and their respective leaders) to act in accordance with moral duty. Opposed to the de-moralized Westphalian conception of states (or at least European states) having an inherent right to war and considering each other, like duelling gentlemen, as just enemies, Kant separates the international order into the realms of moral and immoral state action.

By placing the demand of moral duty above the right of states, Kant locates the inter-state relation and the problem of war firmly within the moral sphere. In this respect, he sets up a higher form of 'legitimate authority' – the authority of a moral universal – which stands above and is set to direct and govern the legitimate authority of state sovereigns. Such an attempt to morally order the problem of war is revolutionary in its attempt to rigorously order peaceful human sociability and freedom at a global level. Through Kant, a modern concept of war begins to take on a firm moral content. Through this content the right to war is no longer an unquestionable right of the juridical person of the state. Rather, states are treated as moral persons, the condition of war as a whole is morally condemned, and moral reasoning is used to determine the boundaries of the legitimacy and illegitimacy of acts of state violence.

While the movement towards the moral condemnation of war has been much celebrated, the re-moralization of inter-state war is also potentially dangerous. Kant's moral ordering of war harks back to an older form of war's ordering when Catholic religious authorities and their theologians set up a religious natural law that attempted to direct and govern the violent actions of Christian states. In certain respects, Kant re-institutes in a secular form a natural law-based theory of just war, which like that of Vitoria, draws upon the use of moral principles and moral reasoning to attempt to limit and regulate the violent interactions between states. Like the Christian just war theories of Aquinas and Vitoria Kant's moral ordering of war is focussed upon the issue of 'right intention'. Indeed, Kant is almost obsessed with the question of moral intention and his moral theory is driven by an ideal of a 'pure' moment of intention within practical reason that is not swayed and corrupted by motivations of utility or by the passions.

To an extent, Kant's secular just war places 'pure practical reason' in the transcendent space once occupied by God and natural law within a Christian hierarchy of creation. Following, in part, within a tradition of Christian, scholastic metaphysics, Kant claims to describe a notion of right which has 'universal' validity over the globe.[99] To be fair to Kant, the rigour of his moral theory keeps his approach from descending into a style of just war thinking, like that given by Vitoria or Grotius, in which the careful use of legal rhetoric clothed any political motive in the garb of universal moral legitimacy. Kant was fully aware of the danger of a moral theory being used to offer sorry comfort to political motivations and his strict use of the categorical imperative separates him from his just war predecessors. However, the many inheritors of Kant's approach to the moral ordering of war do not necessarily replicate Kant's care and rigour. It is within the looser use of a moral theory to justify and legitimate acts of violence that the worst of the Christian just war tradition is revived within modernity in a secular, Enlightenment form.

V

In considering Kant's moral ordering of war and its relevance to the present, a distinction needs to be drawn between, on the one hand, the rigour and discipline of Kant's account of pure practical reason and his account of the moral law, and on the other, a more general conception of morality, or *subjective moralism*, tied to the traditions of Western liberalism, human rights, and individual autonomy. Further, while holding onto this distinction Kant's conception also needs to be situated within the wider socio-political tradition of Western moral thinking, emerging, in part, around the political, social and economic revolutions of the eighteenth century in western Europe and North America. In one sense, Kant's philosophical moral theory develops within an emerging tradition of liberal, bourgeois morality and human rights that, bound to an emerging industrial capitalist economy, had come to hold a degree of dominance within the nineteenth and twentieth centuries through western Europe and North America.

Situated within this context, Kant's philosophical moral theory can be thought of as simultaneously: an expression of a form of moral thinking (liberal, bourgeois, 'moralistic') present within twentieth- and twenty-first century political institutions that developed within the capitalist political economy of the Anglo-European state;[100] and, a rigorous and powerful critique of the relativism, contradiction and subjectivism (subjective moralism) present within a modern, liberal, Western, moral language and culture.

Viewed in terms of this double role, Kant's philosophical moral theory can be seen to be relevant to an understanding of contemporary international law in which Kant's dream of a peaceful federation of states has moved a little closer to becoming a historical reality. In a sense, Kant's writings on war and peace can be thought as one central philosophical foundation, or at least an anticipation, of the twentieth-century re-organization of inter-state relations through the failed League of Nations (1919) and the still current United Nations (1945). Kant's theoretical account of the moral ordering of war prefigures an institutional and cultural moral ordering of war that has developed historically. Understanding Kant's philosophical account might assist in coming to a better understanding of the operation of the moral ordering of war that constitutes a significant element of contemporary, global social reality. A focus upon some of the difficulties faced by the Kantian approach might shed light upon some of the inherent problems within the operation of the moral ordering of war today.

The move towards the moral ordering of war within international law and international relations can be seen to have taken place through the establishment of inter-state federations in the early and middle parts of the twentieth century. Emerging with the League of Nations and later taken up by the United Nations, is a dominant moral discourse that condemns war in the name of peace and security.[101] Under the UN Charter, while war is understood as a right of a particular state, the scope of its legitimacy is severely curtailed.[102] The right of war is limited to the right of self-defence and collective right of self-defence.[103] Most starkly, the act of aggressive war is criminalized.[104] What was once understood as a right of state to wage war to further its own interests begins, in the twentieth century, to be understood as a 'crime' that deserves to be punished.

Such a form of ordering has not washed away the Westphalian international political order. The notion of the sovereign state, based upon the model of the European state, still remains the primary actor within international law[105] and it is the continued agreement, negotiation and participation of states which underpins the success or failure of the operation of any notion of international law. In a sense, the twentieth-century model of international ordering through the notion of an inter-state federation plays out a number of elements of the post-Westphalian civil and political ordering. The duty of non-interference in the internal matters of another state[106] and the de-legitimization of terror and civil war in favour of the curbed legitimization of state war[107] still remain fundamental principles of international law.

Further, to a small extent, the form of an inter-state contract to establish peace sparked by the fear and horror of war replicates in some fashion the ideas of a civil social contract based upon a natural law of minimum content proposed by Grotius and Hobbes. Yet, this Westphalian conception is amended somewhat by the moral ordering of war influenced by a culture and language of Western morality and liberalism with its emphasis upon individual freedom and human rights. As such, contemporary international law portrays an underlying tension between the right of the sovereign state, and a global or cosmopolitan sovereignty of international law and its notions of human rights[108] and human freedom.

Present within both Kant's approach to war and the development of the moral ordering of war within the UN framework is a notion that may be termed the *moral force of international law*. The moral force of international law emerges as a forceless force;[109] it is a radical normative demand which is both immanent within the structures and institutions of international law and stands above, and outside of, all positive international law. The moral force of international law demands that war should end and that global society be organized around the notions of peace, freedom and human rights. In its radical sense the moral force of international law presents a normative demand powered not simply by the notion of what ought (*sollen*) to be, but, by what *must* (*müssen*) be. The moral force of international law can be thought as simultaneously a point of *critique*, a *hope*, and a *demand for action*.

In the first sense, the notion opens a powerful space for denouncing and criticizing the actions of states who trample upon the face of humanity by disregarding human rights internally and by launching into acts of aggressive war. This critical moment of the moral force of international law could be seen in the massive anti-war protests in condemnation of the USA in the Vietnam

War (1964–75) and against the invasion of Iraq by the USA and its allies (2003–). Such a moral force of law gives an authoritative voice to the members of humanity, who not only for the demand of peace, but also in the name of freedom and human rights, may legitimately denounce the violence of politicians, generals, military strategists, and the many media organizations who act as propaganda agencies for states at war.[110]

Further, the moral force of international law presents a moment of hope in a global future that may be better than the present. Part of this hope is contained in the idea that peace, freedom and human rights are *not yet* (*noch nicht*).[111] This involves the sense that while these notions are not fully present today, they may yet come to be more fully present in the future. The vision of hope contained within the moral force of international law is open and pluralistic, it does not outline the formula of a better world, but provides normative and regulative ideas worth believing in, that make the notion of a better world of the future more tangible. One such hope is in a legitimate, independent, and operational international law that is free from the manipulation of state interests, is democratic, and can regulate conflict through a global police force and judiciary.[112]

A hope for a world in which actors do more than pay lip service to the ideals of peace, freedom and human rights creates a demand for action. The moral force of international law contains a strong demand that states and international organizations act in the interests of not only preserving, but also of realizing, peace, freedom and human rights. The moral demand for a better world requires action and moral actors. It depends upon the creation of a better world through human hands, through deeds. The demand is also urgent, human and institutional actors cannot simply wait for a better tomorrow, they must create their own tomorrow today.

The demand for action contained within the moral force of international law opens onto a problem faced by the moral ordering of war more generally. The problem can be thought of as one of *action* or *realization*. In part, this problem emerges when a federation of nations is faced by a state or group of states which threaten peace by acting aggressively, or by grossly violating the human rights of its own citizens or the citizens of its neighbours. In a Kantian sense, it can be assumed that if the federation of nations has been established, to the extent that it can genuinely be called a form of international or cosmopolitan *law*, then such an institution may legitimately use force, coercion and violence to preserve peace, human rights and human freedom. Such an idea follows from Kant's account of law in which the use of coercion or force is *a priori* necessary to the operation of law.

The current international law framework, under the UN Charter, affirms this line of thinking and grants the executive body of the UN the right to use military force or coercion to 'restore peace and security'[113] and in a more ambiguous sense the right to use such force to protect against the violation human rights.[114] However, a practical problem emerges for the moral ordering of war in situations where the UN, because of political stalemates within the

Security Council (and the right of veto), is unable to intervene to preserve peace or protect human rights, or, in situations where the UN executive cannot even pass judgment on particular acts of state violence.

Recent events have shown situations where the UN federation is unable to intervene to legally enforce international law and such a role has fallen upon groups of states who have taken upon themselves the role of enforcement (i.e. NATO's bombing of Serbia-Kosovo, 1999). Further, recent history has witnessed the situation where the world's most militarily powerful state has carried out an act of war and has done so on its own accord without UN authority (i.e. the invasion of Iraq by the USA and its allies in 2003). In both situations the acts of war carried out by inter-state alliances have taken place within the context of broad debates over the legal and moral legitimacy of such actions.

One way of framing the issue, in Kantian terms, is to think the UN Charter as constituting and bringing into existence legislative and executive bodies of international law. However, the existence of international law as a sovereign body is still not yet fully realized. The full realization of a sovereign governing body of international law is made problematic by the UN's inability to consistently enforce international law. The UN is not only reliant upon military forces provided by member states, but further, its executive body is often rendered impotent in particular instances where it is silent upon the issue of enforcement. In this moment of silence, international law as a whole does not disappear but the legal function of judging who may legitimately use violence is, for periods of time, suspended. Here the question of the moral demand of international law comes to the fore. Can states use coercion (i.e. violence) to enforce or realize international law in the situation where the executive authority is silent or cannot itself act? Or, in other words, can a 'universal' moral law legitimate an act of war by states who endeavour to uphold and realize the principles of international law?

In the effort to keep this discussion within a Kantian framework,[115] it is worth turning to an approach to this problem taken by Jürgen Habermas who actively inherits Kant's cosmopolitan tradition and who considered this problem in relation to the bombing of Serbia and Kosovo by NATO in 1999. In this situation, the act of war by NATO was not given legal authority by the executive arm of the United Nations, the Security Council. In an open letter to the German people, Habermas argued that the bombing of Serbia and Kosovo was legitimated by the need to protect human rights abuses against the Kosovo-Albanian population. Habermas argued that due to the lack of an institutionally operative cosmopolitan law, the act of war by NATO, while not technically 'legal', could draw its authority from the normative or moral force of international law. Habermas stated:

> For as long as human rights are institutionalized only weakly on the global scale, it remains possible for the borders between law and morals to become blurred, as they have in the case at hand. Because the Security Council is

> blocked from acting effectively, it is only possible for NATO to appeal to the moral validity of international law – and to norms for which no effective and universally recognized instances assure their application and enforcement.[116]

Habermas argued in favour of the NATO action, claiming:

> The dilemma of having to act as though there were already a fully institutionalized global civil society, the very promotion of which is the intention of the action, does not force us to accept the maxim that victims are to be left at the mercy of thugs. The terrorist misappropriation of state power transforms classical civil war into mass murder. When nothing else is possible, neighbouring democratic states should be allowed to rush to provide emergency help as legitimated by international law. But precisely the unfinished character of global civil society calls out for a special sort of sensitivity. Existing institutions and procedures are the only available controls over the fallible judgments of a party aspiring to act on behalf of the common interest.[117]

While arguing in favour of a particular war, Habermas gave a note of caution to the action, stressing that such self-empowerment should be considered as an exception and not the rule.[118] In this sense, while supporting the action, Habermas still remained critical of some of the motives behind it. Part of his critique invoked the Kantian figures of the political moralist and the moral politician through which he contrasted the actions of the USA to those of Europe. For Habermas, the USA enforced the implementation of human rights as part of the mission of a super-power who 'pursues this goal according to the premises of power politics', while, on the other hand, most European nations regard the enforcement of human rights as necessary in order to establish the rule of law in international relations.[119]

For Habermas, in specific circumstances states can morally draw upon violence to uphold or realize the principles of international law, peace, human rights and freedom. In his account the boundary between law and morality is 'blurred'. He sees groups of states (such as NATO) acting 'morally', however, he claims that such acts are legitimized by international law. Part of Habermas's claim to 'legitimate authority' stems from the fact that, for him, human rights are not moral, but, are juridical in character.[120] For Habermas, while human rights have a moral content, they structurally belong within an order of positive and coercive law in which claims to individual rights may be enforceable.[121] He argues that it is constitutive of the meaning of human rights that they belong within an existing legal order in which they can be protected, be it national, international or global.[122]

Part of this 'blurring' of the boundary between law and morality is significant in thinking about the problem of the realization of international law faced by the moral ordering of war. In the Habermasian sense when the executive body of international law cannot carry out its function of using coercion to enforce international law, then states may step in as the agents that give force or power to international law through violence. In this regard, the *moral force* of international law, understood in the normative sense of 'force', takes upon itself the role and agency of the *force* of international law, understood in the physical, coercive and violent sense. In response to this 'blurring', one may here still ask the question of whether such violence carried out by states is legal or moral. It might be worthwhile thinking a little more here (within the framework of Kant's distinctions) of the boundaries between law and morality in relation to judgment on the use of violence within the international sphere.

For a number of intellectual traditions that attempt to determine what constitutes a sphere of law as opposed to a sphere of morality, the issue of violence plays a significant role. In the Hobbesian tradition the sphere of law is posited or raised as an institution and position of judgment to decide between conflicting moral claims which were often backed by threats and acts of violence. For Hobbes, the sovereign authority of the law adopts the sole right of the use of violence, and judgment on when the use of violence is necessary, to uphold the laws of the commonwealth. In this sense, particular laws and legal rights may have a moral content and citizens may have a moral duty to uphold the law, however, the right to violence is held solely by the sovereign legal authority and not by moral actors.

Much of this tradition is inherited by Kant and extended to the sphere of international relations. For Kant, the point of establishing a cosmopolitan or international law is to respond to the chaotic use of violence by states through setting up a form of legal authority between them that might judge between their claims and, perhaps ideally, possess the sole right to judgment on the legitimacy of the use of violence. In distinguishing between the spheres of legality and morality in the international context, the idea of a competent and objective institution that may *judge* between conflicting claims is important to Kant. In a legal sense, a state cannot be the judge of the validity of its own claims or its own acts of violence, such self-judgment is possible in the sphere of morality but not in law. For Kant, while positive law may have a moral content, legal judgment comes from a sovereign authority and the legal use of violence can only be carried out by a legal authority. In Kant's reasoning, violence carried out at the inter-state level would only be a moral violence (one aimed at instituting the global rule of law), it would only become 'legal' violence after an act was authorized by the established inter-state legal institution. The voice of authorization would need to come from a *body* (the inter-state federation as the global form of sovereignty) and not merely be a moral hope, voiced by a particular state, for a law that is yet to come.

In the UN Charter, whose foundational premises are not too far away from the traditions of thought expressed in Hobbes and Kant, the issue over the right to the use of violence and judgment on violence takes centre stage. Different from the Hobbesian position, the institution of the UN does not have a monopoly upon the right to use violence, or upon the right to judgment on violence. This right[123] is shared, and is set out legally in the form of a contract. In this contract the Security Council is given authority to judge between competing or conflicting state claims that might lead to dispute or friction.[124] If the Security Council deems that the dispute is likely to endanger international peace and security then it may take action,[125] one form of action being the authorization of the use of force in the form of war.[126] On the other hand, the Charter sets out the continuing legal right of states to use violence and the right to make judgments over when the recourse to violence is necessary in the case of self-defence. Article 51 states:

> Nothing in the present Charter shall impair the inherent right of individual or collective self-defence if an armed attack occurs against a Member of the United Nations, until the Security Council has taken measures necessary to maintain peace and security.[127]

Furthermore, Article 52(1) allows the existence of regional arrangements and regional action relating to the maintenance of international peace and security consistent with the purposes and principles of the UN.[128] However, the right of such regional arrangements to use violence is reliant upon authorization by the Security Council.[129]

When concentrating attention upon the differentiation between the spheres of legality and morality with respect to the right to use violence in these intellectual traditions and under the UN Charter, there is not so much a sense of 'blurring' as some might tend to argue. Under international law, as set out by the UN Charter, states retain a legal right to the use of violence in one limited case, that of individual and collective self-defence. In all other cases, including the threat to peace and the violation of human rights, the authority for the judgment upon and authorization of the use of violence resides with the Security Council. When the Security Council cannot act, or is silent on such matters, the legal authority on the use of violence does not pass to individual states or alliances. Rather, these states need to be seen as acting within a moral capacity as *moral agents* who take it upon themselves to uphold international law. As much as they may claim, they do not have legal authority. Rather, they would only have a moral authority, which in the sphere of competing moral claims, is often endlessly contested.[130]

Under international law there is legal authority for the Security Council to protect through violence a broad range of legal rights, such as human rights, and principles, such as peace and human freedom. However, under the UN Charter there is no scope for states to possess legal authority to protect through violence these broad-ranging global rights and principles without express authorization from the Security Council.[131] Many thinkers, including Habermas, have a tendency to confuse the question of the legality of particular rights, such as human rights, with a different question concerning who has the legal authority to uphold and protect legal rights through violence. In contemporary times many states and their theorists claim a legal authority for wars aimed at protecting and upholding peace, freedom and human rights. Within a Kantian reading of the current framework of international law, the legal authority for the use of violence in such cases is monopolized by the legal institution of the Security Council. In the silence or impotence of the Security Council, states who attempt to take on or replicate the Security Council's authority and function may possess moral and but not legal authority. As moral actors, they may only attempt to justify their violence by moral and not legal reasoning. When understood in this sense, the problem faced by the moral ordering of war, that of the realization of international law through moral action, and the slide into subjective moralization, continues to be relevant.

The argument here is not that there is a strict separation between law and morality generally. All forms of law and legal institutions contain moral aspects to the extent that legal traditions and legal actors adhere to some sets of norms and disregard others. Forms of law and legal institutions are not morally 'neutral' in any sense and the realm of law is typified by disingenuous argument and partisan moral and political claims that attempt to hide behind a façade of formal, legal and procedural neutrality. There is, however, a distinction between law and morality within the context of international law with regard to the question of who might authorize the use of violence to protect the cosmopolitan demands of peace and human rights. While all legal violence (including violence authorized by the Security Council) will be driven by moral, political and economic concerns, this legal violence is differentiated from moral violence by the fact that it is authorized by a sovereign legal authority (i.e. the naming of the boundaries of 'legitimate authority' to use violence set out in the UN Charter and the role of the Security Council in enforcing these boundaries). Too often this distinction is overlooked, yet it plays a significant role if one is to properly understand contemporary Kantian approaches to international law and the limitations of the moral ordering of war.

Within the sphere of moral reasoning and moral argument there is wide scope for state actors to justify acts of war on the basis of some form of moral authority. In many cases moral argument over war descends quickly into *subjective moralization*, or in other words, into a moral legitimation of war not based upon any objective, universal standard, but merely based upon subjective choice, private interest or dubious moral reasoning. In some respects what might also be seen to be occurring is the formulation of 'moral' wars that challenge and deny the legitimacy of the executive body (the Security Council), and in this respect challenge the sovereignty of contemporary international law. Such moral wars guided by a claim that they are realizing a new, global 'popular sovereignty' – the universal ideals of freedom, human rights and democracy – replicate in some ways the arguments underlying forms of revolutionary war suggested in the theories of Locke and Rousseau.

Such moral warriors claim, through their violence, to act in the name of a higher, legitimate authority and in so doing move towards dissolving the contract between states and the UN which they see as inadequate to securing freedom, human rights and democracy at a global level. There is no need to be romantic about such a movement, often it can institute a 'reign of terror', and this is one way of interpreting the invasion of Iraq (2003–) by the USA which completely ignored the 'sovereignty' of the inter-state federation, the UN.[132] What renders this movement even more problematic, just like when a moment of revolution turns into civil war, is the multiple claims of differing state actors that their state or alliance properly represents the vision of an international 'legitimate authority' and that they, and not their others, are the proper constituting power which will bring a new law of freedom into existence.[133] The possible competition between differing 'revolutionary' vanguards at the inter-state level fighting over the content of a future international law replicates in some ways the violence of various 'just wars' fought by Christian confessions within the Thirty Years War. Within such a scenario the notion of legitimate authority is itself contested by violence with competing actors all claiming the legitimacy of some form of 'universal' sovereignty.

For Kant, such a scenario would turn the dream of perpetual peace into a nightmare – a return to the chaos of an international state of nature which his moral theory had attempted to overcome. His moral theory aimed at ending war or, at least, strictly regulating it. However, part of the problem of Kant's account is the question of how states, guided by a theory of morality, can bring into existence and realize a workable system of international law when faced by opposition. As Kant gives little advice on how to approach this problem, or the problem of the subjective moralization of war, then these can only be analysed by examining the theoretical tools which Kant makes available – the categorical imperative. For him, the discipline of pure practical reason and the categorical imperative is able to critique and display the arbitrariness of the subjective moralization of war. However, his approach may not fully be able to come to terms with the problem of the realization of the moral law through violence because maxims designed to that effect, when thought of as a universal law, fall into contradiction.

It is worth here considering a number of maxims in the manner in which Kant may have considered them. That is, by considering whether a maxim, when considered as a universal rule of behaviour, would lead to some form of contradiction, and whereby the actions of differing individuals would conflict with the stated ends of the maxim. At a general level a maxim, such as, 'Act in such a way that your actions are directed to the end of peace', when re-considered as a universal law, does not, it would seem, fall into contradiction. Likewise, a maxim with a greater level of content, or detail, that, 'One may legitimately engage in war in the case of self-defence', when re-considered as a universal law, also seems not to fall into contradiction. However, more expansive maxims containing detail related to the issue of the use of war to realize the moral demands of international law, are more likely to fall into contradiction. The maxim 'One may go to war with the aim of gaining or establishing peace', when re-considered as a universal law, falls into contradiction. The act of war, while carried out with the aim of establishing peace would factually create or contribute to the condition of war. If everyone were to make this a guiding rule of their moral action, then there might well be more war than peace. Similarly, the maxim 'One may go to war to protect or establish human rights', when considered as a universal law, falls into contradiction. The act of war, which involves killing, while attempting to protect human rights will detrimentally affect the human rights of those individuals who are killed.[134] If everyone were to make this a guiding rule for moral action, then it could be envisioned that more human rights could be trampled upon than protected and realized.[135]

Kant's moral ordering of war has great difficulty in coming to terms with the problem of the realization of the moral force of international law through violence. At a very general level where the maxims do not involve a great deal of content, Kant's approach works as a basic guide. However, as soon as more detail is added pertaining to the act of war, moral action simply cannot be reconciled with the guiding principles of peace and human rights without contradicting them. If one tries to introduce terms such as 'pre-emptive attack', and distinguish between 'short-term' and 'long-term' peace in an effort to get around contradiction,[136] then moral reasoning merely falls into a form of sophistry that Kant was at pains to avoid.

With regard to this problem, Kant's rigour and discipline of the categorical imperative can only offer negative instruction. Kant's moral ordering of war cannot provide a clear objective standard of how each actor should morally behave with regard to their own acts of violence in the effort to *realize* the moral demands of international law. Given this, Kant's approach can only rely upon a more generalized form of a moral rule in which one's actions are directed towards the ends of peace, freedom and human rights. His account is forced to rest upon the hope that 'moral politicians' may make the appropriately constrained judgments over the 'necessity' of going to war to realize moral ends. Such a general reliance is problematic as moral politicians, being pragmatic actors, are forced to mediate moral demands through economic, political, and strategic concerns. Further, all too often it is difficult to distinguish the moral politicians from the political moralists.

Within the moral ordering of war, how does one tell the difference between the moral politician and the political moralist? The categorical imperative provides some form of critique. However, as soon as states are conceived as moral persons and only given very general objective moral guidance to direct their action towards the realization of peace, freedom and human rights, then there is the high probability that states (and other actors) will use a moral language and moral claims as an effort to legitimate their violent actions and self-interests, or, that these interests themselves become inseparable from moral concerns.

State actors might genuinely believe that their acts of violence, and even aggressive acts of war, invasion and occupation are directed towards the noble ends of the realization of peace, freedom and human rights. Alternatively, warring actors might hypocritically and rhetorically use a moral language to justify their actions when they are motivated by other interests. Within the early phases of the historical moral ordering of war and international law during the twentieth century the rhetorical and strategic use of moral concepts to 'trump' the enemy while disguising other interests was grasped by Carl Schmitt. In response to the criminalization and punishment of Germany following its defeat in World War I and the development of the League of Nations, Schmitt argued:

> When a state fights its political enemy in the name of humanity, it is not a war for the sake of humanity, but a war wherein a particular state seeks to usurp a universal concept against its military opponent. At the expense of its opponent, it tries to identify itself with humanity in the same way as one can misuse peace, justice, progress, and civilization in order to claim these as one's own and to deny the same to the enemy.
>
> The concept of humanity is an especially useful ideological instrument of imperialist expansion, and in its ethical-humanitarian form it is a specific vehicle of economic imperialism. Here one is reminded of a somewhat modified expression of Proudhon's: whoever invokes humanity wants to cheat. To confiscate the word humanity, to invoke and monopolize such a term probably has certain incalculable effects, such as denying the quality of being human and declaring him to be an outlaw of humanity; and a war can thereby be driven to the most extreme inhumanity.[137]

Between the hypocritical use of moral justifications and concepts on the one hand, and the genuine moral intent (including perhaps a reliance upon faulty moral reasoning and erroneous 'intelligence' reports) on the other, emerges within the moral ordering of war a modern form of secular, moralized 'just war'.[138] One example is the case of the invasion of Iraq by the USA and its allies in 2003. The arguments for, and in condemnation of, this act of aggressive war took place as competing moral claims and counter-claims over the legitimacy or illegitimacy of violence. While the 'facts'[139] presented in support of the arguments of the aggressors appear to have been fabricated (or, in the least, were the product of ignorance and error), this does not depart from the point that the aggressors drew upon the moral force of international law – as a moral voice – to empower (morally and rhetorically) their acts of violence.

This is perhaps what is most troubling about the moral ordering of war – the manipulation and creative use of the *moral force* of international law to justify and support immoral acts of state aggression. In the case of Iraq in 2003 (and in numerous other cases), the aggressors did not purely rely upon military power. Rather, so much of their strength came from the ability to mobilize the moral force of international law *as a normative and rhetorical power* through state and media propaganda machines which convinced many individuals of the supposed 'justness of the cause' and drowned out and sometimes silenced the moral voices of the war's critics. Leading up to the invasion a 'universal' moral language was used as a strategy and as a weapon. This moral strategy not only helped to portray a greedy neo-colonial adventure as one which was carried out in accordance with the 'right intention', it also allowed many of the supporters of the war, ordinary men and women, to feel good about themselves.

Aside from those who are bombed and slaughtered by acts of morally trumped-up war, it seems that within the moral ordering of war it is those moral actors who take the Kantian injunction of practical reason most seriously who suffer. Their moral voice becomes lost amidst the noise and endless shouting of competing moral claims. The words of those who take the Kantian injunction seriously are mimicked, lampooned, and turned against them by sovereigns, philosophers, businessmen and 'experts' who, in greater positions of power and public influence, claim *all* moral authority as their own. In such an atmosphere it is the loudest voices, and not the most rigorous adherents to the moral law, who often carry the most weight and influence within a moralized global order.

We are presented with an image of the contemporary operation of the moral ordering of war as being something of a 'secular' replication of the pre-Westphalian condition of chaotic, moralized, religious violence. At a global level, violence takes the form of moral just wars fought by states and inter-state federations and alliances. In this context the condition of war refers not only to the action of physical killing, but also to the figurative sense of a war carried out at the level between thoughts and concepts. Surrounding every act of war is the chaos of moral claims and counter-claims over the legitimacy and illegitimacy of violence: every side claims to have right on its side, every side claims to be acting in the effort to realize a world of peace, freedom and human rights. The tears of the suffering and the genuine tears for those who suffer through war are mixed with the crocodile tears of presidents, academics, lawyers and journalists. Every tear shed is mixed in some way with the shedding of blood. Further, it is not that the injunction to *be more moral* falls upon deaf ears. Rather, when war is moralized, the injunction to be more moral cannot provide a solution to conflict. Instead, the injunction inflames and leads into a vicious cycle of violence where actors, driven by the moral force of international law, find it necessary to carry out war against war – to carry out war in the name of peace.

In this respect, one might identify the *Janus face* of the tradition of the moral ordering of war. On the one hand, the moral ordering of war introduces into modernity a powerful critique of war carried out by state interests, a radical hope for a global future of peace, freedom and human rights, and a demand for action that actors put aside their private interests and realize the moral law. On the other, the moral ordering of war opens onto a profoundly dangerous space marked by the moral just wars of genuine believers,[140] hypocrites and rhetoricians who legitimate their violence by what they conceive or call 'moral reason'.

It is important to note here, however, that contrary to the so-called 'realist' critique of the moral ordering of war the situation does not fully degenerate into one of moral relativism. While the situation may be chaotic, within the parameters of Kant's account of the moral law, determined by pure practical reason, there still remains something of an 'objective criteria' operating as a *negative standard* by which one might say that a particular act or claim is 'immoral': that the form of moral reasoning is faulty and that if considered as a universal law it would fall into contradiction. Short of this negative standard however, the problem of enacting or realizing the moral law through violence places the tradition of the moral ordering of war on tenuous ground. For some, such a negative standard is enough. Perhaps from the standpoint of hope, such a limited, negative standard is far too inadequate. It would seem that hope, and the moral demand of hope, always want something more.

Notes

1 Jean-Jacques Rousseau, *A Project of Perpetual Peace*, trans. E.M. Nuttal, London: Richard Cobden-Sanderson, 1927.
2 Ibid., pp. 129.
3 Ibid., pp. 107–9.
4 Ibid., pp. 113.
5 E. Bloch, *Natural Law and Human Dignity*, trans. D.J. Schmidt, Cambridge, MA: MIT Press, 1996, pp. 61–2.
6 J. Locke, *Two Treatises of Government*, ed. P. Laslett, Cambridge: Cambridge University Press, 2005.
7 Ibid., p. 278.
8 Ibid., pp. 412–13. For Locke, given his interests in the English colonization of North America, this right to resist against slavery was not generally extended to non-European peoples. For a discussion of Locke's theories in relation to colonialism, see J. Tully, *An Approach to Political Philosophy: Locke in Contexts*, Cambridge: Cambridge University Press, 1993. With regard to liberal notions of revolution more generally, see H. Arendt, *On Revolution*, London: Penguin, 1990.
9 J. Locke, *Two Treatises of Government*, at p. 283, Locke argues:

> The *Natural Liberty* of Man is to be free from any Superior Power on Earth, and not to be under the Will or Legislative Authority of Man, but to have only the Law of Nature for his Rule. *The Liberty of Man, in Society*, is to be under no other Legislative Power, but that established, by consent, in the Common-wealth, nor under the Dominion of any Will, or Restraint of any Law, but what the Legislative shall enact, according to the Trust put in it.

10 The accounts of Grotius and Hobbes are also premised upon the preservation of certain 'natural' liberties which gain their concrete realization through the social contract and establishment of a strong sovereign. Locke's account is probably more libertarian and wary of the latter's tendency to justify widespread incursions upon individual liberty in the name of securing 'peace'. One might claim that much of contemporary liberal theory, especially in response to the so-called 'war on terror',

sits within the to and fro between Locke and Hobbes, and is entirely caught within the limits of this theoretical paradigm. As much as the theories of Locke and Hobbes are captivating like shining stars, for many liberal theorists, they operate like blinkers on a horse.

11 J-J. Rousseau, 'Discourse on the Origin and Foundations of Inequality Among Men', in P. Gay (ed.) *Jean-Jacques Rousseau: The Basic Political Writings*, trans. D.A. Cress, Indianapolis, IN: Hacket, 1987.

12 Ibid., p. 53.

13 That Rousseau's theory is one pointing to alienation is clear from the first paragraph of Part II of the text. At p. 60 he argues:

> The first person who, having enclosed a plot of land, took it into his head to say *this is mine* and found people simple enough to believe him, was the true founder of civil society. What crimes, wars, murders, what miseries and horrors would the human race have been spared, had someone pulled up the stakes or filled in the ditch and cried out to his fellow men: 'Do not listen to this impostor. You are lost if you forget that the fruits of the earth belong to all and to no one!'

14 Ibid., p. 61.

15 On this reading of Rousseau, there are aspects of an account of social conflict and inequality driven by desire which are influential upon, and are later developed by, Hegel in his theory of inter-subjective recognition. This reformulation of Rousseau's account of social conflict takes place not only within Hegel's *Phenomenology of Spirit*, but also within his earlier *Jena Manuscripts*.

16 On the significance of '*amour-propre*', see N. Dent, *Rousseau*, London: Routledge, 2005. At pp. 39–40 he argues:

> How and why could a society grow up that contained such inhumanity? For Rousseau, the key factor here is the demands of man's *amour-propre*. There is considerable debate about what exactly we should understand by Rousseau's use of this term, but I interpret *amour-propre* as, in its essence, a desire or need to secure recognition from others, for an acknowledgment of oneself in their eyes and actions. This desire very readily takes on, in Rousseau's view, an aggressive and competitive character, whereby individuals come to feel that they have received their due acknowledgement only if they are preferred above others, have precedence or superiority above others in whose ignominy and abjection they rejoice as a sign that they themselves are better people who count for more, are a 'better class of person'. Inequalities arise and are elaborated and maintained, on this account, in order to afford people a sense of their own significance in society that they crave. Domination and subservience become the key marks of social structures and relations between groups and individuals.

17 J-J. Rousseau, 'Discourse on the Origin of Inequality', p. 64. Unlike some of his predecessors, Rousseau does not call this social condition of competition and conflict 'war'. Generally, he uses this term only with reference to inter-state conflict and in this sense follows to a limited degree the Westphalian conception of war. See J-J. Rousseau, 'On the Social Contract', in P. Gay (ed.) *Jean-Jacques Rousseau: The Basic Political Writings*, trans. D.A. Cress, Indianapolis, IN: Hacket, 1987. At p. 145, he argues:

> War is not therefore a relationship between one man and another, but a relationship between one state and another. In war private individuals are enemies

only incidentally: not as men or even citizens, but as soldiers; not as members of the homeland but as its defenders. Finally, each state can have as enemies only other states and not men, since there can be no real relationship between things of disparate natures.

18 J-J. Rousseau, 'Discourse on the Origin of Inequality', p. 70. In the passage that follows, Rousseau comes quite close to and yet situates himself far away from the account of the international presented by Hobbes. Rousseau claims:

> Societies, multiplying or spreading rapidly, soon covered the entire surface of the earth; and it was no longer possible to find a single corner of the universe where someone could free himself from the yoke and withdraw his head from the often ill-guided sword which everyone saw perpetually hanging over his own head. With civil right thus having become the common rule of citizens, the law of nature no longer was operative except between the various societies, when, under the name of the law of nations, it was tempered by some tacit conventions in order to make intercourse possible and to serve as a substitute for natural compassion which, losing between one society and another nearly all the force it had between one man and another, no longer resides anywhere but in a few great cosmopolitan souls, who overcome the imaginary barriers that separate peoples, and who, following the example of the sovereign being who has created them, embrace the entire human race in their benevolence.
>
> Remaining thus among themselves in the state of nature, the bodies politic soon experienced the inconveniences that had forced private individuals to leave it; and that state became even more deadly among those great bodies than that state had been among the private individuals of who they were composed. Whence came the national wars, battles, murders, and reprisals that make nature tremble and offend reason, and all those horrible prejudices that rank the honour of shedding human blood among the virtues. The most decent people learned to consider it one of their duties to kill their fellow men. Finally, men were seen massacring one another by the thousands without knowing why.

19 Ibid., p. 79.
20 Rousseau, 'On the Social Contract', p. 148.
21 Ibid., Rousseau states: 'Each of us places his person and all his power in common under the supreme direction of the general will; and as one we receive each member as an indivisible part of the whole.'
22 To very broadly use Jean-Luc Nancy's sense of the term. See J-L. Nancy, *Being Singular Plural*, trans. R.D. Richardson and A.E. O'Byrne, Stanford, CA: Stanford University Press, 2000; J-L. Nancy, *The Inoperative Community*, ed. P. Connor, Minneapolis, MN: Minnesota University Press, 1991.
23 Rousseau, 'On the Social Contract', p. 151.
24 Ibid., pp. 150–1. It should be noted that Rousseau's earlier denunciations of private property are tempered somewhat in 'On the Social Contract' which affirms a particular type of private property right mediated by the social. Rousseau does, however, remain critical of moments of colonial conquest. At p. 152, he argues:

> How can a man or a people seize a vast amount of territory and deprive the entire human race of it except by punishable usurpation, since this seizure deprives all other men of the shelter and sustenance that nature gives them in

> common? When Nuñez Balboa stood on the shoreline and took possession of the South Sea and all of South America in the name of crown of Castille, was this enough to dispossess all the inhabitants and to exclude all the princes of the world? On that basis, those ceremonies would be multiplied quite in vain. All the Catholic King had to do was to take possession of the universe all at once from his private bedroom, excepting afterwards from his empire only what already belonged to other princes.

25 Ibid., p. 150.
26 J.W. Goethe, *Faust*, München: Deutscher Taschenbuch Verlag, 1997, p. 67: '*(I)m Anfang war die That!*' (*Im Anfang war die Tat*).
27 This *aporia*, reformulated, in part, as the antinomy of freedom and necessity, is taken up by both Kant and Hegel (among others) who each struggle to find an adequate way of coming to terms with it.
28 At the very least, Rousseau's notion of freedom operates in a negative sense, as a critical test or standard by which we can judge institutions. For such a reading, see J.N. Shklar, *Men and Citizens: A Study of Rousseau's Social Theory*, Cambridge: Cambridge University Press, 1985, p. 17.
29 This line of inheritance of non-sovereign war will be discussed further in Chapter 5.
30 On the links between Rousseau and Kant, see E. Cassirer, *The Question of Jean-Jacques Rousseau*, ed. P. Gay, Bloomington, IN: Indiana University Press, 1967.
31 I. Kant, *The Metaphysics of Morals*, ed. M. Gregor, Cambridge: Cambridge University Press, 1996.
32 I. Kant, *Critique of Pure Reason*, ed. P. Guyer and A. Wood, Cambridge: Cambridge University Press, 1998.
33 Ibid., pp. 99 and 109.
34 Ibid., p. 101A. On Kant's use of juridical metaphors, see O. O'Neil, *Constructions of Reason: Explorations of Kant's Practical Philosophy*, Cambridge: Cambridge University Press, 1989; G. Rose, *The Broken Middle: Out of Our Ancient Society*, London: Blackwell, 1984. On the relations between Kant's critical philosophy and his moral philosophy more generally, see the discussions in H.E. Allison, *Kant's Theory of Freedom*, Cambridge: Cambridge University Press, 1990; P. Guyer, *Kant and the Experience of Freedom*, Cambridge: Cambridge University Press, 1996; A. W. Wood, *Kant's Ethical Thought*, Cambridge: Cambridge University Press, 1999; O. Höffe, *Immanuel Kant*, trans. M. Farrier, Albany, NY: SUNY Press, 1994.
35 I. Kant, *Critique of Pure Reason*, pp. 649–50, A751/B779.
36 Ibid., pp. 106–14, Bvii–Bxxiv. Consider Kant's discussion in I. Kant, *Prolegomena to Any Future Metaphysics*, ed. J.W. Ellington, trans. P. Carus, Indianapolis, IN: Hackett, 1977.
37 I. Kant, *Critique of Pure Reason*, pp. 108–9, Bxiii–xiv.
38 Ibid., p. 112, Bxx.
39 Ibid., p. 110, Bxvi. Kant argues:

> Up to now it has been assumed that all our cognition must conform to the objects; but all attempts to find out something about them *a priori* through concepts that would extend our cognition have, on this presupposition, come to nothing. Hence, let us once try whether we do not get farther with the problems of metaphysics by assuming that the objects must conform to our cognition, which would agree better with the requested possibility of an *a priori* cognition of them, which is to establish something about objects before they are given to us. This would be just like the first thoughts of Copernicus, who when he did not make good progress in the explanation of celestial

motions if he assumed that the entire celestial host revolves around the observer, tried to see if he might not have greater success if he made the observer revolve and left the stars at rest.

40 Ibid., pp. 196–7, A57–58/B81–2. Kant argues:

> In the expectation, therefore, that there can perhaps be concepts that may be related to objects *a priori*, not as pure or sensible intuitions but rather merely as acts of pure thinking, that are thus concepts but of neither empirical nor aesthetic origin, we provisionally formulate the idea of a science of pure understanding and of the pure cognition of reason, by means of which we think objects completely *a priori*. Such a science, which would determine the origin, the domain, and the objective validity of such cognitions, would have to be called a *transcendental logic*, since it has to do merely with the laws of the understanding and reason, but solely insofar as they are related to objects *a priori* and not, as in the case of general logic, to empirical as well as pure cognitions of reason without distinction.

41 Ibid., pp. 193–4, A50–52/B74–B6. Kant argues:

> Our cognition arises from two fundamental sources in the mind, the first of which is the reception of representations (the receptivity of impressions), the second the faculty for cognizing an object by means of these representations (spontaneity of concepts); through the former an object is *given* to us, through the latter it is *thought* in relation to that representation (as a mere determination of the mind). Intuition and concepts therefore constitute the elements of all our cognition, so that neither concepts without intuition corresponding to them in some way nor intuition without concepts can yield a cognition. Both are either pure or empirical. *Empirical*, if sensation (which presupposes the actual presence of the object) is contained therein; but *pure* if no sensation is mixed into the representation. One can call the latter the matter of sensible cognition. Thus pure intuition contains merely the form under which something is intuited, and pure concept only the form of thinking of an object in general. Only pure intuitions or concepts alone are possible *a priori*, empirical ones only *a posteriori*.
>
> If we will call the *receptivity* of our mind to receive representations insofar as it is affected in some way *sensibility*, then on the contrary the faculty of bringing forth representations itself, or the *spontaneity* of cognition, is the *understanding*. It comes along with our nature that *intuition* can never be other than *sensible*, i.e., that it contains only the way in which we are affected by objects. The faculty for *thinking* of objects of sensible intuition, on the contrary, is the *understanding*. Neither of these properties is to be preferred to the other. Without sensibility no object would be given to us, and without understanding none would be thought. Thoughts without content are empty, intuitions without concepts are blind.

42 Ibid., p. 115, Bxxvi. Kant argues:

> To *cognize* an object, it is required that I be able to prove its possibility (whether by the testimony of experience from its actuality or *a priori* through reason). But I can *think* whatever I like, as long as I do not contradict myself, i.e., as long as my concept is a possible thought, even if I cannot give any assurance

> whether or not there is a corresponding object somewhere within the sum total of all possibilities.

A further statement by Kant at p. 406, A335/B392, is more succinct. Kant argues: '(P)ure reason is never related directly to objects, but instead to concepts of them given by the understanding.'

43 Ibid., p. 467, A412/B449. Kant argues:

> If in using principles of the understanding we apply our reason not merely to objects of experience, for the use of principles of the understanding, but instead venture also to extend these principles beyond the boundaries of experience, then there arise sophistical theorems, which may neither hope for confirmation in experience nor fear refutation by it; and each of them is not only without contradiction in itself but even meets with conditions of its necessity in the nature of reason itself, only unfortunately the opposite has on its side equally valid and necessary grounds for its assertion.

44 Ibid., pp. 467–8, A422–23/B450–1. Kant argues:

> A dialectical theorem of pure reason must accordingly have the following feature, distinguishing it from all sophistical propositions: it does not concern an arbitrary question that one might raise only at one's option, but that every human reason must necessarily come up against in the course of its progress; and second, this proposition and its opposite must carry with them not merely an artificial illusion that disappears as soon as someone has insight into it, but rather a natural and unavoidable illusion, which even if one is no longer fooled by it, still deceives though it does not defraud and which thus can be rendered harmless but never destroyed.
>
> Such a dialectical doctrine will relate not to the unity of understanding in concepts of experience, but to the unity of reason in mere ideas, whose conditions, since, as a synthesis according to rules, must first be congruent with the understanding, and yet at the same time, as the absolute unity of this synthesis, must be congruent with reason, will be too large for the understanding if this unity is to be adequate to the unity of reason, and yet too small for reason if they are situated to the understanding; from this there must arise a contradiction that cannot be avoided no matter how one may try.

45 Ibid., p. 519, A506/B535. Kant argues:

> Accordingly, the antinomy of pure reason in its cosmological ideas is removed by showing that it is merely dialectical and a conflict due to an illusion arising from the fact that one has applied the idea of absolute totality, which is valid only as a condition of things in themselves, to appearances that exist only in representation, and that, if they constitute a series, exist in the successive regress but otherwise do not exist all. But one can, on the contrary, draw from this antinomy a true utility, not dogmatic but critical and doctrinal utility, namely that of thereby proving indirectly the transcendental ideality of appearances, if perhaps someone did not have enough direct proof in the Transcendental Aesthetic.

46 Ibid.

47 Ibid., pp. 530–3, A528–32/B556–60.

48 Ibid., pp. 112–13, Bxxi–Bxxii.
49 Ibid., pp. 115–16, Bxxvii–Bxxviii.
50 Ibid., p. 532, A531/B559.
51 Ibid., p. 532, A531/B559.
52 Ibid., p. 533, A534/B562.
53 Ibid., p. 674, A800/B828. Kant argues:

> Pure practical laws ... whose end is given by reason completely *a priori*, and which do not command under empirical conditions but absolutely, would be the products of pure reason. Of this sort, however, are the moral laws; thus these alone belong to the practical use of reason and permit a canon.

54 I. Kant, *Groundwork of the Metaphysics of Morals*, ed. M. Gregor, Cambridge: Cambridge University Press, 1998. Kant also sets out this account in a slightly differing manner within the *Critique of Practical Reason.* I will only consider the account given by Kant from the *Groundwork* here. For a discussion of the differing ways Kant links the critique of pure reason with pure practical reason, see H.E. Allison, *Kant's Theory of Freedom.*
55 I. Kant, *Groundwork of the Metaphysics of Morals*, p. 31.
56 Ibid.
57 Ibid., p. 38.
58 With regard to this negative function of the categorical imperative in general, see O. O'Neil, *Constructions of Reason: Explorations of Kant's Practical Philosophy*, Cambridge: Cambridge University Press, 1989. At p. 24, O'Neil argues:

> In pointing to the Categorical Imperative as the supreme principle of reason Kant is true to his insistence that we can obtain only negative instruction. The Categorical Imperative is only a strategy for avoiding principles of thinking, communicating and acting that cannot be adopted by all members of a plurality whose principles of interaction, let actual interaction (let alone coordination!), are not established by any transcendent reality. The supreme principle of reason does not fix thought or action in unique grooves; it only points to limits to the principles that can be shared.

59 Among many others, Kant's radical inheritors can be seen to include: Hegel, Marx, Nietzsche, Freud, and Derrida.
60 M. Gregor in I. Kant, *The Metaphysics of Morals.* At p. xxii, Gregor states:

> The categorical imperative determines which maxims are acceptable moral principles by their ability to serve as practical norms of conduct for everyone, that is, as laws within a civil community. Moral norms for conduct, therefore, are pre-eminently *public* laws, characterised by the universality of the obligations they impose, especially the obligation of reciprocity. It is important to state this clearly, because today so many people tend to think of morality as concerned mainly or only with one's private standards.

Consider also S. Anderson-Gould, *Unnecessary Evil: History and Moral Progress in the Philosophy of Immanuel Kant*, New York: SUNY Press, 2001. Anderson-Gould argues at p. 45 that:

> The idea of a moral life must include not only the unification of all of one's own acts/maxims but also an essential connection of these acts to the acts/maxims

of other moral subjects. In other words, given the universality of the ascription of this propensity, the 'moral life' must be represented as a social or collective undertaking.

61 I. Kant, *The Metaphysics of Morals*, pp. 17–18. At p. 31, Kant argues:

> No external lawgiving can bring about someone's setting an end for himself (because this is an internal act of the mind), although it may prescribe external actions that lead to an end without the subject making it his end.

62 Ibid., p. 24. Kant states: 'Right is therefore the sum of the conditions under which the choice of one court can be united with the choice of another in accordance with a universal law of freedom.'
At p. 30, Kant argues:

> *Freedom* (independence from being constrained by another's choice), insofar as it can coexist with the freedom of every other in accordance with a universal law, is the only original right belonging to every man by virtue of his humanity.

63 Ibid., p. 24.
64 Ibid.
65 Ibid., p. 25.
66 Ibid.
67 Ibid.
68 Ibid., p. 26. On this point, note O. Höffe, *Immanuel Kant*, at p. 174:

> According to Kant, the rational concept of law is closely connected with the authority to use force. He does not see this authority as irrational violence or as an immoral usurpation on the part of the legal system but instead as an indisputable *a priori* element of all law. As paradoxically as it may seem, without the authority to use force, no legal system, which must nonetheless be committed to the co-existence of free subjects, can be conceived.
>
> Because the law is the very essence of the conditions under which freedom is compatible with the freedom of all others, every action which, in accordance with universal laws, is compatible with the freedom of all others, is legitimate from a legal standpoint. Any interference with this legal authority is illegitimate. Anyone who impedes me in my performance of legal actions does me wrong. Hence, the force preventing illegitimate interference is itself legitimate because it makes freedom of action possible. But with his justification of the forcible nature of law, Kant does not open the door to force of any sort whatsoever. Force is only legal insofar as it prevents injustice. Any other use of force is unjust.

69 I. Kant, *The Metaphysics of Morals*, p. 25.
70 Ibid., p. 96.
71 Ibid., p. 97.
72 Ibid., p. 95.
73 I. Kant, 'Idea for a Universal History with a Cosmopolitan Purpose', in I. Kant, *Political Writings*, ed. H.I. Reiss, Cambridge: Cambridge University Press, 1991. Kant also placed an amount of faith in the notion of 'Enlightenment', its progress and the contribution of 'enlightened monarchs'. See I. Kant, 'An Answer to the Question: What is Enlightenment?' in I. Kant, *Political Writings*.
74 I. Kant, 'Idea for a Universal History', p. 44.

75 I. Kant, 'Perpetual Peace: A Philosophical Sketch' in, I. Kant, *Political Writings*, p. 111.
76 To an extent, wider questions of war's relation to 'progress' and enlightenment are discussed in Chapter 6.
77 I. Kant, 'Perpetual Peace', p. 96.
78 Ibid., p. 105, Kant states:

> There is only one rational way in which states coexisting with other states can emerge from the lawless condition of pure warfare. Just like individual men, they must renounce their savage and lawless freedom, adapt themselves to public coercive laws, and thus form an *international state* (*civitas gentium*), which would necessarily continue to grow until it embraced all the peoples of the earth. But since it is not the will of nations, according to their present conception of international right ... this can at best find a negative substitute in the shape of an enduring and gradually expanding *federation* likely to prevent war.

79 Ibid., p. 102; I. Kant, 'Idea for a Universal History', p. 47; I. Kant, *The Metaphysics of Morals*, p. 119.
80 I. Kant, 'Idea for a Universal History', p. 47.
81 On this point, see G. Bennington, 'Frontiers: Two Seminar Sessions', in *Frontiers, The Oxford Literary Review* 14, 1992, 197–227.
82 J-J. Rousseau, 'On the Social Contract', p. 145.
83 Ibid.
84 This notion of standing things on their head and drawing attention to humans as rightful subjects will be taken up again in Chapter 5.
85 J-J. Rousseau, 'On the Social Contract', p. 145.
86 I. Kant, 'Perpetual Peace', footnote to pp. 98–9.
87 On this point, see M.C. Nussbaum, 'Kant and Cosmopolitanism', in J. Bohman and M. Lutz-Bachman (eds) *Perpetual Peace: Essays on Kant's Cosmopolitan Ideal*, Cambridge, MA: MIT Press, 1997, and M.C. Nussbaum, 'Patriotism and Cosmopolitanism', in M.C. Nussbaum and J. Cohen (eds) *For Love of Country?* Boston, MA: Beacon Press, 2002.
88 On this point, see D. Archibugi, 'Immanuel Kant, Cosmopolitan Law and Peace', *European Journal of International Relations*, 1(4), 1995, 429–56, p. 441. See also T. J. Schlereth, *The Cosmopolitan Ideal in Enlightenment Thought*, Notre Dame, IN: University of Notre Dame Press, 1977.
89 I. Kant, 'Perpetual Peace', p. 108.
90 Ibid.
91 Ibid., p. 103.
92 Ibid., p. 104.
93 Ibid., p. 118.
94 Ibid.
95 Ibid., p. 122.
96 Ibid.
97 Ibid.
98 Ibid., p. 123.
99 For a discussion of the way in which Kant's moral theory sits within a tradition of Christian university metaphysics, see I. Hunter, 'The Morals of Metaphysics: Kant's *Groundwork* as Intellectual *Paideia*', *Critical Inquiry*, 28(4), 2002.
100 I am including the USA within the 'Anglo' of this term.
101 The *Charter of the United Nations* (UN Charter) 1945, http://www.un.org/aboutun/charter/ (accessed on 9 June 2008). The Preamble states:

> We the peoples of the United Nations determined to save succeeding generations from the scourge of war, which twice in our lifetime has brought untold sorrow to mankind, and to reaffirm faith in fundamental human rights, in dignity and worth of the human person, in the equal rights of men and women and of nations large and small, and to establish conditions under which justice and respect for the obligations arising from treaties and other sources of international law can be maintained, and to promote social progress and better standards of life in larger freedom.
>
> And for these ends to practise tolerance and live together in peace with one another as good neighbours, and to unite our strength to maintain international peace and security, and to ensure, by the acceptance of principles and the institution of methods, that armed force shall not be used, save in the common interest, and to employ international machinery for the promotion of the economic and social advancement of all peoples.

Article 1(1) states that the Purposes of the United Nations are:

> To maintain international peace and security, and to that end: to take effective collective measures for the prevention and removal of threats to the peace, and for the suppression of acts of aggression or other breaches of the peace, and to bring about by peaceful means, and in conformity with the principles of justice and international law, adjustment or settlement of international disputes or situations which might lead to a breach of peace.

102 UN Charter, Art. 2(4):

> All Members shall refrain in their international relations from the threat or use of force against the territorial integrity or political independence of any state, or in any other manner inconsistent with the Purposes of the United Nations.

103 UN Charter, Art. 51:

> Nothing in the present Charter shall impair the inherent right of individual or collective self-defence if an armed attack occurs against a Member of the United Nations, until the Security Council has taken measures necessary to maintain international peace and security.

104 *General Assembly Declaration on Principles of International Law Concerning Friendly Relations and Co-operation Among States in Accordance with the Charter of the United Nations* (1970), http://daccessdds.un.org/doc/RESOLUTION/GEN/NR0/348/90/IMG/NR034890.pdf?OpenElement (accessed on 9 June 2008). Article 1 states: 'A war of aggression constitutes a crime against the peace for which there is responsibility under international law.'

105 UN Charter, Arts. 3 and 4(1).

106 The *General Assembly Declaration on Principles of International Law* sets out the 'principle of sovereign equality of states' as involving:

> a States are juridically equal.
> b Each state enjoys the rights inherent in full sovereignty.
> c Each state has the duty to respect the personality of other States.
> d The territorial integrity and political independence of the State are inviolable.

e Each State has the right freely to choose and develop its political, social, economic, and cultural systems.
f Each State has the duty to comply fully and in good faith with its international obligations and to live in peace with other States.

107 Note *The Declaration on Measures to Eliminate International Terrorism*, UN General Assembly Resolution 49/60, December 9, 1994, http://www.un.org/documents/ga/res/49/a49r060.htm (accessed on 9 June 2008):

1 The States Members of the United Nations solemnly reaffirm their unequivocal condemnation of all acts, methods and practices of terrorism, as criminal and unjustifiable, wherever and by whomever committed, including those which jeopardize the friendly relations among States and peoples and threaten the territorial integrity and security of States.
2 Acts, methods and practices of terrorism constitute a grave violation of the purposes and principles of the United Nations, which may pose a threat to international peace and security, jeopardize friendly relations among States, hinder international cooperation and aim at the destruction of human rights, fundamental freedoms and the democratic bases of society.
3 Criminal acts intended or calculated to provoke a state of terror in the general public, a group of persons or particular persons for political purposes are in any circumstance unjustifiable, whatever the considerations of a political, philosophical, ideological, racial, ethnic, religious or any other nature that may be invoked to justify them.

The principles of this resolution were affirmed in the *International Convention for the Suppression of Terrorist Bombings*, New York, January 12, 1998, http://www.un.org/law/cod/terroris.htm (accessed on 9 June 2008).

108 See The *Universal Declaration of Human Rights* (1948) http://www.un.org/Overview/rights.html (accessed on 9 June 2008).

109 The term 'the moral force of international law' bears some reference to Derrida's term 'the force of law'. See J. Derrida, 'The Force of Law: The Mystical Foundation of Authority', in D. Cornell, M. Rosenfeld and D.G. Carlson (eds) *Deconstruction and the Possibility of Justice*, New York: Routledge, 1992. On Derrida's account of law, see S. McVeigh, P. Rush and A. Young, 'A Judgment Dwelling in Law: Violence and the Relations of Legal Thought', in A. Sarat (ed.) *Violence and the Possibility of Justice*, Princeton, NJ: Princeton University Press, 2001.

110 On the role of media with respect to propaganda of state war, see E.S. Herman and N. Chomsky, *Manufacturing Consent: The Political Economy of the Mass Media*, New York: Vintage, 1994.

111 The term is taken from Ernst Bloch. See E. Bloch, *Natural Law and Human Dignity*. In terms of the contemporary 'hope' offered by human rights, see C. Douzinas, *The End of Human Rights: Critical Legal Thought at the Turn of the Century*, Oxford: Hart, 2000.

112 Such a 'hope' is enunciated in differing ways by thinkers such as J. Derrida, *Specters of Marx: The State of Debt, the Work of Mourning and the New International*, trans. P. Kamuf, New York: Routledge, 1994; J. Habermas, *The Postnational Constellation: Political Essays*, trans. M. Pensky, Cambridge: Polity Press, 2001; D. Held, *Democracy and the Global Order: From the Modern State to Cosmopolitan Governance*, Cambridge: Polity Press, 1995; A. Linklater, *The Transformation of Political Community: Ethical Foundations of the Post-Westphalian Era*, Cambridge: Polity Press, 1998; T.W. Pogge, *World Poverty and Human Rights: Cosmopolitan Responsibilities and Reforms*, Cambridge: Polity, 2002, and O. O'Neil, *Faces of*

Hunger: An Essay on Poverty, Justice and Development, London: Allen and Unwin, 1986.

113 UN Charter, Arts. 4 and 42.

114 Under the UN Charter, the notion of human rights is not explicitly cited as a legitimate ground for carrying out war. Under Art. 42, the Security Council is granted authority to carry out the use of force. Per Art. 24(2), in carrying out its responsibilities the Security Council is to 'act in accordance with the Purposes and Principles of the United Nations' which specifically mentions human rights. Under this heading it can be interpreted that the Security Council is given a general, but not explicit, degree of legitimacy to conduct violent action in the interests of protecting and preserving human rights.

115 I am trying to keep the discussion of international law here within the boundaries of a Kantian framework so as to point out the limits of Kant's approach to the moral ordering of war and, at the same time, demonstrate the limits of taking a Kantian position (such as that taken by Habermas, among others) in response to contemporary acts of inter-state war. In this respect my comments are not aimed at providing a general analysis of contemporary international law. This is beyond the scope of this chapter. Such an analysis would need to consider among other things: the colonial foundations of international law and international law's continued operation as a tool which legitimates Western neo-colonial projects; the undemocratic nature of the Security Council and the question of, to what extent can such an institution claim to be a 'legitimate authority'?, the links between international law and a system of global capitalism; the conflicting and competing notions of sovereignty within international law; and, the legal, normative and rhetorical practices that allow contemporary international law to hide its 'indeterminacy'. For a broader analysis and critique of international law which considers some of these issues, see M. Koskenniemi, *From Apology to Utopia*, Cambridge: Cambridge University Press, 2005.

116 J. Habermas, 'Bestiality and Humanity: A War on the Border between Legality and Morality', *Constellations*, 6(3), 1999, 269.

117 Ibid., p. 271.

118 Ibid.

119 Ibid., p. 269. Habermas anticipates to a degree the problem of differing states invoking the language of human rights to secure differing national political goals. He notes at pp. 269–70:

> The USA has taken on the superpower's task of assuring order in a system of states only weakly regulated by the UN. Human rights function thereby as a moral orientation for the evaluation of political goals … From the particularly American national perspective of a normatively orientated power politics, it must appear plausible to continue to pursue the struggle against Yugoslavia rigorously and uncompromisingly, despite all complications and, if necessary, with ground troops. That position at least has the advantage of being consistent. But what do we say when one day the military alliance of another region – for example, in Asia – pursues the politics of human rights with military means in accordance with a very different interpretation of international law or the UN Charter?

120 Ibid. Habermas seems to think that because human rights have a 'juridical character' the scope for states using the moral claim of human rights to pursue their national interests is limited. He claims:

> Things look different when human rights not only come into play as a moral orientation for one's own political activity, but as rights which have to be

implemented in a legal sense. Human rights possess the structural attributes of subjective rights which, irrespective of their purely moral content, by nature are dependent on attaining positive validity within a system of compulsory law.

121 J. Habermas, 'Kant's Idea of Perpetual Peace, With the Benefit of Two Hundred Years Hindsight', in J. Bohman and M. Lutz-Bachman (eds) *Perpetual Peace: Essays on Kant's Cosmopolitan Idea,* Cambridge, MA: MIT Press, 1997, p. 140.
122 Ibid.
123 That is, the classical notion of legitimate authority and the right to the use of violence flowing from this.
124 UN Charter, Art. 34.
125 Ibid., Art. 37(2).
126 Ibid., Arts. 41 and 42.
127 Ibid., Art. 51.
128 Ibid., Art. 52.
129 Ibid., Art. 52(1).
130 It is noted that for international lawyers there is ongoing debate around how broadly one can and should read Art. 51 and the 'legal' right of states to go to war in the situation of 'individual and collective self-defence if an armed attack occurs against a Member of the United Nations'. Especially in attempting to justify the 'legal' legitimacy of state aggression, many governments and lawyers attempt to broaden the notion of 'collective self-defence' beyond the notion of member states to include a defence of 'humanity' as the new 'collective' body. Such efforts are dubious and are attempts to gain a legal authority under international law for acts of violence in situations where there is no such authority. The lawyers who put forward such claims are the 'sorry comforters' whom Kant rightly denounces. The notion of 'pre-emptive self-defence' is more complicated. In the case where two actors within a potential conflict both have a nuclear weapons capability, then the nature of the technology of warfare radically changes what historically 'pre-emption' might have meant. At some point the boundaries between the concepts of 'attack', 'aggression', 'pre-emptive attack', and 'self-defence' begin to merge and attempts to clearly delineate relevant meanings become highly problematic.
131 This account might appear to some as an over-simplification of international law. The alternative (and current practice for some lawyers) is a move towards legal arguments that attempt to broaden notions such as 'self defence' or interpret historical declarations of the Security Council in such a manner that almost any form of violence can be included under the umbrella of 'legal' legitimacy. The approach presented here concentrates instead upon what is meant by the term 'law' specifically in relation to the problem of violence. If international law is to have any continued meaning and significance as *law,* then the issue of who may legally use violence, and who has the authority to pass judgment over violence in global terms, needs to be taken seriously. All else reverts to mere sophistry and either erodes international law as *law* or demonstrates that perhaps international law is not yet fully *law* in any practical and authoritative sense.
132 If the contract was momentarily 'dissolved', then it was quickly re-constituted after the invasion with the UN moving quickly to sanction the continued occupation of Iraq after the illegal invasion. That an invasion by an aggressive state can be 'illegal' but a subsequent occupation by the same state be 'legal' under international law only proves the rhetorical powers and lack of moral convictions held by many international lawyers and the flexibility of a legal system which can, with a straight face, accommodate such a glaring legal and historical contradiction.

133 Consider the contemporary suggestion of the establishment of a parallel, so-called, 'league of democracies' set up and led by the USA as an alternative inter-state executive to that of the current Security Council. See R. Kagan, 'The Case for a League of Democracies', *Financial Times*, 13 May 2008.

134 A maxim that allowed war to be fought 'only for the purpose of establishing a rightful condition of freedom' would also fall into contradiction if considered as a universal law. If, for Kant, a rightful condition of freedom may be thought to involve the case where universally an individual's actions do not hinder another's, then the act of war would occur as a force that hinders another state's immediate autonomy (as a form of freedom) for the purposes of bringing it into a condition of freedom. While such a hindrance through force might be thought allowable at the level of law, it is questionable whether it works at a level of moral action. In a Kantian sense, under the condition of law, the freedom of individuals (moral agents) is limited by a higher institutional authority for the purpose of making freedom possible. When this legal authority is absent and the act of war of a moral agent is considered as a force which 'enables freedom', the situation arises where some moral agents have their freedom limited while others (the enforcers), if even only for a time, are given a wider sphere of freedom in their hindrance of their others. In this respect some moral agents hinder while others are hindered and this seems to contradict the basic principles of Kant's account of freedom. Part of the problem is that Kant's account of morality presupposes the violence of the state which, at times, is exempted from certain requirements of the moral law. The problem arises in the inter-state relation where there is no higher legal authority because Kant's account of the moral law cannot come to terms with foundation questions of violence, as these were, in a sense, always solved through the back door by the acceptance of the historical legitimacy of the monarch's violence. In the inter-state relation Kant's theory cannot get from morality to the establishment of a condition of law because his theory of law refuses to conceptualize the violent origins of the state.

135 Note here I. Kant, *The Metaphysics of Morals*, at p. 117, Kant argues:

> The greatest difficulty in the right of nations has to do precisely with right during a war; it is even difficult to form a concept of this or to think of law in this lawless state without contradicting oneself (*inter alia silent leges*) [*In time of war the laws are silent*]. Right during a war would, then, have to be the waging of war in accordance with the principles that always leave open the possibility of leaving the state of nature among states (in external relation to one another) and entering a rightful condition.

Whether Kant's formulation of this 'right to war' could stand up to the test of the categorical imperative without falling into contradiction is questionable. Kant seems here to be aware of this and is caught between his own moral philosophy which would not allow this kind of war, and a pragmatic view that believes that somehow a condition of international law securing peace, freedom and human rights, must be realized.

136 One attempt to get around this contradiction would be to introduce a notion of 'time' into the maxim. For example, consider the maxim 'I may go to war with the aim of gaining peace and protecting human rights in the long term, knowing that my efforts will not contribute to peace or protect human rights in the short term.' When considered as a universal law, such a maxim still falls into contradiction. It relies upon a promise that one can secure peace or human rights in the long term by sacrificing peace and human rights in the short term. However, the moral actor

is in no position to make such a promise, especially in the case of war, the moral actor has no control over future events, over the length of the war, or over whether the whole of humanity might perish through the escalation of conflict. Further, all of these terms such as 'peace', 'self-defence', 'injury', presuppose particular values and levels of abstraction which are contested socially. Their application to 'facts' within social reality falls back into something of an epistemic and interpretive war of all against all.

137 C. Schmitt, *The Concept of the Political*, trans. G. Schwab, Chicago, IL: University of Chicago Press, 1996, p. 54. To a certain extent, Habermas recognizes also such an operation. See J. Habermas, 'Kant's Idea of Perpetual Peace'. At, p. 147, Habermas argues:

> The politics of human rights undertaken by a world organization turns into a fundamentalism of human rights only when it undertakes an intervention that is really nothing more than the struggle of one party against the other and thus uses a moral legitimation as a cover for a false juridical justification.

See also the discussion in J. Derrida, *On Cosmopolitanism and Forgiveness*, trans. M. Dooley and M. Hughes, London: Routledge, 2001. At p. 29 with a certain Schmittian resonance, Derrida argues: '[H]ere is a human race which would claim to accuse itself all at once, publicly and spectacularly, of all the crimes committed in effect by itself against itself, "against humanity".'

138 On the strengthened re-emergence of this moralist 'just war' in the twentieth century, see C. Schmitt, *The Nomos of the Earth*, trans. G.L. Ulmen, New York: Telos Press 2003, pp. 259–80; C. Douzinas, 'Postmodern Just Wars: Kosovo, Afghanistan and the New World Order', in J. Strawson (ed.) *Law After Ground Zero*, London: Glasshouse Press, 2002; C. Douzinas, *Human Rights and Empire: The Political Philosophy of Cosmopolitanism*, Abingdon: Routledge-Cavendish, 2007.

139 These being the supposed (though non-existent) existence in Iraq of so-called 'weapons of mass destruction' and links between the Iraqi regime and militant Islamicist political organizations for the supply of such weapons. See US Secretary of State, Colin Powell's speech to the UN Security Council, 5 February, 2002, http://www.whitehouse.gov/news/releases/2003/02/20030205–1.html (accessed on 9 June 2008).

140 Their moral 'belief' bears stark resemblance to the religious beliefs held by others in the past and the present.

Chapter 4

The ethics of recognition

I

Both the traditions of the juridical and moral ordering of war continue to exercise a great deal of influence over how a concept of war is understood in late modernity. To a great extent, contemporary thinking about war and the manner through which a notion of right is attached to war are still ordered by these traditions of thinking. Generally, the right to war is understood as state sovereign war, a de-theologized form of violence which excludes from its sphere of legitimacy non-sovereign violence. The right to war is also morally ordered. A Western moral discourse attempts to limit state war and places state actors under a moral obligation to adhere to and realize a form of supra-state cosmopolitan law. In many cases, war is framed as a secular, moral form of just war under which justification is claimed through grand concepts such as peace, freedom, human rights and democracy.

This chapter introduces another form of war's ordering called the *ethical ordering of war*. An account of the ethical ordering of war is developed by Georg Wilhelm Friedrich Hegel. Hegel inherits both the Westphalian juridical notion of war as state sovereign war and Kant's critical and moral philosophy. In part, Hegel re-frames the moral account of war to comprehend the operation of war within a wider theory of ethical life (*Sittlichkeit*). Hegel orders war around an ethical theory which focuses upon the role and status of war in the realization of human freedom within the ethical life of the modern state. At first glance, Hegel's account of war might appear as somewhat dangerous. For some, it conjures up images of authoritarian or Fascist states of the past and the present which justify wars fought for the glory of the nation, race or civilization. The connection of Hegel to absolutism and Fascism has always been tenuous and highly unfair to Hegel.[1] Significantly, such assertions have mischaracterized Hegel's efforts to demonstrate how any account of ethics and ethical life is bound up with the work of violence. From a Hegelian perspective, an account of ethics fails if it does not attempt to understand the position of violence within ethics itself. Many Western accounts of ethics within modernity have ignored the significance of this Hegelian lesson and have run into crippling conceptual difficulties when they are forced to rely upon violence to realize their own particular moral positions.

There are certainly some unsettling moments within Hegel's approach to war and his account of an *ethics of exclusion*. However, it is intellectually dishonest to simply reduce Hegel's account of war to these elements. When Hegel's account of war is placed within his wider philosophical system and method, then his account can be seen to draw attention to some central insights into war which many moderns simply overlook. This chapter shows how Hegel places war within the context of a wider theoretical relation between thinking and violence and within a cognitive and ethical theory of *recognition* (*Anerkennung*). This theory attempts to explain some of the causes of social and institutional violence and how, as a *praxis of recognition*, social violence might be overcome or at least minimized. By reading Hegel's account of war through an interpretation of Hegel's philosophy in which a theory of recognition is given central emphasis, this chapter draws out aspects of the ethical ordering of war and its relevance to thinking about the rightness of war in the present.

II

The account presented here reads Hegel's philosophy with the questions of violence, war and law in mind. One means of considering some of the aspects of Hegel's philosophy that impact upon and are presupposed by his account of war is to focus upon Hegel's inheritance of the notion of the spontaneity of thinking originating in Kant and further developed by Johann Gottlieb Fichte. Central to the tradition of transcendental philosophy developed by Kant, Fichte and Hegel is the idea of *thinking as action, thinking as its own deed*. How Hegel develops this idea into his own original account of thinking has consequences for the attempt to comprehend Hegel's account of war.

In the *Critique of Pure Reason*, Kant argues that cognition arises from two sources in the mind, the first involves the reception of representations (intuition), the second involves an active faculty of cognizing an object by means of these representations. This later notion involves a 'spontaneity' of cognition and is referred to in a general sense by Kant as the faculty of the understanding (*Verstand*).[2] This spontaneous activity of thinking is crucial for Kant. It occurs as a fundamental act of self-emanation without which the cognition of sensible representations would not be possible. Kant argues:

> The *I think* must *be able* to accompany all my representations; for otherwise something would be represented in me that could not be thought at all, which is as much as to say that the representation would either be impossible or else at least would be nothing for me. That representation that can be given prior to all thinking is called *intuition*. Thus the manifold of all intuition has a necessary relation to the *I think* in the same subject in which this manifold is to be encountered. But this representation is an act

> [*Actus*] of *spontaneity*, i.e. it cannot be regarded as belonging to sensibility. I call it the *pure apperception*, in order to distinguish it from the *empirical* one, or also the *original apperception*, since it is that self-consciousness which, because it produces the representation *I think*, which must be able to accompany all others and which in all consciousness is one and the same, cannot be accompanied by any further representation. I also call its unity the *transcendental* unity of self-consciousness in order to designate the possibility of *a priori* cognition from it. For the manifold representations that are given in a certain intuition would not altogether be *my* representations if they did not altogether belong to a self-consciousness; i.e., as my representations (even if I am not conscious of them as such) they must yet necessarily be in accord with the condition under which alone they *can* stand together in a universal self-consciousness, because otherwise they would not throughout belong to me. From this original combination much may be inferred.[3]

For Kant, the 'I think' expresses the act of the thinking self's determination of its existence. It is through the *spontaneous act of thinking* that there is such a thing as intelligence.[4] This activity underlying human intelligence bears degrees of similarity with an intellectual activity that is claimed by Kant as the basis of transcendental freedom within his resolution of the 'third antinomy of pure reason'. While each activity should not be reduced to the other, for Kant, there seems to be something significant that is shared between these two activities – an activity of the 'I' residing at the basis of both human intelligence and human freedom.

An account of the spontaneity of thinking as an *act* or *deed* is given a radical emphasis by Fichte and his broad notion of thinking as '*Tathandlung*'. In *The Science of Knowledge* (1794),[5] Fichte develops an account of the thinking self that is not originally reliant upon a sensible or empirical world but which creates itself or emanates from itself as an act of *self-positing*. For Fichte, while the activity of thinking or the intellect is spontaneous, it is not chaotic or lawless. Fichte argues that the intellect acts, but owing to its nature it can only act in a certain fashion. In this sense, for Fichte, there is a certain 'law of action' of the intellect and there are 'necessary laws of the intellect'.[6]

Taking the place of, or re-interpreting, Kant's notion of the 'transcendental unity of apperception', Fichte introduces a conception of the activity of the thinking intellect as the act of *positing* (*setzen*). Such a move is seen as necessary so that the categories of the understanding (within the framework of Kant's architectonic) can actually be derived. For Fichte, the intellect or the self is not posited by something else but is posited by itself, it is an act of *self-positing*. Fichte argues:

> The self's own positing of itself is thus its own pure activity. The *self posits itself*, and by virtue of this mere self-assertion it *exists*; and conversely, the

> self *exists* and *posits* its own existence by the virtue of merely existing. It is at once the agent and the product of action; the active, and what the activity brings about; action and deed are one and the same, and hence the 'I am' expresses an Act, and the only one possible, as will inevitably appear from the Science of Knowledge as a whole.[7]

For Fichte, this conception of thinking as being an act which posits itself cannot be proved empirically.[8] Rather, it arises as a form of intellectual intuition (*intellektuele Anschauung*) which Fichte compares to the form of sensible intuition (*sinnliche Anschauung*) of space and time presupposed by Kant.[9] On this notion of intellectual intuition, Fichte argues:

> This intuiting of himself that is required of the philosopher, in performing the act whereby the self arises for him, I refer to as *intellectual intuition*. It is the immediate consciousness that I act, and what I enact: it is that whereby I know something because I do it. We cannot prove from concepts that this power of intellectual intuition exists, nor evolve from them what it may be. Everyone must discover it immediately in himself, or he will never make its acquaintance. The demand to have it proved for one by reasoning is vastly more extraordinary than would be the demand of a person born blind to have it explained to him what colours are, without his needing to see.
>
> Everyone, to be sure, can be shown, in his own admitted experience, that this intellectual intuition occurs at every moment of his consciousness. I cannot take a step, move a hand or foot, without an intellectual intuition of my self-consciousness in these acts; only so do I know that *I* do it, only so do I distinguish my action, and myself therein, from the object of action before me. Whosoever ascribes an activity to himself, appeals to this intuition. The source of life is contained therein, and without it there is death.[10]

Fichte attempts to outline the basic operation of the self-positing of the self (*das Ich*). He begins with the basic proposition 'A is A' or 'A = A' and its suggestion that 'if A exists, then A exists'.[11] For Fichte, the necessary connection between 'if' and 'then' (named 'X') expresses a form of positing, in the sense that 'A' is posited, therefore 'A' is.[12] Fichte extends this conception to include a universal notion of self abstracted from empirical content, expressed as 'I = I' or 'I am I'.[13] Fichte argues:

> But the proposition 'I am I' has a meaning wholly different from that of 'A is A'. For the latter has content only under a certain condition. *If* A is posited, it is naturally posited *as* A, as having the predicate A. But this proposition still tells us nothing as to *whether* it actually is posited, and hence whether it is posited with any particular predicate. Yet the proposition 'I

> am I' is unconditionally and absolutely valid, since it is equivalent to the proposition X; it is valid not merely in form but also in content. In it the I is posited, not conditionally, but absolutely, with the predicate of equivalence to itself; hence it really *is* posited, and the proposition can be expressed as *I am*.[14]

This 'I', for Fichte, as the spontaneous act of the intellect, is grounded upon its own activity, it is 'absolutely posited'.[15] For him, the 'I' refers to the 'absolute subject': 'That whose being or essence consists simply in the fact that it posits itself as existing.'[16]

Following the notion of the positing of identity, Fichte introduces the notion of the positing of opposition, through the proposition '~A is not equal to A' (~A ≠ A; which involves: ~A = ~A).[17] Fichte argues that if any ~A were posited, this would presuppose an A, and in this sense the ~A would need to be understood as materially conditioned. For Fichte, in the positing of an ~A, an A must also be posited.[18] Fichte argues: 'As surely as the absolute certainty of the proposition '~A is not equal to A' is unconditionally admitted among the facts of empirical consciousness, *so surely is a not-self opposed absolutely to the self*.'[19] From this basis, Fichte puts forward the notion that the positing of every A involves the implicit positing of the ~A, and vice versa. Fichte extends this to the notion that the positing of the self (I) involves the implicit positing of the not-self (~I) and that the self is posited through the simultaneous positing of both itself and what is other than itself, the not-self. For him, when the self posits itself through its opposite it is positing its limit.[20] He argues that: 'To *limit* something is to abolish its reality, not *wholly* but in *part* only, by negation.'[21] Such limitation through negation points to the notion of divisibility and the notion that the self and not-self are posited as divisible.[22] Fichte argues that: 'In the self I oppose a divisible not self to the divisible self.'[23]

The notion of the spontaneous activity of thinking which posits both itself and its not-self or 'other' is inherited by Hegel.[24] Further, the central idea of thinking as a deed is taken up by Hegel and given a radical re-interpretation, especially in relation to the operation of negation. For Kant and Fichte, the deed of thinking, its self-positing and negation of its self and its other, took place purely in the realm of thinking. In the *Science of Logic* (1812–16),[25] Hegel is similarly concerned with the realm of pure reason and demonstrates, contra Kant, that contradictions are not confined to merely the four 'cosmological antinomies of pure reason' but are contained within every act of thinking. For Hegel, pure reason, as with all human thinking, is *antinomical*, it is characterized by *contradiction* and hence, transcendental philosophy needs to comprehend the role, operation and activity of contradiction within pure reason.[26]

While Hegel in his *Logic* is concerned with the realm of pure reason, the relation between his *Phenomenology of Spirit* (1807)[27] and the *Logic* is such as to make his undertaking consistent with the activity of actual thinking within the living, social world in the realm of *spirit* (*Geist*). In the *Phenomenology of*

Spirit, Hegel shows how the deeds of thinking (drawn into view by Kant and Fichte) occur also as physical, social deeds within an inter-subjective and inter-institutional human world. By making such a move, Hegel forges an original and crucial link between the tradition of transcendental philosophy and the operation of human violence. The link has consequences for any account of morality or ethics that presupposes or develops historically from Kant's notion of transcendental freedom.

III

In the *Phenomenology of Spirit*, Hegel inherits the necessary relationship occurring in the positing of the self between self and not-self, or between self and other, developed by Fichte. Hegel takes this relationship, which for Fichte is implicit in both the notion and existence of the 'I', and places it back within a living world of not only sense experience and perception but also a world containing physical materiality and living, breathing other beings. A notion of 'world' is not added to Fichte's account of the self, it is already implicit in the notion of the not-self, which must include everything *other* than the self. Hegel simply makes this more explicit and asks the question: how does the self come to be itself as distinct from its not-self? Further, how does the self precisely come to draw the limits of itself from its other and thus *become conscious of itself* in a way that it might be *certain* that what it *intuits* as itself (the 'I') is actually itself and not, in fact, something other?

For Hegel, if we can have an immediate sense or intellectual intuition of a particular 'I' that simply *is*, or that exists, then there arises a philosophical problem involving how this specific, immediate 'I' can be distinguished from something else. He claims that if we try to identify the immediate 'I' that we *mean*, then it is taken as something different from something else, it is a 'this' rather than a 'that'.[28] Hegel argues that there is a difference between the 'this' or the object that we might *mean* and the 'this' or the object that is expressed through words. Hegel argues:

> It is a universal too that we *utter* what the sensuous [content] is. What we say is: 'This', i.e. the *universal* This; or 'it is', i.e. *Being in general*. Of course, we do not *envisage* the universal This or Being in general, but we *utter* the universal; in other words, we do not strictly say what in this sense-certainty we *mean* to say. But language, as we see, is the more truthful; in it, we ourselves directly refute what we *mean* to say, and since the universal is the true [content] of sense-certainty and language expresses this true [content] alone, it is just not possible for us ever to say, or express in words, a sensuous being that we *mean*.[29]

In one sense, Hegel can be understood as arguing against a tradition that tries to ground transcendental philosophy upon a notion of *intellectual intuition* and demands that if an account of self-consciousness is to be a subject of philosophy (rather than a subject of aesthetics), then it needs to be explained through a philosophical language. In another sense, by suggesting the 'truthfulness' of language Hegel draws out a speculative theme latent in Fichte but not fully brought to bear in philosophy. The theme involves the notion of *mediation* in general which is most apparent in the use of symbols and words within language which have meaning as points of designation and universality only in some form of relation to their others. The relation between self and not-self occurs as one basic speculative form, each term has meaning only in its relation of distinction from the other. Further, when one term is *meant*, a sense of the distinction from the other, a reference to this other, and thus, the other, is contained within this meaning. For Hegel, comprehending an object concretely, rather than abstractly, involves grasping how its content, or the object itself, is mediated through such a relation.

From Hegel's viewpoint, Kant and Fichte have only presented an abstract account of the 'I' or self-consciousness. They have not yet grasped a concrete account of self-consciousness which would come about through paying attention to how self-consciousness is mediated. Part of the structure of Hegel's *Phenomenology of Spirit* presents a speculative account of self-consciousness by moving from the abstract to the more concrete. Hegel can be seen to do this by drawing attention to the operation of mediation (*Vermittlung*), negation and the manner in which the knowledge of an object gains a greater speculative or determinate content when viewed in terms of its necessary interrelations with its others. In relation to the Fichtean account of the self, this involves comprehending its self-positing in relation to its not-self, this being a world of physical objects and other intelligent human subjects.

For Hegel, the Fichtean self-consciousness exists in a world where it has some immediate sense of itself, the 'I', and where it is confronted by something that is not itself, a world of appearance. In its existence, self-consciousness posits both itself and its not-self, however, it is not completely certain of the boundaries or limits of itself. That is, it cannot be certain of the limits of the self, as determined by the not-self, because this boundary is marked (for Kant and Fichte) by the uncertain and often erroneous world of appearance. Hegel argues that the self wants to become fully conscious of what it is, that is, it wants to become self-conscious and wants to know itself with certainty rather than vagueness.[30] Hegel calls this demand, need or drive that the self know itself and know itself as an identity or unity that is distinct from its not-self, 'desire' (*Begierde*) in general.[31]

By placing the abstract 'I' in the world, Hegel positions the self within a broader category of 'life'.[32] Positioned within a world of life and driven by a desire to know itself with certainty, the self, in the manner of Kant, cannot withdraw from a world of appearance and turn back into itself. If the self withdrew from the world of appearance into itself, it would never be able to know with any certainty the limits of the boundaries of itself – the self would not *know* where *it* ends and where the shadowy world of appearance begins. Rather, for Hegel, the only means by which a self might come to know what *it is*, is through the experience of learning the limits of itself through becoming aware of the independence of its objects, that is, the independence of what *is* the not-self.[33] For Hegel, it is through the outward mediated *experience* of the world and not through some form of purely *internal* knowing or intellectual intuition that a consciousness becomes a self-consciousness. This is not to say that Hegel rejects entirely any immediate knowledge of self. Rather, he draws attention the fact that any form of immediate knowledge is *always* mediated through the self's experience of its implicit relation with the external world.[34]

One aspect of the speculative account Hegel presents involves the sense that through the self's experience of the not-self there occurs a radical change in both the self's knowledge of itself and the self's knowledge of the world. By experiencing a certain independence of an object in the world, for example, in the way that it needs to be moved, or that it can be eaten or chopped down, the self comes to a firmer, more detailed, and more concrete knowledge of its objects. Further, through this greater knowledge of the objects of the not-self, the self comes to a firmer, more concrete and more detailed knowledge of itself: a knowledge of what it *is* through reflecting upon the character, qualities and forms contained within the relations and mediations between itself and what is other than itself.

What was initially a very abstract concept of the self's being, the simple assertion 'I am' has now taken on a more concrete content. What being is for the 'I' is radically different after the process of experiencing and its own reflection upon this process. By drawing attention to how the self's knowledge of itself is *constituted* through its experience of mediation with the not-self and its reflection upon this experience, Hegel draws attention to the *speculative nature* of knowing and the production of knowledge. In this both the knowing *subject* and the known *object* are constituted through each other.[35] For Hegel, grasping the *subject-object* character of all knowledge is central to the task of any critical, or now, speculative philosophy.

For Fichte, the self's relation to its not-self involved the operation of *negation*. The self distinguished or determined itself and maintained its self-identity through the negation of what was other than it. In Fichte, this self-inscription of the unity of the 'I' through negation took place purely at the level of thinking. Negation was an act of thinking and as taking place within the realm of thought, when the not-self was 'negated', no physical harm was done. For Hegel, if we are to consider what self-consciousness in fact *is*, then the self needs to be understood as positioned firmly within the physical and social world, within *life*, where the self's demand for unity and certainty of self-identity operates as both mental and physical desire (the passions).[36] Placed within the realm of life, the self's negation of the object occurs no longer purely as an act of thinking. Rather, this act of thinking occurs also as a physical act whereby the negation of the object by the self involves harm, destruction, killing, violence. For the self which has not yet understood the speculative connection between itself and the other, this negation is easy, it sees the object merely as the negative of itself (without a positive content of its own) and treats it accordingly. Hegel argues:

> Certain of the nothingness of this other, it explicitly affirms that this nothingness is *for it* the truth of the other; it destroys the independent object and thereby gives itself the certainty of itself as a *true* certainty, a certainty which has become explicit for self-consciousness itself *in an objective manner*.[37]

For Hegel, the desire for a self to fully become certain of itself, to become conscious of itself, does not gain satisfaction in the self's relation to the bare world of objects. Part of this rests in the fact that these objects have only a limited independence in relation to the self, and hence they can be negated relatively easily in the self's assertion of its self-identity. Where the self does, however, gain satisfaction, argues Hegel, where it becomes self-conscious, is when it confronts another intelligent self: when the opposing not-self or, other, is an intelligent self. Hegel argues: 'Self-conscious achieves its satisfaction only in another self-conscious.'[38] For Hegel:

> A self-consciousness exists *for a self-consciousness*. Only so is it in fact self-consciousness; for only in this way does the unity of itself in its otherness become explicit for it. The 'I' which is the object of its notion is in fact not 'object'; the object of desire, however, is only independent, for it is the universal indestructible substance, the fluid self-identical essence. A self-consciousness, in being an object, is just as much 'I' as 'object'. With this, we already have before us the notion of *spirit*. What still lies ahead for consciousness is the experience of what spirit is – this absolute substance which is the unity of the different independent self-consciousnesses which, in their opposition, enjoy perfect freedom and independence; 'I' that is 'We' and 'We' that is 'I' [*ich, das Wir, und Wir, das Ich ist*]. It is in self-consciousness, in the notion of spirit, that consciousness first finds its turning point, where it leaves behind it the colourful show of the sensuous here and now and the nightlike void of the supersensible beyond, and steps out into the spiritual daylight of the present.[39]

For Hegel, the self only finds some form of certainty in its pursuit of self-knowledge when it begins to comprehend itself in relation to another intelligent self that stands before it as the not-self. The self may only comprehend its unity or self-identity through a comprehension of how it is *constituted* through a relation of *mediation* with the other. The relation of mediation between self and other constitutes the limits of the self; the boundaries of the self are drawn or produced through the active relation of mediation between self and other, and through the self's reflection upon this relation as the operation of self-inscription and self-positing.

In this respect, the self is not something that exists before coming into contact with the world but is itself *produced* through its relation of mediation with its others. On this side of thinking and self-reflection, the creative, constitutive, spontaneous act of thinking occurs as mediation itself, it is mediation (*Vermittlung*). In a sense, for Hegel, the self or 'I' is always mediated, its act of thinking is always an act of mediation with its self and with its other. The 'I' is a middle term, it is a middle and process of mediation between the self and the other. From such a standpoint, the 'I' needs to be understood as a 'We'. The self cannot be thought of as the merely atomistic individual but is always a process of mediation such that the concept of 'self' now includes within it the process of co-constitution between intelligent beings. For Hegel, self-consciousness is a relation between immediacy and mediation, a relation between the drive of the immediate 'I' for its self-identity and the reflection upon the constitution of selves through their others as a 'We': a relation between the notions of the *subject as spirit* and *spirit as subject*.

For Hegel, understood as a relation between immediacy and mediation, the attempt of the self to know itself involves the effort to see-into or know the other. Only through knowing what the other is, might the self more firmly comprehend itself and come to understand the content and limits of itself. Hegel calls the process of attempting to comprehend the not-self or the other the process of recognition (*Anerkennung*). Hegel sketches two forms or outcomes of this process which are not mutually exclusive.[40] The first involves a successful moment of recognition in which each self recognizes itself as mutually recognizing the other.[41] The second involves an unsuccessful moment of recognition in which one self is recognized and the other is recognizing.[42] This unsuccessful moment involves the operation of *misrecognition*.[43]

In the successful moment, or moment of mutual recognition, each intelligent self is faced by the fact that their not-self is also an intelligent being. In this moment what was formerly simply something other and defined only negatively in relation to the self, is now seen to have a content, as intelligence, which is not completely alien to the self's comprehension of itself. The self's recognition of the other does involve a moment of identification with the other but does not involve the reduction of the other to the same. Rather, in the process of recognition, the self comes to know and appreciate the position and status of the not-self within its own self. The self comes to recognize and appreciate *the other within itself*.

For Hegel, in recognizing the other within itself, the self affirms this otherness and therefore does not try to negate the other, but lets the other go free.[44] What is recognized is not simply the other, but the constitutive role of the other in the self, the necessity of the other for the self to be itself. Recognition involves an affirmation by the self that a necessary and essential element of itself resides in the other and in the relation of mediation with it. Such an encounter involves the possible moment of *transformation* within the self's comprehension of itself – a moment where the self leaves its limited and atomistic view of itself and grasps the 'nature' of itself as epistemologically, socially and ontologically, subject-object.

This road to Damascus-style comprehension of the 'I' as the product of a mediated, inter-subjective 'We', or as *spirit* (*Geist*) more generally, can be read in part, as Hegel's critical reformulation of Rousseau's individual within the social contract who realizes their social being through the notion of the 'general will'.[45] In this sense, Hegel's notion of mutual recognition involves an account of how a human subject may overcome its alienation from its others. For Hegel, this overcoming of alienation occurs at both the level of knowledge – as a dialectical or speculative comprehension of the self – and at a level of praxis, via the affirmation of the other's difference and autonomy. This side of recognition lies at the basis of Hegel's account of how freedom is produced and of how ethical norms develop practically. In his discussion of ethics, law and society in the *Philosophy of Right* (1821),[46] Hegel tries to show how freedom is produced and moments of alienation are overcome through the differing social and institutional *forms* of inter-subjective recognition which occur within modern social and political life.

While Hegel sees in the moment of recognition the possibility of the overcoming of alienation and unfreedom, he also sees in its operation the *production* of alienation, unfreedom and domination though the operation of misrecognition. And just as his accounts in the *Phenomenology of Spirit* and in the *Philosophy of Right* show recognition's positive effects in relation to freedom, he also highlights how particular forms of recognition produce the negative effects of limited freedom, unfreedom, alienation, domination, control, and violent killing within social and material life. By holding onto a diverse range of effects that are produced by a process of recognition Hegel begins to develop a powerful theory that helps to explain social violence and the role of norms, or concepts of right, within such violence.

For Hegel, the moment of successful, mutual recognition is bound up with the moment of unsuccessful recognition, or misrecognition. In the operation of misrecognition the self behaves in relation to its now intelligent other in the same way as it had behaved in relation to the world at large. That is, the self in its drive to self-identity and self-certainty affirms itself by negating its other. In the moment of misrecognition the self does not recognize the other within itself or the relation of mutual co-constitution between self and other, it merely sees its immediate view of self as significant and everything else as insignificant.

Further, misrecognition can be interpreted as involving the operation of *error* within the moment of self-reflection. The *mis* of misrecognition refers to a moment of cognitive error, mistake, and slippage or a moment where self-consciousness cannot get past elements of its own immediacy to comprehend its mediated nature. The *mis* of misrecognition also involves the operation of finitude within human cognition in its efforts to comprehend the infinite. In a sense, the finite self can only comprehend its infinite mediated character, by grasping differing parts that make up a whole. In attempting to grasp itself as a unity or a whole, the self can only grasp fragile, weak, limited moments of itself in its relations to its many others.

For Hegel, the recurrent moment of error does not condemn the self's attempt to know itself and the world to failure. Rather, the process of recognition describes the effort of a spontaneous, creative human intelligence attempting to come to terms with its own errors and limitations. This involves a certain restlessness of thinking which is always pushed by itself to reach beyond its own limitations.[47] The self's recognition of the other does not just happen once, it is an act of thinking that needs to be repeated again and again. Every cognition needs to be continually re-cognized and the self will only come to some form of self-certainty through these ongoing acts and efforts. Further, recognition draws attention to the creative aspect of human thinking whereby it only begins to develop by coming to terms with its own errors. The capacity of thinking to come to terms with error, limitation, and contradiction more generally is given significant emphasis by Hegel.

If operating purely within the realm of thinking, misrecognition, error, mistake and the assertion of a naïve sense of self-certainty against the other would not have violent consequences. Hegel, however, places the recognizing self within a living, physical world of intelligent human subjects. In this context the moment of misrecognition of the other, the refusal to recognize the other, the act of self-positing at the expense of the other, and the negation of the other all have physical, material consequences. Hegel quite clearly describes this as *violence*: the seeking of the death of the other and the staking of the self's own life so that two selves engage in a life and death struggle.[48] In this struggle each self learns not only that the other is independent, but, also, that as a living being, the self may also be treated as an object that can be negated. In a sense, through being negated by the other's misrecognition, the self is faced with its own limits and its extreme finitude within the possibility of death. For Hegel, through relative levels of power and the fear of death, one self succumbs to the other, recognizes the other as master (*Herr*) and assumes the subservient position of slave (*Knecht*).[49]

Through this account Hegel can be seen to be presenting quite a stark and original theory which draws attention to the relation between the act of thinking and the deeds that occur in the natural, physical world.[50] For Hegel, the act of self-positing and the act of negation have physical consequences that impact upon the self's attempt to gain knowledge of itself. In one sense, Hegel's account of recognition draws attention to a certain form of violence, or at least the unaccounted for possibility of violence, residing within the transcendental philosophy of Kant and Fichte. In abstracting from the world, this transcendental philosophy abstracts from violence. However, to the extent that Kant and Fichte speak of a self-consciousness which exists in the world, then their account participates in a form of violence which they remain unaware of or hide. Such an unawareness impacts upon their attempts to construct a practical, moral philosophy.

In another sense, Hegel begins to point to one significant theoretical form of comprehending human, social violence based upon the operation of positing and negation within human thinking. Through Hegel, the *deeds* of thinking become closely related to the physical deeds of human life: a certain violence of positing and negativity. Viewed in such a light, the metaphors drawn upon by Hobbes and Kant of war occurring as a 'war between thoughts' start to become a little closer to being perhaps something more of an appropriate view of human, social reality.

In terms of developing an account of social violence, Hegel's notion of the 'duel' fought between two subjects resulting in the relation of dominance by the master over the slave, is significant. Hegel's account draws together an epistemological desire of an individual to have both knowledge of the world and control over how the world is known, together with the physical passions that manifest in drives for self-realization, self-empowerment and the desire for physical control over territory and over other human bodies. Sitting behind this account, as will be shown shortly through a discussion of Hegel's *Jena Manuscripts* (1802–06), is also a subject's desire to have its normative world-view govern the lives of others. In drawing together these three accounts of human 'nature' – epistemological, biological and normative – into a theory of recognition, Hegel develops an account of social conflict and violence which builds upon and supersedes the preceding accounts delivered by Hobbes and Rousseau. Hobbes's notion of a conflict for the supremacy of differing moral and truth claims is re-framed by Hegel as a struggle for recognition. Rousseau's notions of *amour-propre* and alienation are re-framed by Hegel as the individual's desire for recognition and the moment of misrecognition.

It is important not to reduce Hegel's theory of recognition to the moment of the duel and the resulting master–slave relation. To do so is to focus on only one side of the theory of recognition. With this said, Hegel's image of the duel offers a stark re-conceptualization of social conflict and violence. In it, the moment of violence, desire for objects and power, and the drive towards self-realization, are shown to be fundamentally connected to the production of knowledge and the production of norms. Seen through the theory of recognition, knowledge claims cannot be separated from power relations and moral claims and acts cannot take place without the manifestation of some form of violence.

When Hegel's notion of recognition is interpreted quite freely, then this opens up a level of meaning in his texts which point to the dual nature of recognition operating at multiple levels of social and material life. On such an interpretation, the 'positive' and 'negative' moments of recognition should be seen to simultaneously pepper all acts of recognition. In this respect, moments of strong affirmation such as love or solidarity still involve elements of negation, self-interest and cognitive error and limitation. Further, moments of strong negation such as mastery, domination and annihilation still involve limited elements of affirmation in which a life-form is acknowledged to have some degree of value or worth. Reading the notion of recognition in this way helps to show the very tricky operation of recognition within Hegel's account of social conflict and within his account of how notions of 'legitimate violence' are constituted and dissolved within social, ethical and legal spheres. Such a reading of recognition may also pave the way for the development of a theory of recognition as a way of coming to terms with the problem of war and perhaps even as a basis of social theory more generally.

IV

The theory of recognition stands at the centre of Hegel's theory of ethics, law and the political.[51] The operation of successful, mutual recognition between intelligent subjects lies also at the centre of Hegel's theory of the realization of freedom.[52] Understood in the context of a theory of freedom, Hegel inherits the notion of recognition from Fichte. For Fichte, recognition occurs as a means of conceiving a Kantian notion of right as a 'universal law of freedom' in which an individual acts or limits its action so as not to impair the freedom of another. In the *Foundations of Natural Right* (1795–96), Fichte argues that a conception of a human individual as a rational finite being involves and presupposes the existence of other such beings outside itself.[53] He describes this necessary relation between finite beings as the relation of right (*Rechtsverhältniß*).[54] For Fichte, right occurs as an act of 'mutual recognition' between human individuals.[55] He argues:

> Thus the relation of free beings to one another is necessarily determined in the following way, and is posited as thus determined: one individual's knowledge of the other is conditioned by the fact that the other treats the first as a free being (i.e. limits its freedom through the concept of the first). But this manner of treatment is conditioned by the first's treatment of the other; and the first's treatment of the other is conditioned by the other's treatment and knowledge of the first, and so on *ad infinitum*. Thus the relation of free beings to one another is a relation of reciprocal interaction through intelligence and freedom. One cannot recognize the other as a free being, if both do not mutually treat the other as free.[56]

Fichte's creation of a relation of freedom through mutual recognition adds an element of praxis to Kant's account of determining moral and legal universals. Fichte's praxis, however, remains rather formal and relies upon a model of an atomistic, liberal subject.[57] In contrast, Hegel's use of the notion of recognition is radical. Through recognition, Hegel tries to show how not only moral and legal universals are produced through differing forms of relations and mediations, but further, that within the operation of recognition there resides a certain violence – a violence of misrecognition, negation and alienation, which does not stand outside of ethics but occurs as a central part it.

The development of the notion of recognition as an ethical theory can be seen in Hegel's unpublished *Jena Manuscripts* that precede the publication of the *Phenomenology of Spirit*. The *Jena Manuscripts* include: the *System of Ethical Life* (1802/03),[58] the *First Philosophy of Spirit* (1803/04)[59] and the *Jena Realphilosophie* (1805/06).[60] In these manuscripts, Hegel can be seen to develop an account of inter-subjectivity in which human individuals are understood as mediated beings. Hegel draws attention to three primary forms of inter-subjective mediation that lie at the basis of human life, these are: (1) speech and the use of language; (2) the relations of work and the use of the tool; and (3) family relations and the operation of love.[61] For Hegel, these relations do not simply describe the goings-on of atomistic individuals, rather, these relations are moments through which the individual human subject is *inter-subjectively constituted*.

Through the inter-subjective relations of speech, work and the family, Hegel shows how a universal is produced by recognizing individuals. One example of how a universal is produced is in the notion of property. For him, it is not the physical act of possession of property itself that is significant, but, rather, it is the recognition by others of the individual as being a possessor which is central.[62] In being recognized by others as a possessor, the physical act is raised to a level of universality, as something acknowledged by numerous individuals and given universal significance through mutual affirmation. In this sense, possession, and property are not inherent (or original forms of right), as might be suggested by a number of natural law traditions, but are fundamentally a creation of inter-subjective recognition. For Hegel, legal rights and legal personality are universals generated at a higher level of abstraction underlaid by inter-subjective recognition.[63]

Further, the exchange relation and the determination of *value* (i.e. monetary value) within this relation occur for Hegel as a form of inter-subjective recognition in which a particular value is raised to a level of universality by the recognition of it by a number of human individuals.[64] For him, just as much as the operation of inter-subjective recognition leads to freedom through the determination of universality in a Fichtean sense, so it also leads to 'unfreedom' via misrecognition, inequality, alienation and differential power relations towards mastery and slavery or bondage.[65]

In a general sense, Hegel's account of recognition presents a theory which explains how ethical norms that have a degree of universality come to be produced and sustained. For him, such norms are produced through inter-subjective recognition and develop through the inter-actions and mediations of everyday life. These norms come to be entrenched in customs and institutions and shape the value judgments of individuals. Hegel calls these norms *Sittlichkeit*, or ethical life. Ethical life contains not only differing modes or forms of universality (for example, love, as contrasted to private property, as contrasted to citizenship within the state) but ethical life also contains moments of subjective and *institutional* misrecognition and degrees of oppression, alienation[66] and unfreedom that result from this. Part of the value of Hegel's ethical theory is the placement of misrecognition within the sphere of ethics itself with the acknowledgement that error, mastery, negation, non-recognition and oppression, reside within subjective ethical judgments and within ethical institutions.

The account presented in Hegel's *Jena Manuscripts* can also be read as a response to the problem of how to create a universal position of judgment that might stand above and rule over competing claims and conflicts within the context of widespread social violence. Such a problem of judgment was seen to be present within Hobbes's approach to civil war and within Kant's approach to inter-state war. Hegel's approach sidesteps the formal difficulties of establishing a social contract by paying attention to how universals are produced within social relations even in the context where the social relation is marked by violent conflict. Hegel argues:

> The problem is this: What is right and obligation for the individual in the state of nature? The concept of this individual is taken as the basis; out of this concept the full notion is to be developed. I bring to it the definition of *right*. I show the individual to be a bearer of rights, a person. But this demonstration occurs within me; it is the movement of my thought, although the content is the free Self. This [conceptual] movement, however, does not leave this demonstration as it is; i.e., it is [itself] the movement of this concept.
>
> Right is the relation of persons, in their behaviour, to others. It is the universal element of their free being – the determination, the limitation of their empty freedom. I need not spell out this relation of limitation for myself and produce it; rather, the object, in general, is itself this creation of right, i.e., the relation of *recognition*. In recognition (*Anerkennen*), the Self ceases to be this individual; it exists by right in recognition, i.e., no longer [immersed] in its immediate existence. The one who is recognized is recognized as immediately counting as such (*geltend*), through his *being* – but this being is itself generated from the concept; it is recognized being (*anerkanntes Seyn*).[67]

Partly, Hegel's argument involves the position that even in the conditions of chaotic social violence there already exists forms of inter-subjective recognition and thus forms of shared universals between individuals (for example, in the shared use of language). From this perspective, recognition is not something that has to be created out of nothing. Rather, for Hegel, conflicting individuals are already recognizing each other in significant ways. What becomes important then is the question of how mutual forms of recognition might be established so as to bring some form of resolution to conflict, and to allow the creation of a non-violent public sphere of freedom involving degrees of general normative consensus over certain aspects of public life. Significantly, in Hegel's account, the development of shared, mutual recognition occurs *through* the experience of negation, injury or insult taking place within social conflict. In a sense, for Hegel, the negative aspect of misrecognition plays a formative role in the movement towards mutual recognition and the development of a greater set of shared social, universal norms.

Hegel gives the example of when an individual takes possession of something, claims it as its own, as 'mine', and in doing so excludes another individual from possession of the object.[68] He argues that the movement of recognition begins not with the positive moment of knowing oneself in the other, but with being confronted with the independence of the other and in seeing one's self as being excluded by the other.[69] Hegel argues:

> The excluded party spoils the other's possession, by introducing his excluded being-for-himself into it, his [sense of] 'mine'. He ruins something in it, annihilating [i.e., negating] it as desire, in order to give himself his self-feeling (*Selbstgefühl*) – yet not his empty self-feeling, but rather positing his own Self in another, in the knowing of another. The activity does not concern the negative aspect, the thing, but rather the self-knowledge of the other. A distinction in the knowledge of the other is thereby posited, which only puts one in the existence of the other. He [the excluded] is also angered thereby; he is divided in himself, and his exclusion from being is turned into an exclusion of knowledge. He becomes aware that he has done something altogether different from what he intended. His intention (*Meynen*) was the pure relating of his being to itself, his impartial being-for-itself.
>
> Thus angered, the two parties stand opposed to one another – the one as the insulter, the other as the insulted. The insulter did not intend to insult the other in taking possession, but the insulted did relate himself to the insulter: what the insulter annihilated was not the intrinsic form of the thing, but the form of the other's labour or activity. Thus the fact that the excluded party has restored himself does not produce the equality of the two, but rather a new inequality. Equality [demanded] that *both* parties posit themselves in the thing [asserting themselves with respect to it]. But [here we have] the higher inequality of the positing of the one in the being-for-himself of the other. The first posited [i.e., asserted] himself in the unowned thing, the other in the thing already possessed.[70]

Through the process of excluding and of being excluded, the parties are brought to face not only the relative independence of those who share their social environment, but also the normative expectations of their others and the injury their actions may cause to these others. For Hegel, the development of a shared set of normative expectations arises only through this to and fro of self assertion and injury which introduces the notion that there is a difference of normative expectations within the social environment. On this Axel Honneth argues, that for Hegel:

> On the part of the attacked subject, the experience of having its possessions destroyed generates a certain normative irritation. For in light of the other's aggressive reaction, the attacked subject realizes, in retrospect, that in this social context its own action (that is, the original seizure of property) necessarily acquires a meaning quite different from the one it originally ascribed to the action. In acting, the property-seizing subject had initially been occupied only with itself. It carried out the act of seizure, egocentrically conscious solely of expanding its economic holdings by one additional object. The counter-reaction of its partners to interaction brings home, for the first time, the fact that in acting it related indirectly to its social environment as well, by excluding others from the use of the object. In this sense, the other is constitutively included in the propertied subject's self-perception as well, since the other has enabled it to decentre its initially egocentric way of looking at things.[71]

For Honneth, it is the act of injury, insult, resistance and feelings of shame and humiliation occurring out of the struggle for recognition which generates an awareness of the inter-subjective and vulnerable nature of moral and social norms. He argues:

> For it is the mere fact of the morally decisive resistance to its interaction partner that actually makes the attacking subject aware that the other had come to the situation harbouring normative expectations in just the same way that it itself had vis-à-vis the other. That alone, and not the way in which the other asserts its individual rights, is what allows subjects to perceive each other as morally vulnerable persons, and thereby, to mutually affirm each other in their fundamental claims to integrity. In this sense, it is the social experience of realizing that one's interaction partner is vulnerable to moral injury – and not the existential realization that the other is mortal – that can bring to consciousness that layer of prior relations of recognition, the normative core of which acquires, in legal relations, an inter-subjectively binding form.[72]

The experience of exclusion, vulnerability, injury and humiliation might be thought more generally as the experience of the negative and the experience of the violence of negativity. One of the insights of Hegel's theory of recognition is the manner in which he draws out this experience and shows its significance in the formation of ethical norms and universals. By reflecting upon its exclusion and injury, the individual is given the opportunity to piece together the relation between its own thoughts and acts and the violence that it might inflict upon others through self-assertion or through the claim of the universality of its own moral position. At its most extreme, the experience of being negated introduces a sense of humility which Hegel, in the *Phenomenology of Spirit*, places in the voice of Antigone: 'Because we suffer we acknowledge we have erred.'[73]

Yet, even when this extremely critical moment of self-reflection is lacking, the experience of vulnerability in general, or even that of being challenged through another's self-assertion, places each actor on notice that what is claimed as a universal is always at some point contested. The challenge of recognition occurs then at the level of whether the parties will continue to attempt to sustain a claim over a normative universal through conflict and force, or, of whether the experience of being negated leads to genuine efforts to mutually recognize each other. Significantly, for Hegel the operation of mutual recognition is never one grand, formal act in the sense of a social contract. Rather, it is the many moments of mutual recognition which would precede any formalization of norms via law and it is the ongoing errors, conflicts and efforts of recognition through which ethical norms or universals and laws are developed by including new contents and new parties and through excluding others.

By holding onto the somewhat differing senses of recognition expressed in the *Jena Manuscripts* and in the *Phenomenology of Spirit*, a number of aspects of Hegel's ethical ordering of war that might initially have seemed odd or troubling may become a little clearer. Hegel's account of war, which focuses primarily upon war waged by the state, draws upon Hegel's broader theoretical position on the status of negativity within thinking and ethics and upon the operation of *inter-institutional* recognition between states.

V

Hegel's account of war can be read, in part, as an inheritance of and response to Kant's moral ordering of the problem of war. In contrast to Kant's moral condemnation of war, Hegel attempts to demonstrate the positive significance of war, he suggests that war is 'ethical', or that it contains an 'ethical moment'. Hegel's critique of the moral condemnation of war can be seen in an early comment from *The German Constitution* (1798–1802).[74] Hegel states:

> Right is the advantage of a particular state, specified and acknowledged by treaties; and since, in treaties in general, the different interests of states are specified, despite the fact that these interests, as rights, are infinitely complex, these interests – and hence also the rights themselves – must come into contradiction with each other. It depends entirely on the circumstances, on the combinations of power – i.e. on the *judgment* of politics – whether an endangered interest or right will be defended with all the force a power can muster, in which case the other party can also, of course, adduce a right of its own since it has itself exactly the opposite interest which collides with the first, and hence also a right. Thus, war or some other means must now decide – not which of these rights asserted by the two parties is the genuine right (for both parties have a genuine right), but which right should give way to the other. War or some other means must decide the issue, precisely because both contradictory rights are equally true and hence a

> third factor – i.e. war – must make them unequal so that they can be reconciled, and this occurs when one gives way to the other.[75]

This position expresses an affinity with the Westphalian prioritization of the right of the state and something of a 'realist' and conflictual characterization of the inter-state relation. Yet, to characterize the mature Hegel's approach to war as merely positing a 'reason of state' argument would misunderstand Hegel's position and would place Hegel's thinking along side other reason of state theorists such as Heinrich von Treitschke.[76] Rather, Hegel's position is far more complex and can be seen as an attempt to reconcile the post-Westphalian tradition and its move away from a moral and theological ordering of violence through the juridical figure of the state, with an ethical conception of the state itself inherited from Rousseau and the heritage of the French Revolution that includes an emphasis upon the state's role in the *realization* of human freedom.

Further, in attempting to affect this reconciliation Hegel draws upon an image of the ancient Greek city-state in which an individual's moral life and freedom is lived through the life of the *polis*.[77] Yet, Hegel's conception of the state does not return to the supposed beauty of the Greek conception of ethical life that is lost to history and broken by the development of Roman and modern, bourgeois forms of individual legal personality. Nor, does Hegel's conception of the state merely put forward what can be understood today as a 'communitarian' position.[78] Rather, Hegel's account of the state puts forward a philosophical account of the concept of right understood as the realization of freedom occurring through the juridical entity of the modern state, the social and economic revolutions of the eighteenth century, and the historical emergence of the significance of individual moral judgment and private conscience. These forms are underlaid by a theory of recognition involving the inter-subjective and inter-institutional constitution of ethical norms within modernity. Hegel's *Philosophy of Right* which contains the bulk of his engagement with war, develops his theory of recognition and needs to be read as such.

With regard to Hegel's critique of Kantian morality generally Hegel makes the comment that Kantian morality presents something of an 'empty formalism'.[79] Hegel argues:

> Whereas we earlier emphasized that the point of view of Kant's philosophy is sublime inasmuch as it asserts the conformity of duty with reason, it must be pointed out here that this point of view is defective in that it lacks all articulation. For the proposition 'Consider whether your maxim can be asserted as a universal principle' would be all very well if we already had determinate principles concerning how to act. In other words, if we demand of a principle that it should also be able to serve as the determinate of a universal legislation, this presupposes that it already has a content; and if this content were present, it would be easy to apply the principle. But in this case, the principle itself is not yet available, and the criterion

> that there should be no contradiction is non-productive – for where there is nothing, there can be no contradiction either.[80]

One aspect of the Kantian response involves the point that Kant's practical reason takes place in a world of moral content and its attempt is to determine the relative criteria through which the individual may navigate through this content and the conflicting demands of everyday life. Onora O'Neil argues:

> Practical judgment is *always* a matter of finding a way of achieving a range of aims and objectives while conforming to a plurality of principles of duty, and of doing so while taking account of the varied realities and vulnerabilities of human life.[81]

Hegel's critique that Kantian morality is an 'empty formalism' certainly rides roughly over some of the subtleties of Kant's approach. However, Hegel's critique, developed through the theory of recognition, points to a number of limitations of Kantian moral reasoning and develops an account of ethics that is substantively different to Kant's. One focus within the Hegelian approach is upon the formation of universals within human thought determinations, which for Hegel, proceed from the abstract to the concrete through a process that involves error, mistake, and conflict. Generally a Kantian approach views practical reason as determining a set of universal, regulative ideals to which the world, through human action, *ought* to be brought into a closer approximation. Hegel's account resists this Kantian deontology and sees the operation of practical reason as situated within a process of inter-subjective recognition through which concrete universals are produced. For Hegel, practical reason cannot determine how the world ought to be absolutely because any thought determination necessarily involves limit and error. If we are to grasp ethical standpoints, then we need to come to terms with their concrete, mediated and thick contents which have developed through the errors, conflicts, and corrections of *many* thought determinations within the social and historical process of recognition and misrecognition.[82]

Hegel's *Philosophy of Right* is divided into three sections: abstract right, morality and ethical life (*Sittlichkeit*). Hegel's notion of ethical life contains three forms: the family, civil society (*die bürgerliche Gesellschaft*) and the state. For Hegel, the sphere of the family involves a moment of natural mutual recognition occurring through love. In this, individual members comprehend themselves as part of a unity and are able to direct their action via their speculative awareness of themselves to their moments of unity.[83] Such a self-comprehension in the family is limited by and is in contradiction to the ethical comprehension of an individual in the sphere of civil society.[84]

The sphere of civil society represents a form of mutual recognition in which individuals gain recognition as 'individuals' having a degree of moral, legal and political independence related to their working and commercial life. The sphere refers to the acknowledgement of the value of the freedom of the individual's private will and conscience.[85] Yet, for Hegel, this sphere lacks a moment in which the individual has an awareness of itself as part of an interdependent, concrete whole.[86] Hegel believed that such an awareness could occur within the sphere of the state. In this sphere, individual action is not directed by personal wants and desires, but is directed by a comprehension of the individual's mutual, co-constitution through the state and through a comprehension of the state's significance in the realization of human freedom.[87] Further, Hegel thought that the state could operate as an institution that would overcome the conditions of alienation that resulted from the economic relations of civil society.[88]

Hegel situates Kantian morality within the section named 'morality', he views it as a relevant form of normative thinking in modernity, however, it is only ever a limited, abstract way of describing human welfare or what is good. Such an abstract conception is distinguished from a more concrete account of norms contained within ethical life. In this respect, at a basic level, Hegel draws a contrast between an abstract Kantian morality and a more concrete sphere of ethical life.

Further, Hegel also locates Kantian morality within history, he shows how the abstract form of moral reasoning contained in Kantian morality, and subjective moralism more generally, comes into prominence within one sphere of ethical life, civil society. As emerging in civil society, Kantian morality represents one form of ethical life distinguished from the ethical life of the state. In this manner, Hegel historicized a dominant form of moral thinking that developed out of the social, political and economic revolutions of the eighteenth and nineteenth centuries which emphasized the emancipation of the individual and ownership of private property.[89] By showing Kantian morality to be one historical form of right, Hegel critiqued its pretensions to being an absolute, universal form. Set within the relations of civil society, Kantian morality, as with modern subjective moralism, is shown to be merely *one* form of right among many others.

Viewed from the perspective of his account of war, Hegel's critique of Kantian morality can be considered as two-fold. In one sense, it involves the critique of an abstract form of normative thinking by contrasting it against more concrete forms of ethics. In another sense, it involves a critique of the normative forms of thinking bound up with modern life within civil society contrasted against the ethics of modern political community. In this double sense, Hegel's critique of the moral condemnation of war is an expression of his criticism of an abstract and one-sided conception of right being expressed by both Kantian morality and a liberal (or romantic) subjective moralism. For Hegel, these conceptions naïvely or dishonestly downplay their dependence upon the juridical and political institution of the state and their dependence upon the importance of the state's act of war in the realization of human freedom. For Hegel, such critiques of war given by the moral 'ought', while relevant, overlook the ethical function of the state in favour of civil society, and in doing so, they misinterpret *one* moment of ethical life as the being the *whole*. In this respect Hegel positions the abstract moral 'ought' against the notion of the 'welfare' of the state.[90] Hegel argues:

> There was at one time a great deal of talk about the opposition between morality and politics and the demand that the latter should conform to the former. In the present context, we need only remark in general that the welfare of a state has quite a different justification from the welfare of the individual [*des Einzelnen*]. The immediate existence [*Dasein*] of the state as the ethical substance, i.e. its right, is directly embodied not in abstract but in concrete existence [*Existenz*], and only this concrete existence, rather than any of those many universal thoughts which are held to be moral commandments, can be the principle of its action and behaviour. The allegation that, within this alleged opposition, politics is always wrong is in fact based on superficial notions [*Vorstellungen*] of morality, the nature of the state, and the state's relation to the moral point of view.[91]

In Hegel's account of the ethical ordering of war, the relation between war and right is not ordered by the state as a purely juridical figure that maintains internal peace, nor the state as a moral figure which must act in accordance with duty to secure a universal law of freedom. Rather, the state is understood as an ethical entity, a concrete universal which is (at least potentially)[92] the objective realization of human freedom through the operation of full, mutual recognition between its citizens. For Hegel, when the state is at war, it is this ethical life, this internal freedom, that is put at risk and which asserts itself against its other. Such a position can be seen to underscore what Hegel refers to as the 'ethical moment' in war.[93] One of Hegel's more controversial claims about war is contained in the following statement:

> [W]ar should not be regarded as an absolute evil [*Übel*] and as a purely external contingency whose cause [*Grund*] is therefore itself contingent, whether this cause lies in the passions of rulers or nations [*Völker*], in injustices etc., or in anything else which is not as it should be. Whatever is by nature contingent is subject to contingencies, and this fate is therefore itself a necessity – just as, in all such cases, philosophy and the concept overcome the point of view of mere contingency and recognize it as a *semblance* whose essence is necessity. It is *necessary* that the finite – such as property and life – should be *posited* as contingent, because contingency is the concept of the finite. On the other hand, this necessity assumes the shape of a natural power, and everything finite is mortal and transient. But in the ethical essence, i.e. the state, nature is deprived of this power, and necessity is elevated to the work of freedom, to something ethical in

> character. The transience of the finite now becomes a *willed* evanescence, and the negativity which underlies it becomes the substantial individuality proper to ethical essence. – War is that condition in which the vanity of temporal things [*Dinge*] and temporal goods – which tends at other times to be merely a pious phrase – takes on a serious significance, and it is accordingly the moment in which the ideality of the *particular attains its right* and becomes actuality. The higher significance of war is that, through its agency (as I have put it on another occasion), the 'ethical health of nations [*Völker*]' is preserved in their indifference towards the permanence of finite determinacies, just as the movement of the winds preserves the sea from that stagnation which lasting calm would produce – a stagnation which a lasting, not to say perpetual, peace would also produce among nations.[94]

While Hegel's argument here is dense, at least two claims can be drawn out. In one claim, Hegel argues that war is a part of the ethical life of the state and following this, ethics in general, as ethical life, cannot be abstracted from the historical operation war and violence. War can be viewed as a moment of ethical life in the sense that historically all states either found themselves in, or maintain themselves through, some form of violence. In this respect, as the ethical life of the state has some form of significant relation to war, an individual cannot, without a degree of hypocrisy, condemn war outright. Such condemnation cannot occur without considering the individual's dependence upon the state and the fact that the individual's freedom within civil society sits in a historical and causal relationship with the state's violence. In a historical sense, the human individual is somewhat complicit in the state's violence, or at least, inherits this violence as part of its social self. Moral voices that condemn war as being evil are asked to recognize the historical stains of blood that mark their own hands.

A second claim made by Hegel focuses upon the 'necessary' aspect of war for ethical life. Hegel argues that war performs a function that, at first, is not immediately apparent.[95] Hegel's argument involves the claim, as described by Shlomo Avineri, that war operates as a 'test' of the 'health' of the ethical life of the state.[96] For Hegel, war highlights the internal tensions between civil society and the state, it highlights the fact that much of what is valued in civil society – individual life and property – might be shown to be relative to the higher value of the security of the state itself and the ethical relations of mutual recognition between individuals in the state who value the lives of their fellow citizens as much as their own. As an act of negativity, Hegel considers war to be a test of whether the full, mutual recognition within a state has come into existence, or, of whether the state is nothing more than civil society wherein individuals, holding onto the value of life and property, run away.

Such a conception put by Hegel is not unreasonable. What might be considered less than reasonable is Hegel's suggestion that war 'necessarily' leads to the affirmation of the ethical life of the state over civil society. While the point that an outside threat may bring the citizens to identify with the state may have some relevance, the contention cannot be given any level of proof. Further, there is nothing to suggest that the ethical life of the state might not be realized above the level of civil society without recourse to war and brought about instead through other means, such as good government.

In one sense, Hegel's suggestion might be read as an advice to government and can be seen to draw upon Niccolò Machiavelli's contention that, in the process of time, a republic's 'goodness' becomes corrupted unless something intervenes to bring the state back to its original principles.[97] In the *Phenomenology of Spirit*, through the voice of Creon, Hegel gives a similar form of advice.[98] Such advice, perhaps still taken on board by many governments today draws a much darker picture of the operation of war. While its particular proscription should be rejected, it does, however, point to a relation between violence and ethics highlighted by Hegel.

Hegel's comments upon the 'necessity' of war for ethical life may be considered in the context of his theory of recognition in which human thinking, through negation, is related to acts of violence occurring within the world. In similarity to the human individual positing itself at times in opposition to, or through negation of its others, Hegel portrays the state defining itself in opposition to its others. Like the human individual, the state defines itself, its boundaries, its limits, through a negative relation to itself and a negative relation to its others – civil society and other states. Hegel explains this as the basis of the state's 'individuality'.[99] Such a conception does not need to involve the portrayal of the state as a thinking being but merely reflects the operation of collective thinking defining one group of individuals against others. By drawing the limits of inclusion of a group (spatially, racially, culturally, legally, linguistically, and so on) through the exclusion of others, a group of individuals might be thought to possess (or create for itself the appearance of) an ongoing identity and this identity, organized through institutions, can be thought of as an acting subject: a subject capable of violence and capable of forms of inter-institutional recognition.[100]

On its own, such a conception of how thinking might organize collective human activity does not initially point to an ethicality of war. The other state, or community, might not only be excluded from the first's identity but the negation of other at the level of thought might also involve a physical negation through violence: an act of war, genocide, conquest, or enslavement. At the level of inter-subjective recognition, such an action might be considered a failure or lack of speculative awareness, moment of misrecognition, which is perhaps even 'unethical'. Yet, at the level of the state, at the level of what can be called inter-state recognition, Hegel seems to consider this moment of exclusion and violence as having ethical significance. The state's existence as a 'concrete universal', one which has an already internally mediated ethical content, provides Hegel with the grounds to argue that there is an ethical significance or an ethicality of war. As an ethical entity, the violent negation of the other involves not only the positing of one state interest against another, but the positing of one ethical entity against another. War occurs as the defence and realization of an institution whose existence secures the freedom and ethical life of its members. For Hegel, in this context, the negation and exclusion of the other are an ethical moment.

Hegel can be read as developing here an account of an *ethics of exclusion*. This involves the sense that an ethical-political community comes into being and sustains itself through the often violent negation and exclusion of individuals, contents and institutions that are other than it. The act of negation and exclusion is seen as 'necessary' to the positing and self-inscription of ethical-political community. Rather than viewing the act of negation and exclusion as unethical, the act is understood as a part of ethics. In a sense, the notion of the ethical is broadened to include this sometimes very violent activity. Such an account raises a number of objections.

One immediate objection asks the question of whether an ethics of exclusion can ever be an adequate account of ethics. Drawing upon the Decalogue's injunction 'Thou shalt not kill', many traditions of religious and secular Western ethical thinking (and traditions within Islam) treat acts of killing and violence as unethical and argue that the challenge of ethics involves the effort to develop human behaviours and social relations in which violence and killing are minimized. Further, radical cosmopolitan and humanist elements of these traditions position the role of ethics as involving the effort to overcome or transcend the boundaries and conceptions that exclude individuals from a universal community of humanity and of love.[101] For these dominant traditions the notion of an ethics of exclusion looks more like an aberration or inversion of the ethical demand.

A second objection keeps in mind the historical and contemporary violence of the modern nation-state and the manner in which appeals to nationalism, the *Volk*, and the freedom of the nation and its citizens are drawn upon to justify bloody wars and to conceal underlying commercial, strategic and power interests. Describing the state as having some form of 'ethical being' has been seen to be highly dangerous – often a crude mix of nationalism and militarism drawn on by propaganda machines to whip citizens into a frenzy of self-belief and willingness to sacrifice. From the Nazi state to the contemporary aggression of Israel ('*Ein Land für ein Volk*') and the USA ('God bless America'), an ethics of exclusion might describe an operation of politics but it would seem to be a far cry from anything that might be understood as 'ethical'.

Another objection asks who or what exactly is the 'We' of the ethical-political community that claims an ethical status in war. Further, who declares this 'We' and who decides who and what is to be included and excluded? The objection suggests that an ethics of exclusion is founded upon a moment of indeterminacy and that the proper subject of what is to be ethical (the state, the community, and the people) is merely an image, projection, a fantasy, an 'empty' space. In light of these objections, is there anything that might be held onto within Hegel's account of an ethics of exclusion?

There is something worth holding onto in Hegel's account of an ethics of exclusion, even if it might not be pretty. Hegel's argument that there is an ethical moment in war offers a particular way of thinking about the relation between ethics and political community, it attempts to broaden the notion of ethics by drawing attention to the operation of *ethical-political community*. For Hegel, the modern state is an ethical-political community. It is a political community, it is an institutional form in which public social life, security, economy, territory and competing normative claims are organized and ordered by a form of governance. For Hegel, the state is also an ethical community, it provides a space through which a public set of norms, ethics and customs are encouraged and sustained by institutions. Further, the state provides and allows a certain level of human freedom to be realized, and provides an institutional framework through which individuals might realize their potentialities.

The notion of the state as an ethical institution is not unproblematic, one could name a number of different types of states including the modern welfare state, fascist states, and post-colonial dictatorships, and some of these would seem to be of dubious ethical character. Hegel's assertion that the state occurs as an ethical institution implies a number of normative requirements and a series of graduations towards a level of 'statehood'.[102] One way around this unclarity is to think of the modern, liberal-democratic 'welfare state' and to consider this as one possible embodiment of the Hegelian notion of the state existing as an ethical institution. While not perfect, the modern welfare state could be thought as an example of ethical-political community.[103] If the modern welfare state can be thought as an example of what Hegel might have imagined as an ethical institution, then some aspects of an ethics of exclusion might be less open to objection.

One sense in which the modern welfare state can be considered as an ethical entity involves the sense that it not only allows a space for the negative liberties of its citizens but that the state actively engages in daily human life through education, health care, progressive taxation, the managing of public space, and so on, to *lift up* its citizens to a higher level of freedom (or positive liberty) and a share of the good life. However, the act of lifting up citizens within the realization of ethical-political community also involves the exclusion, suppression and negation of both others and other aspects of human life. In the act of lifting up, something or someone is always *left behind*. One way of thinking about the moment of exclusion is to say that the state is not being ethical enough and that exclusion operates as a failure of ethical action. This might make sense internally as being a failure of ethics (for example, the provision of health care to some citizens and not others). However, at the boundaries of the state, at the drawing of its borders, and the distinction between citizens and non-citizens, the act of exclusion may appear to be 'necessary' to the positing of the state as an ethical-political community.

Part of the point here is that, within the welfare state, ethical life is bound up with and constituted through a notion of political community. Considered in this sense, moral claims are no longer purely free-floating norms that stand apart from political community (and from politics) and which pass judgment over the exclusionary practices of political community. Rather, within the modern welfare state, these norms, as part of the 'ethical', are, in part constituted through political community; the ethical and political community come to be combined in a form in which ethics, as ethical life is realized through the positing and development of political community. In such a manner the ethical is implicated in the exclusionary practices of political community, these exclusionary practices are to be viewed as acts of ethical-political community.

To understand ethics in the sense of the enactment and realization of the notion of ethical-political community involves drawing back into ethics all the moments of exclusion at the borders of community which are normally hidden under bureaucratic silence and historical narrative. Every ethical act within the state, every free breath of every free citizen is implicitly related to and grounded upon the exclusion and negation of preceding territorial occupants and inhabitants, and upon the exclusion of every neighbour, indigenous inhabitant, and asylum seeker who was and continues to be refused citizenship through the rule of law.

By suppressing or ignoring these moments it is often easy to portray the ethical life of the welfare state or ethical-political community as being non-violent. Yet the opposite is the case, the realization of an ethical-political community is profoundly violent, and in this sense, the act of war on behalf of the state can be understood as an exaggerated and highly destructive form of this – war speaks the violence that is normally silent within ethical-political community. In other words, war is the most vivid and destructive element of an act of exclusion and negation lying at the heart of the realization of ethical-political community. It is only moral and political 'beautiful souls' who do not ever pay attention to the violence of ethical-political community who see war and Hegel's notion of an ethics of exclusion as an aberration, an accident, an error, and not something closer to the rule. It was in response to such beautiful souls that the darker moments of Hegel's *Rechtsphilosophie* were often set against.

Rather than ignore, suppress or condemn the violence of ethical-political community, a better approach might be one that recognizes an ethics of exclusion and attempts to come to terms with a certain darkness contained within Western ethics and ethical life. Hiding from or suppressing this unsettling moment within ethics does not make our ethical judgments any stronger, rather, it weakens them, makes them one-sided. Acknowledging an ethics of exclusion does not mean embracing this violence and viewing it as something wonderful. What such an acknowledgment does involve is thinking a little longer about what it means to say that such violence is 'not right' and thinking seriously about what ground we are standing on when making such a statement. Hegel's approach to ethics has value precisely because it does not shy away from a violence residing at the heart of Western ethics, but approaches it head-on.

Importantly, putting forward the notion of an ethics of exclusion presented within the operation of ethical-political community does not imply a reduction of all ethics to this form. Rather, a free-floating account of ethics not bound to community occurring as a Christian-cosmopolitan ethics of love, or a Kantian morality, or even a Levinasian-Derridean ethics of a responsibility to absolute otherness, might still oppose and condemn what they claim as unethical. In the least, the Hegelian position suggests that ethical thinking in modernity may be *caught between* a free-floating ethics and ethical-political community. Further, the Hegelian position argues against a reductionist tendency of understanding the ethics of war purely in terms of the former while disregarding the role of the latter.

At the least, Hegel's conception points to something problematic within ethics in modernity, a seemingly unresolvable contradiction or *aporia* lying at a central point of modern rationality and ethical thinking. On the one hand, much of modern ethics is organized around and reliant upon the belief in the possibility of some form of ethical-political community and the development of ethical life and freedom through institutions such as the state – either in liberal-capitalist, welfare state or revolutionary-socialist formulations. On the other hand, ethical-political communities such as the state have been, and continue to be, profoundly violent. They have relied upon violence to realize ethical ideals and they have produced horrendous forms of violence as a by-product of the attempt to posit a greater sphere of freedom.

This *aporia* spins around the notion that in modernity the attempt to realize freedom by ethical action produces violence through the necessary reliance upon negation. Alternatively, this can be put in terms of the language of recognition. Any sphere of freedom constituted by acts of mutual recognition is undone in some way, or produces irredeemable violence, through the misrecognition of, or refusal to recognize, an other or a number of others. It seems that in thinking (rationality) and in action (actualization, realization, or for Hegel, broadly the concept of *Wirklichkeit*), *negation* is doing a form of work which weaves the activity of exclusion and violence into the fabric of our concepts of freedom and ethics.

Hegel's philosophy does not offer a clear way out of this *aporia*.[104] His use of recognition in relation to inter-state war does make some attempts. However, his approach at times (although not always) has a tendency to redeem the violence of action and realization through broader metaphysical commitments or through philosophical and religious reconciliation.[105]

VI

Hegel inherits the Hobbesian conception of inter-state relations described in terms of a 'state of nature'. Characteristic of the state of nature is the absence of any higher power to judge between conflicting state claims.[106] Unlike Kant, Hegel does not argue for the establishment of a higher power in the form of a federation of states mandated by pure practical reason. This does not mean that Hegel conceived the right of the individual state to be absolute. Rather, Hegel saw the ethical relations between states developing through the process of recognition and not as something declared by practical reason as a universal rule valid across space and time.

For Hegel, treaties occurred as a formal mechanism through which states came to some form of agreement over shared norms. Hegel argued that states should respect their mutual obligations set out under treaties.[107] Yet, for him, the character of inter-state obligations to one another remained at the level of an *ought* and these were subject to the will of each particular state in its consideration of its 'welfare'.[108] In this sense, Hegel characterized the nature of inter-state relations in terms of the operation of 'contracts' in general.[109] These, set within the condition where there exists no higher power to enforce them, are reliant upon the good faith of each party and, in the consequence of a breakdown of agreement, the settlement of disputes by war.[110]

With respect to Kant's argument that a federation of states should be established through a contract to secure peace, Hegel argues:

> Perpetual peace is often demanded as an ideal to which mankind should approximate. Thus, Kant proposed a league of sovereigns to settle disputes between states, and the Holy Alliance was meant to be an institution more or less of this kind. But the state is an individual, and negation is an essential component of individuality. Thus, even if a number of states join together as a family, this league, in its individuality, must generate opposition and create an enemy.[111]

Further, that:

> Kant's idea [*Vorstellung*] of *perpetual peace* guaranteed by a federation of states which would settle all disputes and which, as a power recognized by each individual state, would resolve all disagreements so as to make it impossible for these to be settled by war presupposes an *agreement* between states. But this agreement, whether based on moral, religious, or other grounds and considerations, would always be dependent on particular sovereign wills, and would therefore continue to be tainted with contingency.[112]

Hegel's rejection of Kant's proposal involves a number of elements. In one sense, Hegel's characterization of the state as the highest moment of ethical life and locus through which freedom is realized renders the institution of the state the highest point of political organization in the world. As the state occurs as the highest power on earth,[113] there is no other power that might compel it to act in a particular way. Such a claim takes place within the context of Hegel's argument that philosophy should limit itself to the attempt of describing the world as it *is* rather than as it *ought* to be.[114] Within Hegel's view, at his point in history, the state was the highest power.

Another element of this critique concerns Hegel's characterization of the self-identity of states through the operation of negativity. For Hegel, the negative relation of one state to its others is the state's own highest moment.[115] This is not to say that states cannot overcome their negative relation to each other, but that the notion of perpetual peace is significantly challenged by the operation of the negativity of thinking occurring as the positing of an ethical-political community through physical negation. Along such lines, in the suggestion that a group of states formed together as a family will generate an opposition and create an enemy, Hegel anticipates Carl Schmitt's critique of the League of Nations and his condemnation of pacifism.[116]

Not only is the Schmittian concept of 'enmity' visible here, so is the insight of what might be called a 'paradox of peace' in which the demand for peace in order to realize itself in the world leads into a war in the name of peace against any opposition. Further, by linking the 'Holy Alliance', the continental opponents of Napoleonic France (Austria, Prussia and Russia), to Kant's ideal of an inter-state alliance in the name of peace, Hegel displays an open scepticism of the use by states of abstract moral justifications to legitimize political ends. Such a sceptical view sees that it is often the desire for political power and the operation of state interest which reside behind high moral claims.

One final aspect of Hegel's opposition to Kant's proposal is the argument that a contract in the name of peace 'presupposes agreement between states'. For Hegel, inter-state agreement presupposes the operation of inter-state recognition. In this respect, Hegel's argument is not merely that Kant's vision is practically untenable, but more so, that Kant's approach to the problem, via a social contract conception, is theoretically inadequate and misunderstands the production of ethical norms within the inter-state relation. For Hegel, the production of ethical norms within the inter-state relation occurs through a process of inter-state recognition. Hegel argues:

> The nation-state [*das Volk als Staat*] is the spirit in its substantial rationality and immediate actuality, and is therefore the absolute power on *earth*; each state is consequently a sovereign and independent entity in relation to others. The state has a primary and absolute entitlement to be a sovereign and independent power *in the eyes of others*, i.e. *to be recognized* by them. At the same time, however, this entitlement is purely formal, and the requirement that the state should be recognized simply because it is a state is abstract. Whether the state does in fact have being in and for itself depends upon its content – on its constitution and [present] condition; and recognition, which implies that the two [i.e. form and content] are identical, also depends on the perception and will of the other state.[117]

In this respect, the notions of what constitutes 'legitimate violence' and 'legitimate authority', understood at an inter-state level, are something produced by inter-state recognition. The particular 'universal' moral norms drawn up by scholars or states to govern the violent conduct of international actors, and to operate as a standard of judgment, are dependent upon the mutual recognition by states. The force of these norms ('the force of law') comes by way of mutual recognition by actors who affirm or posit these norms and negate others. Within the context of recognition, these norms are brought into being through the use of and the threat of violence. What was in Kant, and in just war theory, a paradox of peace (the attempt to achieve peace being dependent upon acts of war), is for Hegel, a more basic operation of the process of recognition. Any norm, whether directed towards the end of peace or otherwise is realized through the activity of mutual recognition and the negation and violence against those who refuse to recognize the universality of such a norm. Any concept of 'legitimate violence', or for that matter 'legitimate authority', is produced through the operation of recognition and the negation and violence that is contained within struggles for recognition. Any such concept or norm which attempts to regulate violence is itself the product of violence, the result of conflict, contestation and threat that is implied in Hegel's notion of the duel.

The limits of a Kantian approach and just war theory stems from the fact that each of these approaches disassociates their normative concepts from the social field of recognition and its violence. Such approaches rely on a portrayal of the use of reason and rationality that is falsely abstracted from a social and material context which, per the theory of recognition, is flush with the operation of negation, conflict, struggle and violence. One of Hegel's constant philosophical moves in the field of ethics is to challenge any conception of moral reason which has been abstracted by philosophers and placed in some non-temporal and 'neutral' realm. For Hegel, in the sphere of morality, the thoughts we think and the ideas we produce cannot be abstracted completely from the historical and social lives we live. As such, these normative ideas contain a residue of negation and violence owing to their causal production within the sphere of inter-subjective and inter-institutional recognition. By drawing moral approaches to war back into the context of recognition Hegel's approach shows up the faults contained within more abstract modes of reasoning.

Following this, for Hegel, the state-sovereign's claim to 'legitimate authority' is not purely an internal matter, nor is it something produced purely by reason. Rather, the state's existence and the sovereign's claim to an internal monopoly upon the legitimacy of violence are something which is dependent upon recognition. In the inter-state relation, the state comes to be constituted, in part, through the formal acknowledgment of it by other states. At times, the form of this recognition takes the shape of international law, whereby the state gains its sovereignty through the international recognition of its 'personality'. The state's existence and its rights are dependent upon it having, or acquiring, a certain legal form that is accepted by its others in communion. This involves an acknowledgement of the independence of one state by its others and, with this, an entitlement to have its boundaries respected and its internal matters not interfered with. To be denied recognition of this status is similar to not being acknowledged as a legal person. It means not even being treated at a level of formal equality with other states and, thus, the prospect of being 'acquired' by another state as their property or dominion.

For Hegel, the state comes to be a sovereign political body through the 'perception and will of the other state'.[118] On this, Hegel argues:

> Without relations [*Verhältnis*] with other states, the state can no more be an actual individual [*Individuum*] than an individual [*der Einzelne*] can be an actual person without a relationship [*Relation*] with other persons. On the other hand, the legitimacy of a state, and more precisely – in so far as it has external relations – of the power of its sovereign, is a purely *internal* matter (one state should not interfere with the internal affairs of another). On the other hand, it is equally essential that this legitimacy should be *supplemented* by recognition on the part of other states. But this recognition requires a guarantee that the state will likewise recognize those other states which are supposed to recognize it, i.e. that it will respect their independence; accordingly these other states cannot be indifferent to its internal affairs. In the case of a nomadic people, for example, or any people at a low level of culture, the question even arises of how far this people can be regarded as a state. The religious viewpoint (as in former times with the Jewish and Muhammedan nations [*Völkern*]) may further entail a higher opposition which precludes that universal identity that recognition requires.[119]

Underlying Hegel's account of war is the theory of recognition, which at times, is not fully explicit within his writings. For him, war occurs as recognition and misrecognition. Hegel's account sets out a notion of spatially limited war between European states that recognize the legitimacy of each other. In this sense, war occurs in the manner of a duel between 'just enemies' who keep a future peace in mind when fighting their particular war. Yet, this account of the recognition of statehood also implies the misrecognition or refusal to recognize particular peoples at a so-called 'low level of culture' who might not be regarded as comprising a state. In this sense, war can be understood as acts of misrecognition or non-recognition and as a struggle between competing ethical-political communities to be recognized by each other as independent and autonomous entities.

Unlike Kant's critique of European colonialism, Hegel seems to treat the differing relations between cultures as relations of recognition in which 'higher' or more 'developed' European cultures need only recognize certain aspects of their less 'enlightened' neighbours. In this respect, Hegel's comment on peoples of a 'low level of culture' points to a historically racist conception of western

European culture which viewed itself as 'civilized' and the inhabitants of the rest of the world as sitting on differing levels of a scale moving between the 'civilized' and the 'uncivilized'. For Europeans, in their contact with their others, particular forms of social organization and human behaviour were drawn upon as signs or markers of 'civilization' (family and sexual practices, the cultivation of land, wealth, forms of political organization, military power)[120] within a recognition framework. Historically, the legitimacy of the use of violence was bound up with the question of the recognition of statehood. An ethical-political community that was recognized as a state or quasi-state was engaged with through treaties and even perhaps treated as a just enemy. An ethical-political community that was not recognized as a state was often simply acquired as a territory or as a 'protectorate' and its people enslaved, put to work, or massacred.

In this respect, the contemporary language of a 'clash of civilizations'[121] between the West and actors in the Islamic world, is nothing new. Such a narrative of a war of the so-called 'civilized' against the 'uncivilized' has been used by Europeans since at least the 'age of discovery' to justify the acquisition of wealth and territory. This has involved the production of mythical and racial images of the colonial other as 'barbaric', or 'uncivilized' or 'childlike', who can then be comfortably enslaved or 'protected' by the colonizer.[122] In the colonial moment, recognition operates as misrecognition – the colonizer fails to see in the colonial subject the qualities which it deems worthy of being recognized. As such, the colonizer misses or ignores the worthy qualities of the other and treats the other as an object of lesser value. In the process of recognition, the colonizer also constructs an image of the other in line with its own beliefs and prejudices and in a way which furthers the colonizer's economic and political interests. This false image has the effect of blocking any mutual moments of recognition between subjects and leads to the legitimation of violence and 'just wars' by the colonizer.

Further, such an image of the colonial subject as 'inferior' becomes entrenched within colonial intellectual and scientific discourses, captures a public's imagination and is enforced through the supposed 'neutral' field of law.[123] Within such an operation there are, of course, some 'affirmative' moments of recognition such as when elements of indigenous cultural rights are acknowledged or when elites who might claim to represent the colonized are recognized at a level of quasi-equality. Yet, even these 'positive' moments take place within a framework of recognition which is one of domination, totalization and cruelty, such that often they are no more than merely piecemeal gestures.

This account does not imply that there is a 'genuine' face of the other who hides behind a mask and that all a subject needs to do is to see past the false veil and recognize the other correctly.[124] Such an approach pushes recognition back into a false empiricism and ignores the Hegelian point that what is occurring epistemologically within inter-subjective recognition is the mutual construction of an appearance of the other. For Hegel, this level of appearance is all there ever is for any human subject. Yet, also for Hegel, the conceptual or symbolic realm which we use to construct our images of objects in the world gains its content from norms and cultures in society that change over time. A historical awareness of the different *forms of appearance* in which our knowledge of human and non-human objects have been constructed, as presented in the *Phenomenology of Spirit*, offers a cognitive standpoint for an actor to reflect upon its own mode of recognition and to judge it in relation to other differing historical and contemporary modes. For Hegel, the *goal* of 'absolute knowing', framed not as an achievement, but as an epistemological ought, is set out as *the* task of self-knowledge.[125] In part, the subject can come to know itself as subject-object, as *spirit* (*Geist*), through becoming aware of the historical aspects of its wider constituted self by means of taking into account the differing forms of *spirit* that had preceded it.

Relating this to the colonial moment, subjects who can develop an awareness of the differing forms of *spirit*, and the differing forms of inter-subjective recognition in history, may self-consciously attempt to recognize the other in ways which try to limit totalization, mastery and the desire for self-empowerment. While never complete, and always fallible, such epistemological-ethical praxis can be gleaned from Hegel's theory of recognition even though his own discussion of inter-state recognition is clouded by assumptions of western European cultural superiority.

Generally, underlying these wars of 'civilization' is a structure of interstate recognition that legitimizes the actions of particular communities and delegitimizes the acts and claims of others. War occurs within a wider, historical process of recognition and misrecognition and at times manifests as a struggle for recognition between the colonizers and the colonized. In this respect, contemporary wars for 'peace', 'freedom', and 'human rights', such as the so-called 'war on terror', need to be understood in the historical and theoretical context of wars of recognition. Further, although Hegel participates in a European civilizing narrative, part of his scepticism of Kant's declaration of peace and the idea of an alliance to realize peace, involves an awareness that something like peace cannot be achieved by a declaration of the 'civilized' who claim a monopoly upon 'reason'. The creation of peace would always take place within the context of struggles, conflicts, negotiations and errors of recognition and misrecognition. In this respect, from Hegel's view, periods of peace would always be undone by a certain restlessness of misrecognition and the violence of intellectual and political self-positing.

In terms of the construction of peace, the process of inter-state recognition does not replicate the range of ethical relations developed through inter-subjective recognition. As the acting subject is an institution and not a human individual, forms of mutual recognition like love and genuine friendship are improbable. Yet the inter-state relation is characterized by a number of forms of legal and cultural ethical relations that have come to be produced over time. What Hegel is insistent upon is the notion that it is the absence of an enforcing power which renders inter-state ethical obligations wholly reliant upon the continued mutual recognition of states. In such a process, recognition is not static but is uncertain, open to error and involves a constant effort of political and ethical thinking to come to terms with the violence of thinking's own negativity. For him, the operation of this negativity, combined with the significance of the state's realization of its moment of ethical life over civil society, renders the Kantian project of peace untenable. Yet, while the possibility of inter-state peace does not lie within the horizon of Hegel's conception of ethical life, the central concern of Hegel's thought as a philosophy of the realization of freedom, and the structure of the theory of recognition, opens onto a possibility of peaceful relations being conceived through Hegel's framework.

Hegel gives hints of the development of more peaceful relations occurring in his lifetime through inter-state, mutual recognition. He argues that states reciprocally recognize each other in war, so that even in wartime, the condition of war is something that each understand should come to an end.[126] Hegel argues:

> The European nations [*Nationen*] form a family with respect to the universal principle of their legislation, customs, and culture [*Bildung*], so that their conduct in terms of international law is modified accordingly in a situation which is otherwise dominated by the mutual infliction of evils [*Übeln*].[127]

Thus, there is scope to argue that the operation of inter-state recognition could lead to the possibility of highly co-ordinated ethical relations between states in which states find it less necessary to resort to violence to resolve disputes.[128] However, any such progress towards peaceful relations via mutual recognition needs to be placed within the context of Hegel's cultural and racial assumptions of the value of European customs in relation to non-European peoples. Any such mutual recognition would need to get past racial and cultural moments of misrecognition contained within both Hegel's thought and within many Western forms of thought more generally. If this moment of misrecognition is not taken into account, then one dominant cultural group would simply attempt to extend its so-called 'peace-producing customs' universally to all peoples and this would constitute a form of intellectual and abstract moral *mastery* over the so-called 'less civilized'.[129]

Such a form of inter-state recognition does not lead out of conflict unless the actors involved (especially those in positions of greater power) can acknowledge and find ways of dealing with their own assumptions of racial and cultural superiority. When these assumptions are ignored or suppressed, as is dominantly the case in many simplistic contemporary debates over the relationship between Islam and 'Western' values, then actors fall quickly back into struggles for recognition in which they misrecognize the central role their others play in the historical and ongoing process of inter-cultural and inter-communal constitution.

With this point in mind, Hegel does, however, offer an important insight into the way in which forms of recognition, contained within the conduct of war (the *ius in bello*), lead perhaps to less violent conduct and the possibility of greater peace.[130] In noting the sharing of particular customs over how wars are to be conducted by European nations, Hegel points to a process in which the life of the other comes to be recognized as holding value even in war.[131] The reverse of this is just as telling. When such a moment of recognition is absent and when the warring other is treated with less value than an animal to be slaughtered (for example, in the treatment of the Jew by the Nazi state; or, the treatment of the Palestinian by the Israeli state; or, the treatment of the Aboriginal by the British/Australian colonizer), then the possibility of peace slips away and a limited war of recognition turns into a total war of annihilation. It would seem that within Hegel's account the possibility of peace, just like the rightness of war, is located within an ongoing play of recognition and mis-recognition which is tenuous.

VII

Hegel's ethical ordering of the problem of war can be seen to have come to terms, at least in part, with a number of difficulties present in the approaches to war taken by thinkers such as Hobbes and Kant. By developing a concept of ethical life based upon the operation of inter-subjective recognition, Hegel puts forward a strong account which explains the significance of social violence within epistemic conflict and the struggles over opposing conceptions of right. Through the process of recognition Hegel is able to make sense of the position of social conflict and violence within the production of universal ethical norms and can point to the possibility of the resolution of conflict and violence through moments of successful, mutual recognition taking place in differing forms. In this conceptualization, Hegel is able to forge an important link between the operation of human thinking in general and the occurrence of social violence.

Further, Hegel's account of ethical life as the operation of inter-subjective recognition comes to terms with some of the difficulties encountered in Kant's attempted reconciliation of freedom within the state and the inter-state relation. By understanding that the realization of freedom occurs through moments of successful, mutual recognition, Hegel positions war within a conflict between numerous spheres of recognition in which differing forms or conceptions of freedom are produced: civil society; the state; the inter-state relation. War becomes then not simply a moral question of acting in accordance with 'right' or committing 'wrong', but involves a struggle between institutions or ethical-political communities in the production of ethical universals.

By placing the Kantian conception of moral right firmly within the social and historical conception of civil society, the moral claim becomes one claim that is forced to compete against the claims of its others. In this sense, Hegel strengthens Kant's distinction between man and citizen,[132] between *ius cosmo-politicum* and *ius civitatis*, and portrays them as at least two firm conceptions of how the individual might comprehend itself in its universality. Through a concretization of these conceptions, Hegel points to how individual ethical judgment might be problematic as it is torn between internal, competing conceptions that are not easily reconciled.[133] By conceptualizing such positions, not merely as a tension, but as struggles for recognition between human individuals and their political institutions, Hegel's theory of recognition opens onto a broader understanding of war in terms of global struggles for recognition between differing cultures, political and social ideologies, legal forms and religions, playing out in history.

Viewed thus, the notion of war occurring as a war of ideas is given by Hegel a more concrete content. These ideas do not simply float around in the air, rather, they are the different normative formations of social and material life within which we live and which come into constant conflict in space and time. From this perspective, Hegel turns the problem of the position of judgment over war into a question of history. The concept of history becomes, for the act of war, the 'world's court of judgment [*Weltgericht*]'.[134]

Hegel's tying of judgment to the concept of history positions Hobbes's positing of the sovereign as a judge over civil war and Kant's positing of pure practical reason as a court of judgment over war, within a wider process of the emergence of concepts of right in history in which acts of critique and judgment occur as moments of an ongoing process of inter-subjective and inter-institutional recognition. The notion of history as a court of judgment asks human thinking to reflect upon the process of its own ethical development and upon the relation between the moments of its development and its acts of violence. In one sense, the question of judgment over war becomes the question of: how does the judge, actor, or critic, recognize itself in history and relate the violence of its claim of right to the violence that has gone before it and the violence that opposes it?

The placing of the moment of judgment over war into history is not unproblematic. To a degree it displays something of a therapeutic function in that the horrors of war are given a rationalization (and philosophical redemption) by locating their meaning within a framework and context of historical struggles for recognition. Such an account becomes even more problematic if it is tied up with a historical narrative that attempts to locate the meaning of violence within the context of human 'progress', the work of 'providence', or an uncritical metaphysics of a global or cosmic being.[135]

On the other hand, the placement of judgment in history opens onto a set of important questions involving the relation between human thinking, the realization of freedom and acts of violence. Late modernity, it would seem, is still caught within a somewhat 'Hegelian' problem involving the possibility of rationalizing, or of resisting the rationalization of, acts of violence that are drawn upon in the attempt to realize human freedom. A Hegelian account of a praxis of recognition goes some way in coming to terms with this problem, however, it may not be able to solve it. Paying attention, however, to the *violence of negativity* within one's own thoughts and acts, and within the violence of one's own ethical-political community, is at least one step towards acknowledging the importance of this problem. Recognizing and holding onto this aspect of this problem might be a significant step towards coming to terms with the problem of war more generally.

Notes

1 See the misinterpretations of Hegel given by J. Dewey, *German Philosophy and Politics*, New York: Books for Libraries Press, 1915; L.T. Hobhouse, *The Metaphysical Theory of the State*, London: George Allen and Unwin Press, 1918; and K. Popper, *The Open Society and its Enemies*, Princeton, NJ: Princeton University Press, 1945. For early defenders of Hegel, refuting the linking of him to Prussian militarism and Nazism, see J. Watson, 'German Philosophy and Politics', *Queen's Quarterly*, 22(4), 1915, 366–79; J.H. Muirhead, *German Philosophy in Relation to the War*, London: John Murray, 1917. For theorists who in the latter half of the twentieth century began to turn around the Anglophone misconceptions of Hegel and his position on war and the state, see W. Kaufman, 'Hegel's Myth and Its Method', *The Philosophical Review*, 60, 1951, 486–95; S. Avineri, 'The Problem of War in Hegel's Thought', *Journal of the History of Ideas*, 22, 1961, 463–74; H.G. Bruggencate, 'Hegel's Views on War', *Journal of the History of Ideas*, 22, 1961, 58–60; C.I. Smith, 'Hegel on War', *Journal of the History of Ideas*, 16, 1965, 282–5; D.P. Verene, 'Hegel's Account of War', in Z.A. Pelczynski (ed.) *Hegel's Political Philosophy: Problems and Perspectives*, Cambridge: Cambridge University Press, 1971; E.E. Harris, 'Hegel's Theory of Sovereignty, International Relations, and War,' in D.P. Verene (ed.) *Hegel's Social and Political Thought: The Philosophy of Objective Spirit*, Atlantic Highlands, NJ: Humanities Press, 1980.

2 I. Kant, *Critique of Pure Reason*, eds P. Guyer and A. Wood, Cambridge: Cambridge University Press, 1998, p. 193, A51/B75.

3 Ibid., pp. 246–7, B132–B133.

4 Ibid., p. 260, B158, in footnote.

5 J.G. Fichte, *The Science of Knowledge*, eds P. Heath and J. Lachs, Cambridge: Cambridge University Press, 1982.

6 Ibid., p. 21.

7 J.G. Fichte, *Science of Knowledge*, p. 97.

8 Ibid. Fichte, at p. 93 argues:

> Our task is to *discover* the primordial, absolutely unconditioned first principle of all human knowledge. This can be neither *proved* nor *defined*, if it is to be an absolutely primary principle.
>
> It is intended to express that *Act* which does not and cannot appear among the empirical states of our consciousness, but rather lies at the basis of all consciousness and alone makes it possible.

9 Ibid., pp. 49–51.

10 Ibid., p. 38.

11 Ibid., p. 94.

12 Ibid., p. 95.

13 Ibid., p. 96.

14 Ibid.

15 Ibid., p. 97.

16 Ibid., p. 98. Fichte, at p. 99, argues: 'The self begins by an absolute positing of its own existence'. At pp. 100–1, Fichte argues further:

> That our proposition is the absolutely basic principle of all knowledge, was pointed out by *Kant*, in his deduction of the categories; but he never laid it down specifically *as* the basic principle. *Descartes*, before him, put forward a similar proposition: *cogito, ergo sum* – which need not have been merely the minor premise and conclusion of a syllogism, with the major premise: *quodcumque cogitat est*; for he may very well have regarded it as an immediate datum of consciousness. It would then amount to *cogitans sum, ergo sum* (or as we should say, *sum, ergo sum*). But in that case the addition of *cogitans* is entirely superfluous; we do not necessarily think when we exist, but we necessarily exist whenever we think. Thinking is by no means the essence, but merely a specific determination of existence; and our existence has many other determinations besides this.

17 Ibid., p. 103.
18 Ibid.
19 Ibid., p. 104.
20 Ibid., p. 108. Fichte states:

> Hence, as before, we must make an experiment and ask: How can A and ~A, being and nonbeing, reality and negation, be thought together without mutual elimination and destruction? ... We need not expect anyone to answer the question other than as follows: They will mutually *limit* one another.

21 Ibid.
22 Ibid.
23 Ibid., p. 110.
24 Significant in the movement between Fichte and Hegel is the philosophy of Schelling. See F.W.J. Schelling, *System of Transcendental Idealism*, trans. P. Heath, Charlottesville, VA: University Press of Virginia, 2001. For more general accounts of the philosophical movements between Kant and Hegel, see D. Henrich, *Between Kant and Hegel*, Cambridge, MA: Harvard University Press, 2003; G. Di Giovanni, *Between Kant and Hegel: Texts in the Development of Post-Kantian Idealism*, Indianapolis, IN: Hacket, 2000; L. Kolakowski, *Main Currents of Marxism*, Vol. 1, trans. P.S. Falla, Oxford: Oxford University Press, 1981.
25 In the first half of the *Logic*, Hegel attempts to derive the categories of the understanding. He shows how contradiction is contained at the heart, not just at the peripheries, of pure reason. See G.W.F. Hegel, *Science of Logic*, trans. A.V. Miller, London: Allen and Unwin, 1969; G.W.F. Hegel, *The Encyclopaedia Logic: Part I of the Encyclopaedia of Philosophical Sciences with the Zusätze*, trans. T.F. Geraets, W.A. Suchting and H.S. Harris, Indianapolis, IN: Hackett, 1991.
26 G.W.F. Hegel, *Encyclopaedia Logic*, § 48, p. 91, Hegel argues:

> The main point that has to be made is that antinomy is found not only in the four particular objects taken from cosmology, but rather in *all* objects of all kinds, in *all* representations, concepts, and ideas. To know this, and to be cognizant of this property of objects, belongs to what is essential in philosophical study; this is the property that constitutes what will determine itself in due course as the *dialectic* moment of logical thinking.

For an account of the necessary role of contradiction within human thinking, as it relates to metaphysics, logic and mathematics, see U. Petersen, *Diagonal Method and Dialectical Logic: Tools, Materials, and Groundworks for a Logical Foundation of Dialectic and Speculative Philosophy*, Tönning: Der Andere Verlag, 2002. See also V. Kerruish, 'On Re-staging the Universal: Butler, Hegel and Contesting the Closure of Logic' *Dilemmata: Jahrbuch der ASFPG*, 2006.

27 G.W.F. Hegel, *Phenomenology of Spirit*, trans. A.V. Miller, Oxford: Oxford University Press, 1977.

28 Ibid., p. 58.

29 Ibid., p. 60.

30 Ibid., p. 105.

31 Ibid.

32 Ibid., p. 106.

33 Ibid.

34 On the relation between immediacy and mediation in Hegel's philosophy, see the discussion in D. Henrich, *Hegel im Kontext*, Frankfurt am Main: Suhrkamp, 1971.

35 Hegel's account should not be misconstrued as one which argues that physical objects are completely constituted by the mind. Rather, following Kant's 'Copernican turn', for Hegel, there is no direct knowledge of objects in the world simply by empirical sense experience. For Hegel, sense experience and thus the knowledge of what the object *is*, are mediated by the concepts that structure our thought. Importantly for Hegel, concept formation, as it occurs in the world of spirit (*Geist*), develops inter-subjectively through language and through social, cultural, religious, normative and scientific traditions of thought which change over space and time. The particular knowledge of an object is dependent and partly contingent upon the concepts constructed within social and historical forms of knowledge in general. In this respect an image of what the object *is*, is *produced* by an activity of human, inter-subjective knowledge. This production is for Hegel not simply mental but physical, it occurs through physical labour in which case many of the material objects that surround us are produced by differing forms of human knowledge. One twentieth-century inheritor of aspects of this line of thinking about the production of human knowledge and the world developed by Kant and Hegel is, via Alexandre Koyré, Thomas Kuhn. See T. Kuhn, *The Structure of Scientific Revolutions*, 3rd edn, Chicago, IL: University of Chicago Press, 1996.

36 Hegel's materiality and focus upon the passions, or drives and desires – of which the demand for self-certainty and self-knowledge is one such desire – owe much to Hegel's re-formulation of aspects of Spinoza's philosophy. Spinoza's notion that 'Each thing, as far as it can by its own power, strives to persevere in its being' is important for Hegel's account of the human subject. See B. Spinoza, *Ethics*, trans. E. Curley, London: Penguin, 1996, p. 75. Hegel takes this notion and the role of desire in both physical and intellectual senses and reformulates it around his concept of *Wirklichkeit*, that of realization, or actualization, or of coming into being, which he develops as a reformulation of aspects Aristotle's metaphysics (and against a Newtonian worldview of fixed physical laws of the natural world). The notion of *Wirklichkeit* lying at the basis of Hegel's metaphysics of the subject and thus the constant restless push towards becoming, realization, actualization and empowerment (via contradiction and conflict and physical and linguistic/symbolic acts, deeds, and work as both affirmation and negation) places aspects of Hegel's theory somewhat close to elements of Nietzsche's notion of the 'will to power' which draws together both intellectual and physical drives towards self-empowerment. Re-reading Hegel's theory of recognition in this way is one possible method of producing a better understanding of an *ontology of human violence*. Such an interpretation sits in the background of the theory of war that I am trying to develop.

37 G.W.F. Hegel, *Phenomenology of Spirit*, p. 109. A certain sense of this violence is picked up by Derrida in the essay 'Violence and Metaphysics'. Derrida's interpretation of Hegel, however (influenced by Heidegger), appropriates Hegel's philosophy for his own purposes and presents an account of Hegel's philosophy which he thinks is inadequate in comparison to the philosophy of Levinas. See J. Derrida, 'Violence and Metaphysics: An Essay on the Thought of Emmanuel Levinas', in *Writing and Difference*, trans. A. Bass, Chicago, IL: University of Chicago Press, 1978.

38 G.W.F. Hegel, *Phenomenology of Spirit*, p. 110.

39 Ibid., pp. 110–11.

40 For an account which emphasizes these two moments of recognition, see R.R. Williams, *Hegel's Ethics of Recognition*, Berkeley, CA: University of California Press, 1997. Contrast this to the account given in A. Kojève, *Introduction to the Reading of Hegel*, trans. J.H. Nichols, Ithaca, NY: Cornell University Press, 1980. While Kojève has done much to draw attention to the importance of Hegel's theory of recognition, his account of the theory is somewhat limited. Kojève's account only gives emphasis to the moment of struggle and the master–slave relation and does not give due regard to moments of mutual recognition present within the *Jena Manuscripts*, the *Phenomenology of Spirit* and the *Philosophy of Right*. Another important Marxist account of Hegel's theory of recognition is the interpretation and extrapolation given by Slavoj Žižek. See S. Žižek, *The Sublime Object of Ideology*, London: Verso, 1989; S. Žižek, *Tarrying with the Negative: Kant, Hegel and the Critique of Ideology*, Durham, NC: Duke University Press, 1993. While Žižek's use of recognition is a novel and powerful critique of modern society and culture, his interpretation of Hegel through Lacan has a tendency to reduce or structure recognition around the Lacanian 'void'. For a critique of Žižek's reading of Hegel, see P. Dews, *The Limits of Disenchantment: Essays on Contemporary European Philosophy*, London: Verso, 1995.

41 G.W.F. Hegel, *Phenomenology of Spirit*, p. 112.

42 Ibid., p. 113.

43 The term is taken from Gillian Rose, see G. Rose, *Hegel Contra Sociology*, London: Athlone, 1981; G. Rose, *Mourning Becomes the Law*, Cambridge: Cambridge University Press, 1996. For more general accounts of the *Phenomenology of Spirit*, see R. Pippin, *Hegel's Idealism: The Satisfactions of Self-Consciousness*, Cambridge: Cambridge University Press, 1989; T. Pinkard, *Hegel's Phenomenology: The Sociality of Reason*, Cambridge: Cambridge University Press, 1994.

44 G.W.F. Hegel, *Phenomenology of Spirit*, p. 112.

45 Hegel's account also reformulates, though in a post-Kantian tradition of a *critical* approach to metaphysics, Spinoza's identification of the human individual with 'universal substance', the 'infinite', and 'God'. Hegel's 'I' that understands itself as 'We' and 'We' as 'I' presents an account of how, through recognition, a modern human subject may begin to comprehend its place within the fundamental interconnectedness and flux of the universe. For Hegel, such a transformation in the comprehension of the self has an ethical result. In grasping itself as subject-object, the individual begins to moderate its understanding of desire, autonomy and action in a way which pays attention to its social being and fundamental inter-subjectivity without losing its 'self' in the process. Marx's inheritance of Spinoza's and Hegel's notions of the dialectical comprehension of social being take on this point but argue further that such a transformation of the self cannot occur under the conditions of a political and economic system of modern capitalism which constantly reinforces the alienation of the individual from its social being. Any transformation at the level of self-consciousness, if it is to have an 'ethical result', cannot simply take place at a level of personal morality or at the level of philosophical reconciliation,

rather, it would need to occur as a moment of social, political and economic transformation – the production of freedom through mutual recognition as revolutionary praxis.

46 G.W.F. Hegel, *Elements of the Philosophy of Right*, ed. A.W. Wood, trans. H.B. Nisbet, Cambridge: Cambridge University Press, 1991.

47 On the 'restlessness' contained within thinking as presented by Hegel, see J-L. Nancy, *The Speculative Remark: One of Hegel's Bon Mots*, trans. C. Suprenant, Stanford, CA: Stanford University Press, 2001; J-L. Nancy, *Hegel: The Restlessness of the Negative*, trans. J. Smith and S. Miller, Minneapolis, MN: University of Minnesota Press, 2002.

48 G.W.F. Hegel, *Phenomenology of Spirit*, pp. 113–14.

49 Ibid., p. 115. Many 'post-modern' interpretations of Hegel's theory of recognition, sometimes influenced by Kojève and Derrida, focus only upon the unsuccessful moment of recognition – the moment of struggle, of reducing the other to the same, and the master–slave relation. Emphasizing this violent and totalizing moment is important, especially when applied to colonial and post-colonial contexts, where the non-European has generally not been recognized in their difference, equality and dignity by the European and where recognition has occurred simply as the relation of master and slave. For such an account, see F. Fanon, *Black Skin, White Masks*, New York: Grove Press, 1967. However, it is important to acknowledge that Hegel's theory of recognition is not reducible to the master–slave relation, nor reducible to any one historical moment. In the *Phenomenology of Spirit*, the process of recognition continues through differing phases of *spirit* (*Geist*) in which Hegel describes a plurality of historical and possible forms of reflective inter-relation between self and other. Such a plurality of forms of recognition, all having different consequences in relation to the production of both freedom and alienation and unfreedom, are described by Hegel in the *Jena Manuscripts* and in the *Philosophy of Right*, especially as this relates to the development of different forms of legal rights. Some post-modern interpretations which give an emphasis only to the negative moment of recognition run the risk of being reductionist. Further, such readings risk missing many of the significant epistemological and normative aspects of Hegel's philosophical theory of recognition by interpreting Hegel purely through a post-colonial lens. While the re-interpretation of Hegel through the lens of the colonial encounter is relevant, it is also important not to be trapped by this.

50 For a non-reductionist interpretation which offers an argument that Hegel's theory of recognition represents his attempt to come to terms with the Haitian Revolution, see S. Buck-Morss, 'Hegel and Haiti', *Critical Inquiry*, 26(4), 2000, pp. 821–65. At p. 852, she argues:

> Beyond a doubt Hegel knew about real slaves and their revolutionary struggles. In perhaps the most political expression of his career, he used the sensational events of Haiti as the linchpin in his argument in *The Phenomenology of Spirit*. The actual and successful revolution of Caribbean slaves against their masters is the moment when the dialectical logic of recognition becomes visible as the thematics of world history, the story of the universal realization of freedom. If the editor of *Minerva*, Archenholz, reporting history as it happened, did not himself suggest this on the pages of his journal, Hegel, longtime reader of them, was capable of that vision. Theory and reality converged at this historical moment. Or, to put it in Hegelian language, the rational – freedom – became real. This is the crucial point for understanding the originality of Hegel's argument, by which philosophy burst out of the confines of academic theory and became commentary on the history of the world.

51 For theorists who take this view, see R.R. Williams, *Hegel's Ethics of Recognition*; G. Rose, *Hegel Contra Sociology*; R. Pippin, 'What is the Question for Which Hegel's Theory of Recognition is the Answer?', *European Journal of Philosophy*, 8(2), 2000, 155–72; M. Theunissen, 'The Repressed Inter-Subjectivity in Hegel's Philosophy of Right', trans. W. Watkins, in D. Cornell, M. Rosenfeld and D.G. Carlson (eds) *Hegel and Legal Theory*, New York: Routledge, 1991.

52 See generally, S. Avineri, *Hegel's Theory of the Modern State*, Cambridge: Cambridge University Press, 1972; P. Franco, *Hegel's Philosophy of Freedom*, New Haven, CT: Yale University Press, 1999; M.O. Hardimon, *Hegel's Social Philosophy: The Process of Reconciliation*, Cambridge: Cambridge University Press, 1994.

53 J.G. Fichte, *Foundations of Natural Right*, ed. F. Neuhouser, Cambridge: Cambridge University Press, 2000, p. 29.

54 Ibid. p. 39.

55 Ibid. p. 42.

56 Ibid.

57 On the relationship between Fichte and Hegel on recognition, see R.R. Williams, *Recognition: Fichte and Hegel on the Other*, Albany, NY: SUNY Press, 1992.

58 G.W.F. Hegel, 'System of Ethical Life', in H.S. Harris and T.M. Knox (eds) *Hegel's System of Ethical Life and First Philosophy of Spirit*, Albany, NY: SUNY Press, 1979.

59 G.W.F. Hegel, 'First Philosophy of Spirit', in H.S. Harris and T.M. Knox (eds) *Hegel's System of Ethical Life and First Philosophy of Spirit*.

60 G.W.F. Hegel, 'Jena Realphilosophie', trans. L. Rauch, in *Hegel and the Human Spirit*, Detroit, MI: Wayne State University Press, 1983.

61 G.W.F. Hegel, 'System of Ethical Life', pp. 112–14.

62 Ibid., p. 118.

63 Ibid., p. 118. Holding onto differing forms of levels of recognition in this way can help to show how political acts of recognition of groups such as minorities or indigenous peoples are not always beneficial and sometimes hide more significant forms of oppression. For example, the political act of recognition made by the state of cultural difference and cultural rights of indigenous peoples often hides the ongoing practice of the misrecognition of indigenous ownership of property. In this manner one form of recognition hides another form of misrecognition or the refusal of recognition. Such different *forms* of recognition within the social world, law, ethics, the political and the economic realm are expressed in Hegel's mature thought within the *Philosophy of Right*. While Hegel's account of recognition is limited to the extent that it does not recognize sexual and cultural difference, the model outlined by Hegel can still be understood to explain elements of these contemporary forms of political struggle as 'struggles for recognition'. For feminist critiques of Hegel more generally, see P.J. Mills (ed.) *Feminist Interpretations of G. W.F. Hegel*, Philadelphia, PA: Pennsylvania State University Press, 1996; J. Butler, *Antigone's Claim*, New York: Columbia University Press, 2000; K. Hutchings, *Hegel and Feminist Philosophy*, Cambridge: Polity Press, 2003; J.A. Gauthier, *Hegel and Feminist Social Criticism: Justice, Recognition and the Feminine*, Albany, NY: SUNY Press, 1997.

64 G.W.F. Hegel, 'System of Ethical Life', pp. 121–2.

65 Ibid., pp. 124–5.

66 For accounts of 'alienation' in Hegel's *Jena Manuscripts*, see S. Avineri, S. *Hegel's Theory of the Modern State*; G. Lukács, *The Young Hegel: Studies in Relations between Dialectics and Economics*, trans. R. Livingstone, Cambridge, MA: MIT Press, 1976.

67 G.W.F. Hegel, 'Jena Realphilosophie', p. 111.

68 Ibid., pp. 113–14.
69 Ibid., p. 115.
70 Ibid., pp. 115–16.
71 A. Honneth, *The Struggle for Recognition: The Moral Grammar of Social Conflicts*, trans. J. Anderson, Cambridge: Polity Press, 1995, pp. 44–5. The interpretation of Hegel's theory of recognition taken by Honneth draws a sharp distinction between Hegel's accounts given in the *Jena Manuscripts* and the *Phenomenology of Spirit*. Honneth endorses an interpretation taken by Habermas, see J. Habermas, *Theory and Practice*, trans. J. Viertel, Cambridge: Polity Press, 1988. Habermas and Honneth argue that important elements of Hegel's original social theory of inter-subjectivity developed in the *Jena Manuscripts* were lost or were abandoned in Hegel's attempt to develop a theory of consciousness and account of *spirit* (*Geist*) in the *Phenomenology of Spirit*. My interpretation, which pays attention to some the different senses of recognition operating in these texts, does not follow such a sharp line of distinction made by Habermas and Honneth. Rather, I try to hold onto both senses of Hegel's theory of recognition as they are relevant to Hegel's mature theory of ethics found in the *Philosophy of Right*. For a general discussion of the interpretations taken by Habermas and Honneth, see E. Sembou, 'Hegel's Idea of a Struggle for Recognition: The Phenomenology of Spirit', *History of Political Thought*, 24(2), 2003, 262–81. For Honneth's account of recognition at a more general level of social theory, see N. Fraser and A. Honneth, *Redistribution or Recognition*? London: Verso, 2003.
72 A. Honneth, *The Struggle for Recognition*, pp. 48–9.
73 G.W.F. Hegel, *Phenomenology of Spirit*, p. 284.
74 G.W.F. Hegel, 'The German Constitution', in G.W.F. Hegel, *Political Writings*, ed. L. Dickey, trans. H.B. Nisbet, Cambridge: Cambridge University Press, 1999.
75 Ibid., p. 70.
76 H. Treitschke, *Politics*, trans. H. Kohn, New York: Harcourt, Brace and World Inc., 1963.
77 S. Avineri, *Hegel's Theory of the Modern State*, pp. 15 and 84. For the influence of elements of Greek thought and particularly that of Aristotle upon Hegel's philosophy more generally, see A. Ferrarin, *Hegel and Aristotle*, Cambridge: Cambridge University Press, 2001.
78 See, for example, the 'communitarian' interpretation made popular by Charles Taylor: C. Taylor, *Hegel*, Cambridge: Cambridge University Press, 1975; C. Taylor, *Hegel and Modern Society*, Cambridge: Cambridge University Press, 1979.
79 G.W.F. Hegel, *Philosophy of Right*, § 135, p. 162.
80 Ibid., § 135 Addition, p. 163.
81 O. O'Neil, 'Instituting Principles: Between Duty and Action', in M. Timmons (ed.) *Kant's Metaphysics of Morals: Interpretive Essays*, Oxford: Oxford University Press, 2002, p. 338.
82 In a Hegelian sense, ethics occurs as a praxis of recognition. A praxis of recognition looks towards developing forms of non-coerced, mutual recognition that allow the recognizing parties to realize their freedom through each other. Such a praxis does not attempt to set down a list of universal rules of behaviour valid across global history, but understands the activity of recognizing as the process through which ethical norms or universals are negotiated and developed. Further, such a praxis does not attempt to begin ethics anew but understands that it takes place within a differential life-world understood as ethical life (*Sittlichkeit*) in which particular social norms and customs have come to take on institutionally supported ethical validity over time. These ethical norms involve various shapes or forms and are sustained by ongoing practices of inter-subjective and inter-institutional

recognition. Many of these forms, through being constituted by the operation of misrecognition, contain elements of unfreedom, exclusion and even oppression which, via their equal enactment affect some individuals and not others.

A praxis of recognition attempts to overcome the injurious operation and consequences of forms of misrecognition and does so with the intent of realizing human freedom. In this sense, a praxis of recognition can be understood as a constant work or effort towards the realization of human freedom. As a praxis, this form of ethics is significantly different to the declaratory attitude of Kantian morality, it does not attempt to present an ethics where ethical actors assume the position of speaking or lecturing to the world as if they were delivering the Sermon on the Mount.

83 G.W.F. Hegel, *Philosophy of Right*, § 158 and 159, pp. 199–200. This, for Hegel, involved a particularly strong operation of inter-subjective recognition. Hegel, at § 158 Addition, p. 199, argued:

> Love means in general the consciousness of my unity with another, so that I am not isolated on my own [*für mich*], but gain my self-consciousness only through the renunciation of my independent existence [*meines Fürsichseins*] and through knowing myself as the unity of myself with another and of the other with me ... The first movement of love is that I do not wish to be an independent person in my own right [*für mich*] and that, if I were, I would feel deficient and incomplete. The second moment is that I find myself in another person, that I gain recognition in this person [*daß ich in ihr gelte*], who in turn gains recognition in me. Love is therefore the most immense contradiction; the understanding cannot resolve it, because there is nothing more intractable than this punctiliousness of self-consciousness which is negated and which I ought nevertheless to possess as affirmative. Love is both the production and resolution of this contradiction. As its resolution, it is ethical unity.

84 Ibid., § 177–80, pp. 214–18.

85 Ibid., § 182–7, pp. 220–6. At § 182 Addition, p. 220. Hegel argues:

> Civil society is the [stage of] difference [*Differenz*] which intervenes between the family and the state, even if its full development [*Ausbildung*] occurs later than that of the state; for as difference, it presupposes the state, which it must have before it as a self-sufficient entity in order to subsist [*bestehen*] itself. Besides, the creation of civil society belongs to the modern world, which for the first time allows all determinations of the Idea to attain their rights ... In civil society, each individual is his own end, and all else means nothing to him. But he cannot accomplish the full extent of his ends without reference to others; these others are therefore means to the end of the particular [person]. But through its reference to others, the particular end takes on the form of universality, and gains satisfaction by simultaneously satisfying the welfare of others.

86 For Hegel, one result of the individualistic operation of civil society in modernity is the problem of poverty. At ibid., § 241, p. 265, Hegel argues that individuals having lost the bonds of family and kinship groups are:

> [M]ore or less deprived of all the advantages of society, such as the ability to acquire skills and education in general, as well as the administration of justice, health care, and often even the consolation of religion.

87 Ibid., §§ 257 and 258, pp. 275–81.

88 Marx's critique of Hegel's notion of the state, that it fails to overcome the social, political and economic conditions of alienation generated by civil society – later re-termed 'capitalism' – is discussed in Chapter 5.

89 On this interpretation, see M. Riedel, *Between Tradition and Revolution: The Hegelian Transformation of Political Philosophy*, trans. W. Wright, Cambridge: Cambridge University Press, 1984; J. Ritter, *Hegel and the French Revolution: Essays on the Philosophy of Right*, trans. R.D. Winfield, Cambridge, MA: MIT Press, 1982.

90 G.W.F. Hegel, *Philosophy of Right*, § 337, p. 370.

91 Ibid.

92 In his discussion of the state, sometimes it is difficult to work out whether Hegel is speaking descriptively, as per the method he claims to follow in the Preface of the *Philosophy of Right*, pp. 21–3: 'To comprehend *what is* is the task of philosophy ... ' and 'A further word on the subject of *issuing instructions* on how the world ought to be: philosophy, at any rate, always comes too late to perform this function', or, of whether he is proscribing a form of an institution which has not yet fully taken shape (not yet realized) within Western history. I think that sometimes Hegel has it both ways, being descriptive and proscriptive when it suits him.

93 G.W.F. Hegel, *Philosophy of Right*, § 324, pp. 360–3.

94 Ibid.

95 On some of the different probable meanings of 'necessary' in this context, see S. Walt, 'Hegel on War: Another Look', in *History of Political Thought*, 10(1), 1989, 112–23, at p. 121; S.B. Smith, 'Hegel's Views on War, the State, and International Relations', *American Political Science Review*, 77(3), 1983, pp. 624–32 at p. 630. Consider also Lukács's comments on the young Hegel's conception of Greek conception of the positive role of dying for one's *polis*. See G. Lukács, *The Young Hegel*.

96 S. Avineri, *Hegel's Theory of the Modern State*, p. 199.

97 See N. Machiavelli, *The Prince and the Discourses*, ed. M. Lerner, trans. L. Ricci, New York: Random House, 1950, pp. 397–402. Hegel's comments here might best be interpreted in light of his similar comments in 'The German Constitution'. Here Hegel draws on Machiavelli in a discussion of the radical means necessary in the formation of a unified state out of smaller conflicting political entities. Note Hegel's comment at p. 80:

> Even Machiavelli's basic aim of raising Italy to statehood is mis-construed by those who are short-sighted enough to regard his work as no more than a foundation for tyranny or a golden mirror for an ambitious oppressor. But even if his aim is acknowledged, it is alleged that his means are abhorrent, and this gives morality ample scope to trot out its platitudes that the end does not justify the means, etc. But there can be no question here of any choice of means: gangrenous limbs cannot be cured by lavender-water, and a situation in which poison and assassination have become common weapons permits no-half measures. Life which is close to decay can be re-organized only by the most drastic measures.

In the *Philosophy of Right*, § 350, p. 376, this is repeated in the sense of Hegel's characterization of the 'right of heroes to establish states'.

98 G.W.F. Hegel, *Phenomenology of Spirit*, p. 272:

> In order not to let them become rooted and set in this isolation, thereby breaking up the whole and letting the [communal] spirit evaporate, government

has from time to time to shake them to their core by war. By this means the government upsets their established order, and violates their right to independence, while the individuals who, absorbed in their own way of life, break loose from the whole and strive after the inevitable independence and security of the person, are made to feel in the task laid on them by their lord and master death.

99 G.W.F. Hegel, *Philosophy of Right*, §§ 322 and 323, pp. 359–60.

100 In this sense, Hegel extends his theory of recognition to inter-state relations. This extension obviously has limits, a state cannot love, and the state cannot think or be self-conscious in the organic sense that a human individual can. However, a state through institutional organization can recognize other actors through the operation of legal forms and through linguistic signification and classification and the state can refuse to recognize its others through force and violence.

101 Such an example of ethics could be seen in a particularly Christian sense in the manner in which Jesus from a religious-ethical standpoint criticized the oppressive practices of the Jewish-Roman political order and Jewish religious-political community. As an example of how this form of ethics operates as a critique of political community and the divisions of political community particularly as given by Saint Paul, see S. Žižek, *The Fragile Absolute: Or, Why is the Christian Legacy Worth Fighting For?*, London: Verso, 2000. Žižek draws upon such a cosmopolitan ethics in his response to the contemporary problem of terrorism. See S. Žižek, *Welcome to the Desert of the Real! Five Essays on September 11 and Related Dates*, London: Verso, 2002.

102 G.W.F. Hegel, *Philosophy of Right*, § 349, p. 375.

103 The notion of the liberal welfare state presented by Rawls could be thought of as a form of ethical-political community. See J. Rawls, *A Theory of Justice*, Cambridge, MA: Belknap Press, 1971.

104 In Chapter 6, I develop a theory of *war as positing* in an effort to sketch an approach that might help us better come to terms with this *aporia*.

105 It would seem that today in the wake of the failure of socialist projects, the collapse of communism and the massive violence wrought by Stalinist and Maoist regimes, the Left is quite caught by the contradiction and in a sense paralyzed by it. It seems that the Left is so caught by a history of the violence of the West and the Enlightenment that it cannot imagine a form of a future ethical-political community that could present a viable, non-violent form of ethical life. So troubled by this, and not wanting to repeat the violence of the past, the Left cannot imagine, let alone commit to, a political programme that might bring about an alternative to liberal-capitalism. On the other hand, the Right fluctuates between suppressing its own violence and embracing it. One might say that only by a certain suppression of this contradiction can one fully embrace the use of violence. The Right seems to suppress a history of its own colonial violence that underlies many of the successes of Western capitalism within the modern world. Yet, in a sense the Right also embraces this violence. It re-narrates this violence via notions of progress, civilization, enlightenment and moral intention and through this allows itself to hold a *belief* in the righteousness of its own historical violence. By suppressing, cleansing and redeeming aspects of its historical violence, the Right can embrace the use of violence in the present to defeat its opposition. In a sense, perhaps the gains made by the Left in critically becoming aware of its own historical violence has led to a certain loss in any belief in the possibility of using violence to realize a better future. Until the Left can come to terms with the role and status of violence within modern social life, political economy, emancipatory politics, and ethics, it is doubtful

whether it will be able to *act* so as to create a future for humanity. Part of this challenge involves moving away from the simplistic response which all too often lays the blame for violence upon irrationality, self-interest, structural and economic barriers or on the 'enemy'. Such a passing of blame misses the point. What needs to be comprehended by any actor is the role and status of its *own* violence historically and ontologically as it pertains to action in the present and hope for the future.

106 G.W.F. Hegel, *Philosophy of Right*, §§ 330 and 333 Addition, pp. 366–8.
107 Ibid., § 333, p. 368.
108 Ibid., §§ 333 and 337, pp. 368–70.
109 Ibid., § 332, p. 368.
110 Ibid., § 334, p. 369.
111 Ibid., § 324, Addition, p. 362.
112 Ibid., § 333, p. 368.
113 Ibid., § 331, pp. 366–67.
114 Ibid., p. 23.
115 Ibid., § 323, p. 360.
116 C. Schmitt, *The Concept of the Political*, trans. G. Schwab, Chicago, IL: University of Chicago Press, 1996, p. 36.
117 G.W.F. Hegel, *Philosophy of Right*, § 331, pp. 366–7.
118 Ibid.
119 Ibid.
120 See *Mabo and Another v The State of Queensland (No. 2)* (1991) 175 CLR 1. The case points to how the recognition of various 'markers' of 'civilization' underlie Anglophone jurisprudence in relation to the acknowledgement or lack of acknowledgement of indigenous sovereignty and rights to property. For a (non-Hegelian) discussion of the production of legal 'jurisdictions' more generally, see S. Dorsett and S. McVeigh, 'Jurisprudence, Jurisdiction, and Authority in Yorta Yorta', *Northern Ireland Legal Quarterly*, 59(1), 2005. Consider also S. McVeigh (ed.) *Jurisprudence of Jurisdiction*, London: Cavendish, 2006.
121 See S.P. Huntington, *The Clash of Civilizations and the Remaking of World Order*, New York: Touchstone, 1996.
122 See E.W. Said, *Orientalism*, London: Routledge and Kegan Paul, 1978. See also P. Fitzpatrick, *The Mythology of Modern Law*, London: Routledge, 1992.
123 The treating of the 'uncivilized' as 'outlaws' who need to be 'civilized' under the rule of law lies at the basis of contemporary international law which has historically legalized the acquisition of territory and the operation of hegemony.
124 Consider this in terms of Žižek's discussion of the 'face of the other' in S. Žižek, 'Melancholy and the Act', *Critical Inquiry*, 26(4), 2000, 657–81.
125 G.W.F. Hegel, *Phenomenology of Spirit*, p. 493.
126 G.W.F. Hegel, *Philosophy of Right*, § 338, pp. 370–1.
127 Ibid., 339, Addition, p. 371.
128 On the idea that Hegel's approach suggests a somewhat optimistic view of history, see S. Avineri, *Hegel's Theory of the Modern State*; J. Bohman, 'Hegel's Political Anti-Cosmopolitanism: The Limits of Modern Political Communities', *Southern Journal of Philosophy*, 29, 2001, 65–91; S.V. Hicks, *International Law and the Possibility of a Just World Order: An Essay on Hegel's Universalism*, Amsterdam: Rudolpi, 1999; T. Mertens, 'Hegel's Homage to Kant's Perpetual Peace: An Analysis of Hegel's Philosophy of Right', *The Review of Politics*, 57(4), 1995, 665–91; A. Peperzak, 'Hegel Contra Hegel in His Philosophy of Right: The Contradictions of International Politics', *Journal of the History of Philosophy*, 32(2), 1994, 241–63.
129 An example of such a form of cultural and moral mastery is given by Rawls in his attempt to draw upon the values and practices of 'liberal' and so-called 'decent'

peoples and extend these universally as a means of bringing an end to war. Rawls is oblivious to his own Western racial and cultural assumptions of superiority and because of this does not see how his framework reproduces, rather then ends, wars of recognition and misrecogntion. See J. Rawls, *The Law of Peoples*, Cambridge, MA: Harvard University Press, 1999.

130 G.W.F. Hegel, *Philosophy of Right*, § 339, p. 371.

131 Michael Walzer makes a similar point in his efforts to tie together the elements of the *ius ad bellum* and the *ius in bello*. See M. Walzer, *Just and Unjust Wars*, 3rd edn, New York: Basic Books, 2000, pp. 127–37.

132 On this relation, see A. Linklater, *Men and Citizens in the Theory of International Relations*, London: Macmillan, 1982.

133 Hegel's problematization of moral judgment through the notion of ethical life has been extended to a contemporary approach to international relations. For such approaches, see K. Hutchings, *International Political Theory*, London: Sage, 1999; C. Brown, *Political Restructuring in Europe: Ethical Perspectives*, London: Routledge, 1994; M. Frost, *Ethics in International Relations: A Constitutive Theory*, Cambridge: Cambridge University Press, 1996.

134 G.W.F. Hegel, *Philosophy of Right*, § 340, p. 340.

135 On the interpretation I have taken here, I have presented Hegel as a thinker who inherits and takes seriously the critical philosophy of Kant and who does not return to an uncritical metaphysics of cosmic being. Thus Hegel's re-appropriation of any aspects of Aristotle's physics and metaphysics is done so by Hegel in the tradition of critical philosophy and with the assertion of the logical primacy of contradiction and antinomy. With regard to the idea of human progress, in terms of both human self-understanding and freedom, Hegel can be understood as sharing with Kant a certain Enlightenment mentality that believed humanity was moving towards greater levels of self-knowledge and development (*Bildüng*). Via this notion of progress, Hegel is able to redeem and rationalize moments of negation and violence that occur within action and within the realization of freedom. See G.W.F. Hegel, *Lectures on the Philosophy of World History: Introduction, Reason in History*, ed. J. Hoffmeister and B. Forbes, trans. H.B. Nisbet, Cambridge: Cambridge University Press, 1975. Much of Hegel's comments on history need also to be read with caution and with one eye upon Hegel's own notion of speculative Christianity which is always doing some sort of work in the background. See H. Küng, *The Incarnation of God: An Introduction to Hegel's Theological Thought as a Prolegomena to a Future Christianity*, trans. J.R. Stephenson, New York: Crossword, 1987. Interpretations about Hegel presenting an 'end of history' argument, such as that given by Francis Fukuyama, should be rejected. See F. Fukuyama, *The End of History and the Last Man*, New York: Avon Books, 1992. For a critique of 'end of history' misinterpretation of Hegel, see J. Stewart (ed.) *The Hegel Myths and Legends*, Evanston, IL: Northwestern University Press, 1996.

Chapter 5

A politics of violence

I

The work so far has presented a number of modern lines of inheritance of the problem of war. Each has framed the figure of war within a differing relation to the concept of right and through this has produced divergent accounts of the concept of war. Yet, through the juridical, moral and ethical ordering of war, the idea that war is an act carried out by a sovereign state, and that the problem of war is primarily one of inter-state relations, has remained relatively central. For Hobbes, the sovereign state appeared as the juridical mechanism through which social peace could be secured from the conditions of widespread social violence and civil war. While the radical demand of freedom expressed by Rousseau and the French Revolution threatened to overturn the oppressive state and opened onto a cosmopolitan demand for human freedom, for Kant, the juridical figure of the state remained the central moral actor who, in a world of inter-state relations, was charged with the task of ending war and establishing an inter-state federation. For Hegel, the juridical figure of the state remained in a central position and was imbued with ethical legitimacy as the institution through which freedom was realized in modernity. Through such an account, the concept of war as state war assumed renewed legitimacy and was portrayed as playing a significant role in the realization of human freedom in history.

While these approaches to the ordering of war have placed the state and the concept of state war in a privileged position, each account can be thought to contain a counter-discourse theoretically upsetting the state's monopoly upon the legitimacy of violence. In Hobbes, this could be seen in the role civil war played in the production of the concept of war: a role which could not be completely suppressed and which threatened to re-emerge and upset the stability of the conceptualization of war as state war. In Kant, such a counter-discourse was more open and was expressed in the form of a universal moral and cosmopolitan demand for freedom and justice which placed all state-based political action under moral critique. In Hegel, the constitution of modern life through the relations of private property within the sphere of civil society limited the complete and universal realization of freedom within the ethical life of the state. Further, an individual state's independence was shown to be heavily dependent upon an inter-state relation of recognition and often violent moments of misrecognition contained within this.

This chapter focuses upon how a number of elements of this counter-discourse have been inherited by a loose tradition or set of traditions that re-frame the problem of war. Drawing attention to aspects of the thinking of Karl Marx, Vladimir Ilyich Lenin, Carl Schmitt, and Walter Benjamin, the chapter demonstrates how the concept of war as state war is challenged, and perhaps even undone, by what might be thought of as the *political ordering* or the *political disordering* of war. The use of such a term does not imply that the previous forms of war's ordering were in any way apolitical. On the contrary, each tradition ordered the concept of war around differing visions of political community and each set out differing conceptions of the role that violence played in the constitution of the political. What arises, however, in the tradition of the political (dis)ordering of war, is an explicit emphasis upon the political nature of the previous traditions of war's ordering. The tradition of the political (dis)ordering of war exposes and challenges the particular political conceptions that reside underneath juridical, moral and ethical traditions in their ordering of the legitimacy of violence. Against this, the tradition sets up rival accounts of the political and re-orders the concept of legitimate violence to this purpose.

The chapter begins by discussing Marx's critique of the Hegelian state and of how Marx's idea of class conflict is taken up by Lenin and later by Schmitt to develop an account of war as *political conflict*. The political ordering of war challenges the traditional Westphalian ordering of the boundaries of the legitimacy of violence around the state and turns the notion of war back into a global intra-state civil war in which politics and political ideas are militarized. By bringing a modern concept of war back to its 'origin' within civil war, the tradition of the political ordering of war draws links between the founding violence of states and that of partisan, revolutionary and terrorist violence which challenge the state and attempt to found new political-legal orders. When state war is viewed simply as just another form of political violence, then the violence of the partisan, revolutionary and terrorist does not appear as anything new or obscene, but merely as a continuation and development of a certain approach to politics within modernity. However, rather than reducing legal violence to political violence, this chapter develops an account which shows how a distinction between legal and political violence can be retained. A notion of the rightness of war can be better understood when comprehended in light of an ongoing, dynamic relation between legal and political violence.

II

One entry point into the critique of the legitimacy of state war within modernity is via focusing upon Marx's inheritance of the philosophy of Hegel and the way in which Marx critiques the Hegelian conception of the state. Marx's critique of Hegel's account of the state opens up a line of critique of state war that emphasizes a moment of political and economic conflict underlying all juridical and ethical claims.[1] On the interpretation taken here,[2] the young Marx can be read as arguing that Hegel's conception of freedom within the ethical life of the state represents an 'ought' rather than a comprehensive grasping of social life as it 'is'. In this respect, Marx can be interpreted not as rejecting Hegel's conception of freedom as ethical life, but, in arguing that ethical life or freedom, occurring as the full, mutual recognition of members of humanity, is *yet to be realized* within the state and is reliant upon political action for its full realization.[3]

In the Introduction to *Toward a Critique of Hegel's Philosophy of Right* (1844),[4] Marx prefaces his critique of Hegel's 'idealization' of the state with an account of a form of idealization that occurs in religion. Inheriting and developing Ludwig Feuerbach's critique of Hegel,[5] Marx argues that the 'criticism of religion is the premise of all criticism'[6] and that humanity must seek to grasp its true reality, and not become lost in a reflection of itself in the fantastic unreality of heaven.[7] Further, he argues that religion is a social form of reflection which is produced in response to the yearnings of human life. Religion operates as a theory of consolation and justification of the ills of the human world through positing an idealized realm of human happiness in an after life.[8]

For Marx, the attempt to grasp the 'truth', and doing so in the critical tradition inherited from Kant, involves not being caught in the 'reflected essence' of man. Rather, it involves comprehending the conditions of human suffering within the state and society and changing them. Marx can be understood not as arguing for a simplified critique or dismissal of religion, but of grasping the 'humanist essence' of religion: that religion presents a human ethical demand for the alleviation of suffering and that this demand must be carried out, not by being caught up in a reflected-idealized form, but by *acting* upon the human world which produces this reflection. In this sense, one might understand Marx's argument that:

> *Religious* suffering is the *expression* of real suffering and at the same time the *protest* against real suffering. Religion is the sigh of the oppressed creature, the heart of a heartless world, as it is the spirit of spiritless conditions. It is the *opium* of the people.
>
> The abolition of a people's *illusory* happiness is the demand for their *real* happiness. The demand to abandon illusions about their condition is a *demand to abandon a condition which requires illusions*. The criticism of religion is thus in *embryo* a *criticism of the value of tears* whose *halo* is religion.[9]

For Marx, Hegel's philosophical account of the state presents an idealization similar to a form of religious reflection; it presents a reflection upon the poverty of the political realities of Germany in the nineteenth century which lagged behind the historical political and economic revolutions of France and England. Read in this sense, the ethical account of the state described by Hegel did not represent the historical development of human freedom within nineteenth-century Germany, but rather, presented only an idealization, a dream-history, of German conditions.[10] Marx argues that Hegel's speculative account of the state occurs as an 'abstraction' from the real conditions of human life in Germany and as such satisfies man only in an 'abstract' way.[11] For Marx, what is demanded by Hegel's philosophical 'idealization' of freedom in Germany is really the realization of this demand through *praxis*: the *realization of human freedom through human action*. Marx argues:

> To be radical is to grasp things by the root. But for man the root is man himself. The clear proof of the radicalism of German theory and hence of its political energy is that it proceeds from the decisive *positive* transcendence of religion. The criticism of religion ends with the doctrine that *man is the highest being for man*, hence with the *categorical imperative to overthrow all conditions* in which man is a degraded, enslaved, neglected, contemptible being.[12]

Marx moves away from the emphasis given by Hegel to the role of the political institution of the bourgeois state in the realization of human freedom. This is not to say that Marx does away with institutions, but that he links the question of freedom back to a certain cosmopolitan emphasis.[13] What is sometimes called the 'humanism' of the young Marx carries forth the radical demand of freedom expressed by Rousseau and the French Revolution which is driven beyond the confines of the political-juridical entity of the European state. In this regard, Marx launches the question of the emancipation of humanity as a global question. He can be understood as positioning the demands of *human dignity* (as a social question and not merely a question of liberal rights and individual autonomy) and the *human emancipation from conditions of oppression* as the central concern of social theory, critical political economy and political action.[14]

In another sense, Marx re-shapes or re-orientates the tradition of German Idealism through an emphasis upon the central position of human action. Marx radicalizes Fichte's conception of self-positing and action, '*Tathandlung*',[15] to produce a philosophical viewpoint that focuses upon the creation of the human world through the constituting power of human acts. In Marx, there is a serious inheritance of the creative role of the *deed* and the manner in which the human deed does not simply mechanically affect something in the world, but rather, that the deed *re-creates* the human world. That is, the deed revolutionizes the world through its action, and opens a space of future possibility that was not immediately there before its intervention. Goethe's statement that 'In the beginning was the deed' is taken over by Marx in his claim that 'The philosophers have so far only *interpreted* the world in various ways; the point is, to change it.'[16]

Following from this, Marx's focus upon the centrality of human action can be seen to begin to produce an account which demonstrates how the conditions of human poverty, oppression and suffering are *produced* through human political and economic action and of how these conditions can only be challenged by human action itself. Such an account radicalizes a connection highlighted by Hegel in the *Phenomenology of Spirit* between the operation of the negativity within the deeds of human thinking and thought's physical-political consequences in the shaping of the human world. Marx's emphasis upon the significance of this operation and the connection between political thinking and political action has consequences for the ordering of war.[17]

In the *Economic and Philosophic Manuscripts* (1844), Marx points to what he finds central to Hegel's philosophy. Marx argues:

> The outstanding thing in Hegel's *Phenomenology* and its final outcome – that is, the dialectic of negativity as the moving and generating principle – is thus first that Hegel conceives the self-genesis of man as a process, conceives objectification as loss of the object, as alienation and as transcendence of this alienation; that he thus grasps the essence of *labour* and comprehends objective man – true, because real man – as the outcome of man's *own labour*. The *real*, active orientation of man to himself as a species being, or his manifestation as a real species being (i.e. as human being), is only possible by his really bringing out of himself all the *powers* that are his as the *species* man – something which in turn is only possible through the totality of man's actions, as the result of history – is only possible by man's treating these generic powers as objects: and this, to begin with, is again only possible in the form of estrangement.[18]

Marx argues that Hegel 'grasps labour as the essence of man' but that he sees only the positive and not the negative side of labour.[19] Further, Marx argues that Hegel only recognized 'mental labour'[20] and in this respect Hegel neglected and devalued the importance of 'manual labour'. For Marx, Hegel grasps a powerful conception of labour in the production of 'thinghood' or 'objectification', as a central element of the subject-object relation. In this relation, the objective world (social conditions, laws, ethics, political institutions) do not stand independent of the human subject (as might be conceived in pre-critical, metaphysical accounts of 'natural law') but are *produced* through the intellectual and physical labour and action of the human subject who is then able to hold the product of its labour, a part of itself, as an object, external to itself.

For Hegel, the object is an externalization of the subject's labour and, through its awareness of this, the subject returns to itself via its object and knows itself, therefore, as *subject-object*.[21] Part of Marx's criticism involves the argument that Hegel does not pay close enough attention to the operation of objectification within the capitalist economy and its result as economic and political alienation. That is, Hegel does not fully grasp the alienation of manual labour and the consequences this has within the realm of civil society.[22]

For Marx, Hegel does not draw a firm enough distinction between the positive operation of objectification, thinghood, and externalization (*Entäußerung*) and the negative consequences of alienation (*Entfremdung*) within a capitalist economy.[23] Marx argues:

> Labour produces not only commodities: it produces itself and the worker as a *commodity* – and does so in the proportion in which it produces commodities generally.
>
> This fact expresses merely the object which labour produces – labour's product – confronts it as *something alien*, as a *power independent* of the producer. The product of labour is labour which has been congealed in an object, which has become material: it is the *objectification* of labour. Labour's realization is its objectification. In the conditions dealt with by political economy, this realization of labour appears as a *loss of reality* for the workers; objectification as *loss of the object* and *object-bondage*; appropriation as *estrangement*, as *alienation*.[24]

And, that:

> The alienation of the worker in his product means not only that his labour becomes an object, an *external* existence, but that it exists *outside him*, independently, as something alien to him, and that it becomes a power on its own confronting him; it means that the life he has conferred on the object confronts him as something hostile and alien.[25]

For Marx, due to the alienation of the human subject from its object (in which case the object sits as an alien power over the subject), Hegel's moment of speculative return, or moment of recognition, in which the subject comes to know itself in the object, occurs only in 'thought'. The speculative return occurs in the same sense of the idealization of religion, as an 'illusory reconciliation', which expresses the lack of reconciliation between subject and object within inter-human relations and in the relation between humans and the natural world. For Marx, the reconciliation between subject and object occurring in thought develops as an 'abstraction'[26] from the concrete economic, political and social relations of the world of *spirit* (*Geist*) and the state in which many human subjects have no control over their labour, are exchanged as commodities, and are held in a relation of subservience by the legal and political ordering of the state that stands over them.[27]

For Marx, Hegel's inability to constantly return to the alienation of the living, breathing, suffering human within the movement of *spirit* (*Geist*) and the state fails to adequately address the fractures within the subject-object relation within modern political economy – that is, within the capitalist system of the production and exchange of commodities. Instead, for Marx, Hegel treats 'real man' as a mere predicate of an idealized or 'unreal man'[28] who has its freedom in the movement of the state as the historical subject. In treating real humans as mere predicates of the state, Marx thought that Hegel did not correctly grasp the concrete social relations within modern political economy and instead gave greater value to the objectification of human labour over and above the labouring human.[29]

In this sense, part of Marx's so-called 'inversion' of Hegel involves bringing attention back to the living, breathing, suffering human who is caught within the web of complex political, economic and social relations. These human subjects are held against moments of their objectified existence as the ethical life of the state, which for Hegel assumes the position of an acting (and sometimes, a self-reflecting) subject. For Marx, Hegel's philosophy has a tendency towards over-idealization in situations where he treats *spirit* (*Geist*) and the state as acting subjects at the expense of ignoring the human individuals who are really doing the active *work* at the heart of any objectified form of life. In a manner, Hegel's tendency to over-emphasize the role of the state and treat it as having a life of its own displays a number of similarities with elements of the mature Marx's notion of the commodity fetish.

In *Capital* (1867), Marx speaks of the fetishism of commodities and their mystical value. He argues:

> A commodity appears at first sight an extremely obvious, trivial thing. But its analysis brings out that it is a very strange thing, abounding in metaphysical subtleties and theological niceties. So far as it is a use-value, there is nothing mysterious about it, whether we consider it from the point of view that by its properties it satisfies human needs, or that it first takes on there properties as the product of human labour. It is absolutely clear that, by his activity, man changes the forms of the materials of nature in such a way as to make them useful to him. The form of wood, for instance, is altered if a table is made out of it. Nevertheless the table emerges as a commodity, it stands on its head, and evolves out of its wooden brain grotesque ideas, far more wonderful than if it were to begin dancing of its own free will.[30]

For Marx, the operation of the fetishism of commodities is analogous to moments in religion when products of the human brain appear as autonomous figures endowed with a life of their own and which enter into relations with each other and with humans.[31] For Marx, there is nothing mysterious about use of the commodity. But its value represents the objectification of human labour, the measure of its value being related to the proportion or quantity of labour contained in its production.[32] Where the mysterious nature of the commodity arises is in its forms of value, as exchange value. In the exchange relation the commodity, as the product and objectification of labour, occurs as a thing which is given value in relation to other things.[33] The social production of the value of commodities within the exchange relationship develops for Marx in a similar way to which norms are produced between recognizing subjects within Hegel's theory of recognition. For Marx, through their exchange, the products of labour acquire a socially uniform objectivity as values, which are distinct from their sensuously varied objectivity as objects of use and utility.[34] Marx argues:

> Men do not therefore bring the products of their labour into relation with each other as values because they see these objects merely as the material integuments of homogenous human labour. The reverse is true: by equating their different products to each other in exchange as values, they equate their different kinds of labour as human labour. They do this without being aware of it. Value, therefore, does not have its description branded on its forehead; it rather transforms every product of labour into a social hieroglyphic.[35]

In a sense, the Hegelian state might be understood as a form of fetish object, an objectification whose value is built up by various thought determinations and over-idealizations. Hegel's claim that there is an ethical moment in war may be seen as the high point of this fetishism in which the ethical 'value' of war is far removed from the lives of many citizens who live in a state of poverty and unfreedom. With this comparison in mind, it is worth turning briefly to an account that links the commodity fetish to modern legal forms given by Marxist jurist Evgeny Pashukanis.

In *A General Theory of Law and Marxism* (1924),[36] Pashukanis links the development of the modern legal subject to the production and exchange of commodities in the exchange relation within modern capitalism. Pashukanis argues that in Marx the analysis of the form of the subject follows directly from the analysis of the commodity form.[37] Pashukanis argues that while the commodity acquires its value independently of the will of the labouring subject, the determination of the commodity's value presupposes and relies upon an act of will on behalf of the owner of the commodity.[38] He quotes Marx's statement in *Capital* that:

> Commodities cannot themselves go to market and perform exchanges in their own right. We must, therefore, have recourse to their guardians, who are the possessors of commodities. Commodities are things, and therefore lack the power to resist man. If they are unwilling, he can use force; in other words, he can take possession of them. In order that these objects may enter into relation with each other as commodities, their guardians must place themselves in relation to one another as persons whose will resides in these objects, and must behave in such a way that each does not appropriate the commodity of the other, and alienate his own, except through an act to which both parties consent. The guardians must therefore

> recognize each other as owners of property. This juridical relation, whose form is contract, whether as part of a developed legal system or not, is a relation between two wills which mirrors the legal relation. The content of this juridical relation (or relation of two wills) is itself determined by the economic relation. Here the persons exist for one another merely as representatives and hence, owners, of commodities.[39]

Pashukanis argues that at the same time that the product of labour becomes a commodity and bearer of value, man acquires the capacity to be a legal subject and bearer of rights.[40] For Pashukanis, 'Legal fetishism complements commodity fetishism.'[41] He argues:

> Simultaneously with this, social life disintegrates, on the one hand into a totality of spontaneously arising reified relations (including all economic relations: price level, rate of surplus value, profit rates and so forth) – in other words, the kind of relations in which people have no greater significance than objects – and, on the other hand, into relations of a kind where man is defined only by contrast with an object, that is, as a subject. The latter exactly describes the legal relation. These are the two basic forms, which differ from one another in principle, but are at the same time interdependent and extremely closely linked. The social relation which is rooted in production presents itself simultaneously in two absurd forms: as the value of commodities, and as man's capacity to be the subject of rights.
>
> Just as in the commodity, the multiplicity of use-values natural to a product appears simply as the shell of a value, and the concrete types of human labour are dissolved into abstract human labour as the creator of value, so also the concrete multiplicity of the relations between man and objects manifests itself as the abstract will of the owner. All concrete peculiarities which distinguish one representative of the *genus homo sapiens* from the another dissolve into the abstraction of man in general, man as legal subject.[42]

For Pashukanis, the natural law account of the juridical state arising through a social contract of free willing, recognizing individuals presupposes the production of commodities and the exchange relation.[43] What is portrayed as 'natural' and 'universal' within the natural law tradition is really the historical development of a form of legal subjectivity that emerges out of increasingly complex stages of commodity production through which legal rights and the legal system come to coordinate, organize and protect the exchange of commodities and the accumulation of property and capital.[44] He claims:

> Just as chance acts of exchange and primitive forms of exchange, such as the exchange of gifts, preceded the exchange transactions of developed commodity production, so too the armed individual (or, more often, group of people, a family group, a clan, a tribe, capable of defending their

> conditions of existence in armed struggle), is the morphological precursor of the legal subject with his sphere of legal power extending around him. This close morphological link establishes a clear connection between the law court and the duel, between the parties to a lawsuit and the combatants in armed conflict. But as socially regulative forces become more powerful, so the subject loses material tangibility. His personal energy is supplanted by the power of the social, that is, of class organization, whose highest form of expression is the state. In this form, the impersonal abstraction of state power functioning with ideal stability and continuity in time and space is the equivalent of the impersonal, abstract subject.[45]

For Pashukanis, within theories of natural law, legal coercion is presented as an objective, impartial norm, emanating from the abstract collective person (the state).[46] He argues, however, that in fact all the theorists of natural law (for example, Grotius) have done is to develop a theme of power representing the connecting link between owners of commodities.[47] He argues that what theorists of natural law describe in a non-historical and abstract, rationalistic manner, when describing state power and coercion, is the affirmation and protection of an economic relation between commodity owners and enforcement of contacts in the market. He argues:

> In the intercourse between commodity owners, the necessity for authoritarian coercion arises whenever the peace is disturbed or a contract not fulfilled voluntarily. The doctrine of natural law therefore reduces the function of state power to keeping the peace, and sees the state's sole determining feature as being the instrument of law. After all, in the market, one owner of commodities is a commodity owner by consent of the others, and all of them are commodity owners through their collective will. That is why the theory of natural law deduces the state from the contract between isolated individuals.[48]

By highlighting the relation between legal rights and the commodity form, Pashukanis is able to draw attention to a Marxist theory of law which does not reduce law and the state to a simple account of class power.[49] Rather, by showing how the modern form of legal subjectivity is bound to and develops with the production and exchange of commodities within capitalism, the legal use of force and violence by the state is shown to be linked to the protection of the free exchange of commodities. To the extent that legal rights and the state develop (through property ownership) by favouring the owners of property and commodities to the disadvantage of those whose labour is alienated, then law can be understood as underlying and sustaining a form of 'class' rule.

Yet, the use of force and violence by the state and the rule of law does not occur as the crude and direct form of coercion of one class by the other, such as in the direct sense of the coercive power relation between master and slave. Rather, as law regulates the free actions of legal subjects, it affirms the right to dispose of one's property as one sees fit, equally and universally for all legal subjects. In this manner the perpetuation of the legal form institutionalizes the alienation of labour and actively disadvantages individuals who form part of a propertyless class. Further, the power of state violence is mobilized under the rule of law to punish anyone who challenges or upsets the peaceful, exchange of commodities or who challenges the setting of the value of commodities (and human life) by the market. In this manner, while the law is applied uniformly and equally to all sectors of society, it entrenches a particular form of economic and social ordering understood as modern capitalism. The law legitimizes and enforces through the threat and use of violence the economic coercion of the market.

In such a manner, the juridical forms of the legal subject and the state can be seen to mask or veil concrete economic relations in which labour is alienated and large sectors of society are driven into poverty. While the law carries out an economic function, the *legal form* abstracts from this function and presents law as a neutral space. Abstracted from the concrete, raised, and at times deified, legal subjectivity and the state appear as living personas that interact in the world with their others. Yet, these personas as fetish characters hide, placate and purify a muddied and dirty realm of economic conflict, coercion and social and political struggle. Viewed in this light, both the state's suppression of internal violence and the efforts of international law to regulate state war in the name of peace are questioned.[50] The 'peaceful' operation of modern capitalism is placed under the direct challenge of class conflict, and the extension of this via the notion of class war, each of which play out at a global level.

In Marx's theory of economic and social relations and in Pashukanis's Marxist theory of law, at least two accounts of violence can be seen to have been developed. The first involves the legal order of the state which carries out the role of enforcing the economic system of modern capitalism. In the guise of a supposedly neutral 'rule of law' and through championing of liberal individual rights as property rights, the law, via the threat and use of violence, provides the coercive force that protects property owners, upholds exploitative employment contracts, and allows some individuals to accumulate greater wealth through the labour of others who are precluded from this. Law renders legitimate and enforces an economic system that entrenches alienation, inequalities of bargaining power, unfreedom and the process of the ongoing commodification of society and culture. Within Marx's account, however, lies a deeper idea of the operation of violence which is linked to coercion, force and power within economic relations. The legal violence of the state develops as a formalization of this economic violence through law's redescription of certain economic conditions as having the status of 'right'.

In part, Marx's account draws upon and re-develops aspects of Hegel's theory of recognition as an economic-social theory. Marx adopts Hegel's notion of self as subject-object which is dialectically and inter-subjectively produced within the symbolic realm of social relations and within the physical-material activity of labour. The operation of inter-subjective recognition takes place within a modern economy structured by historical inequalities of wealth – property and accumulated money or capital – which give some actors control over the means of production and a greater purchasing power over labour. Set within the production of commodities as objects or things which take on fetish values, the exchange and valuing of labour as a commodity, the valuing of things as higher than human lives, and the drive by those actors who possess property and capital to make ever greater profits on the production and exchange of commodities, then the individual and its desire for freedom through full, mutual recognition are continually *negated* by a system of economic relations that hampers the realization of freedom for all individuals, equally.

Within Hegel's notion of the struggle for recognition as a 'duel' one self succeeds in part through being able to overpower the other and establish itself as a master over the slave. This power relation could be seen also within the construction of normative universals, through recognition, which underlay the production of notions of right. For Marx, this notion of conflict and enslavement takes place within the economic and social realm of modern capitalism with particular actors being empowered in economic sense through possessing greater property and capital and being backed by the coercive weight of the market and the legal system.

Such a power relation allows the capitalist to recognize the value of the worker's labour only in limited ways. The moment of recognition occurring within the agreement or contract between capital and labour is one-sided and coercive. The capitalist, possessing greater resources and wealth, holds a greater bargaining power over its workers who are forced out of necessity (and in competition with other workers) to accept less payment for the product of their labour. Inequality of economic power, backed by law, transforms the labour contract into a contract of subservience and further allows the capitalist to recognize and treat its human labourers merely as things.[51] Pushed by the drive for greater profits and out of the fear of economic ruin, the capitalist is compelled to play out multiple struggles for recognition with other capitalists in their competitive exchange of commodities.[52] Again this takes place on the playing field of unequal economic power and the treatment and valuing of others as dehumanized things.

In this context, moments of mutual inter-subjective recognition are partly blocked by conflict and violence created by struggles for recognition between actors who attempt to survive and realize their individual freedom within the compulsion and coercion of competitive markets. Further, mutual recognition is also partly blocked by the endemic economic-cultural practice of commodification in which individuals are socialized into comprehending their selves and their others as things – viewed and valued in the same way as the commodity objects produced by human labour.

Under such conditions the individual is blocked from fully recognizing itself and its others in their social being and instead has its view of the world caught by a particular phase of *spirit* (*Geist*) – the commodity form of modern capitalism – which it reproduces and re-inscribes continually through the world through every thought and act.[53] The shape of *spirit* (*Geist*) as the commodity form starts to infect all levels of inter-subjective recognition within social and material life. For Marx, what saves, in part, this shape of *spirit* (*Geist*) from becoming absolute is the unsustainability of capitalism as a historical economic system, and the possibility of some sectors of society understanding both their social being and the transformative social power of their activity (their deeds) through the experience and comprehension of the special dialectical status of labour. In this respect, struggles for recognition play out as struggles between sectors of society over working conditions[54] and as revolutionary struggle to transform the whole sphere of economic, social, political and juridical relations.

For Marx, Hegel's notion of the bourgeois state cannot realize freedom through mutual, inter-subjective recognition because it cannot overcome the forms of negation, coercion, force, compulsion and violence that constitute the economic relations of the market and commodification within modern capitalism. What is needed in its stead is a radical, re-ordering of human economic, social, political and juridical life which transcends the conditions of economic violence and posits a new set of social and economic relations which will more fully realize human emancipation and human happiness.

For Marx, moral regulation by the state with the purpose of minimizing some of the inequalities and lessening some of the harmful consequences of negation within the economy is not enough. Rather, freedom demands an entirely new social, economic and politic community be constituted – a freedom of human recognition which could only come about through social, economic and political revolution. To the extent that those who uphold the system of capitalism through the state and its rule of law desire to defend the status quo through force and violence, then those guided by a revolutionary socialist idea of freedom may be forced to oppose this violence with violence. Within such a Marxist conception of the positing of a new social order reliant, if only in part, on counter-violence, a problem arises as to what extent the old form of state violence is done away with and not replicated or renewed in order to protect and police the newly constituted political community.

III

While Marx is critical of Hegel's conception of the state, he holds onto Hegel's notion of civil society and develops this account and its global implications.[55] Hegel recognized that the demand created by civil society for markets and resources pushed it to reach out beyond its own political boundaries and create colonies.[56] Marx radicalizes this conception and points to the role of the political and economic relations within civil society which underlie state action and state violence. Such an account is given a powerful expression within *The Communist Manifesto* (1848).[57]

For Marx and Friedrich Engels, the state represents the interests of a particular class of property owners and entrepreneurs, the 'bourgeoisie', who have risen in modernity to control the political benefits of the economic relations of civil society.[58] Religious and political claims veil the economic exploitation and alienation of labour perpetuated by the bourgeois class within the state and at a global level. For Marx, the form of economic ordering of the modern capitalist economy (controlled by the bourgeois class) is driven to universalize itself: civil society in both its positive and negative consequences becomes a universal, cosmopolitan, and global form of social organization. Marx argues:

> The need of a constantly expanding market for its products chases the bourgeoisie over the whole surface of the globe. It must nestle everywhere, settle everywhere, establish connections everywhere.
>
> The bourgeoisie has through its exploitation of the world market given a cosmopolitan character to production and consumption in every country. To the great chagrin of Reactionists, it has drawn from under the feet of industry the national ground on which it stood. All old-established national industries have been destroyed by new industries, whose introduction becomes a life and death question for all civilized nations, by industries that no longer work up indigenous raw material, but raw material drawn from the remotest zones; industries whose products are consumed, not only at home, but in every quarter of the globe. In place of the old wants, satisfied by the productions of the country, we find new wants, requiring for their satisfaction the products of different lands and climes. In place of the old local and national seclusion and self-sufficiency, we have intercourse in every direction, universal inter-dependence of nations. And as in material, so also in intellectual production. The intellectual creations of individual nations become common property. National one-sidedness and narrow-mindedness become more and more impossible, and from the numerous national and local literatures, there arises a world literature.[59]

Marx was not unaware of the benefits of such a cosmopolitanism arising through emerging global economic and political inter-relations and the inter-dependency of societies. Yet these benefits could not mask the grave forms of oppression resulting from a particular class having control over, or guiding, human economic relations whose negative consequences were justified in the name of greater enlightenment or 'civilization'.[60] Further, rather than considering poverty as a natural condition, Marx argued that the control over economic and political relations held by the bourgeoisie led to the *production* of an oppressed and exploited class, the 'proletariat'.[61]

Through Marx, the justification of state violence in terms of notions of sovereignty, national interest, morality or ethical life, as presented by traditions stretching from Grotius and Hobbes, to Kant and to Hegel, is re-formulated via an account of global economic-political relations. The juridical form of the state and its moralization is rendered subservient to a cosmopolitan political conception which portrays opposing groups within society, stretching across state boundaries, struggling over the control of the economic basis of social organization. In this respect, questions of law and morality are re-framed as political and economic questions of ordering, organization and social antagonism.

Marx can be understood as reformulating the Hobbesian conception of moral-political life as warring, violent struggle, through building upon a Hegelian conception which attempts to grasp the objective conditions of human relations and social life. The epistemic conflict presented in Hobbes, arising from an inability of social thought to reconcile religious, political and moral truth claims, is expressed as a conflict between worldviews that reflect opposing positions within the process of economic, social and political production. Social antagonism and violence are explained by the exploitation of some sectors of society, carried out by others, who control the operation of political and economic organization and the means of production. What was described by Hegel as contradiction and conflict within the realm of *spirit* (*Geist*) is re-described by Marx as social antagonism and conflict between differing groups within modern political economy.

By grasping the very real differences in the quality and power of human life based upon an individual's position within material-economic conditions of society, Marx can relate the epistemic conflict between human subjects, and their attempts to negate their others, to the objective causes of social antagonism and civil war. The negative aspect of human thought, as negation, and its connection to social violence becomes more apparent. The ability to order and organize economic and social relations has a direct impact upon the lives of particular members of society whose alienation, exploitation and suffering generate political demands against the ruling class. The inability to reconcile the political demands of various opposing sectors of society leads to the use of violence to maintain or affirm political demands.

The position suggests that war is no longer the struggle of all against all (either physically or at the level of ideas), nor is war simply the act of violence between states. Rather, underlying the concept of war is a conflict between competing groups (classes) over the control of wealth, the means of production, the ownership of property, and the authority and power to order and organize social, legal, political and economic relations.[62] In the sense that each of these groups presents a differing viewpoint over how social, economic and political life is to be organized, there exists a conflict or war at the level of concepts or ideas. This conflict is, however, related to and a result of the differential objective conditions of social life. In general terms, war becomes a conflict between those who suffer[63] and those who benefit from capitalism. As such, the concept of war is re-framed by Marx as a history of 'class struggle'.[64]

One wider step from Marx into 'Marxism' involves the re-framing of 'class struggle' as 'class war'. In some interpretations of Marxism, war is re-conceptualized as a Manichean struggle between two classes: the bourgeoisie and the proletariat. In others, the notion of class war militarizes the whole of social and political life and even the realm of ideas. While only certain elements of these movements might be found in Marx, they are found quite strongly in some of his inheritors and in the way in which they develop a political concept of war and a warlike conception of politics.

Marx's critique of the state through an account of global political economy (global capitalism) and the characterization of global politics as class struggle are given firmer expression by Lenin.[65] Lenin develops a critique of state war and re-formulates politics more clearly as class war. In *Imperialism, the Highest Stage of Capitalism* (1917),[66] Lenin places European inter-state and colonial wars firmly under the hammer of ideology critique. The wars of European states are placed within the context of the global operation of finance capital.

For Lenin, the monopolization of markets via 'cartels' (companies grouped together to establish monopolies) transforms capitalism into *imperialism* when the holders of finance capital, and the states whose interests are bound up with capital (or controlled and directed by capitalist interests), establish monopolies within foreign markets and divide these markets among themselves.[67] The outward reach of economic interests creates a world market in which domestic markets become inter-dependent and reliant upon the movement and control of finance capital.[68] The inter-dependence binds state interests to the attempt to control markets abroad, which, for Lenin, are best secured through the acquisition of colonies.[69]

Through such an account, Lenin portrays inter-state war as the attempt by 'capital-rich' countries to establish colonies and the struggle between capital-rich countries to control, divide and re-divide world markets.[70] For Lenin, when the economic interests of states come into conflict and cannot be reconciled, then their only resolution is through war.[71] Further, within the conflict between imperialist states, moments of 'peace' are nothing other than temporary 'truces' which prepare the groundwork for new wars as the growing economic strength of emerging imperialist powers comes to challenge the monopolization of markets held by established powers.[72]

Such an analysis is not out of place today. The 'imperialistic' character of the 'war on terror' fought out in the Middle East and Central Asia can be understood as a war fought between capital-rich countries to control oil and gas resources and their respective markets. In this sense, the war fought by the USA and the UK in Afghanistan and Iraq is, in one respect, a conflict between competing capital rich countries (or state economies) such as China, Russia, and the European Union (centred around France and Germany).[73] This imperialist war is merely a continuation in a long series of conflicts for economic and strategic control over the Middle East and Central Asia, which has been continually carved up and re-carved as the balance of power between capital-rich states has historically shifted.[74] In one sense, groups of Iraqi and Afghani resistance forces who are fighting against US and European occupation, and other militant Islamicist political organizations carrying out acts of violence at an international level – at the level of a global 'front' – are fighting a war against imperialist aggression, an anti-imperialist war located firmly within global capitalism. In another sense, some of these actors are also merely the pawns used within wider strategic conflicts between capital-rich powers in the context of a changing global status quo.

Turning back to Lenin, his account can be understood as affirming and attempting to extend a connection Marx made between the operation of politics, political struggle and violence. For capital-rich states, war takes place as the extension or positing of their economic interests and the attempt to gain control over the ordering of world markets. On the other hand, for the alienated and oppressed, war is the struggle to gain political control over the economic and social ordering of society. Significantly, Lenin, in his re-formulation of war, cites and draws upon the Prussian war theorist, Carl von Clausewitz, and his famous statement that 'War is merely the continuation of politics by other means' ('*Der Krieg ist eine bloße Fortsetzung der Politik mit anderen Mitteln*').[75] In 'The Military Programme of the Proletarian Revolution' (1916),[76] Lenin argues:

> Theoretically, it would be absolutely wrong to forget that every war is but the continuation of policy by other means. The present imperialist war is the continuation of the imperialist policies of the two groups of Great Powers, and these policies were engendered and fostered by the sum total of relationships of the imperialist era. But this very era must also necessarily engender and foster policies of struggle against national oppression and of proletarian struggle against the bourgeoisie and, consequently, also the possibility and inevitability; first, of revolutionary national rebellions and wars; second, of proletarian wars and rebellions *against* the bourgeoisie; and, third, of a combination of both kinds of revolutionary war, etc.[77]

In 'War and Revolution' (1917),[78] Lenin argues:

> War is a continuation of policy by other means. All wars are inseparable from the political systems that engender them. The policy which a given state, a given class within that state, pursued for a long time before the war is inevitably continued by that same class during the war, the form of action alone being changed.[79]

For Lenin, such an account changes the notion of 'peace' which must be understood within the context of global economic and political struggles. Most importantly, the securing of peace in one region needs to be understood in terms of how this peace is sustained through war and bloody oppression in other parts of the world. Peace is a concept which is mediated through the operation of war. Lenin argues:

> Peace reigned in Europe, but this was because domination over hundreds of millions of people in the colonies by the European nations was sustained

> only through constant, incessant, interminable wars, which we Europeans do not regard as wars at all, since all too often they resembled, not wars, but brutal massacres, the wholesale slaughter of unarmed peoples. The thing is that if we want to know what the present war is about, we must first of all make a general survey of the policies of the European powers as a whole.[80]

For Lenin, one of the consequences of imperialist wars was the militarization of the whole of social life. In this, all social life was caught up in ongoing, global struggles over the political and economic control of the earth.[81] Significantly, Lenin's argument was not that socialism should demand peace or disarmament, but, rather, that socialism must engage in a legitimate, 'just war' against the imperialist bourgeoisie.[82] Lenin argues that at some points the proletariat ripens into a 'fighting party'. In 'Guerrilla Warfare' (1906),[83] he argues:

> [A] Marxist cannot regard civil war, or guerrilla warfare, which is one of its forms, as abnormal and demoralizing *in general*. A Marxist bases himself on the class struggle, and not social peace. In certain periods of acute economic and political crises the class struggle ripens into direct civil war, i.e., into an armed struggle between two sections of the people. In such periods a Marxist is *obliged* to take the stand of civil war. Any moral condemnation of civil war would be absolutely impermissible from the standpoint of Marxism.[84]

For Lenin, in the conditions of exaggerated social antagonism, socialist political struggle may adopt the strategies of war. Further, Lenin grasped the importance for socialist political struggle of adopting strategies of warfare different from the ordered and regimented structure of nineteenth-century European inter-state warfare. Lenin argues that, at times, socialist revolutionary politics must develop through adopting forms of warfare such as 'guerrilla warfare' and even 'terrorism'.[85] Through such a move Lenin forges a link between a change in the philosophical ordering of war and a change in the strategy and form of warfare and does so by tying the political notion of war as *revolutionary violence* to an emerging strategy of unconventional military fighting.[86] This link between political struggle and guerrilla war was inherited and developed by numerous influential socialist, revolutionary leaders of the twentieth century such as Mao Tse-tung[87] and Ernesto 'Che' Guevera.[88]

One consequence of the line of thinking developed by Lenin is a *militarization of the political*. In the context of imperialist war, class struggle moves more openly to assuming the position of class war. Through such a movement it is not only the concept of war that is altered, but also the concept of the political. Politics and the realm of political ideas are treated as warlike and, in such a context, every idea is seen to both express and to hide a partisan position. The extension of this notion is that all ideas within society display the operation of partisan political struggle. Nothing is neutral, neither science nor philosophy. One such example of this notion is given in Lenin's comment that:

> [B]ehind the epistemological scholasticism of empiro-criticism one must not fail to see the struggle of parties in philosophy, a struggle which in the last analysis reflects the tendencies and ideology of the antagonistic classes in modern society. Recent philosophy is as partisan as was philosophy two thousand years ago.[89]

In such an approach, intellectual discussion or debate becomes a form of fighting and disputes a form of battle. From such a position, notions of class, or revolutionary war, or, partisan political struggle, come to pervade and re-characterize human social life, such that every aspect of life gets sucked into a hyper-aggressive re-formulation. Here the Hobbesian metaphor of a conflict between ideas being a war of all against all is taken to its logical limit. Within such a climate how else is a war of ideas, or a war between political positions, to be resolved if not with the raising of a sovereign authority to dictate a 'party line' over all aspects of human social life and over the world of ideas? It would seem that any political system or institution founded upon such a militarized conception of the political would have extreme difficulties in ever being able de-militarize. Once the move is made to consider the political as essentially warlike, then it becomes difficult to separate a notion of critique from armed attack.

Further, within a militarized conception of the political, there occurs a certain snowball effect bound up with the concept of war. The traditional notion of war as state war is broken down into a partisan war between competing political groups and economic-political conceptions. Following this, as social life is understood as being more and more warlike, the concept of war starts to assume a larger and larger content. War becomes life and life becomes war. At such a point any discernible content of a concept of war perhaps fades into oblivion. Every act of violence, every act of government, any closing of a factory, demonstration or denunciation comes to be known as war.[90] Every political actor, every poet, every stone-throwing child, by being portrayed as partisan warriors are treated like enemy soldiers – imprisoned, tortured, shot. Public life is ordered by a logic of military strategy and all is pushed to the side that stands in the way of victory.

IV

The reformulation of war as class war, or as a global intra-state civil war between political actors, has not widely upset the dominance of the traditional Westphalian conception of state war within the discourse of contemporary international law. Few jurists would be willing to recognize this form of political violence as 'war proper'. One jurist, who against the grain, paid attention to the changing nature of warfare within the twentieth century and argued that the concept of war itself needed to be revised to take account of these changes was Carl Schmitt. Schmitt, with his ambiguous Nazi heritage, grasped the significance of socialist and anti-colonial nationalist struggles of the twentieth century and the manner in which they challenged the dominant, Westphalian conception of war. Schmitt referred to this emerging form of warfare as 'partisan war'.

Schmitt's *The Theory of the Partisan* (1963)[91] attempts to trace a historical change in the phenomenon of war, or at least a changing dynamic within the sphere of war, which has consequences for the concept of war. For Schmitt, the change gained momentum in the twentieth century and involved an emphasis upon forms of 'irregular' or 'guerrilla' warfare fought very successfully by non-sovereign actors against traditional, uniformed armies of European states. This form of warfare was deployed in the anti-colonial wars against the French in Indochina (1946–54) and Algeria (1954–62) and had developed during World War II (1939–45) in Europe particularly against the German invasion of the Soviet Union and, earlier, by the Chinese communists against the invading Japanese army (1932–45).[92]

For Schmitt, the initial moments of this form and strategy of non-sovereign violence occurred successfully in the Spanish Guerrilla War (1808–14) against Napoleonic France.[93] Schmitt referred to this form of fighter as the 'partisan': a figure, who becoming increasingly prevalent, put in question the traditional European concept of inter-state war. In contrast to the classical model of regular European inter-state war, Schmitt saw the war of the partisan as a form of warfare that was becoming increasingly important. For Schmitt, a modern concept of war would need to be adjusted in light of this emerging phenomenon which could be no longer be regarded as a mere 'exception' to regular warfare. Schmitt attempts to provide something of a definition of the notion of the partisan. He points to four criteria: irregularity; increased mobility; a tellurian character; and an intensity of political commitment.[94]

For Schmitt, the partisan carries out an irregular form of fighting, this is of course defined through negation of whatever counts as 'regular' warfare, but at least it might be thought to involve not wearing a military uniform, not carrying weapons openly, using secrecy, sabotage, and so on.[95] The partisan is characterized by agility, speed, surprise attack and increased mobility which develop with the further mechanization and motorization of warfare.[96] Further, the tellurian character is important for the partisan, it involves the partisan's relation to the earth, to the population and to the geographical specificity of the region which is the sphere of warfare.[97] In this sense, the partisan is primarily defensive in character and, for Schmitt, the nature of the partisan changes somewhat when the partisan takes on a world revolutionary form, whereby 'justice', formerly tied to one portion of the earth, land, soil, becomes a de-territorialized, universal concept.[98]

Perhaps, most importantly, what characterizes the partisan is for Schmitt a certain 'political character'. He argues that an intense political character is crucial as it distinguishes the partisan from other fighters, from the thief and criminal, or the pirate, whose violence is carried out only for private enrichment.[99] Schmitt notes that the partisan fights on a political front, and it is precisely this character which brings to the fore the original sense of the word 'partisan'.[100] In drawing attention to the political nature of partisan warfare, Schmitt gives particular attention to the theories of Clausewitz and Lenin.

Schmitt notes that Clausewitz's formula that 'War is merely the continuation of politics by other means' is the theory of the partisan in nutshell.[101] For Schmitt, the development of the theory of the partisan as moving beyond of form of military classification towards properly a 'political theory' came about through an intellectual climate in Berlin in the early nineteenth century.[102] In one sense it was a development of the Prussian *Landsturm* edict (1813), lasting only for three months before its revocation, which under Prussian royal edict prepared for a partisan war against the invading armies of Napoleonic France.[103] This '*Magna Carta* of partisanship'[104] called for all citizens to obey no orders from the enemy and to instead resist the intruding enemy with whatever means were at hand.[105] For Schmitt, the ideas behind this short-lived document which 'legitimated the partisan in the interest of national defence'[106] became theorized by intellectuals in Berlin.

This intellectual climate included the young Clausewitz who in his lectures at the military academy spoke of the possibilities of this political form of guerrilla and insurrectional war of the *Parteigänger* – 'conducted by a people in its own fields [*Fluren*] on behalf of their freedom and independence'.[107] Schmitt notes that Clausewitz's conception was limited by the still prevalent classical conception of war in his thought, and that the theory of the partisan was to be developed and radicalized as a political theory by Lenin.[108] In this move, the shift in the conception of the partisan from being primarily defensive to that of taking part in a revolutionary civil war is significant.[109]

Schmitt argues that Lenin was the first who consciously conceived of the partisan as an important figure of national and international civil war.[110] Schmitt states:

> What Lenin learned from Clausewitz, and he learned it well, was not just the famous formula of war as the continuation of politics. It involved the larger recognition that in the age of revolution the distinction between friend and enemy is the primary distinction, decisive for war as for politics. Only revolutionary war is true war for Lenin, because it derives from absolute enmity. Everything else is a conventional game.[111]

For Schmitt, the importance of Lenin's reformulation lies in the sense that today the partisan's 'irregularity' refers not simply to the military line or formation, as it did in the eighteenth century when the partisan was merely a lightly-armed troop standing in contrast to the uniformed regular troop.[112] Rather, for Schmitt, the irregularity of the class struggle calls not just the military line, but, *the whole edifice of political and social ordering into question*.[113] He argues that Lenin raised this new strategy and military reality to a level of philosophical consciousness, whereby the alliance of philosophy with the partisan unleashed new, unexpected and explosive forces.[114] In this formulation, the traditional legal ordering of states and state violence is put under threat by a global partisan civil war guided by competing conceptions of what is 'good' and 'just'.[115]

Schmitt argues that while some forms of international law have taken small steps to address the position of regular fighters (for example, on the treatment of partisan prisoners as possessing the rights of regular soldiers and not as 'criminals'),[116] on the whole, the juridical response to the phenomenon of the partisan has been to ignore the facts on the ground, to 'criminalize' the partisan, and to re-affirm the classical conception of European inter-state war fought by regular armies.[117]

However, the relation between the sovereign state and the partisan is more ambiguous than the standard account given by international law. Schmitt notes that the partisan, as an irregular fighter, is always dependent in some way upon a regular power.[118] This dependency occurs through economic and military assistance and through political acts of recognition. In this respect the position of the partisan is linked to a relation with an 'interested third party'.[119] For Schmitt, the interested third party offers not only money, munitions and material assistance, but further, offers a form of political recognition which is required by the partisan if it is to avoid falling into the sphere of the 'unpolitical': that is, the sphere of the 'criminal', including the thief and the pirate.[120] Schmitt argues that in the longer view of things the 'irregular must legitimize itself through the regular'.[121] For the partisan this involves only two possibilities: recognition by an existing regular state power, or, the establishment of a new regularity by its own force.[122]

For the partisan, neither of these two options is unproblematic. Schmitt notes that when dependent upon the recognition of powerful political actors, the partisan is bound into a global political context. In a sense, the partisan becomes something of a pawn within a larger power's own aggressive aims.[123] Schmitt argues:

> At this point the partisan ceases to be essentially defensive. He becomes a manipulated cog in the wheel of world-revolutionary aggression. He is simply sent to the slaughter, and betrayed of everything he was fighting for, everything the telluric character, the source of his legitimacy as an irregular partisan, was rooted in.[124]

For Schmitt, under this conception, the partisan operates within a wider political context of 'friend and enemy'. In being dependent upon an interested third party so as not to sink into the realm of criminality, the partisan presupposes not only an enemy but also a friend.[125] Situated within this context of a multiplicity of potential friends and enemies, the partisan is forced to decide who constitutes the 'real enemy'.[126]

Schmitt's account of partisan war and the recognition of the partisan by interested third parties is not out of place within contemporary international relations and the 'war on terror'. Often the claim is made that the question of the legitimacy of 'terrorist' violence is a matter of perspective in the sense of the saying that 'one man's terrorist is another's freedom fighter'. Yet Schmitt's placing of the partisan within a politics of recognition, driven by conflicts between larger powers, structured around a friend–enemy relation, moves the question of legitimacy away from that of mere 'perspective'. The question of legitimacy becomes a question of recognized legitimacy, and, a moral just cause becomes a question of the politics and political recognition of friends and enemies. In this sense, the contemporary criminalization of particular violent actors as 'terrorists' sits firmly within a politics of recognition. Many contemporary actors (both states and non-sovereign actors) carry out acts of terrorism, yet only some are named and denounced as 'terrorists'.

Through such a notion one might make more sense of the relation between the USA and militant Islamicist political organizations such those represented by the figure of Osama Bin Laden and the 'group', '*al-Qa'ida*'. In the 1980s Bin Laden and other Arab and Afghan fighters were funded, encouraged, legitimized by the USA as 'freedom fighters' against the invasion and occupation of Afghanistan by the Soviet Union. In that time and for that purpose, for the USA, these people were 'friends' in a struggle against the 'evil empire' and were even celebrated in Hollywood cinema.[127] At some point long before the bombings in New York and Washington, DC, in 2001, these very same 'freedom fighters' had moved over to the category of the enemy and were described by Western governments and Western media as 'terrorists'.

Behind this movement is a complex set of political and strategic manoeuvres explaining the shift in the recognized moral and political status of these partisans from friends to enemies. For the discussion here what is most important is not how historically this shift has occurred but, of the question mark *any* such shift places over contemporary legal and ethical claims to the illegitimacy of particular acts of non-sovereign, irregular, partisan violence. The West's general celebration of a partisan war of resistance to the Soviet Union's occupation of Afghanistan and the subsequent denunciation of a partisan war of resistance to the occupation of Iraq by the USA, points to an affirmation of the Schmittian account of partisan war. That is, all too often, judgment on the legitimacy or illegitimacy of non-sovereign, irregular, partisan war is not a matter of law and ethics. Rather, it is purely a matter of political decision – of supporting friends and of condemning enemies. Significantly, in politics, for reasons of expediency, friendships do not seem to last very long, and in this respect what is at issue here is not really friendship as such, in any firm ethical sense,[128] but merely the pragmatic affirmation of one, who for the time being helps to further your interest and is not your enemy.

While there is much to learn from the Schmittian account, there is a certain danger in reducing not only partisan war, but all forms of war, to Schmitt's friend–enemy distinction. In one sense, the friend–enemy distinction, set out by Schmitt in *The Concept of the Political* (1932) perfectly describes how many on the 'Left' and on the 'Right' think about politics. Yet the notion presents a danger of simplifying political analysis into purely binary, Manichean structures and strips away much of the complexity and detail of political life. Taken too seriously, the reduction of the world to that of friends and enemies becomes a form of abstraction which actively shuts out the detailed inter-relations of the concrete. Further the idea, as an affirmation of the political, risks a certain militarization of the political in a similar manner to the characterization of politics as class war present within elements of Lenin's thought.

For Schmitt, the categorical distinction which determines the political is the relation between 'friend and enemy'.[129] Schmitt argues:

> The political enemy need not be morally evil or aesthetically ugly; he need not appear as an economic competitor, and it may even be advantageous to engage with him in business transactions. But he is nevertheless, the other, the stranger; and it is sufficient for his nature that he is, in a specially intense way, existentially something different and alien, so that in the extreme case conflicts with him are possible. These can neither be decided by a previously determined general norm nor by the judgment of a disinterested and therefore neutral third party.[130]

Schmitt argues that only actual participants can recognize their concrete condition of conflict. He argues that: 'Each participant is in a position to judge whether the adversary intends to negate his opponent's way of life and therefore must be repulsed or fought in order to preserve one's own form of existence.'[131] Placing the friend–enemy distinction in the context of its relation to war Schmitt argues:

> War is neither the aim nor the purpose nor even the very content of politics. But as an ever present possibility it is the leading presupposition which determines in a characteristic way human action and thinking and thereby creates a specifically political behaviour.[132]

There is a question here over whether the existential threat of war and the subsequent determination of the other as either a friend or enemy constitutes the whole, or, just a part of the political. The question goes beyond the present discussion and leads away from a focus upon war towards a focus upon the political.[133] While the question cannot be taken up any further here, it does at least draw attention to some form of relation between war and the political. If the political, or politics in general, is understood as being marked in some way by struggle, conflict and even open war between opposing partisan, political conceptions, then a firm juridical or ethical concept of war is challenged as the realms of law and ethics are themselves placed under contestation. In other words, when the juridical and ethical are characterized as merely forms of justifying political violence and the outcome of violent political struggle, then it becomes difficult to distinguish a distinct juridical, moral or ethical concept of war from a more general category of *political violence* which lays claim to numerous forms of legitimacy.[134] Part of the challenge of developing a modern concept of war involves the attempt to present an account that can hold onto a notion of war that is placed within a context of political violence but is not reduced to this.

V

One way of coming to terms with the challenge the political (dis)ordering of war poses to thinking about war more generally is to attempt to hold onto some sort of relation and distinction between law and politics. While forms of law such as state sovereignty or international law are placed under political critiques which claim that their legitimacy is flawed (and that law is really the working of politics in disguise), there still exist legal structures in the world that exert a degree of power over societies and territory which thinking has to come to terms with. Further, in the sense put forward by Pashukanis, the establishment of the ideological nature of particular concepts in no way exempts us from the obligation of seeking and coming to terms with their objective reality.[135]

In this sense, while from a political viewpoint, one might claim that state war and partisan war, or what will be called, *non-sovereign war*, each occur as a particular violent means to secure political ends, there still remain important elements of difference contained within their legal forms which has certain consequences within legal, political and social life. Viewed from the perspective of positive law, part of the difference involves the sense that one form of violence is enacted by an existing legal structure which has a degree of universality, control, power and sovereignty over a particular society and territory, while the other lacks and, to an extent, desires this.

In holding onto this difference, one might be able to discern a certain *dynamic* operating within a wider concept of political violence. The dynamic involves a continual process of the drawing, challenging, and re-drawing of the legitimacy of the boundaries of violence by the law in relation to those who stand outside the law, or whose political claims are *not yet* law. In this dynamic, legal violence is not reduced to political violence but stands as a particular form towards which political violence strives and as which it wants to realize itself. In this striving, political actors want their conception of the world to become law, to be realized in actuality, and to be endowed with the universal status and authority of law – even if this 'universal' is limited to a particular territory. In such a manner, a juridical concept of war is not reduced to political violence but is placed within a dynamic where political violence strives towards the status of legal legitimacy, and in this sense, strives towards the status of becoming 'war properly so called'.

The basic argument here is that there is at least *one* form of law which remains universal and continues even after all other legal forms have been transformed or displaced by political and social revolution. This form arises around the need of any political or social organization to designate a single authority which determines the legitimate use of violence, that is, a body which reserves for itself the final right to pass judgment on who may legitimately use violence.[136] A dynamic relation between legal and political violence can be thought to revolve around this basic form of law and the question of who might occupy the absolute, authoritative position of judgment.

The outline of the political ordering of war presented so far involves a distinction between state sovereign war and irregular forms of guerrilla, terrorist, and revolutionary war understood generally as partisan or non-sovereign war. Both of these are placed within a wider context of ongoing struggles and conflicts over the political control of society and the economy fought at local and global levels. Given that this conflict, often occurring between the state and the non-sovereign or partisan group, takes place within an existing structure of legal relations, the non-sovereign group is often placed at the disadvantage of being criminalized and of having its acts of violence condemned as illegal. Any chance of a non-sovereign group having a claim to the legal and non-criminal use of violence is dependent upon it being recognized as a 'friend' of a powerful interested third party or by a system of international law. Even if this occurs, such recognition takes place within a context of both legal and political contestation.

Opposed to the condemnation by the state or legal order is the claim by the non-sovereign group and its supporters and sympathizers that the state's, or a legal order's, legality is founded upon political violence and that its legality is in many ways nothing more than the result of a previous violent political victory. In a manner, part of the challenge of non-sovereign war is the argument that law is in many ways nothing more than a glorified, mystified, and fetishized, form of political violence. Or, at least, that legal orders have their *origin* in political violence, and that when viewed from this perspective, legal violence cannot be too dissimilar from other forms of political violence that contest it. In considering this claim, it is worth turning briefly to a number of conceptions given by Walter Benjamin.

Benjamin in the *Critique of Violence* (1921),[137] draws attention to the role and characterization of violence within law, legal orders and the state. In focusing upon positive law's affirmation of legal violence and its condemnation of other forms of violence, he argues:

> The meaning of the distinction between legitimate and illegitimate violence is not immediately obvious. The misunderstanding in natural law by which a distinction is drawn between violence used for just and unjust ends must be emphatically rejected. Rather, it has already been indicated that positive law demands of all violence a proof of its historical origin, which under

> certain conditions is declared legal, sanctioned. Since the acknowledgement of legal violence is most tangibly evident in a deliberate submission to its ends, a hypothetical distinction between kinds of violence must be based on the presence or absence of a general historical acknowledgement of its ends. Ends that lack such acknowledgement may be called natural ends, the other legal ends. The differing function of violence, depending upon whether it serves natural or legal ends, can be most clearly traced against a background of specific legal conditions. For the sake of simplicity, the following discussion will relate to contemporary European conditions.
>
> Characteristic of these, as far as the individual as legal subject is concerned, is the tendency not to admit the natural ends of such individuals in all those cases in which such ends could, in a given situation, be usefully pursued by violence. This means: this legal system tries to erect, in all areas where individual ends could be usefully pursued by violence, legal ends that can only be realized by legal power. Indeed, it strives to limit by legal ends even those areas in which natural ends are admitted in principle within wide boundaries, like that of education, as soon as these natural ends are pursued with an excessive measure of violence, as in the laws relating to the limits of educational authority to punish. It can be formulated as a general maxim of present-day European legislation that all the natural ends of individuals must collide with legal ends if pursued with a greater or lesser degree of violence. (The contradiction between this and the right of self-defence will be resolved in what follows.) From this maxim it follows that law sees violence in the hands of individuals as a danger undermining the legal system. A danger nullifying legal ends of the executive? Certainly not; for then violence as such would not be condemned, but only that directed to illegal ends. It will be argued that a system of legal ends cannot be maintained if natural ends are anywhere pursued violently. In the first place, however, this is a mere dogma. To counter it one might perhaps consider the surprising possibility that the law's interest in a monopoly of violence vis-à-vis individuals is not explained by the intention of preserving legal ends but, rather, by that of preserving the law itself; that violence, when not in the hands of the law, threatens it not by the ends that it may pursue but by its mere existence outside the law.[138]

One distinction that might be understood as present within Benjamin's account involves a separation between the form of law, or more properly, the form of positive law, and the political content of positive law. The form of positive law invoked by Benjamin involves a sense reminiscent of the juridical ordering of violence contained within the Hobbesian tradition (and the traditions of early modern legal sovereignty more generally) involving a positing or establishment of an authority over a particular territory in which the sovereign has universal authority to pass judgment on and draw the boundaries of the legitimate use of violence. Such a form of positive law is not empty or neutral; it contains within it a particular political content and endorses a particular approach to the organization of social and economic relations within society. As such, every positive legal order contains within it a particular set of political ends, conceptions of the good or of political justice, which law realizes universally with the backing of legal violence.[139]

What Benjamin might be seen to draw attention to is the idea that the positive law's de-legitimization of non-sovereign violence is not so much directed at suppressing the realization of competing claims of political justice through violence, but rather, of protecting and defending the role or form of law itself. Benjamin should not be read here as excluding the fact that positive law is of course defending a particular account of political justice (for example, liberal capitalism) against the demands of other groups (for example, revolutionary socialists, anarchists, and today, radical Islamicists). While Benjamin takes note of this account, he refuses to reduce legal violence to simply a moment within a conflict between competing political groups over political justice. In a sense, Benjamin's account tries to keep open a space of law and legal violence as something distinct from politics and political violence. Part of this distinction involves the modern form of positive law as an authority which judges the legitimacy of the use of violence. In holding onto this, it can be understood that while a political group may want to do away with a particular political content of positive law, it does not want to do away with this central element of the modern form of law as such. Rather, such a group wants to occupy this position and give to law a new political content. In this manner, legal violence may be considered as somewhat different to political violence.

Legal violence, for Benjamin, involves both law-making and law-preserving functions.[140] In its law-preserving function, legal violence maintains, secures and defends the form of positive law. It marks the clear separation between legitimate and illegitimate violence by calling 'legitimate' only that violence which it proscribes within limits or which is done by legally authorized agents – the police, prison guards, and the military. Further, law-preserving violence maintains the form of law by crushing any actors who claim the authority of judgment on the use of violence. While law may delegate moments of this judgment, it reserves the absolute right of judgment for itself and enforces this right through violence.

Law-making violence points to a creative function within law by which the authority of positive law over territory and over persons is extended through the violence of law's agents. Benjamin gives the example of the intervention of police for 'security reasons' in situations where no clear legal situation exists.[141] In this sense, the violence of positive law, and the violence that stands behind it as a potential threat, occur as a form of organizing or ordering human life at the boundaries of what is prescribed by statute. This sense of organizing involves a broad sense of the German verb '*walten*', as both a form of reigning or ruling (*herrschen*, *gebieten*) and as something of a working power (*Kraft*) which affects and comes to influence or order things. The verb '*walten*', is related to the term '*Gewalt*', which contains not only the sense of violence, but also that of power and authority. Understood in this sense, the law-preserving and law-making functions of legal violence (*Gewalt*) are related to the perpetuation and continual re-creation of the form of law as an authority and power (and in particular, an authority over the use of violence). In a manner, part of the creative or law-making function of *Gewalt*, as authority and power, involves the organizing and ordering of space, human bodies and human behaviours in a manner that expands the *order* and reach of law without necessarily relying upon acts of physical violence.[142]

For Benjamin, in the exercise of legal violence, and in particular in the exercise of legal violence over life and death, 'something rotten in law' is revealed.[143] Part of this involves the sense that in the operation of legal violence, moments of the origin or foundation of positive law are reflected. Systems of positive law, legal orders and states do not historically emerge out of the ether. Rather, most often they are founded, created and posited through acts of political violence and methods of military violence – revolutions, coups, seizures of power, and wars. What is rotten in the law, what makes law stink, is its origin in political violence which positive law continually tries to hide, deny and purify. Law seems to stink the most when it condemns acts of non-sovereign violence as 'terrorism' while ignoring or suppressing the historical fact that so many particular legal orders have been founded, and often initially maintained, through terror. On the relation between the founding of positive law in political violence and the hiding of this violence, Jacques Derrida argues:

> *All* Nation-States are born and found themselves in violence. I believe that truth to be irrecusable. Without even exhibiting atrocious spectacles on this subject, it suffices to underline a law of structure: the moment of foundation, the instituting moment, is anterior to the law or legitimacy which it founds. It is thus *outside the law*, and violent by that very fact. But you know that this abstract truth could be illustrated (what a word, here!) by terrifying documents, and from the history of all states, the oldest and the youngest ... This foundational violence is not only forgotten. The foundation is made in *order* to hide it; by its essence it tends to organize amnesia, sometimes under the celebration and sublimation of the grand beginnings.[144]

Rather than collapsing legal violence into a more general category of political violence, what might be sketched is a certain dynamic relation between political and legal violence. Within this dynamic a legal order or a state is founded by acts of political violence and at this moment of founding a form of law is posited which holds within it, and attempts to realize, a particular conception of political justice determined by the victorious parties. What was political violence now adopts the form of law. Or rather, at the moment of positing a legal authority, what was raw political violence is now transformed, changed, taken up, and re-cast under the form of law. In this form, the old act of political violence is de-legitimized as positive law adopts the position of being the sole authority that may pass judgment on acts of violence. This moment of positing and transformation involves also an act of re-narration of law's beginnings, involving purification, collective forgetting and the suppression of law's foundation. In this sense, law's self-narrative presents law, not emerging from political violence, but as emerging from itself – as a law or legal sovereignty that has been somehow posited by the law, a law that has been and continues to be *self-posited.*

Against this legal fiction stand non-sovereign groups or partisans who challenge positive law's inherent political content and who understand the historical fact that law is founded upon political violence. These partisans are completely modern, they view their acts of violence as that which will destroy an old legal order and through which a new order will emerge: they wish to posit, raise up and create a new human order through action, and if necessary, through violence. For some, this new order may involve simply replacing those in ruling positions at the top of a regime, for others, this positing may involve a complete transformation and revolution of all aspects of society and the economy. These various partisans seek to found a new political justice through acts of violence and to universalize this in the form of law. For these partisans, when standing outside the law, the difference between political and legal violence, between war proper and revolution or terror is irrelevant and occurs only in the realm of 'thought'. However, for positive law, this distinction is critical. By drawing the distinction between legal and political violence, positive law attempts to consistently maintain the separation between law and politics and to maintain the idea of law as a realm which is distinct from the political.

In this dynamic, the non-sovereign group or partisan wants to both destroy a regime of positive law, and occupy the place of law so as to become the legal authority. Against the attempt of the political partisan to realize itself as the law, a positive legal order draws upon all violence it considers 'necessary' to defend its posited legal order and its status and position as *law*. The drawing of the legal distinction between an act of violence as 'war', as opposed to non-sovereign violence, including terrorism and revolution, can be seen as an outcome of this dynamic. At the level of international law, non-sovereign violence is de-legitimized and only the violence of states is understood in the legal sense of war and even this is limited by the legal notions of the regulated use of force and 'war crime'. Within the state, non-sovereign violence is de-legitimized and treated as crime and set against the legitimate and legal operation of military and police violence. For non-sovereign political actors who oppose the political content of international and state law, these distinctions remain a farce. That is, up until and shortly after the time of victory, in which case these categories are drawn upon and put to use again to preserve and maintain a newly constituted legal order.

VI

Outlining a dynamic between political and legal violence involves a number of difficulties. At its core, law can never be separated from politics, no form of law will be 'neutral' and every posited order of law will contain a political content – a particular account of political justice. Just as the critique of the supposed 'neutrality' of law is politically motivated, so is the attempt by legal positivism to draw a strict line of distinction between law and politics.

Further, a certain account of law that follows on from Hobbes in an Anglo-European tradition of coming to terms with the problem of public violence, runs into difficulty in extreme cases of civil war. In such cases, when the former sovereign authority who had decided over legitimacy of the use of violence can no longer back this decision with any power and this position of authoritative judgment is claimed by another or a number of competing groups, via violence, then the typical question is raised of whether or not *the law* still exists. Following a Hobbesian line of thought, the law in this case does not exist until a new sovereign authority who may judge universally on the use of violence can be posited effectively. Certainly, for many, this is a very thin and limited account of what law is. Yet with regards to the specific question of the public use of violence and the manner in which a legal sphere of violence may be carved out of political violence to peacefully mediate between claims, this account of law still holds some degree of historical and contemporary purchase.

One way getting around this impasse is by arguing that in a situation of civil war 'law' does not disappear entirely. Rather, it remains to the extent that it involves a set of customary, inter-subjective norms that are still honoured by people as habitual, intact aspects of ethical life, for example, the laws of marriage, or of purchasing of goods. Where the law seems to fall apart in this situation is at the point of its enforcement, that is, when parties no longer uphold the law voluntarily, or come into a dispute which needs to be reconciled by legal judgment and legal violence. At the point of judgment on violence and enforcement through violence, the law, in such a context might be thought to break down. In this respect it might be important to identify and separate at least two aspects of modern law: on the one hand, an inter-subjective operation of universal norms, and, on the other, a standpoint of judgment on conflicting claims containing the authority to decide the legitimate use of violence. In the chaos of civil war the latter sense may be seen to be rendered problematic while the former may still function until such a point that circumstances drive it towards a dependency upon the latter. Thinking about law in such a way avoids a reduction of the concept of law to a bare Hobbesian position, but has the benefit of holding onto the central significance of an aspect of law identified by both Hobbes and Benjamin, each centred upon the position of judgment on the legitimate use of violence.

More generally, the difficulty in attempting to outline a dynamic between political and legal violence suggests something more central within the political ordering of war which is worth paying attention to. The political ordering of war points to the central operation of *contestation* within the ordering of the legitimacy of violence. The operation of political contestation and conflict upsets law and legal violence because modern law demands order. Opposed to this it would seem that the political is more chaotic, involves ongoing irreconcilable conflicts between opposing positions which resists being ordered.

An endless contestation which drives and sits at the heart of the political renders any moment of judgment on violence fundamentally problematic. To the extent that legal judgment on violence does not want to be problematic, law suppresses the political moment within itself, and abstracts from the political, economic and social conditions in which it lives and from which it has been produced. At this point, crisp and reified legal definitions such as that of 'war proper' rise up, take on a life of their own and begin to dance. It would seem that these definitions can continue to dance only so long as they are backed by power. When this starts to evaporate, legal judgment and legal definitions are forced to more openly fight it out in the muddy world of political conflict and contestation. At this point the claims over the authority to pass judgment on violence begin to look more like the contested claims for legitimacy in the to and fro of civil war.

Notes

1 The account presented here focuses primarily upon juridical and political questions and the ordering of the concept of war within a relation between differing conceptions of legal and political violence. In this respect, I am not attempting to present a comprehensive Marxist economic critique of war and international relations.

2 On the relation of the young Marx to Hegel more generally, see L. Kolakowski, *Main Currents of Marxism*, Vol. 1, trans. P.S. Falla, Oxford: Oxford University Press, 1981; H. Marcuse, *Reason and Revolution: Hegel and the Rise of Social Theory*, 2nd edn, London: Routledge & Kegan Paul, 1955; G. Lukács, *The Young Hegel: Studies in Relations between Dialectics and Economics*, trans. R. Livingstone, Cambridge, MA: MIT Press, 1976; J. Hyppolite, *Studies on Marx and Hegel*, trans. J. O'Neil, London: Heinemann, 1969.

3 For such a positioning of Marx with regard to the conception of freedom and ethical life as presented by Hegel, see S. Avineri, *The Social and Political Thought of Karl Marx*, Cambridge: Cambridge University Press, 1968.

4 K. Marx, 'Toward a Critique of Hegel's Philosophy of Right: Introduction', trans. L.D. Easton and K.H. Guddat, in L.H. Simon (ed.) *Karl Marx: Selected Writings*, Indianapolis, IN: Hacket Publishing, 1994.

5 L. Feuerbach, *The Essence of Christianity*, trans. G. Eliot, New York: Harper & Row, 1957. L. Feuerbach, *Principles of the Philosophy of the Future*, trans. M.H. Vogel, Indianapolis, IN: Bobbs-Merrill, 1966.

6 K. Marx, 'Toward a Critique of Hegel's Philosophy of Right: Introduction', p. 28.

7 Ibid.

8 Ibid.

9 Ibid. Note that sometimes the term 'opium' in this passage is better read as 'opiate'.

10 Ibid., p. 32.

11 Ibid., p. 33.

12 Ibid., p. 34.

13 On the 'cosmopolitan' aspects of Marx's theory, consider the accounts in: A. Linklater, *Men and Citizens in the Theory of International Relations*, London: Macmillan, 1982; D. Boucher, *Political Theories of International Relations: From Thucydides to the Present*, Oxford: Oxford University Press, 1998.

14 My interpretation here is influenced by the work of Ernst Bloch. For Bloch, the concerns of human dignity, human freedom and human happiness are not simply concerns of a young 'humanistic' Marx. Rather, these lie at the core of any present or future account of Marxism or socialism which must remain aware of its historical inheritance of the radical elements of the tradition of natural law. See E. Bloch, *Natural Law and Human Dignity*, trans. D.J. Schmidt, Cambridge, MA: MIT Press, 1996.

15 On the relation between knowledge and action and the influential position of Fichte's notion of '*Tathandlung*' on the radicalization of Hegel's philosophy by his socialist inheritors and of how this extends through to critical theory, see G. Kortian, *Metacritique: The Philosophical Arguments of Jürgen Habermas*, trans. J. Raffan, Cambridge: Cambridge University Press, 1980. Consider also the accounts in K. Löwith, *From Hegel to Nietzsche: The Restoration of Nineteenth Century Thought*, trans. D.E. Green, London: Constable, 1964; J. Habermas, *The Philosophical Discourse of Modernity*, trans. F.G. Lawrence, Cambridge, MA: MIT Press, 1990; L.S. Stepelevich (ed.) *The Young Hegelians: An Anthology*, Atlantic Highlands, NJ: Humanities Press, 1997.

16 K. Marx, 'Theses on Feuerbach' Introduction', in L.H. Simon (ed.) *Karl Marx*, p. 99.

17 Consider the comment in K. Marx, 'Toward a Critique of Hegel's Philosophy of Right: Introduction', pp. 29–30:

> *War* on German conditions! By all means! They are *below the level of history, beneath all criticism*, but they are still an object of criticism just as the criminal below the level of humanity is still an object of the *executioner*. In its struggle against these conditions criticism is not a passion of the head but a head of passion. It is not a lancet, it is a weapon. Its object is an *enemy* it wants not to refute but to *destroy*. For the spirit of these conditions has already been refuted. In and for themselves they are objects not *worthy of thought* but *existences* as despicable as they are despised. Criticism itself does not even need to be concerned with this matter, for it is already clear about it. Criticism is no longer an *end in itself* but simply a *means*. Its essential pathos is *indignation*, its essential task, *denunciation*.

18 K. Marx, *Economic and Philosophic Manuscripts of 1844*, trans. M. Milligan, Amherst, MA: Prometheus Books: 1988, pp. 149–50.

19 Ibid., p. 150.

20 Ibid.

21 On the significance of the notion of subject-object, see E. Bloch, *Subject-Object: Erläuterung zu Hegel*, Frankfurt am Main: Suhrkamp Verlag, 1962.

22 With this said, Hegel's *Jena Manuscripts* do pay more attention to the alienation of manual labour (as opposed to Hegel's treatment of this in his mature work) and share a number of similarities with elements the young Marx's account presented in the *Paris Manuscripts*. See G.W.F. Hegel, 'System of Ethical Life', in H.S. Harris and T.M. Knox (eds) *Hegel's System of Ethical Life and First Philosophy of Spirit*, Albany, NY: SUNY Press, 1979, pp. 117–22; 125–6; 170–1. Hegel, at p. 167, argues:

> The system of need has been conceived formally above as a system of universal physical dependence on one another. For the totality of his need no one is

> independent. His labour, or whatever capacity he has for satisfying his need, does not secure its satisfaction for him. Whether the surplus that he possesses gives him a totality of satisfaction depends upon an alien power (*Macht*) over which he has no control. The value of that surplus, i.e. what expresses the bearing of the surplus on his need, is independent of him and alterable.

23 For an account of this critique, see G. Lukács, *The Young Hegel*, pp. 537–67.
24 K. Marx, *Economic and Philosophic Manuscripts*, p. 71.
25 Ibid., p. 72.
26 Ibid., p. 150.
27 This conception might be thought as one element of Theunissen's critique of the 'suppression' of mutual recognition within Hegel's account of the ethical life of the state. See M. Theunissen, 'The Repressed Inter-Subjectivity in Hegel's Philosophy of Right', in D. Cornell, M. Rosenfeld and D.G. Carlson (eds) *Hegel and Legal Theory*, New York: Routledge, 1991.
28 K. Marx, *Economic and Philosophic Manuscripts*, p. 162.
29 For Marx, labour stands at the centre of human life and is dialectical. See K. Marx, *Capital*, Vol. 1, trans. B. Fowkes, London: Penguin, 1990, pp. 283–4:

> Labour is, first of all, a process between man and nature, a process by which man, through his own actions, mediates, regulates and controls the metabolism between himself and nature. He confronts the materials of nature as a force of nature. He sets in motion the natural forces which belong to his own body, his arms, legs, head and hands, in order to appropriate the materials of nature in a form adapted to his own needs. Through this movement he acts upon external nature and changes it, and in this way he simultaneously changes his own nature. He develops potentialities slumbering within nature, and subjects the play of its forces to his own sovereign power. We are not dealing here with those first instinctive forms of labour which remain on the animal level. An immense interval of time separates the state of things in which man brings his labour-power to market for sale as a commodity from the situation when human labour had not yet cast of its first instinctive form. We presuppose labour in a form in which it is an exclusively human characteristic. A spider conducts operations which resemble those of the weaver, and a bee would put many a human architect to shame by the construction of its honeycomb cells. But what distinguishes the worst architect from the best of bees is that the architect builds the cell in his mind before he constructs it in wax. At the end of every labour process, a result emerges which had already existed ideally. Man not only effects a change in the form of the materials of nature; he also realizes [*verwicklicht*] his own purpose in those materials. And this is a purpose he is conscious of, it determines the mode of his activity with the rigidity of law, and he must subordinate his will to it. This subordination is no mere momentary act. Apart from the exertion of the working organs, a purposeful will is required for the entire duration of the work.

30 Ibid., pp. 163–4.
31 Ibid., p. 164. Marx argues:

> The mysterious character of the commodity-form consists therefore simply in the fact that the commodity reflects the social characteristics of men's own labour as objective characteristics of the products of labour themselves, as the socio-natural properties of these things. Hence it also reflects the social relation

> of the producers to the sum total of labour as a social relation between objects, a relation which exists apart from and outside the producers. Through this substitution, the products of labour become commodities, sensuous things which are at the same time suprasensible or social. In the same way, the impression made by a thing on the optic nerve is perceived not as the subjective excitation of that nerve but as the objective form of a thing outside the eye. In the act of seeing, of course, light is really transmitted from on thing, the external object, to another thing, the eye. It is a physical relation between physical things. As against this, the commodity-form, and the value-relation of the products of labour within which it appears, have absolutely no connection with the physical nature of the commodity and the material [*dinglich*] relations arising out of this. It is nothing but the definite social relation between men themselves which assumes here, for them, the fantastic form of a relation between things. In order, therefore to find an analogy we must take flight into the misty realm of religion. There the products of the human brain appear as autonomous figures endowed with a life of their own, which enter into relations both with each other and with the human race. So it is in the world of commodities with the products of men's hands. I call this the fetishism which attaches itself to the products of labour as soon as they are produced as commodities, and therefore inseparable from the production of commodities.

32 Ibid. At p. 168, Marx argues:

> [I]n the midst of the accidental and ever-fluctuating exchange relations between the products, the labour-time socially necessary to produce them asserts itself as a regulative law of nature. In the same way, the law of gravity asserts itself when a person's house collapses on top of him. The determination of the magnitude of value by labour-time is therefore a secret hidden under the apparent movements in the relative values of commodities.

33 Ibid., p. 165.
34 Ibid.
35 Ibid., pp. 166–7.
36 E.B. Pashukanis, *Law and Marxism: A General Theory*, trans. B. Einhorn, ed. C. Arthur, London: Links, 1978.
37 Ibid., p. 112. Consider also V. Kerruish, *Jurisprudence as Ideology*, London: Routledge, 1991.
38 Ibid.
39 K. Marx, *Capital*, p. 180. Note that Pashukanis only quotes the first four sentences. The rest of paragraph is relevant in that it points to a certain inheritance by Marx of Hegel's notion of recognition between property owners and the way in which Marx uses this aspect of Hegel's theory to develop his concept of exchange value. Not that Marx is solely reliant upon Hegel in this respect. Both Hegel and Marx drew much from Adam Smith and the 'speculative' nature of his discussion of the exchange relation.
40 E.B. Pashukanis, *Law and Marxism*, p. 112.
41 Ibid., p. 117.
42 Ibid., p. 113.
43 Pashukanis takes this critique a number of steps further to attempt to historicize the idea of an individual 'will' as presented by bourgeois natural law. His critique is not unproblematic given that Pashukanis presupposes an account of 'will' (the will of the 'guardians of commodities' who 'recognize' each other) which he does not develop an account of.

44 E.B. Pashukanis, *Law and Marxism*, pp. 114–16. For Marx, such theories of natural law are the product of, and attempt to legitimize an economic and social system of 'capitalism', which importantly is linked to the theft of property, imposition of slavery, and commodification of labour within the history of the European colonization of the non-European world. In *Capital*, at p. 247, Marx argues:

> The circulation of commodities is the starting-point of capital. The production of commodities and their circulation in its developed form, namely trade, form the historic presuppositions under which capital arises. World trade and the world market date from the sixteenth century, and from then on the modern history of capital starts to unfold.

And, at pp. 915–16:

> The discovery of gold and silver in America, the extirpation, enslavement and entombment in mines of the indigenous population of that continent, the beginnings of the conquest and plunder of India, and the conversion of Africa into a preserve for the commercial hunting of blackskins, are all things which characterize the dawn of the era of capitalist production. These idyllic proceedings are the chief moments of primitive accumulation. Hard on their heels follows the commercial war of the European nations, which has the globe as its battlefield. It begins with the revolt of the Netherlands from Spain, assumes gigantic dimensions in England's Anti-Jacobin War, and is still going on in the shape of the Opium Wars against China, etc.
>
> The different moments of primitive accumulation can be assigned in particular to Spain, Portugal, Holland, France and England, in more or less chronological order. These different moments are systematically combined together at the end of the seventeenth century. For England the combination embraces the colonies, the national debt, the modern tax system, and the system of protection. These methods depend in part on brute force, for instance the colonial system. But they all employ the power of the state, the concentrated and organized force of society, to hasten, as in a hothouse, the process of transformation of the feudal mode of production into the capitalist mode, and to shorten the transition. Force is the midwife of every old society which is pregnant with a new one. It is itself an economic power.

And, at p. 918:

> Today, industrial supremacy brings with it commercial supremacy. In the period of manufacture it is the reverse: commercial supremacy produces industrial predominance. Hence the preponderant role played by the colonial system at that time. It was the 'strange God' who perched himself side by side with the old divinities of Europe on the altar, and one fine day thew them all overboard with a shove and a kick. It proclaimed the making of profit as the ultimate and sole purpose of mankind.

45 E.B. Pashukanis, *Law and Marxism*, p. 118.
46 Ibid., p. 143.
47 Ibid., p. 144.
48 Ibid.
49 Pashukanis's account of law is not unproblematic. His adherence to the notion that legal forms such as modern legal subjectivity will 'wither away' in the replacement

of bourgeois legal systems by bureaucratic and technical administration is questionable and overly utopian. Ibid., pp. 132–3.

50 On the critique of international law more generally, see C. Miéville, *Between Equal Rights: A Marxist Theory of International Law*, London: Pluto Press, 2006.

51 Marx describes the system of capitalist accumulation as a 'coercive relation'. K. Marx, *Capital*, pp. 424–5:

> Capital developed within the production process until it acquired command over labour, i.e. over self-activating labour-power, in other words the worker himself. The capitalist, who is capital personified, now takes care that the worker does his work regularly and with the proper degree of intensity.
>
> Capital also developed into a coercive relation, and this compels the working class to do more work than would be required by the narrow circle of its own needs. As an agent in producing the activity of others, as an extractor of surplus labour and an exploiter of labour-power, it surpasses all earlier systems of production, which were based on directly compulsory labour, in its energy and its quality of unbounded and ruthless activity.

52 For Marx, the systemic pressure of market which forces the capitalist to constantly act so as to secure a profit operates as a form of compulsion that limits the possibility of the capitalist making any substantive 'moral' acts. Any less selfish thoughts are tempered by the fear of economic ruin. Self-preservation of the capitalist occurs by way of a greater exploitation of the labour power of its workforce. Unfreedom produced via the force of market competition. Ibid., p. 739, Marx argues:

> Moreover, the development of capitalist production makes it necessary to constantly increase the amount of capital laid out in any industrial undertaking, and competition subordinates every individual capitalist to the immanent laws of capitalist production, as external and coercive laws. It compels him to keep extending his capital, so as to preserve it, and he can only extend it by means of progressive accumulation.

53 For more detailed accounts of the negative consequences of commodification and the violence this produces within all aspects of social life within modern capitalism, see, generally, G. Lukács, *History and Class Consciousness*, trans. R. Livingstone, London: Merlin Press, 1990; M. Horkheimer and T.W. Adorno, *Dialectic of Enlightenment*, trans. E. Jephcott, Stanford, CA: Stanford University Press, 2002; H. Marcuse, *One Dimensional Man*, London: Abacus, 1964.

54 In relation to struggles over the working day between the capitalist and the labour force over the value of the labour-commodity, Marx notes that this negotiation between 'right' and 'right' (which constructs a norm) is backed by force and represents the 'duel' of class struggle. K. Marx, *Capital*, p. 344:

> There is here therefore an antinomy, of right against right, both equally bearing the seal of the law of exchange. Between equal rights, force decides. Hence, in the history of capitalist production, the establishment of a norm for the working day presents itself as a struggle over the limits of that day, a struggle between collective capital, i.e. the class of capitalists, and collective labour, i.e. the working class.

55 See K. Marx, 'Preface to A Contribution to the Critique of Political Economy', trans. S. Ryazanskaya, in L.H. Simon (ed.) *Karl Marx*, pp. 210–11. Marx argues:

> The first work which I undertook to dispel the doubts assailing me was a critical re-examination of the Hegelian philosophy of law; the introduction to this work being published in the *Deutsch-Französische Jahrbücher* issued in Paris in 1844. My inquiry led me to the conclusion that neither legal relations nor political forms could be comprehended whether by themselves or on the basis of a so-called general development of the human mind, but that on the contrary they originate in the material conditions of life, the totality of which Hegel, following the example of English and French thinkers of the eighteenth century, embraces within the term 'civil society'; that the anatomy of this civil society however, has to be sought in political economy.

56 G.W.F. Hegel, *Elements of the Philosophy of Right*, trans. H.B. Nisbet, ed. A.W. Wood, Cambridge: Cambridge University Press, 1991, § 248, p. 269.
57 K. Marx and F. Engels, *The Communist Manifesto*, trans. S. Moore, Harmondsworth: Penguin, 1969.
58 Ibid., pp. 81–2.
59 Ibid., pp. 83–4.
60 Ibid., p. 84. Marx argues:

> The bourgeoisie, by the rapid improvement of all instruments of production, by the immensely facilitated means of communication, draws all, even the most barbarian, nations into civilization ... it compels all nations, on pain of extinction, to adopt the bourgeois mode of production; it compels them to introduce what it calls civilization into their midst, i.e. to become bourgeois themselves. In one word, it creates a world after its own image.

61 Ibid., pp. 87–9.
62 The question of 'who' engages in this revolutionary struggle need not be narrowly defined. Consider Laclau and Mouffe's contemporary re-formulation of the notion of 'class' around a diverse range of alienated and oppressed groups whose struggle is aimed at achieving some political and economic hegemony. See E. Laclau and C. Mouffe, *Hegemony and Socialist Strategy: Towards a Radical Democratic Politics*, 2nd edn, London: Verso, 2001.
63 Although often the sufferers are played against each other, such as in the mass mobilization of the poor to fight in state armies against the poor of another state, or in the rise of elites within particular social groups (i.e. the colonial elite) who often direct their struggle downwards against the colonized instead of upwards against the colonial power.
64 K. Marx, and F. Engels, *The Communist Manifesto*, p. 79.
65 See V.I. Lenin, 'The State and Revolution', in D. McLellan, *The Essential Left*, London: Unwin Books, 1960. At p. 152, Lenin argues:

> The state is the product and the manifestation of the irreconcilability of class antagonisms. When, where, and to what extent the state arises, depends directly on when, where and to what extent the class antagonisms of a given society cannot be objectively reconciled. And, conversely, the existence of the state proves that class antagonisms *are* irreconcilable.

At p. 153:

> According to Marx, the state is the organ of class *domination*, the organ of oppression of one class by another. Its aim is the creation of order which

legalizes and perpetuates this oppression by moderating the collisions between classes.

66 V.I. Lenin, 'Imperialism, the Highest Stage of Capitalism', in H.M. Christman (ed.) *Essential Works of Lenin*, New York: Dover Publications, 1987.
67 Ibid., pp. 179–90. At p. 186, Lenin argues:

> Capitalism in its imperialist stage arrives at the threshold of the most complete socialization of production. In spite of themselves the capitalists are dragged, as it were, into the new social order, which marks the transition from complete free competition to complete socialization. Production becomes social, but appropriation remains private. The social means of production remain private property of a few. The framework of formally recognized free competition remains, but the yoke of a few monopolists on the rest of the population becomes a hundred times heavier, more burdensome and intolerable.

68 Ibid., pp. 219–66.
69 Ibid., pp. 226–36.
70 Ibid., pp. 244–5.
71 Ibid., p. 244.
72 Ibid., pp. 262–3.
73 In terms of understanding this action as one guided by the desire to safeguard US global hegemony, particularly against the emerging threat of China, see D. Kagan and G. Schmitt *et al.*, *Rebuilding America's Defenses: Strategy, Forces and Resources for a New Century. A Report for the Project for the New American Century, September 2000.* http://web.archive.org/web/20020923154604/www.newamericancentury.org/RebuildingAmericasDefenses.pdf (accessed on 9 June 2008).
74 For various accounts of this, see T. Ali, *The Clash of Fundamentalisms*, London: Verso, 2003, R. Fisk, *The Great War for Civilization: The Conquest of the Middle East*, London: Harper Perennial, 2005; S. Žižek, *Iraq: The Borrowed Kettle*, London: Verso, 2005; M. Hardt and A. Negri, *Empire*, Cambridge, MA: Harvard University Press, 2001.
75 C. von Clausewitz, *On War*, ed. M. Howard and P. Paret, New York: Everyman's Library, 1993, p. 99. Note that I have changed the translation here from 'policy' to 'politics', the original translation reads: 'War is merely the continuation of policy by other means'.
76 V.I. Lenin, 'The Military Programme of the Proletarian Revolution', in V.I. Lenin, *Collected Works*, Vol. 23, ed. M.S. Levin, London: Lawrence and Wishart, 1974.
77 Ibid., p. 80.
78 V.I. Lenin, 'War and Revolution', in V.I. Lenin, *Collected Works*, Vol. 24, trans. I. Bernard, London: Lawrence and Wishart, 1974.
79 Ibid., p. 400.
80 Ibid., p. 401.
81 V.I. Lenin, 'The Military Programme of the Proletarian Revolution', p. 82.
82 Ibid., p. 79.
83 V. Lenin, 'Guerrilla Warfare', in V.I. Lenin, *Collected Works*, Vol. 11, trans. C. Dutt, London: Lawrence and Wishart, 1972.
84 Ibid., pp. 219–20.
85 Ibid., pp. 219–21. It should be noted that Lenin does not endorse all acts of guerrilla war or terror. Rather, he argues that acts of anarchism and terrorism which are not controlled politically may demoralize the workers and injure the revolution. In this sense, just as Lenin condemns acts of imperialist war, he is keen to

draw a line of legitimacy between acts of violence of a political nature controlled by the revolutionary party and those acts standing outside this framework.

86 This linkage is noted by Carl Schmitt, see the discussion below.

87 T. Mao, *On Guerrilla Warfare*, trans. S.B. Griffith, Urbana, IL: University of Illinois Press, 2000. Note Mao's comments at p. 41 that:

> [G]uerrilla operations must not be considered as an independent form of warfare. They are but one step in the total war, one aspect of revolutionary struggle. They are the inevitable result of the clash between oppressor and oppressed when the latter reach the limits of their endurance.

And at p. 89:

> It is to be hoped that the world is in the last era of strife. The vast majority of human beings have already prepared or are preparing to fight a war that will bring justice to the oppressed peoples of the world. No matter how long this war may last, there is no doubt that it will be followed by an unprecedented epoch of peace. The war that we are fighting today for the emancipation of the Chinese is a part of the war for freedom of all human beings, and the independent, happy, and liberal China that we are fighting to establish will be part of that new world order.

88 E. Guevara, *Guerrilla Warfare*, ed. M. Becker, Lincoln, NE: University of Nebraska Press, 1998, Guevera argues at p. 9, 'Guerrilla warfare, the basis of the struggle of a people to redeem itself, has diverse characteristics, different facets, even though the essential will for liberation is the same.' And at p. 10:

> We must come to the inevitable conclusion that the guerrilla fighter is a social reformer, that he takes up arms responding to the angry protest of the people against their oppressors, and that he fights in order to change the social system that keeps all his unarmed brothers in ignominy and misery. He launches himself against the conditions of the reigning institutions at a particular moment and dedicates himself with all the vigour that circumstances permit to breaking the mould of these institutions.

89 V.I. Lenin, *Materialism and Empirio-criticism: Critical Comments on a Reactionary Philosophy*, Moscow: Progress Publishers, 1977, p. 336.

90 Aspects of this militarization of the political can be seen today in contemporary capitalist states in the way in which the language of war is invoked to combat social problems – the 'war on crime', the 'war on drugs', the 'war on poverty', and so on.

91 C. Schmitt, *The Theory of the Partisan: A Commentary/Remark on the Concept of the Political*, trans. A.C. Goodson, East Lansing, MI: Michigan State University Press, 2004.

92 Ibid. At p. 8, Schmitt states:

> Serious partisan battles have been raging in large (-scale) areas of the world for thirty years now. They began already in 1927, before World War II, in China and other Asian countries that would later take up arms against the Japanese invasion of 1932–45. During World War II, Russia, Poland, the Balkans, France, Albania, Greece, and other regions became arenas for this kind of war. After it the partisan struggle continued in Indochina, where the Vietnamese communist leader Ho Chi Minh, and the victor of Dien Bien Phu, General Vo Nguyen Giap, were particularly effective against the French colonial army.

93 Ibid. At p. 4, Schmitt states:

> The partisans of the Spanish Guerrilla War of 1808 were the first who dared to wage irregular war against a regular modern army. In autumn 1808, Napoleon had defeated the regular Spanish army; the real Spanish Guerrilla War began only after the defeat of the regular army.

And at p. 5:

> A spark flew north from Spain at that time. It did not kindle the same flame that gave the Spanish Guerrilla War its world-historical significance. But it started something whose continuance today in the second half of the twentieth century changed the face of the earth and its inhabitants. It produced a *theory* of war and of enmity that culminates in the theory of the partisan.

94 Ibid., p. 14.
95 Ibid., pp. 9–10.
96 Ibid., p. 11.
97 Ibid., p. 13.
98 Ibid.
99 Ibid., p. 10.
100 Ibid.
101 C. Schmitt, *The Theory of the Partisan*, p. 5. Compare this to Schmitt's comment in C. Schmitt, *The Concept of the Political*, trans. G. Schwab, Chicago, IL: University of Chicago Press, 1996. In the earlier work, Schmitt argues that war for von Clausewitz is the *ultima ratio* of the friend–enemy grouping: that is, the possibility and fundamental character of the political. At pp. 34–5, he states:

> The military battle itself is not the 'continuation of politics by other means' as the famous term of Clausewitz is generally incorrectly cited. War has its own strategic, tactical, and other rules and points of view, but they all presuppose that the political decision has already been made as to who the enemy is … War is neither the aim nor the purpose nor even the very content of politics. But as an ever present possibility it is the leading presupposition which determines in a characteristic way human action and thinking and thereby creates a specifically political behaviour.

102 C. Schmitt, *Theory of the Partisan*, pp. 32–3.
103 Ibid., p. 29
104 Ibid.
105 Ibid.
106 Ibid., p. 30.
107 Ibid., pp. 31–2.
108 Ibid., p. 32. Schmitt probably does not do complete justice to Clausewitz here. See C. Clausewitz, *On War*, p. 578. Clausewitz argues:

> In the civilized parts of Europe, war by means of popular uprisings is a phenomenon of the nineteenth century. It has its advocates and its opponents. The latter object to it either on political grounds, considering it as a means of revolution, a state of legalized anarchy that is as much of a threat to the social order at home as it is to the enemy; or else on military grounds, because they feel that the results are not commensurate with the energies that have been expended.

The first objection does not concern us at all: here we consider a general insurrection as simply another means of war – in its relation, therefore to the enemy. The second objection, on the other hand, leads us to remark that a popular uprising should, in general, be considered as an outgrowth of the way in which conventional barriers have been swept away in our lifetime by the elemental violence of war. It is, in fact, a broadening and intensification of the fermentation process known as war. The system of requisitioning, and the enormous growth of armies resulting from it and from universal conscription, the employment of militia – all of these run in the same direction when viewed from the standpoint of the older, narrower military system, and that also leads to the calling out of the home guard and arming the people.

The innovations first mentioned were the natural, inevitable consequences of the breaking down of barriers. They added so immensely to the strength of the side that first employed them that the opponent was carried along and had to follow suit. That will also hold true of the people's war. Any nation that uses it intelligently will, as a rule, gain superiority over those who disdain its use. If this is so, the question only remains whether mankind at large will gain by this further expansion of the element of war; a question to which the answer should be the same as to the question of war itself. We shall leave both to the philosophers.

109 For Schmitt, this distinction goes to the question of who might be an 'authentic' partisan. Schmitt's discussion of Raoul Salan, leader of the OAS, a group which attempted to assassinate Charles de Gaulle in the hope of re-starting the war against the independence movement in Algeria, points to the difficulties of what might be an 'authentic' partisan fighter in modern life. For Schmitt, there seems to be a certain sense of the tragic attached to such partisan figures. See C. Schmitt, *The Theory of the Partisan*, p. 43.
110 Ibid., p. 34
111 Ibid., p. 35
112 Ibid. p. 36
113 Ibid.
114 Ibid.
115 Ibid., p. 35.
116 Ibid., pp. 21, 22, 26. Consider *Geneva Convention Relative to the Treatment of Prisoners of War 1950*, Article 4, A.
117 Ibid., p. 25.
118 Ibid., p. 52.
119 Ibid., p. 53.
120 Ibid.
121 Ibid.
122 Ibid.
123 Ibid., p. 52. It should be noted that Schmitt's account of international relations contained in the theory of the partisan changes, or, rather, adds a new dimension to his account of international law contained within his earlier work, *The Nomos of the Earth*. The theory of the partisan would need to be seen as developing Schmitt's central notions of '*Ordnung*' and '*Ortung*'. See C. Schmitt, *The Nomos of the Earth*, trans. G.L. Ulmen, New York: Telos Press 2003.
124 C. Schmitt, *Theory of the Partisan*, p. 52.
125 Ibid., p. 65.
126 Ibid., p. 61.
127 See *Rambo III*, P. MacDonald (dir.), 1988.

128 For a critique of Schmitt's notion of 'friendship', see J. Derrida, *The Politics of Friendship*, trans. G. Collins, London: Verso, 1997.
129 C. Schmitt, *The Concept of the Political*, p. 26.
130 Ibid., p. 27.
131 Ibid., p. 27.
132 Ibid., p. 34.
133 Such a characterization also leads to critiques of Schmitt and of whether one accepts his account of the 'political'. For at least two reasons we should approach Schmitt's account of the political with a great deal of caution. Schmitt's account presupposes a certain Catholic worldview and a pessimistic human anthropology in which a 'sinful' humanity is understood as essentially evil. For Schmitt, there is a long tradition of political theory that is connected to theological dogmas of sin. He argues that the fundamental theological dogma of evilness in the world and in man leads, just as does the distinction of friend and enemy, to a categorization that renders impossible any undifferentiated optimism of a universal conception of man. Schmitt, at pp. 61–5, argues that Machiavelli, Hobbes and Fichte presuppose a pessimistic conception of man and argues that 'The methodical connection of theological and political presuppositions is clear.' The assumption of a pessimistic human anthropology allows Schmitt to describe social relations as fundamentally violent and threatening. The creation of community through the affirmation of friends against enemies occurs as a form of human behaviour in response to a threatening original condition. Further, Schmitt's account of the friend–enemy relation can be understood as an over-emphasis upon the ethics of exclusion contained within Hegel's account of war. In many ways, Schmitt (with some similarity to Kojève) takes a one-sided reading of Hegel's theory of recognition reducing it, and all social relations, to that of a 'struggle to the death'. Any appropriation of Schmitt needs to come to terms with his particular form of Hegelianism (and one-sided or antagonistic interpretation of Hegel) and his religious-pessimistic human anthropology which he uses to support this.
134 On the question of violence more generally, there are a number of differing conceptions that are of relevance but cannot be engaged with here. See, for example, G. Sorel, *Reflections on Violence*, ed. J. Jennings, Cambridge: Cambridge University Press, 1999; S. Freud, *Totem and Taboo*, ed. J. Strachey, New York: W.W. Norton & Co., 1950; M. Foucault, *Society Must Be Defended*, trans. D. Macey, London: Penguin Books, 2003; E. Fromm, *The Anatomy of Human Destructiveness*, New York: Owl Books, 1973; R. Girard, *Violence and the Sacred*, Baltimore, MD: Johns Hopkins University Press, 1977; M. Minow, M. Ryan and A. Sarat (eds) *Narrative, Violence and the Law: The Essays of Robert Cover*, Ann Arbor, MI: University of Michigan Press, 1995. Any comprehensive account of violence would need to take into account or begin with human violence carried out against non-human animals. See P. Singer, *Animal Liberation*, New York: HarperCollins, 1975.
135 E.B. Pashukanis, *Law and Marxism*, p. 75.
136 It is asserted here that this form is *universal* and *necessary* within modern law and as such cannot 'wither away'.
137 W. Benjamin, 'Critique of Violence', in W. Benjamin, *Reflections*, trans. E. Jephcott, New York: Schocken Books, 1986.
138 Ibid., pp. 279–81.
139 The relation between law and politics is a complex one occupying traditions of Marxism, Legal Realism and Critical Legal Studies. The account given here does not attempt to look at the relationship between law and politics as a whole but focuses upon a more specific relationship centred around the issue of public violence and the question of who has the authority to pass judgment on the legitimate

use of violence. Even in focusing upon this specific question, this section should only be seen to examine only a small portion of this relationship.

140 W. Benjamin, 'Critique of Violence', p. 284.

141 Ibid., p. 287.

142 H.L.A. Hart's account of the authority of law which is not simply reliant upon the threat of physical force but based upon the relation between primary and secondary rules, power of tradition, and force of custom and social pressure and the operation of recognition is relevant here as a form in which the authority of the law orders social life. See H.L.A. Hart, *The Concept of Law*, 2nd edn, Oxford: Oxford University Press, 1994, pp. 44–8, 80–7, 94–9.

143 W. Benjamin, 'Critique of Violence', p. 286.

144 J. Derrida, *On Cosmopolitanism and Forgiveness*, trans. M. Dooley and M. Hughes, London: Routledge, 2001, p. 57.

Chapter 6

Developing a theory of war

I

Looking back over the differing traditions of the ordering of war and the way in which aspects of each tradition are draw upon generally and ambiguously by contemporary warring actors, it seems that each is set against its others. Each tradition orders the relationship between war and right in a differing way, each stakes out a claim over the rightness of war. Yet, each tradition is also limited and cannot claim to represent the whole of the relationship between war and right. In this respect, the conflicts between the differing traditions of war's ordering represent a certain chaos – a chaotic conflict between words and deeds that lies at the centre of the modern problem of war. Perhaps, though, the realm of war is not completely chaotic. In the sense that it involves at least these influential forms of war's ordering, then there resides a certain degree of order amidst the chaos.

From this perspective the account of the ordering of war given so far provides something of a template or map that allows contemporary thinking to navigate through many of the competing claims of right that accompany acts of violence in the present. Yet, the picture presented here does not pretend to be complete and questions remain over the role of human thinking, or human reason, in the ordering of violence and over whether thinking can adequately order the use of violence to realize future ends such a peace, freedom and human dignity. By drawing upon the resources given by these modern traditions of war's ordering and in particular, upon the emphasis on the *activity of thinking* developed within the tradition of German Idealism, this chapter looks more closely at the relationship between thinking, action and violence. In an attempt to come to terms with some of the remaining questions related to reason's ordering of war, this chapter develops a contemporary theory of *war as positing.*

II

In developing a modern theory of war, it is worth spending a little time on clarifying terminology. In light of the tradition of the political ordering of war, it would seem somewhat overzealous to reserve the term 'war' solely for acts of violence carried out by one state against another. It would be more appropriate if the term 'war' was used to refer to both acts of state sovereign war and non-sovereign war. Limiting the term 'war' to merely sovereign war excludes a history of warfare within the twentieth century in which wars of national liberation, revolutionary wars and civil wars have moved non-sovereign war closer to the norm. Acts of sovereign and non-sovereign war are not mutually exclusive. The twentieth century saw numerous examples where states were engaged in conflict with non-sovereign, partisan forces and where acts of non-sovereign war were supported by the money, arms, intelligence and soldiers of sovereign states acting as 'interested third parties'.

Using the term 'war' to refer to both sovereign and non-sovereign war is not unproblematic. The lines that separate acts of non-sovereign war from crime or isolated acts of public violence are sometimes not easy to draw and remain as points of contestation between those who wish to draw firm definitions. Many acts of non-sovereign war will be simultaneously wars and 'crimes' to the extent that they breach the internal positive law of a particular state in which they are carried out. Yet, to follow a purely legal positivist line of definition and treat such acts *only* as crimes is to close one's eyes to the significant role of non-sovereign war in shaping the social landscape of late modernity and the manner in which traditions of war's ordering continually re-inscribe and shift the boundaries of what constitutes 'legitimate authority' and 'legitimate violence'. Any strict positivist definition also shuts its eyes to the acts of foundational violence that have historically created all legal and political institutions. In this respect, the term *war* should be understood as referring to *both sovereign and non-sovereign war*. While there will occur ongoing problems of clearly defining non-sovereign war, this is not an isolated case. The problem is one related to all conceptual definitions whereby, at some point, every concept at its limits or at its borders begins to break down and merges into ground covered by neighbouring concepts. The blurring of the boundaries between sovereign war, non-sovereign war and crime reflects a broader moment of conceptual indeterminacy contained within all thinking and speaking which will always be contained within any definition of 'war'.

At this point it is also worthwhile considering the terms 'war' and 'terrorism'. One definition of terrorism is noted by Noam Chomsky. He argues:

> We might ask why the concept of terror should be considered particularly obscure. There are a range of US government definitions that fall well within the range and clarity of other usages that are regarded as unproblematic. A US Army manual defined *terrorism* as 'the calculated use of violence or threat of violence to attain goals that are political, religious, or ideological in nature … through intimidation, coercion, or instilling fear'. The official US Code gave a more elaborate definition, essentially along the same lines. The British government's definition is similar: 'Terrorism is the use, or

> threat, of action which is violent, damaging or disrupting, and is intended to influence the government or intimidate the public and is for the purpose of advancing a political, religious, or ideological cause'. These definitions seem fairly clear. They are close enough to ordinary usage, and are considered appropriate when discussing the terrorism of enemies.[1]

Terrorism can be thought then to refer to a particular military *strategy*. Commonly, under the rhetoric of the 'war on terror', particular non-sovereign actors (predominantly militant Islamicist political organizations) who use the strategy of terrorism are described as 'terrorists'. Yet, because 'terrorism' is a strategy its use is open to both sovereign and non-sovereign actors alike and has been commonly used in recent history by states such as the USA.[2] What was described by the US military as 'shock and awe', the massive aerial bombing campaign of both military and civilian targets before the invasion of Iraq by ground troops in 2003, was a strategy in which tremendous violence was used to terrorize a population. Such an act, which initiated a war against a civilian population, was an act of terrorism. It could be compared to a similar act of terrorism against a civilian population carried out against the USA in 2001 by a group of Islamicist militants in which civilian airlines were used in the place of guided missiles and crashed into the World Trade Center and the Pentagon. Both were acts calculated to kill large numbers of civilians with the aim of striking fear and terror in the heart of the adversary.

If contemporary thinking is to take the problem of war seriously, it needs to acknowledge that terrorism is a strategy that can be used by all sides at the initiation of or, within, a conflict. Its use is gruesome and horrible. Yet, to call a particular group of non-sovereign actors 'terrorists' is to use a term which has a certain loaded, rhetorical meaning. Such groups do not have a monopoly upon the strategic use of terror. Both states and non-state actors, in the sphere of war, and in conditions of relative peace, draw upon acts of terror – both terrorize. In this regard, the term 'war' can be thought as a more general act of violence, 'terrorism' can be thought as a more specific strategy of violence, which given its extent, frequency and the historical context may take place within the conditions of war. To avoid loaded meanings, it might be more appropriate to use the term 'non-sovereign war' instead of the term 'terrorists' or at least to speak of both state and non-state terror. With this in mind, it is worth turning to examine a general definition of war.

Perhaps the standard modern definition of war is given by Carl von Clausewitz. In *On War* (1832).[3] Clausewitz argues:

> War is nothing but a duel on a larger scale. Countless duels go to make up war, but a picture of it as a whole can be formed by imagining a pair of wrestlers. Each tries through physical force to compel the other to do his will; his *immediate* aim is to *throw* his opponent in order to make him incapable of further resistance.

> *War is thus an act of force to compel our enemy to do our will.*
>
> Force, to counter opposing force, equips itself with the inventions of art and science. Attached to force are certain self-imposed, imperceptible limitations hardly worth mentioning, known as international law and custom, but they scarcely weaken it. Force – that is, physical force, for moral force has no existence save as expressed in the state and the law – is thus the *means* to war; to impose our will upon the enemy is its *object*. To secure that object we must render the enemy powerless; and that, in theory, is the true aim of warfare. The aim takes the place of the object, discarding it as something not actually part of war itself.[4]

Further, Clausewitz argues that 'War is merely the continuation of politics by other means'.[5] Clausewitz can be understood as presenting an instrumental definition of war, in which war appears as a *means* used to compel an enemy or to secure a political end. Such a definition makes sense, and the operation of war as an instrument can be seen throughout the differing forms of war's ordering. For the sovereign state, both police violence and military violence are drawn upon to suppress internal challenges to its authority and war is used as a means of settling interstate disputes when disagreements cannot be resolved peacefully. At the level of cosmopolitan morality, war is drawn upon as an instrument used by federations and individual states to realize the ends of peace and human rights or to maintain international security and punish human rights abuses. In this respect, Clausewitz's instrumental definition of war should not simply be restricted to the 'continuation of politics'. Rather, war is a means drawn upon to secure a large number of ends, these being religious, legal, moral, ethical, economic and political. Taking into account a broader understanding of war involves the notion that war is a means drawn upon by both sovereign and non-sovereign actors to secure a number of ends through violence.

In contemporary times, such a definition of war is relevant. However, is such a purely instrumental definition of war adequate? If war is understood as a means in the sense of an instrument or a tool (Clausewitz speaks of force equipped with the inventions of art and science), then describing war as purely a 'means' might not pay enough regard to the *creative* function of war within modernity. Within the process of the ordering of war there were a number of examples of the creative and constitutive function of war. Within Hegel's notion of an ethics of exclusion, war played an important creative function in the sense that ethical-political communities were created and produced through a process of ongoing exclusionary violence.[6] Such violence was not only directed outwardly but was applied inwardly, as described by Benjamin's characterization of legal violence as having a law-making character.

Further, a purely instrumental account of war does not pay enough regard to the creative, constitutive and revolutionary role that the instruments and tools of modern warfare have played within modern human life. In modern life, *tools* have played a major role in the re-shaping and transformation of the social and physical world. The tools of war and their technological development driven by arms races have contributed to the transformation of modern life. In particular economies, the 'military-industrial complex' has created profoundly powerful forms of technology (nuclear, computer and now genetic and nano-technology) which have revolutionized the way in which many humans live their daily lives. Seen in such a light, war cannot simply be defined a means drawn upon to realize a predetermined end or objective. Rather, war has a creative function and any theory of war needs to take this creative character into account.[7]

Thinking about war in terms of 'positing' takes into account both the instrumental and creative aspects of war. Part of the notion of war as positing might already be seen to reside within Clausewitz's formula that 'War is merely the continuation of politics by other means'. In German, the original sentence reads: '*Der Krieg ist eine bloße Fortsetzung der Politik mit anderen Mitteln*'.[8] In thinking about Clausewitz's definition in relation to the process of the ordering of war, his idea of war as the 'continuation of politics' and his use of the term '*Fortsetzung*' is significant. The verb '*fortsetzen*' is commonly translated as 'continuing' in the sense of a continuation of an act or thing or condition. However, more literally, the term '*fortsetzen*' can be read to involve the sense of 'setting forth' and is related to the German verb '*setzen*' meaning to 'put', 'place', 'set' and in some circumstances, to 'posit'.

To interpret Clausewitz's use of the term '*Fortzetzung*' as setting-forth or positing is perhaps to stretch the German too far and introduce a meaning Clausewitz might not have intended. However, my point here is to emphasize the *active* element contained within the definition. Such an emphasis pays attention to the operation of war as an act, as a deed. Thought of in this manner, the notion of war as an act of positing a political body or political objective makes a certain amount of sense. Whether or not such a meaning is at the heart of Clausewitz's definition is not at issue. Rather, thinking about war *as positing* draws the operation of war into the context of an activity that resides at the heart of modern life.

III

The act of positing, or perhaps more properly, creative self-positing, may be understood as one of the central themes of modern life. The modern human creates much of its own world, it produces its own world through acts and deeds. For modern humans, both positive law as sovereignty and the moral law, as something which brings normative content to positive laws and floats above them, are products of human self-legislation. In this sense, drawing attention to the role of creative self-positing contained within modern law Hegel plays with the German term for law '*Gesetz*' and its active heart, its kernel of activity, as positing, as '*setzen*'.[9] Further, modern political community is built upon a notion of the positing of a commonwealth or state and the myth of a collective self-positing by the 'people' (constitutive power).

The notion of modern constitutionalism either in liberal or socialist forms is grounded upon a moment of self-creation, a self-positing of a political community which is declared by a people's voice ('We the people'; 'the proletariat') and lifted up by human hands. Such a moment of creative positing in modernity is not always democratic, often the law, or the creation of a new sovereign community, is declared by the monarch and in such a case the 'self' of self-positing is the voice, image or body of the monarch (or the empty place it sustains)[10] who speaks for the populace. There occur both democratic and non-democratic elements of positing scattered throughout the writings of Hobbes, Locke, Rousseau, Kant and Lenin.

The modern notion of positing is not completely severed from its ties to an older world of the transcendent authority of God and the moral law. These, together with ideas of natural law, fate and providence, still hold a great deal of sway over some and are appealed to on a regular basis in the authorization and legitimization of human acts. Modern forms of thinking are still bound up with or occur as strange perversions of older forms of thinking, religious or otherwise.[11] Further, notions of sovereignty and the figures of the monarch and president still contain residues of more ancient, religious systems of organizing authority.[12] While a modern notion of positing can never fully escape from the clutches of an older world which it inherits, much of its character develops from the belief and hope that it can escape from the workings of fate, providence and from the rejection (or at least partial rejection) of the idea of an intervening God. The modern notion involves the effort of moving from a positing reliant upon some external thing towards a complete self-positing, a moment where humanity becomes fully reliant upon itself.[13] The idea of an absolute self positing involves humanity attempting to move from its position as the created into a new status as the creator. Such a hope is not unproblematic.

Part of the modern notion of positing involves a particular sense of the relation between human thinking and action. Drawn into view by Kant, given emphasis by Fichte and Schelling and radicalized by Hegel and Marx, both thinking and action are understood as creative. While giving differing degrees of emphasis, both Hegel and Marx[14] present accounts of the inter-relatedness of thinking and action and the manner in which this inter-relation produces the human world. In a general sense, the creative faculty of humans who are able to use tools draws together most clearly the relation between thinking and action. Through the use of the tool the individual subject is able to shape its immediate environment and re-shape matter creatively into new forms. Ideas, imagination and the ever present hope for a life which is better than the present one, help to push the human subject into creating a new world around itself.

In this creative process, human thoughts are not held separate from matter but are combined with matter in ways that radically transform its use. In the making of the plough, the knife, the bowl, or the chair (or the machine, or computer), human thinking or 'reason' is combined with physical activity to create an object with a specific form and use.[15] In the creation or production of the object a particular form of reason is embedded within the thing. The created object's form contains within it, and is partly shaped by, modes of human reasoning. Through the production of an object, a human's thoughts, or a tradition of human thinking (i.e. an artistic, cultural, technical or scientific tradition), can be seen to 'live' within the form and use of the object. In the sense that human life involves the use of and constant inter-relation with made objects, the form of human reason contained within these objects contributes to the active, creative and productive character of everyday life. In the manner in which a particular form of thought becomes embedded and continues to live within the use of a produced object, then particular traditions of human thinking, characters and manners of human life, and norms of reason, are posited through both the human subject's action and through the activity of the object. Through such a subject-object relation, an initial act of positing becomes a re-positing. In such a relation between thinking and action understood as active-creative production, human thinking becomes properly a *deed*.

The relation between thinking and action understood in the sense of labour or production involves a certain snowball effect. The objects that are created by human hands, through their use, begin to re-create the human world. The ideas or reason contained within them begin to affect the human environment, creating new as-yet-unthought realities. In particular, the production and use of machines begin to speed up the creative process and allow the production of not only endless commodities, but of other producing machines, whereby at the point when computer technology is introduced into industrial and factory production, machines begin to take over reproductive, and sometimes, creative moments of production.

In this context, the creativity of the human deed can be seen to involve a transformation of human realities.[16] Through the deed, the human world can be affected in such a way that a range of possibilities for action or new ways of living are opened up. These possibilities, while present in a very latent sense at the beginning only become actual potentialities after a deed (or series of deeds) have transformed the world enough to make specific, new potentialities possible.[17] In political terms, this is sometimes referred to as an 'event'.[18] One example would be the French Revolution (1789) which, as an 'event', allowed other Europeans to see more firmly that radical political change (the political destruction of the remnants of the feudal order) could well be possible in their own lands. The creative act of the revolution shook European thought in such a manner that it transformed the framework and boundaries of human possibility. The act allowed what was previously unthinkable to begin to be thought. Another example could be the first landing of a human on the moon (1969).[19]

However, to call such acts 'events' is to tend towards a certain fetishization of particular aspects of social reality. The manner in which human action (and the thinking contained within this action) reshape not only human reality but the boundaries of human possibilities is firmly entrenched within the everyday mundaneness of life. Many acts of daily life constitute 'events' to the extent that they transform aspects of an individual's existence. Further, viewed from the perspective of the *mundane*, this transformative character of action is both chaotic and unpredictable. There is always an uncertainty contained in what is produced such that the whole range of consequences of any deed can never be completely calculated with certainty beforehand. While human thinking tries to order its acts in a 'rational' manner, the operation of chance and contingency, the emergence of unintended and unforseen consequences, and the creation of new conditions which upset previous methods of planning, combined with the constant errors, limits and failures of human foresight and action, render the idea of an ordered march of reason through history fundamentally untenable. Although modern humans are able to create much of their own existence, there is no necessary operation of historical *progress* contained within a historical *process* of creative self-production. There is a creative process, but not necessarily any firm form of teleology or providence within it.

As much as this modern relation between thinking and action is creative, it is also profoundly destructive. Every act of positing and affirmation involves some degree of negation. In physical labour or material production some matter is always used up or some life killed. The process of the self-creation of human social life in the modern world has been bound up with the transformation of much of our physical environment. Such a changing of matter from one form into another has involved the mass destruction of both living and non-living forms. Within the social realm itself, the positing of individuals and groups over and above others has involved the eradication of peoples, their cultures and the holding of large swathes of humanity under the conditions of bondage and slavery.

More subtly the re-creation of the human world by its production of things or objects contains also negative consequences. Not only does industrial production under modern capitalism produce workers alienated from their labour and a world of commodities valued higher than numerous human lives, but also juridical, political and moral institutional objects are produced and these assume lives of their own. Such objects are not merely passive, but become active agents in a wider process of creative positing within human life. Through such institutional objects, certain forms of human thinking, cultures and manners of arranging social life (predominantly economic and political), come to occupy the 'life' of institutional bodies which posit themselves in the world through force and violence and negate what stands in their way. Directed by living humans who perpetuate the institutional object's mystical character, these often monolithic things re-create aspects of human reality in frequently profoundly destructive and violent ways. War is both an instrument and manifestation of such creative destruction.

IV

War is an act of positing. The theory of war as positing involves the notion that humans in modernity[20] attempt to control, shape and re-create our physical and social world through activity and action. Such activity is not always reliant upon physical violence. However, physical violence is one important aspect of human activity, it is not merely an instrument of action, but is a manifestation of aspects of a specific relationship between thinking and action.

Thinking and action are combined within the concept of *positing*. Thoughts, discourses, and the physical acts of individuals and institutions are posited. Positing involves both *affirmation* and *negation*, closely bound and sometimes indistinguishable. Positing, which Fichte described as the act or deed of the transcendental 'I', is also the activity of the subject and the institutions created by the many subjects within social and material life, as described by Hegel. The act of positing is inter-subjective and dialectical. It takes place as a moment of linguistic, social, intellectual and symbolic mediation between subjects who reflectively constitute themselves inter-subjectively through recognition. Positing occurs also as the physical and mental acts through which the human subject mediates itself with nature, as per Hegel and Marx, via work or labour.

Human beings posit themselves, their individual and collective wills, in and through the world, affirming and negating aspects of themselves and their others. Through creative acts of thought, solidarity, work and violence, human subjects produce and constitute forms of political, social, economic, juridical and religious institutions and systems which *lift up* (*aufheben*) and affirm the lives of some and negate the lives of others. Human beings are also posited, their wills are pushed forward through the world by the *normative force* of traditions, discourses and inherited ideas – the notions of right which constitute and guide their beliefs – and by institutional and systematic forms of political, legal, economic and social coercion. Groups and individuals are caught within an ongoing flux in which they posit and are posited by notions of right and are continually affirmed and negated by the positing of forms of right by others. In this sense, positing – and 'the rightness of war' as positing and being posited – take place within a life-world of *normative contradiction.*

The theory of war as positing involves both subjective and objective elements. Each of these contains instrumental and creative aspects. On the subjective side, war is drawn upon by active, human subjects usually organized into groups, who attempt to realize particular designated ends. In this sense, war is used as a means or instrument to attain a goal or objective and to actively order social relations around a set of normative ends. These ends might be religious, legal, moral, ethical, economic, or political and most commonly a mixture of these forms of thought. As a means, the tools of war become an extension of bodily human action. Through developments in the technology of production, the tools of killing have become more powerful and more destructive. As an instrument, war occurs as one means of resolving conflicts within social life. When different interests or ends come into conflict or contradiction, sometimes human actors posit their interests against their others by attempting to negate or subdue their others via war.

The subjective side of war is not, however, purely instrumental. By human subjects positing their demands and interests via war they re-shape and re-create the social world around them and sustain and maintain particular forms of living. Through the act of war, subjects break institutions, they destroy cultures and draw and re-draw national boundaries. Through war, human subjects create and constitute political communities and legal institutions which come to govern and order human life in particular ways. Through war, human subjects establish forms of ethical life. The creative and constitutive function of revolutionary war is most visible here. From such a viewpoint, the act of war is bound up with the activity of the creative self-positing of human life, it has its source in the self-emanation and the becoming of human life which seeks to order and shape its life in a particular fashion. The act of war as positing has much of its ground in the modern designation of the creative, productive, labouring self and the self's realization of itself through its relation with its others.

On the objective side, war can be seen as an instrument or tool drawn upon by large objective institutions, such as states, to achieve particular designated ends. Yet, war as positing also involves the non-instrumental manifestation of objective forms of life, of institutions, discourses and traditions, which become or realize their selves through war. One sense of this occurs in the notion of state sovereignty. War is not merely a tool drawn upon by sovereignty but is more firmly an integral moment within the becoming of sovereignty, sovereignty's self-realization.[21] War can be thought of as a manifestation of sovereignty, and equally, as the self-manifestation of ethical-political community. Thought of at an even more general level, war is the manifestation or self-realization of concrete forms of right which have an existence in social reality via the manner in which they structure the direction or immanence of ends of large objective institutions within modernity. In this light the end or goal of war is the continued existence of an objective institution that embodies a form of right and the manifestation or realization of this institution against its others.

What helps to make the violence of this objective side of war so profound is the incomplete and future character of objective forms of *right* – normative force – contained within social life. The *sittlich* or objectively present normative character of differing 'forms of life' (or what would be described by Hegel as '*Sittlichkeit*', 'ethical life'), contains what Ernst Bloch calls the 'not yet' (*noch nicht*) and Jacques Derrida the 'yet to come' (*à venir*).[22] In a general sense, each can be understood to refer to the eternal moment of unrealized potentiality that resides at the heart of *right*: simultaneously right is incomplete and demands fulfilment, and, right is always impossible to fulfil, it presents an impossible demand. Social life which is both guided and judged by right, shares and is agitated by the incompleteness of right and its overwhelming futural demand.

Under this conception the present is ripped open, scattered with chips of what Walter Benjamin calls 'messianic time'.[23] Human subjects in the present, whose social being is constituted by the *sittlich* character of norms, are driven restless and crazy by their own lack. The fundamental normative incompleteness of human subjects and their social-political institutions propels and drags them forward into the future.

The moment of 'lack' which I am drawing attention here to is not necessarily the moment that occurs in the passions, or in desire more generally, which commonly underlies the notion of the 'will' as presented in differing models by Hobbes, Spinoza, Hegel and Nietzsche or in its psychological reformulation through Freud. Nor am I speaking here of an idea of an ontological lack or void. While aspects of all of these accounts are relevant, in differing ways, to better understanding normativity, they are not sufficient to explain the meaning of the concept of normative force sitting within the operation of positing.

The 'lack' which I am describing here is contained necessarily within every act of concept formation. It occurs as the moment of contradiction or antinomy. Further, this condition of lack also describes the inadequacy or limit of every concept. That is, every thought determination is limited in that it is contingent upon others which it necessarily presupposes for it to have any meaning. The condition of lack within the act of concept formation, due to contradiction and contingency, generates a 'drive' or 'desire' within human thinking to overcome this inadequacy and to determine a concept whose meaning has a greater level of stability and certainty. In the *Science of Logic*,[24] Hegel shows how the drive of human thought or reason to overcome its own contradiction and contingency operates at the level of pure thought. That is, thinking strives to overcome its inadequacy, and to better know itself. It does this by thinking itself (reflecting upon itself, positing itself) which is necessarily dialectical, creative and constructive – *thinking that thinks itself*.

For Hegel, this drive within thinking also takes place within the realm of *spirit* (*Geist*) and characterizes the operation of a concept of *right* (*Recht*) within the social and material world. Human thinking (reason or rationality), faced with the inadequacy of right, is driven to realize a more adequate concept of right within thought and within physical reality (social and material life, ethical life). Hegel calls this drive towards both comprehending and realizing a more adequate concept of right *Wirklichkeit* – that right strives to become more rational and actual, that it is driven to realize or actualize itself.[25] This drive towards the greater realization of right is constantly upset by contradiction and contingency which renders thinking and social and material life unstable and at times indeterminate. However, this process also makes social and material life restless and it is consistently driven to overcome its inadequacy and become more rational and more free. Within the field of social and material life, I call this operation 'normative force' and 'normative contradiction'.

The notion of normative force involves a sense of normative incompleteness or lack which characterizes every norm, every notion of right. Every norm is orientated in some way towards the future, it occurs as an *ought*. As an ought, every norm demands to be realized and in this demand exposes its own, as yet, unrealized potentiality. A potentiality that demands to be realized exerts a certain 'power' that is something like a compulsion or pressure – a pressure of the incomplete to become complete. A coercive pressure of becoming that need not be the consequence of an uncritical metaphysics, but which merely arises out of the linguistic and conceptual structure and meaning of normativity itself. Norms like freedom and justice display this normative force, consequent of their incompleteness and their demand for realization. The norm, driven by its status as *not yet*, is driven to become more fully actual, to actualize itself.

The social being of human life is driven and pushed forward, in part, by normative force. The social character of human life is infused with norms, inter-subjectively constituted, and which orientate our individual lives and institutions. While these norms are created and posited by humans, they have a tendency to assume a life of their own, dancing like shadows on our walls when we forget that our own light produces and sustains them. Such norms, as notions of right (justice, the good) and as institutions and systems (the state, international law and the market) rise up like deities and demand their realization through us, through our mouths, bodies and hands. They drive us into action through the hope and desire of a better future and push us on from behind through fear, threat, habit and the sting of the whip. In this sense, human subjects both posit norms and are posited by them – compelled to act out of force of habit, the 'gut feeling', prejudice or 'common sense' of right and justice which is part of us, but which is always something other, clipping us in the back of the head and pushing us forward. In this sense, normative force can be thought of as something similar to Benjamin's notion of the 'storm blowing from paradise', getting caught in our wings and driving us ever forward while we look back at the pile of our own wreckage growing higher and higher.[26]

Maybe things would not be so bad if there was only one norm, only one form of right. There is not, however, there are many, and they stand in a relation of contradiction and interdependency with one another. Stuck within a life-world of normative contradiction, and driven by the attempt to overcome the contradictions contained within their claims to right, and to render a particular form of right as absolute, humans swim around blindly within a muck of conflict, positing themselves and their rights and being posited by them. Propelled by the demand of an open and irresistible future, these bodies claw at each other wildly as they try to raise and realize themselves above their others. The demand of every norm that it be realized and realized *now* without hesitation, throws the positing of the rightness of war into a future-orientated, historical frenzy.

The operation of war as positing involves an ongoing interplay between these subjective and objective sides. War as positing has a subject-object character. One aspect of this character is a relation between positing and ordering. The thinking subject's attempt to order the rightness of war takes place within and is, in part, ordered by objective forms of right and the manner in which the manifestation of these objective forms re-shape the social world. To the extent that the act of war as positing emerges out of a particular relationship between thinking and action, every act of positing involves an attempt to order the world set within a broader context of competing and contradicting orders of human life.

Human reason is not brought to the problem of war 'externally', rather, it is a part of the ongoing play of positing and ordering caught within a subject-object relation. Human reason which attempts to order the 'rightness' of war and which assumes that it can draw upon war to realize historical ends is caught up in a sea of competing orders of war and competing acts of reason that posit one order against another. Reason cannot stop and calm the waters, it itself is caught up in its own future demand of the not yet character of right which unceasingly propels it forward.

This demand of the future of right, right's as yet unrealized potentiality, which pushes the positing and ordering of war around into differing, contradictory directions, cannot be reduced to human self-interest or reason's demand that it become master of this dense, swarming ocean. Such a desire for mastery is indeed present and the notion of ordering cannot be thought without it, however, it takes place alongside and is bound up with genuine beliefs that a better life is possible and that the not yet realized rightness of this life might be brought about, in part, by violent action. Caught up in the seemingly unending swirl of positing and ordering, the whole range of differing human future demands becomes so mixed and confused that human reason finds it difficult to separate them and separate itself from the to and fro. With this said, human thinking and human action continue on, creating, producing and destroying, positing and ordering, caught between a future of hope and a history of despair.

V

If the act of war as positing involves a creative aspect, then it is also profoundly destructive. In many cases the act of war destroys more than it creates. If war is considered as something similar to labour, then it can only ever be a limited form of labour, a labour which at times does not produce anything. As a tool, the act of war is often too brutal, too blunt, it is too chaotic and uncontrollable and its devastating consequences can too quickly snowball and get out of hand. If war is like a tool, then often it resembles the weeding of a garden with a flame thrower, or the playing of a piano while wearing boxing gloves. When orders of thought and objective institutions manifest themselves through war, too often they clear away all opposition that stands before them, blasting away all the complexities and intricacies of life and positing nothing but a vacuum. If war is an act of positing, then often this positing turns over into bare or pure *negation*.

A strong sense of the manner in which the act of positing through violence turns quickly into pure negation is present in Hegel's critique of the turning of the French Revolution into the 'Reign of Terror'.[27] One sense of Hegel's critique focuses upon the manner in which the Jacobins attempted to transform and revolutionize the whole of the political and social realm via the abstract thoughts of 'general will', 'absolute equality' and 'absolute freedom'. The revolutionary actors attempted to posit or realize their thought of how the world should be through acts of violence – they tried to create a new world by smashing the old. However, by treating their abstract thought determinations as *absolute*, the only way a new world could be created was by negating all of the differences contained within the political, social and economic inter-relations that constituted the world of the concrete. Driven by an abstract account of how the world *should* be, the revolutionary actors were forced to destroy everything which contradicted their vision. For Hegel, the revolutionary act of positing was unable to produce any positive work or deed and could only remain at the level of negation. Hegel labelled this the 'the fury of destruction' and argued:

> The sole work and deed of universal freedom is therefore *death*, a death too which has no inner significance or filling, for what is negated is the empty point of the absolutely free self. It is the coldest and meanest of all deaths, with no more significance than cutting off a head of cabbage or swallowing a mouthful of water.[28]

Hegel comments upon how the elevation of an abstract moment of thought, in which all limits, differences and contradictions are dissolved – a moment which occurs within many forms of religious, philosophical and political thinking – represents a form of 'fanaticism'. With regard to the fanaticism of the notions of absolute freedom and equality, Hegel argues:

> An example of this was the Reign of Terror in the French Revolution, during which all differences of talents and authority were supposed to be cancelled out [*aufgehoben*]. This was a time of trembling and quaking and of intolerance towards everything in particular. For fanaticism wills only what is abstract, not what is articulated, so that whenever differences emerge, it finds them incompatible with its own indeterminacy and cancels them [*hebt sie auf*]. This is why the people, during the French Revolution, destroyed once more the institutions they had themselves created, because all institutions are incompatible with the abstract self-consciousness of equality.[29]

Hegel's comments should not be read as limited to the specific case of revolutionary violence but should be seen to apply to the problem of war more generally. In a sense, somewhat reminiscent of Hegel's critique of the Reign of Terror, it is today common to label militant Islamicist political organizations that carry out acts of terrorism as 'fanatics'.[30] Historically much religious violence has walked hand in hand with fanaticism. However, the West is not immune to such fanaticism. Contemporary 'just wars' in the name of 'freedom' and 'human rights' are just as, or perhaps even more, fanatical than the 'terrorists' many so quickly condemn. The brutalization of Iraq under its occupation by the USA (and its allies) and the attempt to reshape its complex social relations by crude, naïve, abstract categories of 'democracy' and 'freedom' has so far produced not much more than a fury of destruction.

In a broader sense, the notion of fanaticism draws attention to something that is strongly problematic within the positing of thought determinations by war and violent action. A fixed thought determination of how the world should be, based upon an idea, a theory, a concept or set of concepts, always involves some form of abstraction from the complexities, interrelations and contradictions of everyday life.[31] The effort to reshape and order an aspect of the living world often involves the attempt to transform the concrete to suit the image of the abstract thought determination, to re-create the world in one's own image. To the extent that this effort involves action, force and violence and at its most extreme, war, then this act of positing, in its affirmation and negation, is a positing of both *word* and *deed*: in the beginning was the word – in the beginning was the deed. In war, which is *always* in some manner fanatical, the act of positing attempts to replicate the creative act of God. War's act of positing attempts to re-create the *whole* through the word and the word's deed.[32]

Yet, self-positing humans are not God. Humans are limited, finite, frail and contingent beings prone to error, and misjudgment who are only capable of re-creating small parts of the social and physical world, small pieces at a time. In the attempt to re-create a *whole world* for ourselves through violent action and war, a world which is consistent with an abstract image, ideal or desire, we are bound to fail. In misjudging our own finitude, our attempts to posit ourselves through war are less likely to create and will more often simply destroy.

Within this relationship between creation and destruction the notion of sovereign power and the emergence of one contemporary global 'superpower' perhaps stands as an exception to an idea of human frailty. A superpower, such as the USA, can recreate much of the world through war and sustain and maintain forms and orders of living through violence and the threat of violence. At times, a superpower might even appear God-like and perhaps some people too readily confuse such immense power with the divine. Yet, even a superpower cannot posit a complete new realm of human existence through violence; it may re-create parts but it cannot re-create the whole. By placing too much faith in the power of its own deeds, a superpower tricks itself into believing that it can transform the world in accordance with its own abstract thoughts. Such an actor places too much emphasis upon the subjective power of its deeds and overlooks the other ways in which social transformation occur: through speech, discourse and culture; through changing economic relations; and, through conflicts between social and economic conditions and between differing forms of ethical life and notions of right. Each of these pushes the actor around in the world and forces it to behave in particular ways. In this sense, even a global superpower is limited and what are now viewed as the most powerful warring acts of creative positing, will one day be viewed as merely yet another arrogant, naïve moment within the nonsense of human history.

With this said, our abilities to transform our material and social world have become immensely powerful in certain respects, through the production of more powerful and efficient tools for killing. Humanity has reached a point where, through the production of nuclear weapons, the tools of warfare have begun to outstrip the possibilities of their strategic use.[33] It was not long ago when during the Cold War the notion of 'Mutually Assured Destruction' (MAD) was a popular term. The term refers to the situation where the nuclear capabilities of a number of states are such that an attack by one involves the high possibility of a reciprocal attack and the resulting destruction of both.[34]

Such a possibility challenges the notion of *war as positing*. The notion of war as positing still makes sense with regard to the use of nuclear weapons in the situation where the enemy, or its allies, have no nuclear capability for a counter-attack. In such a case a particular sovereignty, strategic interest or claim, may be posited through the partial destruction of the enemy. An example of this case may be thought to have occurred in the atomic bombing of the Japanese cites of Hiroshima and Nagasaki by the USA (1945). However, in a context in which both or all warring parties possess nuclear technology and their weapons capability[35] is such that both parties, and perhaps large sections of humanity, will perish through the operation of MAD, then all that might be seen to be *posited* by a state or political actor in an act of nuclear war is its own destruction. In this later context, war as positing becomes negation and self-negation. The act of nuclear war tied to the operation of MAD transforms war as positing into *war as pure negation*. All that can be created by such acts of nuclear war is apocalypse.[36]

The idea of nuclear apocalypse[37] has slipped over the horizon of recent history. Some attention is paid to the threat of so-called 'rogue' or 'outlaw' states who have acquired or are attempting acquire nuclear technology. The demonization of states such as North Korea or Iran involves an active forgetting that it is the so-called 'civilized' states of the West that have carried out much of the killing and destruction within modernity and have done so aggressively. There is as much a threat of nuclear war being carried out by 'civilized' states as by their others. Further, it is not too difficult to foresee new arms races developing as new economic and political world powers emerge to challenge the current military supremacy of the USA. It is not too difficult to foresee the possibility of new 'cold wars' as states and non-state actors attempt to posit themselves through the threat and use of nuclear weapons. In such scenarios the operation of war as positing might well turn into a fully fledged war of pure negation. In such a case, humanity's last creative act may well be an act of its self-destruction. In the end was the deed.

Notes

1 N. Chomsky, *Hegemony or Survival*, Crows Nest: Allen & Unwin, 2003, p. 188. Chomsky at p. 189, goes on to argue that the 'difficulty' of defining terrorism stems from the fact that the definition of 'counter-terror' ('low-intensity conflict', 'counter-insurgency') given in US military manuals is exactly the same as its own definition of 'terror'. Chomsky argues that as counter-terror is official US policy, the definitions of terror produced via the Reagan administration are no longer used because they clearly point to the fact that the USA is officially committed to terrorism.
2 For a documentation of the USA's use of terrorism, particularly in Central and South America, see N. Chomsky, *Deterring Democracy*, New York: Hill and Wang, 1991.
3 C. von Clausewitz, *On War*, trans. M. Howard and P. Paret, New York: Everyman's Library, 1993.
4 Ibid., p. 83.
5 Ibid., p. 99.
6 Part of this creative role of action and violence is expressed in Hegel's statement that it is the right of heroes to establish states. See G.W.F. Hegel, *Elements of the Philosophy of Right*, trans. H.B. Nisbet, Cambridge: Cambridge University Press, 1991, § 350, p. 376.
7 A certain sense of this creative function might be found in the statement of Heraclitus that 'war' is the 'father of all things'. The account of war given here will, however, be limited to a concentration upon the creative character of war within the modern world.
8 C. von Clausewitz, *Vom Krieg*, Bonn: Ferd. Dümmlers Verlag, 1991, p. 210.
9 See G.W.F. Hegel, *Grundlinien der Philosophie des Rechts*, Frankfurt am Main: Suhrkamp, 1970. At p. 16, Hegel argues: '*Die Rechtgesetzte sind Gesetztes, von Menschen Herkommendes*'.
10 On the 'empty place of sovereignty', consider: J-L. Nancy, *Being Singular Plural*, trans. R.D. Richardson and A.E. O'Byrne, Stanford, CA: Stanford University Press, 2000; J-L. Nancy, *The Inoperative Community*, trans. P. Conner *et al.*, Minneapolis, MN: University of Minnesota Press, 1991. Consider also C. Douzinas, 'Jurisdiction or *Diken Didonai* in Relation to the Role of the Critic and the Sovereign', in S. McVeigh (ed.) *Jurisprudence of Jurisdiction*, London: Cavendish, 2006.
11 On some of the religious forms of thinking that underlie 'secular' Western political institutions, see W.E. Connolly, *Why I Am Not a Secularist*, Minneapolis, MN: University of Minnesota Press, 1999; J. Milbank, *Theology and Social Theory: Beyond Secular Reason*, Oxford: Blackwell, 1993. See also R. Tuck, *Natural Rights Theories: Their Origin and Development*, Cambridge: Cambridge University Press, 1979.
12 See C. Schmitt, *Political Theology: Four Chapters on the Concept of Sovereignty*, ed. G. Schwab, Chicago, IL: University of Chicago Press, 2006.
13 A desire within modernity away from an acceptance of natural necessity and contingency, and towards a conception of freedom as the self-positing of the subject.
14 It is important to put to one side the unhelpful and naïve characterizations of Hegel as an 'idealist' and Marx as a 'materialist'. Both were aware of the relationship between thinking and matter contained within creative operation of human labour and much of their philosophy makes little sense if this basic insight is ignored. This being said, there are differing points of emphasis in each of their works and Marx's own criticism that Hegel plays too much attention to the labour of thinking and not enough to physical labour remains at a general level, a fair criticism.
15 When one concentrates upon the physicality of action (i.e. the shaping of clay by the human hand) it becomes difficult to draw a firm line of distinction between the working of 'thoughts' and 'matter'. There is a whole history of scientific research

concentrating upon the relation between thinking and action and this work does not pretend to claim any authority here. It is, however, important to note that a strict set of distinctions between thoughts and matter, reason and objects, ideas and things, theories and facts, begin to break down as soon as one takes the time to reflect upon some of the basic relations between these terms within acts of creative activity and production that occur in all aspects of everyday life. The account presented here merely tries to draw attention to how the understanding of war changes once we begin to pay attention to the inter-relation and blurring of thinking and action contained within human labour.

16 Of course, this transformation has limits. Humans are not all powerful and this is evidenced by the fact that only small changes in temperature, across a global level, put into jeopardy the existence of the human species. Through the use of machinery and technology humans might think that they are gods. Facing the incredible power of the natural world (or the universe for that matter), humans are really not much more than children, and often very naïve children at that.

17 For a more detailed account of this process, see E. Bloch, *The Spirit of Utopia*, trans. A.A. Nassar, Stanford, CA: Stanford University Press, 2000; E. Bloch, *The Principle of Hope*, trans. N. Plaice and S. Plaice, Cambridge, MA: MIT Press, 1995. See W. Hudson, *The Marxist Philosophy of Ernst Bloch*, London: Macmillan, 1982; T. Moylan and J.O. Daniel (eds) *Not Yet: Reconsidering Ernst Bloch*, London: Verso, 1997; V. Geoghegan, *Ernst Bloch*, London: Routledge, 1996. Consider also: W. Hudson, *The Reform of Utopia*, Aldershot: Ashgate, 2003. It should be noted that the account I am giving here of the role of labour in the transformation of human reality at a general level does not attempt to say anything more than that which has been previously been more convincingly expressed by Hegel, Marx, Ernst Bloch and Walter Benjamin.

18 On the notion of the 'event', see A. Badiou, *Infinite Thought: Truth and the Return to Philosophy*, New York: Continuum, 2005.

19 In a highly exaggerated example, if a second sun were to instantly appear beside our own and not seem to adversely affect human life, the earth's temperature or its orbit, then such an occurrence might be thought to constitute an 'event' in the sense that human thinking would need to radically revise its conceptions of reality and the laws of the universe. Such an event would reveal to human thought a whole range of possibilities which before were not simply not considered as possibilities, but were off the scale of possibility completely. The example is rather extreme, however, the assertion is here that such 'events' constitute the everyday mundaneness of human life, so much so, that we overlook this continually creative and upsetting character of our existence.

20 It should be noted that I am not referring to all humans here but only to those influenced by Anglo-American and Western European culture under the conditions of capitalism. There are many other ways in which groups of humans relate to each other and to the physical world that are very different to the general level of analysis presented here. I am not trying to argue that any particular form of life is more valid or more worthwhile. I am merely trying to track a particular form of thinking which is quite dominant within the West within modernity.

21 Jean-Luc Nancy gives also a non-instrumental account of war with respect to sovereignty. See J. Nancy, 'War, Right, Sovereignty – Technē', in J. Nancy, *Being Singular Plural*. At pp. 121–2, Nancy argues:

> This is why accusing a sovereign power of wanting war so obviously falls short of the mark. The execution of this desire [*vouloir*] for war is not only one of the proper ends of the executive organ; it also represents the extreme mode of

> these ends. So that it is no longer an organ with regard to the execution of such desire; instead, it is sovereignty itself in its finishing – insofar as we think sovereignty according to the only concept that is at our disposal. In war, there is something that immediately goes beyond all the possible goals of war, whether they be defensive or offensive: the accomplishment of the Sovereign as such in a relation of absolute opposition with another Sovereign. War is indissociably the *physis* and *technē* of sovereignty.

Further, that:

> Thus, war borders on art. This is not to say that it borders on the art of war, the technology of the strategist; it is to say, rather, that it borders on art understood absolutely in its modern sense, *technē* as a mode of the execution of Being, as its mode of finishing in the explosive brilliance [*éclat*] of the beautiful and sublime, that doubled rivalry of sovereignty that occurs within the blossoming [*éclosion*] of *physis*.

Nancy's account of war which relies upon a particular account of the 'Being' of sovereignty and '*technē*' draws much from Martin Heidegger and his conceptualization of technology as *technē*. Such an approach is rather different from the account of war that I am attempting to develop here built upon the operation of positing and ordering. See, generally, M. Heidegger, 'The Question Concerning Technology', in M. Heidegger, *The Question Concerning Technology and Other Essays*, trans. W. Lovitt, New York: Harper and Row, 1969.

22 See J. Derrida, 'The Force of Law: The Mystical Foundation of Authority', in D. Cornell, M. Rosenfeld and D.G. Carlson (eds) *Deconstruction and the Possibility of Justice*, New York: Routledge, 1992; J. Derrida, *Specters of Marx: The State of Debt, the Work of Mourning and the New International*, trans. P. Kamuf, New York: Routledge, 1994. While Derrida's notion of the 'force of law' is certainly informative, in many respects his account is also unhelpful in that it displays a tendency towards mystification and often flies into the 'misty realm of religion'. For a rough account of how Derrida's notion of the 'yet to come' replicates much of Bloch's conception of the 'not yet' and is, in some respects, inferior to Bloch's account of law, see T. Kochi, 'Anticipation, Critique and the Problem of Intervention: Understanding the Messianic: Derrida Through Ernst Bloch', *Law and Critique*, 13, 2002.

23 W. Benjamin, 'Theses on the Philosophy of History', in W. Benjamin, *Illuminations*, trans. H. Zohn, New York: Schocken Books, 1969, p. 263.

24 G.W.F. Hegel, *Science of Logic*, trans. A.V. Miller, London: Allen and Unwin, 1969; G.W.F. Hegel, *The Encyclopaedia Logic: Part I of the Encyclopaedia of Philosophical Sciences with the Zusätze*, Indianapolis, IN: Hackett, 1991.

25 G.W.F. Hegel, *Grundlinien der Philosophie des Rechts*, p. 24: *Was vernünftig ist, das ist wirklich; Und was wirklich ist, das ist vernünftig.*

26 Ibid., pp. 257–8. In a number of respects, my attempt to develop a theory of war is aimed at trying to answer a number of questions raised by Benjamin's 'Angel of History'.

27 G.W.F. Hegel, *Phenomenology of Spirit*, trans. A.V. Miller, Oxford: Oxford University Press, 1977, pp. 355–63. On Hegel's position in relation to the French Revolution, see J. Ritter, *Hegel and the French Revolution: Essays on the Philosophy of Right*, Cambridge, MA: MIT Press, 1982; J. Habermas, *Theory and Practice*, trans. J. Viertel, Cambridge: Polity Press, 1988; J. Hyppolite, *Studies on Marx and Hegel*, London: Heinemann, 1969.

28 G.W.F. Hegel, *Phenomenology of Spirit*, p. 360.
29 G.W.F. Hegel, *Philosophy of Right*, § 5 Addition, pp. 38–9, see also § 258, pp. 275–81.
30 See the various discussions in G. Borradori, *Philosophy in a Time of Terror: Dialogues with Jürgen Habermas and Jacques Derrida*, Chicago, IL: University of Chicago Press, 2003; S. Benhabib, 'Unholy Wars', *Constellations*, 9(1), 2002. For a discussion of the 'fanatic', see D. Nassar, 'Heroes and Fanatics: Discernment and Critique in Hegel's Political Philosophy', *Idealistic Studies*, 34(2), 2004.
31 For Hegel, abstraction is a central moment within the activity human thinking. See G.W.F. Hegel, *Encyclopaedia Logic*, §§ 79–82, pp. 125–33. Abstraction itself is not problematic, rather, what is at issue is the manner in which human actors attempt to re-order the world in accordance with an abstract conception of how the world should be. Thinking will always involve the formation of abstract thought determinations and in this sense all attempts to order aspects of everyday life will involve an activity grounded upon abstractions made in thought. One case where political action runs into difficulty is when an actor holds so firmly (perhaps fanatically) to their abstract thought determination so that the actor ignores all aspects of social reality which render incomplete or contradict the abstract thought determination. When holding fast to this abstract thought determination and attempting to realize it or bring it into being through coercion, violence and war, the actor attempts to force the thick complexity of the social world into a thin form which simply cannot be attained nor sustained. The way in which human actors organize their world in accordance with fixed, abstract thought determinations perhaps always involves, through positing's moments of affirmation and negation, a level of violence, or at least a form of coercion. Mostly in everyday life, because actors are only positing themselves in relation to small parts of the world, this violence goes largely unnoticed. However, when the scope and intensity of an actor's positing increase and an actor attempts to order large sections of the social world – when it tries to order the whole – then the violence of the *word* and its expression through the *deed* become more visible, they are felt more readily, and its consequences become more severe. In this sense, the act of war and its negative consequences can be seen to be related to the positing of human thought. While the act of positing will always involve some form of violence to someone or something somewhere, *how violent* this positing is, is dependent upon the manner in which the human actor comprehends its world and acts in relation to it.
32 Some contemporary actors, whether leaders of Western states or leaders of militant Islamicist political organizations (as opposed to similar organizations which are non-violent, being the majority), would claim that they are simply following the word of God and that therefore they are not occupying a creative God-like position. It is highly possible that such actors can genuinely believe in their self-narrative yet through their actions they still attempt to re-create the whole through their own acts. It should be remembered that such actors are a part of modernity and even if they are unaware (or deny) the very modern character of their violent action, they may still be understood as attempting to play the role of the creators rather than the created. Such actors play out an internal contradiction in that they orientate themselves in terms of an older religious world, yet their actions and their violence are fully modern and highly creative in character.
33 For a similar claim, see H. Arendt, *On Violence*, San Diego, CA: Harcourt Brace & Company, 1970.
34 The notion of MAD also involves a notion of deterrence. Nuclear deterrence, however, places a great deal of faith in the predictability of human action. The notion does not give enough emphasis to the operation of human error and the existence of groups and individuals who are willing to enter into apocalyptic scenarios.

35 Sometimes referred to as a 'second strike capability'.
36 Such a notion must always include the possibility of new and old technologies that may allow parts of the human species to escape nuclear annihilation.
37 The term 'apocalypse' might be also more applicable to a contemporary situation where a number of religious actors are driven by competing futural demands of religious ethical life. The contemporary conflict between many 'fundamentalist' Jews, Christians and Muslims represents not a 'clash of civilizations' but rather, *a clash of messianisms*. For religious actors, comforted by the future belief in an after-life, the threat of nuclear war might not seem so horrible, but might actually be welcomed as a final apocalyptic scenario within a religious-teleological, historical, world process.

Chapter 7

Judging war and terror

I

The future casts a shadow, though its shape is not easily discernible. One silhouette is that of apocalypse. As if human life has not been bloody enough already, a shadow of apocalypse hanging over our heads, a grand suicidal act of our own making, plays the present with a melody of dread. Perhaps we are already there and we simply do not know it. We cannot step outside our own world to catch a view of our terrible historical process as a complete whole, as one brutal instant within which moments of quiet and peace are perhaps merely slices of respite from, and preparation for, greater brutality. Yet, the shadow cast by the future is also our own shadow, one fired by our own light behind our backs, our burning spirit, our beautiful idea. We cast our own future shadow before our selves, and are drawn to it; it seems, like a moth, but towards its own flame. Standing under the shadow of apocalypse we are offered a glimpse of a past and a future of our own making. Catching this glimpse we might realize that it is still too early to talk about inevitability and that, even from the point of view of what is the worst in ourselves, the worst aspects of our species, we might still be allowed to hope.

This concluding chapter looks at the problem of judgment on war and the manner in which continued efforts to reach an objective standpoint of judgment fail and contribute instead to a war of competing judgments. The chapter focuses upon how each tradition of war's ordering contributes to a wider war of ideas in which judgments are posited together with acts of violence. Such positing and counter-positing involve something of a reciprocal violence within judgment itself, driving differing actors further into the darker moments of a war of some against some and all against all. Residing within a war of ideas there remains, however, a little bit of hope that can still be held onto. This hope might be grasped if a radical attitude towards judgment is taken, an attitude guided by a *praxis of recognition*. Such an attitude involves suspending the constant demand to condemn the other's violence and instead engage in the effort of *recognizing the ethics of the other's war*. By taking up such an attitude a small sphere of objectivity within judgment on war might be possible.

II

The numerous conflicts that constitute the so-called 'war on terror' involve a war at the level of ideas, a war between competing claims of right, competing claims over the legitimacy of violence. Within this conflict, warring actors, critics and commentators make judgments on the rightness of war, all judge particular acts of violence, justifying some and condemning others. The theory of war as positing has shown that these *thoughts* about right are not detached from the physicality of violence. Thinking, action and violence are bound – thoughts are deeds and the positing of differing thoughts against each other involves both negation within the realm of thinking and violence within the social world. In this respect, judgments on the rightness of war participate in the violence of war and there occurs a certain *violence of judgment* which humans can perhaps never escape from.

In moments of highly emotive conflict, when the drums of war beat up such a fury that every man, woman and child seems to carry the rightness of war within their hearts, then judgments on war participate more actively within the positing of differential claims of right. For many in the West, the 'war on terror', like the 'cold war', is framed as the ultimate battle between right and wrong, good and evil, freedom and unfreedom, civilization and barbarism. While the bulk of the actual violence, the fighting, the bombing and the killing, within the 'war on terror' is carried out somewhere else, somewhere far away (somewhere on television), many in the West feel the need to pass judgment on the legitimacy of their violence and the illegitimacy of their others – or, for the bulk of the critics, the illegitimacy of their violence and the illegitimacy of their others. Often such normative judgments on war are highly partisan and the legitimacy of violence is not measured by any 'objective' standard but merely by the *feeling* of an inherent rightness of one's own party (i.e. one's state, one's race, one's civilization, one's religion, one's inter-national political community) against the other.

Judgment on war is most often *partisan judgment*. It is a moment of positing of a particular claim of right, a particular concrete form of life, or ethical life, a particular imaginary domain of communal self-reference, which hides behind dazzling claims to universality or transcendent authority. Most often the moment of judgment is a moment within the battle of thoughts against thoughts, a partisan claim to right dressed up in rhetorical finery or emotional simplicity. All too often those casting judgment are not aware of their partisan nature, their judgments are so deeply immersed within the bounded realm of their ethical universe that they simply assume that their little piece of right constitutes the whole.

Viewed from the perspective of the differing and conflicting traditions of war's ordering, contemporary, partisan judgments on the rightness of war lose much of their brilliance. They appear more often as confused, limited, self-contradictory claims over the legitimacy of violence that reflects a number of differing lines of mediation between war and right. By holding onto the differing traditions of war's ordering and their moments of conflict, contemporary claims that an act of war is 'right' or is 'not right' are brought back to earth and shown to be highly fragile and erroneous. No longer dazzling with a transcendent luminescence, these judgments become more clearly the claims of groups of humans positing their selves in the world through violence, drawing upon differing normative traditions to justify their acts, and being driven, pushed or propelled into forms of action by the restless, future-oriented, ethical demands of their social-material world that lie incomplete, unrealized and not yet.

There are some, however, who reject the partisan nature of judgment, who instead want to move beyond this and reach an objective standpoint of judgment on the legitimacy of violence. The differing traditions of war's ordering can be seen to have been pushing towards such a goal. Each, to differing degrees, rejected the absolute chaos of wars of right waged by all against all and attempted to set the chaos of the rightness of war into some form of order. Such a desire for order did not necessarily involve the attempt to stop all forms of violence, rather, for some of these traditions it involved the attempt by philosophical reason to comprehend and enunciate the rightness of war – to have the chaos of war ordered within the realm of thought. Yet, even this latter demand involved, to a certain extent, a search for some degree of objectivity.[1] One concern of the demand for objectivity rejected the suggestion that the rightness of war was merely an issue of subjective opinion or interest. The demand for a certain objective standpoint of judgment on war involved the attempt to say something about the relationship between war and right that might have some form of universal relevance and applicability and which could be drawn upon as some form of measure from which to judge the 'rightness' of individual acts of war.

The differing traditions of war's ordering have been partially successful in producing 'objective' positions of judgment on the rightness of war. Within the conceptual boundaries claimed by each tradition, a certain objective character of the relation between war and right is framed and posited and allows judgments on the rightness of war to be measured against a standard that might claim a degree of universality. However, what thinking is left with after examining these traditions is not one, absolute, universal, objective standpoint of judgment on the legitimacy of violence, but rather, a number of standpoints of judgment that intersect and conflict with one another. Each tradition has been unable to produce a final and comprehensive account of the relation between war and right that might be drawn upon for all time to judge the rightness of acts of war in both the past and the future. The way in which each tradition has only grasped certain limited aspects or particular lines of mediation between war and right points to the suggestion that human thinking will never be able to produce a comprehensive objective standpoint of judgment on the rightness of war that could be valid for all acts all of the time.

There seems to be a certain *impossibility of judgment* here. Much of this relates to the infinite complexity of the relations between right and violence stretching from the most basic, micro levels of everyday life through to the grand acts of inter-state war and wars to end all wars. It appears that any theoretical account simply cannot grasp *all* (the whole, the totality) of the differing and often conflicting relations between war and right and hold them together in a way which can then say that 'this' act of violence is 'right' and that 'this' act of war is 'wrong'.

All that is left for judgment, it seems, is to operate within a certain formal realm of 'objectivity', constructed by thought via abstracting from particular historical and conceptual presuppositions and contradictions. Here judgments on war are made by particular modes (traditions, discourses or paradigms) of thought which assume or draw (posit) the conceptual boundaries of what counts as meaningful and relevant. Within these zones of judgment particular levels of the density and complexity of the relations between violence and right within social and material life are acknowledged, while others are suppressed and ignored. By narrowing the boundaries of a field of inquiry and not accounting for concepts, ideas and historical moments which might upset one's ideological position, or formal line of reasoning, and expose it to irresolvable contradiction, then a certain, limited zone of 'objective' judgment can be said to be created.

Such judgments on violence work to a limited extent in that they provide the parameters from within which a level of consistency in judgment might be brought about. The claims of the rightness of acts of violence carried out by some of the differing traditions of war's ordering offer forms of judgment in which some degree of consistency is maintained within a limited, formal sphere of reasoning. For example, the just war tradition and Kantian moral theory each uses a defined set of principles and sets up something of an 'objective' zone of judgment within limited conceptual and historical parameters. However, such formal approaches to judgment and claims to objectivity are inadequate and are always challenged and upset by forms of violence and right that stand outside the designated boundaries of inquiry. Sometimes formal approaches to judgment recognize their own limitations. At other times these forms of judgment turn into fanaticism – in their zealous drive to ignore and suppress contradiction.

One consequence of the inadequacy of judgment is that contemporary thought is marked by a battle within the discursive realm between forms of judgment. Often contemporary thinkers who inherit differing traditions of war's ordering do not realize the limitations contained within their own forms of judging and that their approach to judgment presupposes the framing of the relation between war and right in particular, abstract ways. In their assertion of their judgments as having universal validity, many contemporary thinkers are partisan actors who do not recognize themselves as such. In coming to terms with contemporary partisan judgments, it is often important to point out the limits of judgment contained within each of the traditions of war's ordering.

The partisan nature of judgment can perhaps be most clearly seen within the tradition of the juridical ordering of war.[2] Hobbes creates something of an objective position of judgment within the state through granting the sovereign the monopoly upon the legitimacy of violence. However, such an ordering is limited to the level of state sovereignty and is not extended beyond the state. Hence, while there is a sphere of objective judgment within states, between states, there still exists the chaos of ongoing war and the partisan interests of the *reason of state* posited against its others. With this said, the sphere of objectivity over judgment opened within state sovereignty is also questionable. While the form of the rule of law presents itself as neutral and independent, it contains a political, economic and moral (and religious) content and underlying conflicts between these contents which the *form of law* continually tries to hide. The more this content is examined and brought into the light, the less 'objective' law's standpoint of judgment appears to be.

Similarly, the tradition of the moral ordering of war fails also to produce an objective standpoint of judgment on the legitimacy of violence. Kant's notion of pure practical reason can only offer a negative standpoint of judgment on violence. It can never be drawn upon to objectively affirm the use of violence for a moral end once differing moral content is admitted. Yet, because states (and non-state actors) are framed as moral actors, charged with the injunction to be moral and to act so as to realize the moral law, what occurs through the moral ordering of war are ongoing secular-moral 'just wars' that replicate the chaotic violence of the religious just wars of the past. Often within these modern, moral, just wars, differing, violent partisan actors claim that they are attempting to realize the same set of universal moral concepts – peace, freedom, human rights, democracy, human dignity. Within such a context the chances of any viable objective standpoint of judgment is lost as all actors and critics use the same universal moral concepts (sometimes honestly, sometimes dishonestly) to realize completely differing ends.

If there is only a limited degree of success involved in the production of an objective standpoint of judgment on the legitimacy of violence given by both the traditions of the juridical and moral ordering of war, then this can perhaps be found in the operation of international law. As an inheritor of both of these traditions, to a limited extent, contemporary international law might present something of an objective standpoint of judgment. At the least, there is a global executive body which, through an inter-state contract, is given the mandate to legally judge when the use of violence may be legitimate or not. However, this executive is highly dysfunctional and is constantly rendered impotent by the openly partisan infighting of its member states. Further, the same critique of the 'objectivity' of the form of law within the state applies also to international law which also contains political, economic, moral and religious contents and underlying conflicts between these contents that are hidden by the legal form's claim to neutrality. As being predominantly a European tradition, and lacking direct democratic accountability, the contemporary form of international law is challenged from many quarters.

What perhaps renders a moment of objective judgment on violence within international law most problematic is its dual inheritance of the traditions of the juridical and moral ordering of war. Contemporary international law (at least since 1945) is built upon the structure of the juridical ordering of violence around the sovereign state. As a form of law which moves between states and sits above them, contemporary international law presupposes and relies upon a particular form of the ordering of the rightness of violence within the state which it affirms in its continued operation. Yet, contemporary international law also inherits the tradition of the moral ordering of war, which can be radical and revolutionary in its outlook. International law contains within it a form of the ordering of the legitimacy of violence around notions of freedom, human rights and human dignity, each of which challenge the state sovereign's authority over the legitimate use of violence. This internal conflict between two intertwined lines of inheritance is carried through into every moment of judgment on violence. The conflict can be seen most clearly in international law's attempt to come to terms with contemporary non-sovereign war. On the one, hand it condemns the illegitimacy of these acts because they challenge the state's monopoly upon the legitimacy of violence. On the other hand, to the extent that acts of non-state violence are carried out in the name of freedom, democracy, human rights and human dignity – a certain terror in the name of human rights – then the radical emancipatory and moral heart of international law might be forced to extend a certain sympathy, and even support, for such actions. If nothing else, this dual inheritance of international law contributes to its ongoing indeterminacy.

The failure to produce an objective standpoint of judgment on violence troubles also the tradition of the ethical ordering of war. For Hegel, if there can be such a standpoint, then it takes place as a form of historical knowledge, the notion of history as a 'court of judgment'. Such a standpoint pushes beyond abstract conceptions of right and demands that we grasp the whole,[3] the concrete, which involves the flux, movement and conflict and contradiction of differing forms of right clashing with each other throughout history. Such a standpoint does not, however, offer a comprehensive position of judgment, in one sense it is always limited to the extent that an individual's judgment can never grasp the whole, which is the infinite. If anything, Hegel's position suggests a certain impossibility of judgment, an impossibility of the finite human mind ever comprehending the complex infinite relations that make up the whole.

In another sense, the ethical ordering of war leaves judgment with a sense of lacking, it can only watch the differing shapes of the world pass by, dancing like a conga line of partisans. It can describe them, and show how each is a form of right, concrete and developed, yet such judgment cannot really condemn. It can describe a 'wrong' in a historical context, but it cannot be drawn into condemning or supporting an act absolutely. There are benefits contained within this lack, it creates a distance and detachment from the world's violence and this approach is bound up with Hegel's view of the role of philosophy, always arriving too late on the scene to do anything but attempt to comprehend what has passed. Yet, the notion of an objective standpoint of judgment (for some) perhaps demands something more. Perhaps judgment wants to be more engaged and not simply be forced to sit on the sidelines watching the passing parade – Hegel's 'slaughter-bench' of history.

The tradition of the political ordering of war given by Marx and his inheritors shares certain aspects of the demand to grasp the whole, however, it does away with any passivity of the old Hegel and is built upon the foundations of radical critique and the radical demand for action. While Marx looks towards a certain degree of objectivity within his economic and social analysis, his inheritors radicalize his insights into the social conflicts contained within differing forms of economic, political and legal ordering. They re-interpret conflict in terms of ongoing intra-state civil wars fought for the control of the political and economic ordering of the social world. The political ordering of war shows the question of the rightness of war, the legitimacy of violence, to be in complete disorder, thrown into chaos and containing at its heart a partisan war of some against their others fought out both physically and at the level of ideas. The tradition shows the boundaries of legitimacy and illegitimacy drawn between sovereign and non-sovereign violence to be both imaginary and necessary, and the standpoint of any objective position of judgment being an object of contestation itself. For elements of this tradition, if we are to reach an objective position of judgment on the legitimacy of violence, then this cannot be done by thought alone, but must be brought about by fighting.

Perhaps more than any other, this tradition grasps the nature of a war carried out within the realm of ideas and the darker consequences of this, as it leads to a complete militarization of all aspects of social life. Viewed from such a perspective, there is very little hope for the production of an objective position of judgment on violence. Any such hope is undone by the reciprocal violence contained within judgment itself. If there is to be any hope, then thinking must attempt to leap out of the reciprocal violence of judgment, it needs to turn its back upon the old demand of judgment and walk a different track, a differing path, or different way. The final section of this work will set out a different way, one that does not pretend to offer any major solution, but one that allows us to hold onto a little slice of hope.

III

One approach that offers a partial solution to the lack of objectivity within our judgments on war develops from an account of inter-subjectivity and ethics within Hegel's theory of recognition. While certain radical aspects of this theory were not taken up and developed by Hegel himself, they can be drawn upon in the present in an effort to come to terms with the battlefield and reciprocal violence of judgment. Contemporary thought can better come to terms with the problem of judgment on war by turning towards a *praxis of recognition*. Such a praxis involves the development of an attitude towards judgment, an attitude that might be thought to change the practice of judging itself. The practice also opens up a space for a degree of 'objectivity' within judgment and in this sense it allows us to hang onto a certain amount of hope. An attitude towards judgment on war guided by a praxis of recognition is not easy and it may make some feel uncomfortable. As a standpoint, it involves breaking free from the constant demand to condemn the enemy's violence, the other's war and terror. In place of this what is required for judgment is a difficult task – *recognizing the ethics of the other's war.*

Confronted by the other's war, the immediate reaction for most is that of condemnation. The violent acts of another sovereign or non-sovereign group are condemned and this other violent actor is comprehended as the enemy. It seems that judgment never fully escapes this initial moment of condemnation of the other's violence and all subsequent acts of judgment are influenced by the lingering sense that the other's violence is wrong. Why should judgment not feel this way? Certainly it feels 'natural' or 'common sense' to condemn the warring actor who attacks your political community, kills your fellow citizens and sometimes kills your family and friends. Certainly there is a right of condemnation here, or, is there?

Feeling is one thing, and no one should be denied the right to feel aggrieved. But, judgment on the legitimacy of violence is something different. Judgment should not be confused with the feeling of being aggrieved. Contemporary thinking must attempt to set judgment apart from a certain degree of personal feeling, from that initial highly partisan sense of condemnation – of right and wrong – that we feel in our breast or gut in response to the latest act of war. Judgment demands something more, it demands more than just simple condemnation; it demands that we push beyond what seems most natural for ourselves and take hold of what is at stake within the ongoing process in which the rightness of war is posited. Judgment involves trying to get away from what is closest to ourselves and to think about the rightness of something other – the forms of right within differing spheres of concrete, social-material life which brush up against and work through our own.

Judgment guided by a praxis of recognition seeks to push beyond the initial moment of condemnation, it attempts to overcome the normally overwhelming subjective sense of rightness attached to our actions and wrongness attached to the acts of the enemy. A praxis of recognition represents a certain method, a method of judging which seeks to grasp something objective about the rightness of violence, it does this by attempting to comprehend our own claims of right in relation to the claims made by the other. Such a praxis asks judgment to attempt to comprehend the rightness of the other's actions, the thick forms of right that coordinate the other's acts by a certain promise of the future. Recognition asks judgment to consider that there is a certain rightness embodied within the other's act of war. This rightness needs to be acknowledged, it needs to be recognized and not simply dismissed as lunacy or evil. The other's violent acts may be aggressive, their attempt to transform the world through violence might even, at times, be fanatical. However, the other's acts of violence do not take place within a normative vacuum, that is, their acts posit certain ethical claims and are driven by the attempt to realize the as yet unrealized potentialities of particular forms of social-material life. Recognizing the ethics of the other's war involves attempting to acknowledge and perhaps better comprehend this normative content which is bound up with the other's act of violence.

Such an approach is not directed out of sympathy for the other's cause, nor is it an expression of an injunction to love one's neighbour, nor does it involve an ethics of alterity. The demand of recognizing the ethics of the other's war need not be understood as an overarching cosmopolitan ethic.[4] Rather, the primary concern of such a standpoint is in addressing a lack of objectivity within judgment on war. The concern of recognition in this case is with our own judgments and with moving beyond the subjectiveness of our own judgments about violence. The demand that we recognize the ethics of the other's war involves the attempt to come to terms with a rightness of violence that is not our own, it opens onto the possibility that we might understand the rightness of our violence in relation to the rightness of the violence carried out by the other.

If judgment is able to make this initial step, it might then proceed to consider how our claims of right are related to the other's and the points of similarity and difference between conflicting positions. If judgment can make it this far, then it might even begin to grasp how our claims of right, and our acts of positing, are mediated through the other and of how our claims and acts have been mutually co-constituted through our relationship with the other. The hope of such an approach is that judgment might be able to step out of its blinkered, overly subjective view and begin to consider the question of what the rightness of violence might mean to a number of differing actors who at times come into conflict with one another. From such a position, judgment leaves behind its initial moment of condemnation, one might still feel aggrieved, yet one no longer confuses this with the question of right attached to the other's violence and to our own.

Judgment guided by a praxis of recognition should not be reduced to an argument of cultural relativism. Partisan judgment is already a form of cultural relativism, each party thinks its judgments on violence are 'universal', however, most often actors are merely arguing from the standpoint of an ethics of exclusion hidden behind claims to universal notions such as freedom, democracy and human rights. A praxis of recognition attempts to move away from this relativism of subjective judgment. Only by beginning to comprehend how the other's war might possibly be *right*, might the individual passing judgment begin to come closer to comprehending the rightness of violence which is in some respects 'universal'. Even if this universality is limited to the rightness of war stretching between only two conflicting actors, it is more universal than the initial moment of judgment in which one party thinks its own account of right is valid for all others.

Further, by not attempting to recognize the ethics of the other's war, we will never fully understand our own claims about the rightness of violence. Because our claims of right are mediated through our others, by cutting ourselves off from them our comprehension of what is 'right' remains one-sided and inadequate. It is because the rightness of violence is something more than ourselves that we have to push beyond our own limited view of the world and comprehend how our claims relate to and have developed though our relationships with our others. The answer to the question of what is the rightness of war cannot be solved simply by looking inwardly into ourselves. We will not find the answer there, no matter how we try. If judgment is to have any purchase on the world, it must attempt to grasp the differing forms of judgment in the world, it must attempt to grasp the ethics of the other's war.

To a certain extent, the method of such recognition mirrors the method of this book as a whole. Yet, instead of judgment grasping the differing historical-theoretical traditions of the ordering of the rightness of war, judgment attempts to grasp practically the differing orders of right residing behind our own acts of violence and the violence of our others. In the attempt to comprehend a certain degree of objectivity within the relationship between war and right, the method remains similar and what changes is the move from theory to praxis. In each case, thinking attempts to move beyond its own initial feelings or insights into what acts of violence are right and seeks to comprehend the outlines of differing forms of the rightness of violence. Within such a process, thinking begins to move towards a certain degree of objectivity in its comprehension of the relation between war and right. This degree of objectivity within judgment may not be absolute but, in a double movement of self-suspension and other-comprehension, it does open a pathway that leads towards a degree of objectivity that is normally lacking within so many contemporary judgments on war.

It should be noted that an approach to judgment guided by a praxis of recognition does not aim at bringing an end to all conflict.[5] The approach is not put forward as an answer to war, but only as an approach to remedying a certain lack of objectivity within judgment. Wars will probably continue as long as conflicting future, normative demands of forms of social-material life (forms of ethical life), whose claims of right cannot be resolved non-violently, are posited against each other by acts of violence. With this said, the adoption of a praxis of recognition may help in some cases to bring to an end to war and conflict. *If* warring actors are able to recognize the ethics of the other's war, then they might leave behind a naïvety or fanaticism residing in their belief that their own acts of violence are naturally or inherently right. If an actor can begin to view their enemy as no longer being crazy or as the embodiment of some transcendent evil, but instead, as an actor (a group of humans) who posits its claims of right through violence, then the pragmatics of negotiation, rather than a war of extermination, might appear a more viable option.

Further, even judgments guided by a praxis of recognition will not completely escape a certain degree of violence. Every attempt to recognize the ethics of the other's war is bound to involve mistake, error, slippage, and moments of epistemic and hermeneutical limitation. Such a moment of misrecognition contains a degree of violence in its misunderstanding and mischaracterization of the other and the reduction of elements of the other's complexity and difference to preconceived images and historical-cultural biases. The recognition of the ethics of the other's war involves the constant work and effort of remaining aware of these moments of misrecognition and attempting to remedy them. Recognition is not a one-off exercise, it is a form of *epistemic labour*,[6] something that is ongoing and which must be self-critically aware of its own inadequacies.

The recognition of the other's war does not simply rely upon effort, it relies upon something more, upon *honesty*. Judgment guided by recognition requires being honest about the nature of the porous boundaries that frame the concept of 'legitimate violence'. These boundaries are produced by human thoughts and deeds, they are posited and shift over time to legitimize differing actors within differing spaces. Especially in relation to the present boundaries that mark the lines of legitimacy between sovereign and non-sovereign violence, judgment has to be historically honest. Judgment must recognize that the distinction between crime and legitimate violence is not fixed eternally but is posited and re-posited by human actors and their institutions. There is not so great a gap between the legality of sovereign violence and the criminality of non-sovereign violence. Most often the institutions of the former have been founded upon the deeds of the latter. Being honest about this historical relation between violence and law is necessary if one is to be able to recognize the ethics of the other's war. A certain aspect of honesty was well noted by Augustine in his discussion of the parable of Alexander and the pirate. Augustine argues:

> Justice removed, then, what are kingdoms but great bands of robbers? What are bands of robbers themselves but little kingdoms? The band itself is made up of men; it is governed by the authority of a ruler; it is bound together by a pact of association; and the loot is divided according to agreed law. If, by the constant addition of desperate men, this scourge grows to such a size that it acquires territory, establishes a seat of government, occupies cities and subjugates peoples, it assumes the name of kingdom more openly. For this name is now manifestly conferred upon it not by the removal of greed, but by the addition of impunity. It was a pertinent and true answer which was made to Alexander the Great by a pirate whom he had seized. When the king asked him what he meant by infesting the sea, the pirate defiantly replied: 'The same as you do when you infest the whole world; but because I do it with a little ship I am called a robber, and because you do it with a great fleet, you are an emperor.'[7]

If we want our judgments on war to escape from a perpetual battlefield, then judgment must be guided by a praxis of recognition – we must attempt to recognize the ethics of the other's war. In contemporary times, this involves the demand that Western actors and critics attempt to recognize the ethics of the acts of war carried out by militant Islamicist political organizations, the ethics of what is commonly denounced as 'terrorism'.[8] Such a task of recognition is not easy. Yet, should it be easy? Should we expect that coming to terms with the problem of war, even if only to comprehend it, let alone solve it, should be easy? Between the historical passages of conflicting forms of war's ordering and our continued positing through violence, recognizing the ethics of the other's war is a difficult path to take. Yet, such a path remains open.

Notes

1 I am using the term 'objective' here in relation to judgments on war in a limited way. I am using the term in relation to the number of meanings it has been given within the differing traditions of the ordering of war. The question of 'objectivity' of judgments within the social world (and the philosophy of science) more generally is large and is highly contested, and my engagement with this wider question here is limited to working through the positions set forth within the traditions war's ordering.

2 As I have already discussed the highly limited and partisan nature of just war theory in Chapter 1, I do not need repeat my critique in this section.

3 G.W.F. Hegel, *Phenomenology of Spirit*, trans. A.V. Miller, Oxford: Oxford University Press, 1977, p. 11. Hegel argues: 'The true is the whole' ['*Das Wahre ist das Ganze*'].

4 In this respect, the account of recognition presented here should contrasted to a cosmopolitan ethic of Christian love put forward by Žižek, and an ethics of alterity put forward by Derrida. See S. Žižek, *Welcome to the Desert of the Real! Five Essays on September 11 and Related Dates*, London: Verso, 2002; S. Žižek, *Iraq: The Borrowed Kettle*, London: Verso, 2005; J. Derrida, *Specters of Marx: The State of Debt, the Work of Mourning and the New International*, trans. P. Kamuf, New York: Routledge, 1994; J. Derrida, *On Cosmopolitanism and Forgiveness*, trans. M. Dooley and M. Hughes, London: Routledge, 2001. Consider also D. Cornell, *The Philosophy of the Limit*, New York: Routledge, 1992; W.E. Connolly, *Why I Am Not a Secularist*, Minneapolis, MN: University of Minnesota Press, 1999. My account of a praxis of recognition does involve elements of a cosmopolitan ethic, however, this aspect is secondary to the use of recognition I am drawing upon here as a partial solution to a lack of objectivity in judgment – that is, recognition as an *epistemic praxis* which may or may not bring an ethical result. The difference is significant as I am not putting forward a praxis of recognition as an ethics that is to bring conflict to an end. In my account, even after you recognize the ethics of the other's war, you might still see the need to fight and even kill the other. In this respect, my account of judgment, guided by a praxis of recognition, runs secondary to my theory of war as positing. Further, my approach is careful not to fall into a current dilemma faced by the Left which is turning to secularized forms of religious ethics (the misty realm of religion) as a means of coming to terms with contemporary political problems. While there is a certain religious aspect to the demand to recognize the ethics of the other's war, I am not putting this forward as a general solution to social problems, but merely as a way of practically guiding our judgments on the legitimacy of violence.

5 My account of judgment guided by a praxis of recognition should not be reduced to a simple return of the notion of the 'just enemy', and the plea for such a return made by Schmitt. See C. Schmitt, *The Nomos of the Earth*, trans. G.L. Ulmen, New York: Telos Press, 2003. An account of judgment guided by a praxis of recognition does hold out a small degree of hope that the recognizing parties might give up their conflict. Such a hope is not great but it is there. Further, my approach should also not be reduced to a simple liberal account of 'toleration'. The cognitive or epistemic aspect of a praxis of recognition demands more than merely tolerating the other, it involves leaving the liberal standpoint of atomized individuality and instead attempting to grasp the dialectical and speculative moment of mutual constitution between self and other. The epistemic hope within recognition which may or may not produce an ethical result is that the self and its claim of right can be re-comprehended as subject-object. The hope is that this new standpoint of comprehension transforms the self's understanding of a particular conflict and the other's claim against it.

6 This involves the labour of dialectical self-comprehension as subject-object and the labour of dialectical concept-formation.

7 Augustine, *City of God against the Pagans*, ed. R.W. Dyson, Cambridge: Cambridge University Press, 1998, pp. 147–8.

8 In principle, recognition involves reciprocity and there is a demand also for Muslims to recognize the ethics of the other's war. Such a demand would, however, need to be placed within the context of an account of the differing forms of war's ordering within Islamic historical-theoretical traditions. This work has not considered these traditions and has instead focused upon Anglo-European traditions of war's ordering. For this reason the political claim is addressed here not to Muslims, but to those in the 'West' who have been so far unable to come to terms with the ethicality of their other's violence.

Bibliography

Abu-Rabi, I.M. (1996) *Intellectual Origins of Islamic Resurgence in the Modern Arab World*, Albany, NY: SUNY Press.

Agamben, G. (1998) *Homo Sacer: Sovereign Power and Bare Life*, trans. D. Roazen-Heller, Stanford, CA: Stanford University Press.

Ali, T. (2003) *The Clash of Fundamentalisms*, London: Verso.

Allison, H.E. (1990) *Kant's Theory of Freedom*, Cambridge: Cambridge University Press.

Anderson-Gould, S. (2001) *Unnecessary Evil: History and Moral Progress in the Philosophy of Immanuel Kant*, Albany, NY: SUNY Press.

Anghie, A. (2005) *Imperialism, Sovereignty and the Making of International Law*, Cambridge: Cambridge University Press.

Aquinas (1988) *St. Thomas Aquinas on Politics and Ethics*, ed. P. Sigmund, New York: Norton & Co.

Archibugi, D. (1995) 'Immanuel Kant, Cosmopolitan Law and Peace', *European Journal of International Relations*, 1(4): 429–56.

Archibugi, D. and Held, D. (eds) (1995) *Cosmopolitan Democracy: An Agenda for a New World Order*, Cambridge: Polity Press.

Arendt, H. (1970) *On Violence*, San Diego, CA: Harcourt Brace & Company.

—— (1990) *On Revolution*, London: Penguin.

Aristotle (2001) *The Basic Works of Aristotle*, ed. R. McKeon, New York: Modern Library.

Aron, R. (1966) *Peace and War: A Theory of International Relations*, Garden City, NY: Doubleday and Co.

Augustine (1998) *City of God against the Pagans*, ed. R.W. Dyson, Cambridge: Cambridge University Press.

Austin, J. (1971) *The Province of Jurisprudence Determined*, London: Weidenfeld and Nicolson.

Avineri, S. (1961) 'The Problem of War in Hegel's Thought', *Journal of the History of Ideas*, 22: 463–74.

—— (1968) *The Social and Political Thought of Karl Marx*, Cambridge: Cambridge University Press.

—— (1972) *Hegel's Theory of the Modern State*, Cambridge: Cambridge University Press.

Badiou, A. (2005) *Infinite Thought: Truth and the Return to Philosophy*, trans. O. Feltham and J. Clemens, New York: Continuum.

Bauman, Z. (2000) *Liquid Modernity*, Cambridge: Polity Press.
Beaulac, S. (2004) *The Power of Language in the Making of International Law*, Leiden: Martinus Nijhoff Publishers.
Beck, U. (1992) *Risk Society: Towards a New Modernity*, London: Sage.
Benhabib, S. (2002) 'Unholy Wars', *Constellations*, 9(1).
Benjamin, W. (1969) *Illuminations*, ed. H. Arendt, trans. H. Zohn, New York: Schocken Books.
—— (1986) *Reflections*, ed. P. Demetz, trans. E. Jephcott, New York: Schocken Books.
Bennington, G. (1992) 'Frontiers: Two Seminar Sessions', *Frontiers*, *The Oxford Literary Review*, 14.
Bloch, E. (1962) *Subject-Object: Erläuterung zu Hegel*, Frankfurt am Main: Suhrkamp Verlag.
—— (1995) *The Principle of Hope*, trans. N. Plaice and S. Plaice, Cambridge, MA: MIT Press.
—— (1996) *Natural Law and Human Dignity*, trans. D.J. Schmidt, Cambridge, MA: MIT Press.
—— (2000) *The Spirit of Utopia*, trans. A. Nassar, Stanford, CA: Stanford University Press.
Bohman, J. (2001) 'Hegel's Political Anti-Cosmopolitanism: The Limits of Modern Political Communities', *Southern Journal of Philosophy*, 29: 65–91.
Borradori, G. (2003) *Philosophy in a Time of Terror: Dialogues with Jürgen Habermas and Jacques Derrida*, Chicago, IL: University of Chicago Press.
Boucher, D. (1998) *Political Theories of International Relations: From Thucydides to the Present*, Oxford: Oxford University Press.
Brierley, J.L. (1936) *The Law of Nations: An Introduction to the International Law of Peace*, Oxford: Clarendon Press.
Brown, C. (1994) *Political Restructuring in Europe: Ethical Perspectives*, London: Routledge.
Bruggencate, H.G. (1961) 'Hegel's Views on War', *Journal of the History of Ideas*, 22: 58–60.
Buck-Morss, S. (2000) 'Hegel and Haiti', *Critical Inquiry*, 26(4): 821–65.
Bull, H. (1977) *The Anarchical Society*, London: Macmillan.
Butler, J. (1987) *Subjects of Desire: Hegelian Reflections in Twentieth-Century France*, New York: Columbia University Press.
—— (2000) *Antigone's Claim*, New York: Columbia University Press.
Cassirer, E. (1967) *The Question of Jean-Jacques Rousseau*, ed. P. Gay, Bloomington, IN: Indiana University Press.
Cheah, P. and Robbins, B. (eds) (1998) *Cosmopolitics: Thinking and Feeling Beyond the Nation*, Minneapolis, MN: University of Minnesota Press.
Chomsky, N. (1991) *Deterring Democracy*, New York: Hill and Wang.
—— (2003) *Hegemony or Survival*, Crows Nest: Allen & Unwin.
Clark, I. and Neumann, I.B. (eds) (1996) *Classical Theories of International Relations*, London: Macmillan.
Clausewitz, von C. (1991) *Vom Krieg*, Bonn: Ferd. Dümmlers Verlag.
—— (1993) *On War*, ed. M. Howard, and P. Paret, New York: Everyman's Library.
Coates, A.J. (1997) *The Ethics of War*, Manchester: Manchester University Press.
Connolly, W.E. (1999) *Why I Am Not a Secularist*, Minneapolis, MN: University of Minnesota Press.

Cornell, D. (1992) *The Philosophy of the Limit*, New York: Routledge.

Dent, N. (2005) *Rousseau*, London: Routledge.

Derrida, J. (1978) 'Violence and Metaphysics: An Essay on the Thought of Emmanuel Levinas', trans. A. Bass, in *Writing and Difference*, Chicago, IL: University of Chicago Press.

—— (1992) 'The Force of Law: The "Mystical Foundation of Authority"', trans. M. Quaintance, in D. Cornell, M. Rosenfeld and D.G. Carlson (eds) *Deconstruction and the Possibility of Justice*, New York: Routledge.

—— (1994) *Specters of Marx: The State of Debt, the Work of Mourning and the New International*, trans. P. Kamuf, New York: Routledge.

—— (1995) *The Gift of Death*, trans. D. Wills, Chicago, IL: University of Chicago Press.

—— (1997) *The Politics of Friendship*, trans. G. Collins, London: Verso.

—— (2001) *On Cosmopolitanism and Forgiveness*, trans. M. Dooley, and M. Hughes, London: Routledge.

Dewey, J. (1915) *German Philosophy and Politics*, New York: Books for Libraries Press.

Dews, P. (1987) *The Logics of Disintegration: Post-Structuralist Thought and the Claims of Critical Theory*, London: Verso.

—— (1996) *The Limits of Disenchantment: Essays on Contemporary European Philosophy*, London: Verso.

Di Giovanni, G. (2000) *Between Kant and Hegel: Texts in the Development of Post-Kantian Idealism*, Indianapolis, IN: Hacket.

Dorsett, S. and McVeigh, S. (2005) 'Jurisprudence, Jurisdiction, and Authority in Yorta Yorta', *Northern Ireland Legal Quarterly*, 59(1).

Douzinas, C. (2000) *The End of Human Rights: Critical Legal Thought at the Turn of the Century*, Oxford: Hart.

—— (2002) 'Postmodern Just Wars: Kosovo, Afghanistan and the New World Order', in J. Strawson (ed.) *Law After Ground Zero*, London: Glasshouse Press.

—— (2006) 'Jurisdiction or *Diken Didonai* in Relation to the Role of the Critic and the Sovereign', in S. McVeigh (ed.) *Jurisprudence of Jurisdiction*, London: Cavendish.

—— (2007) *Human Rights and Empire: The Political Philosophy of Cosmopolitanism*, Abingdon: Routledge-Cavendish.

Dussel, E. (2003) *Beyond Philosophy*, ed. E. Mendieta, Lanham, MD: Rowman & Littlefield.

Dworkin, R.(1986) *Law's Empire*, Cambridge, MA: Belknap Press.

Elias, O. (1999) 'Regionalism in International Law-Making', in C. Harding and C.L. Lim (eds) *Renegotiating Westphalia*, The Hague: Martinus Nijhoff.

Elshtain, J.B. (2003) *Just War Against Terror: The Burden of American Power in a Violent World*, New York: Basic Books.

Esposito, J. (ed.) (1983) *Voices of Resurgent Islam*, New York: Oxford University Press.

—— (1999) *The Islamic Threat: Myth or Reality*? New York: Oxford University Press.

Fanon, F. (1967) *Black Skin, White Masks*, New York: Grove Press.

Ferrarin, A. (2001) *Hegel and Aristotle*, Cambridge: Cambridge University Press.

Feuerbach, L. (1957) *The Essence of Christianity*, trans. G. Eliot, New York: Harper & Row.

—— (1966) *Principles of the Philosophy of the Future*, trans. M.H. Vogel, Indianapolis, IN: Bobbs-Merrill.

Fichte, J.G. (1982) *The Science of Knowledge*, ed. P. Heath and J. Lachs, Cambridge: Cambridge University Press.

—— (2000) *Foundations of Natural Right*, ed. F. Neuhouser, Cambridge: Cambridge University Press.
Fisk, R. (2005) *The Great War for Civilisation: The Conquest of the Middle East*, London: Harper Perennial.
Fitzpatrick, P. (1992) *The Mythology of Modern Law*, London: Routledge.
Foucault, M. (1965) *Madness and Civilisation: A History of Insanity in the Age of Reason*, New York: Random House.
—— (1970) *The Order of Things: An Archaeology of the Human Sciences*, New York: Random House.
—— (1977) *Discipline and Punish: The Birth of the Prison*, trans. A. Sheridan, New York: Vintage Books.
—— (2003) *Society Must Be Defended*, trans. D. Macey, London: Penguin Books.
Franco, P. (1999) *Hegel's Philosophy of Freedom*, New Haven, CT: Yale University Press.
Frank, M. (1989) *What is NeoStructuralism?*, trans. R. Gray, Minneapolis, MN: University of Minnesota Press.
Fraser, N. and Honneth, A. (2003) *Redistribution or Recognition*? London: Verso.
Freud, S. (1950) *Totem and Taboo*, ed. J. Strachey, New York: W.W. Norton & Co.
—— (1961) *Civilisation and its Discontents*, ed. J. Strachey, New York: W.W. Norton & Co.
—— (1962) *The Ego and the Id*, ed. J. Strachey, New York: W.W. Norton & Co.
Frost, M. (1996) *Ethics in International Relations: A Constitutive Theory*, Cambridge: Cambridge University Press.
Fukuyama, F. (1992) *The End of History and the Last Man*, New York: Avon Books.
Gauthier, J.A. (1997) *Hegel and Feminist Social Criticism: Justice, Recognition and the Feminine*, Albany, NY: SUNY Press.
Geoghegan, V. (1996) *Ernst Bloch*, London: Routledge.
Gert, B. (1996) 'Hobbes's Psychology', in T. Sorell (ed.) *The Cambridge Companion to Hobbes*, Cambridge: Cambridge University Press.
Giddens, A. (1991) *Modernity and Self Identity*, Cambridge: Polity Press.
Girard, R. (1977) *Violence and the Sacred*, ed. P. Gregory, Baltimore, MD: Johns Hopkins University Press.
Goethe, J.W. (1997) *Faust*, München. Deutscher Taschenbuch Verlag.
Grotius, H. (2005) *The Rights of War and Peace*, ed. R. Tuck, Indianapolis, IN: Liberty Fund.
Guevara, E. (1998) *Guerrilla Warfare*, ed. M. Becker, Lincoln, NE: University of Nebraska Press.
Guyer, P. (1996) *Kant and the Experience of Freedom*, Cambridge: Cambridge University Press.
Habermas, J. (1988) *Theory and Practice*, trans. J. Viertel, Cambridge: Polity Press.
—— (1990) *The Philosophical Discourse of Modernity*, trans. F.G. Lawrence, Cambridge, MA: MIT Press.
—— (1997) 'Kant's Idea of Perpetual Peace, With the Benefit of Two Hundred Years Hindsight', in J. Bohman, and M. Lutz-Bachman (eds) *Perpetual Peace: Essays on Kant's Cosmopolitan Ideal*, Cambridge, MA: MIT Press.
—— (1999) 'Bestiality and Humanity: A War on the Border between Legality and Morality', *Constellations*, 6(3).
—— (2001) *The Postnational Constellation: Political Essays*, trans. M. Pensky, Cambridge: Polity Press.
Hampton, J. (1986) *Hobbes and the Social Contract Tradition*, Cambridge: Cambridge University Press.

Hardimon, M.O. (1994) *Hegel's Social Philosophy: The Process of Reconciliation*, Cambridge: Cambridge University Press.

Hardt, M. and Negri, A. (2001) *Empire*, Cambridge, MA: Harvard University Press.

Harris, E.E. (1980) 'Hegel's Theory of Sovereignty, International Relations, and War', in D.P. Verene (ed.) *Hegel's Social and Political Thought: The Philosophy of Objective Spirit*, Atlantic Highlands, NJ: Humanities Press.

Harrison, R. (2003) *Hobbes, Locke and Confusion's Masterpiece*, Cambridge: Cambridge University Press.

Hart, H.L.A. (1994) *The Concept of Law*, 2nd edn, Oxford: Oxford University Press.

Heckel, M. (2001) *Deutchsland im Konfessionellen Zeitalter*, Göttingen: Vandenhoeck-Ruprecht.

Hegel, G.W.F. (1969) *Science of Logic*, trans. A.V. Miller, London: Allen and Unwin.

—— (1970) *Grundlinien der Philosophie des Rechts*, Frankfurt am Main: Suhrkamp.

—— (1975) *Lectures on the Philosophy of World History: Introduction, Reason in History*, ed. J. Hoffmeister and B. Forbes, trans. H.B. Nisbet, Cambridge: Cambridge University Press.

—— (1977) *Phenomenology of Spirit*, trans. A.V. Miller, Oxford: Oxford University Press.

—— (1979) *Hegel's System of Ethical Life and First Philosophy of Spirit*, ed. H.S. Harris and T.M. Knox, Albany, NY: SUNY Press.

—— (1983) *Hegel and the Human Spirit*, trans. L. Rauch, Detroit, MI: Wayne State University Press.

—— (1991a) *Elements of the Philosophy of Right*, ed. A.W. Wood, trans. H.B. Nisbet, Cambridge: Cambridge University Press.

—— (1991b) *The Encyclopaedia Logic: Part I of the Encyclopaedia of Philosophical Sciences with the Zusätze*, trans. T.F. Geraets, W.A. Suchting and H.S. Harris, Indianapolis, IN: Hackett.

—— (1999) *Political Writings*, ed. L. Dickey, trans. H.B. Nisbet, Cambridge: Cambridge University Press.

Heidegger, M. (1969) *The Question Concerning Technology and Other Essays*, trans. W. Lovitt, New York: Harper and Row.

Held, D. (1995) *Democracy and the Global Order: From the Modern State to Cosmopolitan Governance*, Cambridge: Polity Press.

Henrich, D. (2003) *Between Kant and Hegel*, Cambridge, MA: Harvard University Press.

Herman, E.S. and Chomsky, N. (1994) *Manufacturing Consent: The Political Economy of the Mass Media*, New York: Vintage.

Hicks, S.V. (1999) *International Law and the Possibility of a Just World Order: An Essay on Hegel's Universalism*, Amsterdam: Rudolpi.

Hirst, P. (2001) *War and Power in the 21st Century*, Cambridge: Polity.

Hobbes, T. (1996) *Leviathan*, ed. R. Tuck, Cambridge: Cambridge University Press.

—— (1998) *On the Citizen*, ed. R. Tuck and M. Silverthorn, Cambridge: Cambridge University Press.

Hobhouse L.T. (1918) *The Metaphysical Theory of the State*, London: George Allen and Unwin Press.

Höffe, O. (1994) *Immanuel Kant*, Albany, NY: SUNY Press.

—— (2002) *Demokratie im Zeitalter der Globalisierung*, München: Beck.

Holsti, K.L. (1991) *Peace and War: Armed Conflicts and International Order 1648–1989*, Cambridge: Cambridge University Press.

Honneth, A. (1995) *The Struggle for Recognition: The Moral Grammar of Social Conflicts*, trans. J. Anderson, Cambridge: Polity Press.
Hood, F.C. (1964) *The Divine Politics of Thomas Hobbes*, Oxford: Clarendon Press.
Horkheimer M. and Adorno, T.W. (2002) *Dialectic of Enlightenment*, trans. E. Jephcott, Stanford, CA: Stanford University Press.
Hudson, W. (1982) *The Marxist Philosophy of Ernst Bloch*, London: Macmillan.
—— (2003) *The Reform of Utopia*, Aldershot: Ashgate.
Hunter, I. (2001) *Rival Enlightenments: Civil and Metaphysical Philosophy in Early Modern Germany*, New York: Cambridge University Press.
—— (2002) 'The Morals of Metaphysics: Kant's *Groundwork* as Intellectual *Paideia*', *Critical Inquiry*, 28(4).
Huntington, S.P. (1996) *The Clash of Civilizations and the Remaking of World Order*, New York: Touchstone.
Hutchings, K. (1999) *International Political Theory*, London: Sage.
—— (2003) *Hegel and Feminist Philosophy*, Cambridge: Polity Press.
Hyppolite, J. (1969) *Studies on Marx and Hegel*, London: Heinemann.
Ignatieff, M. (2004) *The Lesser Evil: Political Ethics in an Age of Terror*, Edinburgh: Edinburgh University Press.
Johnson, J.T. (1981) *The Just War Tradition and the Restraint of War*, Princeton, NJ: Princeton University Press.
—— (1999) *Morality and Contemporary Warfare*, New Haven, CT: Yale University Press.
Johnston, J.T. (1975) *Ideology, Reason, and the Limitation of War: Religious and Secular Concepts, 1200–1740*, Princeton, NJ: Princeton University Press.
Kagan, R. (2008) 'The Case for a League of Democracies', *Financial Times*, May 13.
Kant, I. (1977) *Prolegomena to Any Future Metaphysics*, ed. J.W. Ellington, trans. P. Carus, Indianapolis, IN: Hackett.
—— (1991) *Political Writings*, ed. H.I. Reiss, Cambridge: Cambridge University Press.
—— (1996) *The Metaphysics of Morals*, ed. M. Gregor, Cambridge: Cambridge University Press.
—— (1997) *Critique of Practical Reason*, ed. M. Gregor, Cambridge: Cambridge University Press.
—— (1998a) *Critique of Pure Reason*, ed. P. Guyer and A. Wood, Cambridge: Cambridge University Press.
—— (1998b) *Groundwork of the Metaphysics of Morals*, ed. M. Gregor, Cambridge: Cambridge University Press.
Kaufman, W. (1951) 'Hegel's Myth and Its Method', *The Philosophical Review*, 60: 486–95.
Keene, E. (2002) *Beyond the Anarchical Society: Grotius, Colonialism and Order in World Politics*, Cambridge: Cambridge University Press.
Kennedy, D. (1986) 'Primitive Legal Scholarship', *Harvard International Law Journal*, 27(1): 1–98.
Kerruish, V. (1991) *Jurisprudence as Ideology*, London: Routledge.
—— (2006) 'On Re-staging the Universal: Butler, Hegel and Contesting the Closure of Logic', *Dilemmata: Jahrbuch der ASFPG*.
Knutsen, T.J. (1992) *A History of International Relations Theory*, Manchester: Manchester University Press.
Kochi. T. (2002) 'Anticipation, Critique and the Problem of Intervention: Understanding the Messianic: Derrida Through Ernst Bloch', *Law and Critique*, 13.

—— (2007) 'The Pope and the Ethics of Exclusion', *Logos*, 6(3).

Kojève, A. (1980) *Introduction to the Reading of Hegel*, trans. J.H. Nichols, Ithaca, NY: Cornell University Press.

—— (2000) *Outline of a Phenomenology of Right*, ed. B. Frost and R. Howse, Lanham, MD: Rowman and Littlefield.

Kolakowski, L. (1981) *Main Currents of Marxism*, Vol. 1. trans. P.S. Falla, Oxford: Oxford University Press.

Kortian, G. (1980) *Metacritique: The Philosophical Arguments of Jürgen Habermas*, Cambridge: Cambridge University Press.

Koskenniemi, M. (2005) *From Apology to Utopia*, Cambridge: Cambridge University Press.

Kotzsch, L. (1956) *The Concept of War in Contemporary History and International Law*, Geneva: Librairie E. Droz.

Kuhn, T. (1996) *The Structure of Scientific Revolutions*, 3rd edn, Chicago, IL: University of Chicago Press.

Küng, H. (1987) *The Incarnation of God: An Introduction to Hegel's Theological Thought as a Prolegomena to a Future Christianity*, trans. J.R. Stephenson, New York: Crossword.

Laclau, E. and Mouffe C. (2001) *Hegemony and Socialist Strategy: Towards a Radical Democratic Politics*, 2nd edn, London: Verso.

Las Casas, B. (1992) *A Short Account of the Destruction of the Indies*, trans. N. Griffin, London: Penguin.

Lauterpach, H. (1946) 'The Grotian Tradition in International Law', *British Yearbook of International Law*, 23: 1–53.

Lenin, V.I. (1972) *Collected Works*, Vol. 11, London: Lawrence and Wishart.

—— (1974a) *Collected Works*, Vol. 23, London: Lawrence and Wishart.

—— (1974b) *Collected Works*, Vol. 24, London: Lawrence and Wishart.

—— (1977) *Materialism and Empirio-criticism: Critical Comments on a Reactionary Philosophy*, Moscow: Progress Publishers.

—— (1987) *Essential Works of Lenin*, ed. H.M. Christman, New York: Dover Publications.

Linklater, A. (1982) *Men and Citizens in the Theory of International Relations*, London: Macmillan.

—— (1998) *The Transformation of Political Community: Ethical Foundations of the Post-Westphalian Era*, Cambridge: Polity Press.

Locke, J. (2005) *Two Treatises of Government*, ed. P. Laslett, Cambridge: Cambridge University Press.

Löwith, K. (1964) *From Hegel to Nietzsche: The Restoration of Nineteenth Century Thought*, trans. D.E. Green, London: Constable.

Lukács, G. (1976) *The Young Hegel: Studies in Relations between Dialectics and Economics*, trans. R. Livingstone, Cambridge, MA: MIT Press.

—— (1990) *History and Class Consciousness*, trans. R. Livingstone, London: Merlin Press.

Machiavelli, N. (1950) *The Prince and the Discourses*, ed. M. Lerner, trans. L. Ricci, New York: Random House.

Macpherson, C.B. (1965) 'Hobbes's Bourgeois Man', in K.C. Brown, *Hobbes Studies*, Oxford: Blackwell.

McLellan, D. (ed.) (1960) *The Essential Left*, London: Unwin Books.

McVeigh, S. (ed.) (2006) *Jurisprudence of Jurisdiction*, London: Cavendish.
McVeigh, S.P. and Young, A. (2001) 'A Judgment Dwelling in Law: Violence and the Relations of Legal Thought', in A. Sarat (ed.) *Violence and the Possibility of Justice*, Princeton, NJ: Princeton University Press.
Mao, T. (2000) *On Guerrilla Warfare*, trans. S.B. Griffith, Urbana, IL: University of Illinois Press.
Marcuse, H. (1955) *Reason and Revolution: Hegel and the Rise of Social Theory*, 2nd edn, London: Routledge & Kegan Paul.
—— (1964) *One Dimensional Man*, London: Abacus.
Martinich, A.P. (1992) *The Two Gods of the Leviathan: Thomas Hobbes on Religion and Politics*, Cambridge: Cambridge University Press.
Marx, K. (1988) *Economic and Philosophic Manuscripts of 1844*, trans. M. Milligan, Amherst, MA: Prometheus Books.
—— (1992) *Capital*, Vol. 1, trans. B. Fowkes, London: Penguin Classics.
—— (1994) *Karl Marx: Selected Writings*, ed. L.H. Simon, Indianapolis, IN: Hacket Publishing.
Marx, K. and Engels, F. (1969) *The Communist Manifesto*, trans. S. Moore, Harmondsworth: Penguin.
Mertens, T. (1995) 'Hegel's Homage to Kant's Perpetual Peace: An Analysis of Hegel's Philosophy of Right', *The Review of Politics*, 57(4): 665–91.
Miéville, C. (2006) *Between Equal Rights: A Marxist Theory of International Law*, London: Pluto Press.
Milbank, J. (1993) *Theology and Social Theory: Beyond Secular Reason*, Oxford: Blackwell.
Mills, P.J. (ed.) (1996) *Feminist Interpretations of G.W.F. Hegel*, Philadelphia, PA: Pennsylvania State University Press.
Morgenthau, H.J. (1952) *In Defense of the National Interest*, New York: Alfred A. Knopf.
Moylan T. and Daniel J.O. (eds) (1997) *Not Yet: Reconsidering Ernst Bloch*, London: Verso.
Muirhead, J.H. (1917) *German Philosophy in Relation to the War*, London: John Murray.
Nancy, J-L. (1991) *The Inoperative Community*, trans. P. Conner *et al.*, Minneapolis, MN: University of Minnesota Press.
—— (2000) *Being Singular Plural*, ed. R.D. Richardson, trans. A.E. O'Byrne, Stanford, CA: Stanford University Press.
—— (2001) *The Speculative Remark: One of Hegel's Bon Mots*, trans. C. Suprenant, Stanford, CA: Stanford University Press.
—— (2002) *Hegel: The Restlessness of the Negative*, trans. J. Smith and S. Miller, Minneapolis, MN: University of Minnesota Press.
Nasr, S.H. (2002) *The Heart of Islam*, New York: HarperCollins.
Nassar, D. (2004) 'Heroes and Fanatics: Discernment and Critique in Hegel's Political Philosophy', *Idealistic Studies*, 34(2).
Nietzsche, F. (2000) *The Basic Writings of Nietzsche*, ed. P. Gay, trans. W. Kaufman, New York: The Modern Library.
Nussbaum, A. (1947) *A Concise History of the Law of Nations*, New York: Macmillan.
Nussbaum, M.C. (1997) 'Kant and Cosmopolitanism', in J. Bohman and M. Lutz-Bachman (eds) *Perpetual Peace: Essays on Kant's Cosmopolitan Ideal*, Cambridge MA: MIT Press.
—— (2002) 'Patriotism and Cosmopolitanism', in M.C. Nussbaum and J. Cohen (eds) *For Love of Country?* Boston, MA: Beacon Press.

Oakeshott, M. (1975) *Hobbes on Civil Association*, Indianapolis, IN: Liberty Fund.
O'Donovan, O. (2003) *The Just War Revisited*, Cambridge: Cambridge University Press.
O'Neil, O. (1986) *Faces of Hunger: An Essay on Poverty, Justice and Development*, London: Allen and Unwin.
—— (1989) *Constructions of Reason: Explorations of Kant's Practical Philosophy*, Cambridge: Cambridge University Press.
—— (2002) 'Instituting Principles: Between Duty and Action', in M. Timmons (ed.) *Kant's Metaphysics of Morals: Interpretive Essays*, Oxford: Oxford University Press.
Orford, A. (2007) *Reading Humanitarian Intervention: Human Rights and the Use of Force in International Law*, Cambridge: Cambridge University Press.
Padgen, A. (1982) *The Fall of Natural Man: The American Indian and the Origins of Comparative Ethnology*, Cambridge: Cambridge University Press.
Pashukanis, E.B. (1978) *Law and Marxism: A General Theory*, ed. C. Arthur, trans. B. Einhorn, London: Links.
Peperzak, A. (1994) 'Hegel Contra Hegel in His Philosophy of Right: The Contradictions of International Politics', *Journal of the History of Philosophy* 32(2): 241–63.
Petersen, U. (2002) *Diagonal Method and Dialectical Logic: Tools, Materials, and Groundworks for a Logical Foundation of Dialectic and Speculative Philosophy*, Tönning: Der Andere Verlag.
Pinkard, T. (1994) *Hegel's Phenomenology: The Sociality of Reason*, Cambridge: Cambridge University Press.
Pippin, R. (1989) *Hegel's Idealism: The Satisfactions of Self-Consciousness*, Cambridge: Cambridge University Press.
—— (1991) *Modernism as a Philosophical Problem: On the Dissatisfactions of European High Culture*, Malden, MA: Blackwell Publishers.
—— (2000) 'What Is the Question for which Hegel's Theory of Recognition is the Answer?', *European Journal of Philosophy*, 8(2): 155–72.
Pogge, T.W. (2002) *World Poverty and Human Rights: Cosmopolitan Responsibilities and Reforms*, Cambridge: Polity.
Popper, K. (1945) *The Open Society and its Enemies*, Princeton, NJ: Princeton University Press.
Ramadan, T. (2004) *Islam, the West and the Challenges of Modernity*, trans. S. Amghar, Leicester: The Islamic Foundation.
Ramsey, P. (1961) *War and the Christian Conscience: How Shall Modern War Be Conducted Justly?* Durham, NC: Duke University Press.
Rawls, J. (1971) *A Theory of Justice*, Cambridge, MA: Belknap Press.
—— (1993) *Political Liberalism*, New York: Columbia University Press.
—— (1999) *The Law of Peoples*, Cambridge, MA: Harvard University Press.
Riedel, M. (1984) *Between Tradition and Revolution: The Hegelian Transformation of Political Philosophy*, trans. W. Wright, Cambridge: Cambridge University Press.
Ritter, J. (1982) *Hegel and the French Revolution: Essays on the Philosophy of Right*, Cambridge, MA: MIT Press.
Rose, G. (1981) *Hegel Contra Sociology*, London: Athlone.
—— (1984) *Dialectic of Nihilism: Post-Structuralism and Law*, Oxford: Basil Blackwell.
—— (1992) *The Broken Middle: Out of our Ancient Society*, Oxford: Blackwell.
—— (1996) *Mourning Becomes the Law*, Cambridge: Cambridge University Press.
Rousseau, J-J. (1927) *A Project of Perpetual Peace*, trans. E.M. Nuttal, London: Richard Cobden-Sanderson.

—— (1987) *Jean-Jacques Rousseau: The Basic Political Writings*, ed. P. Gay, trans. D. A. Cress, Indianapolis, IN: Hacket.

Russell, F.H. (1975) *The Just War in the Middle Ages*, Cambridge: Cambridge University Press.

Said, E.W. (1978) *Orientalism*, London: Routledge and Kegan Paul.

Saunders, D. (1997) *Anti-Lawyers*, London: Routledge.

Schelling, F.W.J. (2001) *System of Transcendental Idealism*, trans. P. Heath, Charlottesville, VA: University Press of Virginia.

Schlereth, T.J. (1977) *The Cosmopolitan Ideal in Enlightenment Thought*, Notre Dame, IN: University of Notre Dame Press.

Schmitt, C. (1996) *The Concept of the Political*, trans. G. Schwab, Chicago, IL: University of Chicago Press.

—— (2003) *The Nomos of the Earth*, trans. G.L. Ulmen, New York: Telos Press.

—— (2004) *The Theory of the Partisan: A Commentary/Remark on the Concept of the Political*, trans. A.C. Goodson, East Lansing, MI: Michigan State University Press.

—— (2006) *Political Theology: Four Chapters on the Concept of Sovereignty*, ed. G. Schwab, Chicago, IL: University of Chicago Press.

Scott, J.B. (1934) *The Spanish Origins of International Law: Francisco De Vitoria and His Law of Nations*, Oxford: Clarendon Press.

Sembou, E. (2003) 'Hegel's Idea of a Struggle for Recognition: The Phenomenology of Spirit', *History of Political Thought*, 24(2): 262–81.

Shklar, J.N. (1985) *Men and Citizens: A Study of Rousseau's Social Theory*, Cambridge: Cambridge University Press.

Silva, D.F. (2007) *Toward a Global Idea of Race*, Minneapolis, MN: Minnesota University Press.

Simpson, G. (2004) *Great Powers and Outlaw States*, Cambridge: Cambridge University Press.

Singer, P. (1975) *Animal Liberation*, New York: Random House.

—— (2002) *One World: Ethics and Globalization*, New Haven, CT: Yale University Press.

Skinner, Q. (1978) *The Foundations of Modern Political Thought*, Vol. 2, Cambridge: Cambridge University Press.

—— (1996) *Reason and Rhetoric in the Philosophy of Thomas Hobbes*, Cambridge: Cambridge University Press.

Smith, C.I. (1965) 'Hegel on War', *Journal of the History of Ideas*, 16: 282–5.

Smith, S.B. (1983) 'Hegel's Views on War, the State, and International Relations', *American Political Science Review*, 77(3): 624–32.

Sorel, G. (1999) *Reflections on Violence*, ed. J. Jennings, Cambridge: Cambridge University Press.

Spinoza, B. (1996) *Ethics*, trans. E. Curley, London: Penguin.

Steinvorth, U. (2005) 'On Carl Schmitt's Interpretation of Hobbes', in L. Foisneau, J. Merle and T. Sorell (eds) *Leviathan Between the Wars*, Frankfurt am Main: Peter Lang.

Stepelevich L.S. (ed.) (1997) *The Young Hegelians: An Anthology*, Atlantic Highlands, NJ: Humanities Press.

Stewart, J. (ed.) (1996) *The Hegel Myths and Legends*, Evanston, IL: Northwestern University Press.

Strauss, L. (1963) *The Political Philosophy of Hobbes: Its Basis and its Genesis*, trans. E.M. Sinclair, Chicago, IL: University of Chicago Press.

—— (1965) 'On the Spirit of Hobbes's Political Philosophy', in K. Brown (ed.) *Hobbes Studies*, Oxford: Blackwell.

Swift, L.J. (1983) *The Early Fathers on War and Military Service*, Wilmington, DE: Michael Glazier.

Taylor, C. (1975a) *Hegel*, Cambridge: Cambridge University Press.

—— (1979b) *Hegel and Modern Society*, Cambridge: Cambridge University Press.

Theunissen, M. (1991) 'The Repressed Inter-Subjectivity in Hegel's Philosophy of Right', in D. Cornell, M. Rosenfeld and D.G. Carlson (eds) *Hegel and Legal Theory*, New York: Routledge.

Thucydides (1954) *The History of the Peloponnesian War*, trans. R. Warner, London: Penguin Classics.

Tooke, J.D. (1965) *The Just War in Aquinas and Grotius*, London: SPCK.

Treitschke, von H. (1963) *Politics*, trans. H. Kohn, New York: Harcourt, Brace and World Inc.

Tuck, R. (1981) *Natural Rights Theories: Their Origin and Development*, Cambridge: Cambridge University Press.

—— (1999) *The Rights of War and Peace: Political Thought and the International Order from Grotius to Kant*, Oxford: Oxford University Press.

Tully, J. (1993) *An Approach to Political Philosophy: Locke in Contexts*, Cambridge: Cambridge University Press.

Verene, D.P. (1971) 'Hegel's Account of War', in Z.A. Pelczynski (ed.) *Hegel's Political Philosophy: Problems and Perspectives*, Cambridge: Cambridge University Press.

Vitoria, de F. (1991) *Political Writings*, ed. A. Padgen and J. Lawrance, Cambridge: Cambridge University Press.

Walt, S. (1989) 'Hegel on War: Another Look', *History of Political Thought*, 10(1): 112–23.

Waltz, K. (1959) *Man, the State and War*, New York: Columbia University Press.

Walzer, M. (2000) *Just and Unjust Wars: A Moral Argument with Historical Illustrations*, 3rd edn, New York: Basic Books.

—— (2004) *Arguing About War*, New Haven, CT: Yale University Press.

Warrender, H. (1957) *The Political Philosophy of Hobbes: His Theory of Obligation*, Oxford: Clarendon Press.

Watson, J. (1915) 'German Philosophy and Politics', *Queen's Quarterly*, 22(4): 366–79.

Weber, M. (1958) 'Politics as a Vocation', in H.H. Gerth and C.W. Mills (eds) *From Max Weber: Essays in Sociology*, New York: Oxford University Press.

Williams, R.R. (1992) *Recognition: Fichte and Hegel on the Other*, Albany, NY: SUNY Press.

—— (1997) *Hegel's Ethics of Recognition*, Berkeley, CA: University of California Press.

Windas, S. (1964) *Christianity Versus Violence*, London: Sheed & Ward.

Wood, A.W. (1999) *Kant's Ethical Thought*, Cambridge: Cambridge University Press.

Žižek, S. (1989) *The Sublime Object of Ideology*, London: Verso.

—— (1993) *Tarrying with the Negative: Kant, Hegel and the Critique of Ideology*, Durham, NC: Duke University Press.

—— (2000a) 'Melancholy and the Act', *Critical Inquiry*, 26(4).

—— (2000b) *The Fragile Absolute: Or, Why is the Christian Legacy Worth Fighting For?* London: Verso.

—— (2002) *Welcome to the Desert of the Real! Five Essays on September 11 and Related Dates*, London: Verso.

—— (2005) *Iraq: The Borrowed Kettle*, London: Verso.

Index